Selected Writings

of

BOLIVAR

SELECTED WRITINGS

of

BOLIVAR

Compiled by Vicente Lecuna

Edited by Harold A. Bierck, Jr.
Assistant Professor of History
University of North Carolina

Translation by Lewis Bertrand

Volume Two
1823-1830

Published by
BANCO DE VENEZUELA

New York, N. Y.
THE COLONIAL PRESS INC.
1951

Manufactured in the United States of America
By The Colonial Press Inc.

LIST OF DOCUMENTS—VOLUME II

LIST OF ILLUSTRATIONS—VOLUME II

LIST OF MAPS—VOLUME II

Selected Writings

of

BOLIVAR

1823

[*Original*]

Guayaquil, March 12-14, 1823.

My dear General:

I have much to tell you, and I do not know where to begin. I have heard nothing officially from Perú, and I have only a confused idea of her present situation, which, it appears, is indeed lamentable. Her government is so despicable that, as yet, it has not written me one word; without doubt it plans to perpetrate some infamy upon that miserable people. A vessel, recently arrived from Lima, reports that Canterac is still in Arequipa, although others assert that he has gone in haste to the outskirts of Lima. The fact is that the enemy may be close to Lima by the end of April; there are hardly 4,000 men to defend it, whereas the enemy may bring twice that number of first-rate troops. Everything there is in disorder; there is no government, no army. President La Mar has always been a *godo,* and most of the army heads have always been *godos,* and the naval commander at Callao as well. The chief of staff, the commanding officer of engineers, and the commanding officer of artillery are also *godos.* In these circumstances, I am going to make every effort to send 3,000 of our men to Lima, under the orders of General Valdés. These troops, although not one has been requested, will enter, for they may help prevent the surrender of Lima and Callao. A large number of troops is not being sent for the present because it is impossible. I have no ships, no provisions, and no troops here. We have already spent a hundred thousand *pesos,* and we are just beginning the enterprise. In order to send the next 3,000, God knows what we shall have to do, for we are burdened with debts, and we do not have the slightest credit. But it shall be done, cost what it may. We must hope that all will go well with this first expedition, for it will encounter considerable risk. Valdés has orders to go to Callao and to disembark there if they will permit him. If they do not allow it, he will land at Trujillo, which is a hundred leagues north of Lima, returning the transports to me to take the other 3,000 men to Trujillo. I shall then begin my march toward Lima.

I should like to accompany this first expedition, and I believe it would be a very good thing. But I also believe that, unless I raise the second expedition, it will never be done. By ill-chance Sucre is in Quito speeding the loan, the recruiting, and the outfitting of the troops there. The intendant of that department seeks to make himself popular and therefore is of no help. Sucre will come here within a month and will assume command in the south. Salom will stay on as commanding general in Quito. Aguirre will remain as governor of that province, and Flores will be in command in Pasto. You will try to reinforce the garrison at Pasto with men from Popayán, as otherwise there will be another uprising. Quito will retain its battalion of militia, and the *Yaguachí* or the *Bogotá* battalion will remain here. This city cannot now be left without a garrison of Colombian troops, for every day we are more disliked because of the sacrifices we demand of the population, who are mercantile and greedy, every single one. Fortunately, we are procuring enough supplies to sustain a strong garrison.

If Morales does not stand in the way, I think that the executive power should send me 3,000 more men to defend these departments in case of a setback in Perú or an uprising here.

You can be sure that, if we do not go to Perú now, we shall lose everything there without fail. By going, we can avail ourselves of all her resources: three hundred leagues of land, 300,000 free inhabitants, an excellent garrison in Callao, and the prestige of a capital like Lima. Meanwhile, we must prolong the struggle. We must gain time in which to collect reinforcements and conclude some sort of peace treaty with Spain. When we are in Lima or Callao we shall have more to yield to Spain, and she shall have more to ask of us. We shall have more, hence we will ask for more. In short, you understand me.

I cannot picture to you how I long to go and take possession of Lima and Callao. In my hands those places would never be taken, whereas in the hands of those people they are already lost.

Inform the Congress of my resolution to go to Lima, so they may render their decision in that matter. If I were to be granted discretionary powers, I think that I would be entitled to enter enemy territory which is occupied by the Spaniards in Perú, for the enemy will come here if I do not go there to forestall him. Furthermore, enemy territory should not be regarded as foreign territory, but as conquerable territory. Since conquest is the aim of war, it is my duty to drive the enemy from all the countries with which we have contiguous boundaries. To sum up, I think that I would not be violating the Constitution by marching to meet the enemy, for enemy territory is not foreign territory, just as New Granada was not foreign territory for Venezuela. Whoever says differently is a fool, and a fool's opinion cannot prevail.

The 13th.

Today the mails came from Perú, though greatly delayed. General Santa Cruz writes Castillo that, if I do not come quickly, Perú will most certainly be lost; that La Mar, unfortunately, continues to head the government, which hampers everything. He says that not more than 1,300 of the men who were defeated at Moquegua have arrived at Lima and that Alvarado has stayed in the south with 800 or 1,000 men to occupy the attention of the enemy in that quarter. A merchant by the name of Sarratea, a very prominent man, wrote a letter to a friend of his. I am enclosing it together with Santa Cruz' letter, so that you may be fully informed.

To all appearances, the members of the government are more jealous of us than they are fearful of the Spaniards. But the people and the army want us, for Perú without Colombia is lost. Within forty days I shall be on the march with 2,000 or 3,000 more men, so as to reach Lima at the same time as the Spaniards, or not long after. For the present, four battalions are on their way, comprising 2,800 men besides the officers. Later, three squadrons will follow: the *Rifles* battalion of 1,200, and some 1,500 recruits; the *Bogotá* and *Yaguachi* cadres will remain here to be brought up to strength as quickly as possible. These battalions, formed of men recruited locally, will never amount to much, and, if the 3,000 men whom I have requested do not arrive, we can expect nothing. Send these 3,000 to the Isthmus, and I shall have them picked up there.

As yet I know nothing definite respecting the fate of Morales. However skilful General Clemente's operations may have been, Morales will always give us much to do. I cannot foresee what combination of forces would be needed for that difficult operation of destroying a determined and active, though stupid and cowardly, foe on the Gulf. For, to tell the truth, if Morales does not commit some gross blunder, he can prolong the struggle for quite some time; and, should our forces commit another indiscretion like that of Clemente and Sardá,[1] you can expect to see the enemy in Bogotá.

Here we badly need three more naval officers like Beluche and two more junior officers. They should not be the sort that make off with the ships, whatever their other shortcomings. Order them to come here by way of the Isthmus. If Beluche should not be able to come, send someone else who is with us not in words but in deeds. We have no lack of passable junior officers here, but most of them are drunkards. And we never know but that some fine day they will disappear and the ships with them, which is what I fear most.

I am sending you Alvarado's report on his unfortunate encounter.[2]

The 14th.

Two days ago I began this letter and refrained from closing it in the hope that meantime I might receive some definite and fresh news from Perú and Bogotá. I know no more now than I did then, from either place. A post is expected soon from Perú and will of course bring a few items on the situation in that country. I have heard nothing more from Bogotá than what was reported in the dispatch of February 4, which vaguely mentioned Morales' retreat toward Maracaibo and the loss of a good part of his army. A post departed two days later but brought me not a word about these developments. It seems that the more important communications were sent by way of San Buenaventura.

By the same post I received some of your correspondence and the copies of the *Gaceta de Colombia*, which also say nothing. The fact is I am in a very critical situation: I am working blindly, as I do not know the true state of affairs in either Perú or Colombia. If I lose time, the situation may grow worse, and if I hurry who knows but that my concern for Perú may be detrimental to Colombia? In that case most of the blame should fall on the one responsible for delaying communications. The expedition for Perú will leave the eighteenth of this month; it positively cannot be detained, for war and the tide write their own orders. I am therefore steering my course by dead reckoning and not by the information with which I should have been supplied.

----

[1] These men commanded the province of Santa Marta where a revolt took place against the patriots in January, 1823 (ed.).

[2] See note 1, p. 366 (ed.).

As soon as I receive further intelligence I shall let you know by special messenger.

I am your devoted

BOLÍVAR

P.S. I have just learned that on the island of Tumaco, in the Cauca territory, a revolt broke out which the Colombian Captain Farrera managed to put down. I think that the intendant of Cauca should take all necessary measures to control that island and the adjacent coasts. The commotion was caused by an officer named Nieto, who had brought dispatches from Cauca. He asserted that all was lost, that the people and the soldiers, too, were overcome by the heavy demands made upon them.

158. To F[rancisco] de P[aula] Santander,
   Vice President of Colombia

[*Original*]

Guayaquil, April 29, 1823.

My dear General:

You cannot imagine my concern at receiving no letters from Bogotá. There have been three posts with no news from that quarter, but a similar number have failed to arrive. I do not know how to account for this delay or, rather, this interception [of the mails]. I understand, as they write regularly from Popayán, that throughout Pasto there is nothing new whatsoever. At this very moment Demarquet tells me that he has a letter from the capital dated March 6, a none too recent date. The last post that we received was dated February 21, and that of February 6 came later. The two March mails must have gone around by San Buenaventura and Barbacoas, if, indeed, they have not been lost. This leaves me desperate, for my decision is contingent upon events in the north.

Another mission has come from Perú to urge me to take command of their troops. Commanding General Martínez and General Santa Cruz, who commands the Peruvian division, also urge me most strongly. I do not know what to say since I must await the decision of the Congress and the operations of Morales. Everyone says that, unless I go, Perú and 15,000 men from four American nations will be lost for lack of a leader to command them; for among equals no one is willing to take orders. You can well imagine how proud I should be to command such an army, but I have arrived at a point where neither my country's welfare nor glory itself make the slightest impression on me if they conflict with the letter of my duty. The north may need me, but Congress has not given me permission to leave Colombia. These two factors force me to remain inactive. All may be lost because of my inaction, but I cannot, in all sincerity, become another Don Quixote and aid the helpless against the commands of the law. I have committed enough acts of that nature in the course of my life, and I have been roundly criticized for doing what was right in defiance of my duty. I expect the reply of Congress within two weeks, and, if it permits me to march to Perú, I shall leave immediately. Meanwhile, I shall have heard from General Sucre, and, in the meantime also, Lima may have fallen to the army, if Canterac and his forces are approaching, as it has been reported. I shall be unable to stop this thrust if it occurs during this month or in the beginning of the next; but by May it will be impossible for Canterac to give battle at Lima, for by then we shall be the stronger. Chile is reported to be sending 3,000 men, and Lima is said to have 7,000. We shall send 6,000, of whom 4,600, not counting officers, are now at sea. Next week the rest will follow, including the *Bogotá* battalion, which is now on its way to this port. It may seem to you that this is a large number, but you know that the enemy has no less, and they are excellently commanded and far superior in resources, positions, horses, etc.

I previously told you that I had sent General Sucre with instructions to postpone the beginning of the campaign, if he can obtain this advantage. In this way many other important advantages may be gained. We shall have time to wait for political developments, for the north to dispose of Morales, and for you to send me recruits from a warmer climate, as those from these parts all die off to the last man. Guayaquil is the most important point in the south, and requires 3,000 or 4,000 good men for its defense. There are men here, but greater foes of the service you cannot imagine. I can say the same of the *quiteños*. The other day there was a terrible riot in Quito because it had been proposed that a few men be taken for the *Bogotá* [battalion]. The result was that fifteen or more persons were killed, with General Salom commanding the troops. What a people! The next day saw little improvement, though fewer, if any, were killed. People arriving from Quito say that there is not a living soul to be found between that city and this, for fear of the miserable levy that has been ordered. Thus, whether it pleases or displeases you, unless men are sent from Venezuela and the Magdalena, we cannot form an army here. I might be able to send the entire available population to Lima, but I could not raise a single corps capable of defending the south; for, as you very well know, recruits are of no use in their own country.

At this moment I have received a new post from Perú. Although it says nothing, it nevertheless bears out what I have been telling you. I am therefore sending these communications to you for your information. All those who write to me are military commanders, mostly generals—the Minister of War, Chief of Staff, etc.—as I have many examples of this type of communication, I am sending you the originals.

I can assure you that, having read these appeals, I do not know how I can remain in this city a moment longer. On the one hand, the public interest, and on the other, my personal glory—everything calls me there. In short, the temptation is great, and I may be unable to resist, unless God takes me by the hand. The force that calls me to Perú is so strong that I am beside myself with impatience. In the next six or eight days, when the *Bogotá* [battalion] leaves, I shall know what I must do, and I will notify you by the following post.

General Salom has been appointed Field Commander in the south, although such was not his desire. The Advocate General is intendant *pro tempore* of Quito, pursuant to the law. Colonel Aguirre is the Commanding General of that province. Thus everything will be in the best possible order.

Every day we receive news of Emperor Iturbide and of his troubles at Vera Cruz. The *Gaceta de Guayaquil* will give you an idea of the insurrectionary proclamations of Iturbide's generals. These proclamations appear to me to seal the fate of that empire. It is a case of saying: *He sinned against the principles of freedom and was struck down*—as Bonaparte said of himself. What a lesson, my friend, for those who rule today! He who is not for liberty can expect the chains of misfortune and of universal condemnation. Abbé de Pradt has rightly said that, while it was once very profitable to rule, today there is no better station than that of plain citizen; that the offices of kings, ministers, prelates, etc., are meaningless offices, for today we are guided by inflexible Reason and not by an imposed despotism.

I make my general confession daily, or, rather, I search my conscience, and truly I tremble for the sins that I have committed

against my will for the sake of the cause and because of the guilt of
the *godos*. Who knows but that one day I shall be made to suffer
extreme penance for my misguided patriotism? My friend, it is a
problem; one can now rule only for love of his neighbor and with a
profound humility. The citizens are very sensitive [*cosquillosos*], and
they will not hear of Gothic architecture, or reasons of state, or excuses. What they want is constitutional architecture, legal geometry,
the most perfect and meticulous symmetry—nothing that might offend the sight, the hearing, or any of the other senses. For our own
protection, beg Its Holiness, the Congress, for a dispensation to sin
against liberal principles with remission of sins and punishment; else
we, like Iturbide, O'Higgins, and San Martín, shall have gained
nothing by saving our country. For the worthy citizens are not anxious to fight in battles, nor even to provide pay for their matadors,
lest they break the Ten Commandments and the sacred laws of Phi-
lanthropy. Once the fight is won, however, they demand a share in
the spoils, while roundly condemning the shedders of blood; for it is
a very proper and holy thing to condemn and to collect.

I have just learned that the pirate brig *Belgrano* is off the coasts
of Esmeraldas and Chocó with several prizes. I greatly fear that two
of our vessels, which sailed to pick up arms and troops on those coasts
and at the Isthmus of Panamá, may have been seized, as they are long
in returning. I am awaiting our war vessels, which are due at any
moment, in order to send them in pursuit of the pirate brig. It would
be a sad blow if we were to lose the 2,000 rifles and 300 men that are
coming from Panamá and Chocó, or, rather, from Tumaco, where
men are being recruited daily; and, as these men are from a warm
country, they are especially useful, that is, far from home, the only
place where they are fit for anything.

It seems that all is going well in Chile, and there is a strong sentiment in favor of Perú. I know nothing of Mosquera other than that
he has arrived in Buenos Aires. I hope for his early arrival, for it is
time that the mission returned. His being in Buenos Aires at the
time of the Moquegua mishap[1] will have been very useful, as he must
have taken pains to assist Perú, however ineffectually, for the paralyzed condition of Buenos Aires promises nothing for the present.
In that country all minds are concentrated on Montevideo and internal dissension. I believe that Montevideo will now be handed over

---

[1] At the battle of Moquegua, January, 1823, the Peruvian forces under
General Rudecindo Alvarado were defeated by the Spanish army (ed.).

to Buenos Aires as a result of the disagreement between Brazil and Portugal. This will work to our advantage, as they can then aid Perú.

Were I not well informed on current events in America and Europe by the prompt and frequent advices which I receive from those parts, I should be disconcerted by the absence of news from Bogotá. But news by way of the Isthmus helps me greatly in this regard. I do not for a moment doubt but that, should war break out with Spain, either party would come to terms with us, of its own accord or under pressure from the English. This thought gives me great satisfaction. For I have always found comfort in the thought of peace and recognition, as you know, and I have often been laughed at for my peace mania [pazomania].

I have no news of the Congress, not even hearsay. I understand that it has been inaugurated, but there is no communication whatsoever between this world and that. The senators that you have commended so highly to me will not go, for these gentlemen wish to be neither sovereigns nor legislators, saying, like Bamba [sic],[1] that they would prefer death to the throne. This modesty and moderation cannot be overcome, my friend, for it is disarming, and it cannot be denied that we are the most moderate of men. We wish neither to rule nor to be ruled. Some want centralized liberty, it being the strongest type of liberty, yet they would have it moderated by federacy. Others would not make the laws, to avoid the harsh penalty and ostentation of representing an august constituency.

Do you know that I have not had word from Venezuela for years? Please ask Briceño to write me of my family and friends, if he knows anything, and to give them news of me. By this channel I am sending a message to my sister María Antonia. Please deliver it to Briceño.

I am your most devoted and affectionate friend,

BOLÍVAR

159. To GENERAL ANTONIO JOSÉ DE SUCRE

[Blanco y Azpurúa, IX, 177]

Guayaquil, April 30, 1823.

My dear General:

I shall be very happy when I learn that you have arrived safely at Callao and have found that area ready to defend itself and capable of repulsing any attack Canterac may make upon it.

---

[1] Wamba, King of Spain (672-680) (ed.).

Envoys have arrived here from Perú requesting that I march to that country and bringing me the treaty with General Portocarrero,[2] unratified. I am returning it for ratification, as we have done our part and, moreover, it is a just request. Governments must maintain dignity; above all, strong governments, which remain within the bounds of moderation.

As I have had no news from Colombia, two mails having failed to arrive, probably because they were sent by way of Barbacoas, I know nothing of Morales or of anyone else. Neither have I received congressional permission to go to Perú, though I expect such permission within two weeks so that I can get under way. Meanwhile, I am embarking the remaining 1,500 men, and I am expecting your report of what you have seen and done in your area.

Furthermore, if any major event is to occur, it should take place early next month, as it is unlikely that the enemy will approach Lima after the *Rifles* battalion has arrived; and I shall not be able to be there by then. You know what I have planned and what we must do in the future; in any case, as I have told Villafuerte, it is my final opinion that we must emulate Fabius and not Caesar in the present situation. I insist, therefore, upon the greatest possible caution until Europe has decided our quarrel with Spain; but, if by ill chance some unfortunate event should occur, you must make every effort to defend Callao and to see that the free territory of Perú makes its own defense. It is because of such a probability that I am most anxious to be there, for then authority, zeal, energy, and intelligence will be needed most. You have these qualities, and you must put them to the best possible use.

Six or eight hundred men of the *Bogotá* [battalion] will leave in a week and the remainder will follow in ships of war or in such others as can be found. In any event, they will all be under way within a fortnight.

Please impress upon the president everything that I have said in this letter.

With the greatest esteem, I am, my friend, your most affectionate and devoted

BOLÍVAR

---

[2] The treaty stipulated the conditions under which the Colombian troops would go to the aid of Perú, namely, Perú was to pay and supply the Colombian forces from the time of their departure until their return (ed.).

160. J[osé] Gabriel Pérez to [Joaquín Campino],
    Chilean Minister to Colombia[1]

[Original]

Guayaquil, April 30, 1823.

I have the honor of advising you that His Excellency the Liberator
has received your favored note of April 12, in which Your Excellency
acquaints him with the object of the mission entrusted to your distinguished talents by the government of Chile. Nothing, indeed, is
more worthy of the free governments of America.

Chile and Colombia must unite their forces in order to complete
the liberation of the New World; His Excellency the Liberator is
truly gratified to note the eagerness with which Chile is ready to
make fresh sacrifices for the sacred cause of humanity in Perú.

The Liberator would have been most pleased to receive Your Excellency with the distinctions merited by your high office, and he is
consoled by the hope that he will have that satisfaction later in Lima,
provided that the Colombian Congress grants him permission to leave
the territory of the Republic in order to unsheathe his sword in Perú.

General Sucre, our Envoy Extraordinary to the government of
Perú, is authorized by His Excellency to enter into correspondence
with the governments of Chile and Buenos Aires with respect to the
war in Perú. By this time the General will have arrived in that capital and will no doubt have approached Your Excellency respecting
this matter.

I must not fail to point out to Your Excellency, as the diplomatic
Minister of Chile, how gladly His Excellency would welcome prompt
and substantial aid from Chile to Perú. One great and concerted effort
might end the war upon a single field of battle, whereas piecemeal
sacrifices can only prolong the agonies of the New World.

His Excellency the Liberator orders me to express to Your Excellency his most cordial appreciation of the gracious and flattering terms
with which it has pleased you to honor him.

It is with great satisfaction that I take this opportunity to express
the respect and esteem with which I am Your Excellency's obedient
servant. God keep you, etc.

J. GABRIEL PÉREZ

---

[1] This envoy reached Lima but did not proceed to Bogotá (ed.).

161. J[osé] Gabriel Pérez to [Bernardo Rivadavia],
    Minister of Foreign Relations, Buenos Aires

[Letterbook]

Guayaquil, May 2, 1823.

Since the time when His Excellency the Liberator of Colombia
learned of the unfortunate defeat of the Peruvian army at Moquegua,
he has, in this southern part of Colombia, done everything possible
to prepare a powerful force to be placed at the service of Perú. In
fact, forty-five hundred men have already departed, and, in twelve
days at the most, the remaining fifteen hundred will follow, thus
completing the six thousand promised by His Excellency to that state.

In spite of this aid from Colombia and the three thousand men
promised by Chile, it is possible that the enemy, maneuvering with
great rapidity, will take possession of the capital of Lima before these
auxiliary forces have arrived in sufficient numbers to oppose him, or
before they can recover from the fatigue of their arduous journey.
In such an event Perú's position would be seriously compromised,
and we would be unable to carry out our operations with the same
ease and facility as if we were masters of that city. An Argentine division operating in Upper Perú would, in all probability, meet with
excellent success; this could be accomplished with ease, as the main
body of recruits, being at a great distance from the Buenos Aires provinces, would be obliged to resist, watch, and counter a strong army
within its sight—an army which is prepared to take advantage of the
first opportunity to destroy these recruits, particularly if they move
toward the sierra.

Prior to the events at Moquegua, His Excellency the Liberator of
Colombia had undertaken to urge your government and that of Chile
to join their forces in a concerted effort to destroy the only royalist
army remaining in South America, which menaces, because of its
triumphs, the existence of all the independent governments. The victories recently won by the royalists may serve to alarm those
concerned to such an extent that nothing will be left undone to accomplish their annihilation.

To send a division into Upper Perú, as suggested by His Excellency to your government, would at the same time free the depend-
encies of your state in that territory and seriously embarrass the
enemy, who would find himself attacked from the rear and thus
threatened with the loss of one of his sources of supply.

His Excellency instructs me to remind your government of the importance of this operation, which is so vital to the interests of South America.

As it is assumed that Mosquera, our minister plenipotentiary to your government, has by now returned to Chile, His Excellency has instructed me to address Your Excellency directly so that you may convey his views to your government.

God keep you, etc.

J. GABRIEL PÉREZ

---

162. J[OSÉ] GABRIEL PÉREZ TO JOAQUÍN MOSQUERA, COLOMBIAN MINISTER TO CHILE AND BUENOS AIRES

[Letterbook]

Guayaquil, May 2, 1823.

Since the end of last December, when you reported that you were going to Buenos Aires, I have not had the honor of receiving any communication from you, and it was only from the public papers of Buenos Aires that His Excellency the Liberator learned of your arrival in that capital.

At the end of February this year, from Babahoyo, I addressed an important communication to you in which His Excellency repeated to the governments of Chile and Buenos Aires his desire that they coöperate effectively and in concert to accomplish the destruction of the only royalist army which still exists in South America. This army, strengthened by its newest triumphs, particularly at Moquegua, is an imminent threat to Perú and a source of alarm to the other independent governments. The government of Chile, at the first news of this disaster, promised three thousand men, which we have been assured are already en route. Colombia has sent 4,500 soldiers, and she will send 1,500 more within twelve days, thus completing the 6,000 which she promised. If an Argentine division were to move upon Upper Perú, the destruction of the enemy would inevitably follow. His Excellency, accordingly, has instructed me to address to the government of Buenos Aires a note, a copy of which is enclosed, and charges you to insist upon such an expedition, if you are still in that capital. I earlier informed you that Morales, having advanced through the province of Trujillo as far as Bailadores in La Grita, was attacked in the rear and routed; hence, the invading division was dispersed. He lost all of this division's equipment and baggage. Following that incident, he withdrew to Maracaibo, where he was surrounded by our forces both on land and sea. News of his final destruction in that city is expected daily. Our navy has grown so large that the Spanish cannot cope with it in the northern waters. The Vice President has informed His Excellency the Liberator that he thinks it improbable that even Morales himself will escape. He further states that Puerto Cabello will be occupied before Maracaibo, and that the rest of the Republic is completely quiet. God keep you, etc.

J. GABRIEL PÉREZ

163. To GENERAL ANTONIO JOSÉ DE SUCRE

[Blanco y Azpurúa, IX, 178]

Guayaquil, May 24, 1823.

My dear General:

Yesterday Colonel Heres arrived, bringing me a large number of papers and dispatches. I conversed with him at length, asking him about everything that would merit explanation, for I have given much thought to the fate of Perú and the Army of Liberation.

As yet I know nothing of the outcome of the expected decisive battle between Montilla and Morales, nor have I had any notice respecting the installation of the Congress; it may be the 15th of next month before I receive the reply of Congress concerning my going to Perú. I do not deeply regret this delay, for in the meantime our troops can arrive and recover their strength, our recruits can be trained, and we can learn the outcome of events in Europe before undertaking anything decisive in Perú.

After the most profound and careful reflection of which I am capable, I am more than ever confirmed in my original plan. Each day

I receive added support for my political opinions: everything strongly confirms my conjectures regarding an early peace. England is the principal interested party in this matter. She desires to form an alliance with all the free peoples of America and Europe against the Holy Alliance, in order to place herself at the head of those peoples and rule the world. It does not suit England's purpose for any European nation, like Spain, which is powerful by reason of position, relations, and former dominion, to retain a colony in America, such as Perú. England would prefer to see her independent, weak in authority, and precarious in government; she will therefore use any pretext to support the independence of Perú. She could be given no more plausible pretexts than the patriot possession of the capital, the port, and the fortress, a navy and an army; the support of the people; the spirit of independence; and neighbors allied to maintain this independence—in short, whatever pretext serves the purposes of a power only too willing to espouse a cause that is to its own advantage. England knows that, should she support Spain's claim to Perú, she would estrange all those nations of the New World that desire absolute independence. England, no less than Spain, must also know that Spanish possession of Perú would forever be a seed of war. There would always be national antipathy between the old Spaniards and the new; and, accordingly, we would all unite to drive them out of the New World, so that they would never be able to revive their rights of possession. Consequently, if the dominion which England hopes to form with the league of free peoples is not to suffer from disturbances which might imperil all or part of that colossus, she must necessarily make plans to destroy the seed of discord that would be implanted were any European power to continue to dominate any part of this new continent.

There is not the slightest doubt but that our present situation vigorously demands that we maintain our foothold in Perú with the utmost tenacity until we can secure her independence. Perú's independence would be placed in dire peril if it should be exposed to the fortunes of war at a time when America waits upon a European policy, which will not keep us long in suspense but has, in fact, already decided our fate because of the speed necessitated by Spain's danger and England's prosperity. Everything would turn against Perú were we to lose but a single battle. Appearances as well as actuality would then favor the Spaniards, for they would at once besiege Callao and occupy the province of Trujillo, which is the part of Perú that we hold. You are aware that no troops remain in this quarter and that the companies now being raised consist of local garrisons which, although indispensable, cannot be moved. The forces expected from the northern coast will not arrive here for another two or three months; hence, it would be impossible for us to defend the province of Trujillo or to keep Pasto in submission, were we to suffer a defeat in that area. All this means that, until the campaign against Morales has been decided, we cannot count upon security in the south; that, as long as military results are dependent upon the political situation, any efforts we might make would be futile; and that, until the coordination of negotiations, of preparatory measures, and of all the armies has reached a degree of perfection that will guarantee the success of a military venture, it would be madness to interfere with the natural course of events.

This, then, is what I think about the new campaign that we are supposed to initiate. I shall tell you now: it would be preferable to do nothing. Let our troops diminish from inactivity rather than give the enemy added trophies, thereby lending a more brilliant lustre to his past victories and surrendering to him arms, troops, and every other means for augmenting his already superior strength and haughty pretensions.

I am as certain as I am of my own existence that anything we might do would be lost, because: first, the greater part of our troops are recruits, while theirs are veterans; second, our men are allied troops, and theirs obey a single chief and government; third, we have neither supplies nor horses, and they have both; fourth, we cannot obtain provision on the coasts, while they can in the sierra; fifth, we lack their defensible and continuous positions; and, lastly, they have enjoyed victory, and we have suffered defeat.

If these premises are in error, my deductions are false; but, if the facts that I have just enumerated are true, our defeat and rout are certain. Fortune cannot change the necessary order of things—it can exert an influence in altering something, but it cannot undo the whole. To pretend that, in our position, we can expect a favorable outcome is like trying to plant cacao trees on the peaks of the Andes: we could plant all the seeds in the world and not bring forth a single pod.

Who can change the essence of things? I cannot persuade myself that you or anyone else can believe that any one man possesses a magic virtue or power that will enable him to quell the passions that inflame the breasts of men, to produce horses and mules in a day, to transform raw recruits into veterans, to give water to the deserts, to level the mountains, and to provide nourishment from manna. I believe that no one can perform these miracles, and I less than any man.

So it is my unalterable resolution that Perú should seek her independence in the realm of politics and time, but under no circumstances on the battlefield. I have always had the satisfaction, or the presumption, of holding the Spanish generals and their entire nation in contempt; but I cannot, on that account, say that I feel the same contempt for the enemies of Perú. It seems to me that I, in making this confession, have a right to make a case for my sincerity. Neither Canterac nor Valdés is to be feared; but their resources, positions, and victories give them a decided superiority that cannot be overcome immediately, but slowly and by progressive stages.

The expedition of Santa Cruz is the third act—the climax of the tragedy of Perú. Canterac is the hero; Tristán, Alvarado, and Santa Cruz are the victims. The men may change, but the elements remain the same: nothing can change them.

However proper and wise the instructions given Santa Cruz, the results will not, on their account, be the less disastrous. Tristán received the same instructions, and he had the same chief of staff as Santa Cruz. I have in mind the soul of both expeditions; he possessed great courage and ability, but he lacked the means to alter the facts. Alvarado is able beyond question, yet he did not fare any better. Thus it can be seen that we must not rely too strongly on the Santa Cruz expedition, however much that officer may have done and may yet be expected to accomplish by his ability and valor. He will go to Intermedios;[1] he will encounter small forces which will lure him on, and in the end one of three things will happen: first, his division will lose men in marches and countermarches, sickness, and skirmishes; second, he will be beaten at once if Valdés has 3,000 men, or he will defeat Valdés if the latter has less; hence, the third possibility is that he will be trapped in Arequipa and Puno, where Canterac and the troops of Upper Perú will either finish off his division from either side or force it to take to sea, if the transports are still on the beach. This development might prove disastrous; how much so remains to be seen. A raw detachment like that of Santa Cruz, in a retreat through barren country, needs only to be pursued by infantry and cavalry in order to succumb. If the enemy did not pursue before,

---

[1] This name was given to the so-called "intermediate" ports of Quilca, Ica, and Arica (ed.).

he will do so now, for to do things properly it is necessary to do them twice; that is to say, the first attempt teaches experience to the second. The expedition of Santa Cruz, no matter how well it may fare, will leave half of its arms and forces to the enemy, thereby increasing his margin of superiority. In all this no mention has yet been made respecting the Spanish fleet, which, should it appear, would make the total destruction of the Santa Cruz division doubly certain. In that case not one man would escape to tell the tale.

The enemy, in his present position, will either act as I have indicated or be termed an idiot, which he is not. He knows that 5,000 of our men are on the march; he expects to defeat them with 3,000 of those under Valdés and Olañeta at the Desaguadero River, where they will probably join forces and await Santa Cruz. Canterac will remain with his division intact at Jauja, with advance detachments near Ica and Pisco to cut off our supplies when we advance into that area. He will reason that we have sent that expedition to divert his attention to Upper Perú, knowing it can serve no other purpose, for it is incapable of defeating his division in the ultimate test, even though it may win an occasional encounter. Canterac's cavalry is far superior and has many good horses; our soldiers are inexperienced, while his are seasoned troops. Canterac, therefore, will first devote his attention to the allied troops because they are more hardened and numerous and because he expects me to command them, as, in fact, I shall, as soon as Congress and Morales' position permit. This means that Canterac will abandon the Desaguadero to deal with Arequipa, or with Cuzco if necessary. His best division will continue to cover ours in Lima. These two are more or less equal in numbers, but in quality ours suffers from comparison: first, one-third of our infantry will be composed of raw recruits, weak, half-hearted, and timid, as we know the *quiteños* to be; second, our cavalry will be inferior in numbers, and its horses will not reach the battlefield; third, Canterac's division will have one commander, while ours will be under three commanders who will not be in agreement. Add to this the fact that Canterac has two definite advantages on his side: the first being that his infantry is entrenched in strong positions, and, should we take these at whatever cost, he has only to wait for us on the plains where his cavalry will make retribution; and the second is that he has everything he needs, while we can carry only enough for our immediate requirements. This marks the beginning of our destruction.

The reasoning above leads me to conclude that the division of Santa Cruz can never take Perú and that the division in Lima cannot defeat Canterac. We must therefore combine all our forces to deliver a blow capable of deciding the fate of the country. I shall be told that this cannot be done, for lack of resources and mobility. I shall reply that, if it cannot, let us not do anything. I shall be told that we lack the very means of subsistence even to remain inactive; and to this I will reply that Perú still has resources, credit, and expectations. Let all these be put to use before we commit ourselves to our downfall. When in doubt as to what course to take, wisdom counsels inaction, in order to secure time to change the scene and to develop new ideas. For, when all this is taken into account, the counsel of wisdom coincides with the dictates of necessity. Our recruits must be trained, and our horses and baggage carriers must be fattened and rendered fit for service. Moreover, I need a few days before getting started, as I positively cannot leave at this moment, for a thousand and one reasons.

If the government of Perú will make arrangements to feed our troops in that country, we, in return, can assist them with rice, firewood, meat, vegetables, and other things that are cheaper here. If that government cannot maintain the troops with the assistance we can offer, then, in the last and final resort, having exhausted all resources and all arguments, we can make the sacrifice of 2,000 men from Colombia, to be thrown away in an expedition that must inevitably prove disastrous. These 2,000 men will be the *Voltíjeros* and *Pichincha* battalions, and, to complete the 1,000 each, the men in the Guard from Guayaquil, Tumaco, the Isthmus, and Santa Marta will be added. In short, the 2,000 men will be good soldiers from warm climates, and they will be commanded by General Lara with Colonel Urdaneta as the chief of staff. The other three Colombian battalions will remain to train our recruits and to garrison Callao and Lima. But we must ask that government not to have that place commanded by Anaya or any such officer, but to appoint a general or another officer whom the government and you yourself can trust— a man, that is, who will not betray us under any circumstances, as the present governor did once before—a traitor once is a traitor always. Demand outright the ousting of all the *godos* and enemies who are in positions of command. Unless this is done, do not permit our battalions to take part in any expedition, for with such people nothing is safe either in Lima or in the army.

This proposed new expedition must consist of the allied troops and all those which Perú has in Lima, Callao, or any other region. Otherwise, the troops of Colombia must take part in no expedition, for they are not to be sacrificed alone, no matter what the cause. This expedition will move as the daily situation indicates, with one of the following objectives in view: first, to relieve General Santa Cruz in Intermedios; second, to occupy the enemy's attention around Jauja or Ica; or, third, to occupy any territory the enemy may leave open that can provide subsistence. But on no account will I consent to our troops' exposing themselves in unpredictable combats, especially if they should be regarded as decisive. I repeat here my order of the day: Do not fight, but wait for political developments.

If the government of Perú is unwilling to follow any one of these plans, you can suggest to it that our troops can proceed to the province of Trujillo, in the neighborhood of Cajamarca, leaving the necessary garrison at Callao. That territory will then yield some provisions, and I shall supply the rest. Our battalions can then deploy themselves in suitable cantonments over Huánuco or other points that threaten the enemy, although from afar, changing locations from time to time to ease the burden upon the population. Wherever they go they will constantly receive intensive training and will somehow manage to survive until I come to lead them. I might say in passing that I personally shall undertake nothing unless we have those means which guarantee mobility and strong horses for the cavalry. Movement is the essence of war as it is of life. For this purpose, you must make urgent representations to that government to redouble its efforts to obtain horses, to take the best possible care of them, and to shoe and re-shoe them; to let no one mount these horses and to have them cared for by men who will treat them as if they were their own women. If General Santa Cruz' expedition accomplishes its purpose and returns to Pisco or Callao with no excessive losses, I am inclined to believe it will then be the time for a general movement of all the troops combined, with myself at their head; otherwise, internal dissension will be our Nemesis. But I must add further that this movement is not to start until we have been informed that the Spaniards will not recognize the independence of Perú; for this alone would make it a necessity for us to wrest by force of arms a decision which politics would thus have pronounced against us. To put it more clearly: When all hope is lost, we must seek life in the desperation of a struggle which, if lost, will neither aid nor hamper Perú; but which, if won, will brighten her hopes of independence. This is my last word.

I am your most affectionate friend and servant,

BOLÍVAR

Addendum: Regard this letter as official. I so acknowledge it, and it can therefore serve you as an authentic document at all times.

---

164. J[osé] GABRIEL PÉREZ TO [JOAQUÍN CAMPINO],
 CHILEAN MINISTER TO PERÚ

[Letterbook]

Guayaquil, May 25, 1823.

To the Minister Plenipotentiary:

His Excellency the Liberator of Colombia has instructed me to submit to Your Excellency, for the information of the government of Chile, a brief sketch of the news that he has received from Europe through various channels. The Holy Alliance has delivered an ultimatum to Spain, which states, in formal terms, that she must restore to her monarch his liberty and the exercise of his absolute rights. England has authorized her minister in Madrid to conclude an offensive and defensive treaty of alliance with Spain against those powers. England is working tirelessly to induce Spain to recognize the sovereignty of the South American states, and it is to England's interest to reduce the number of Spain's enemies and to increase those of the Holy Alliance. England knows that we must be recognized if we are to interest ourselves in this tremendous struggle or if she is to provide herself with an immense new market for her industry and manufactures. England knows that, unless the independence of the American states is recognized, Spain will be harassed and, further, even her commerce will be destroyed by our fleets and by the embargo placed in our ports upon the natural and industrial products of the Peninsula.

Portugal has proposed to Buenos Aires that a defensive league be formed against the Holy Alliance, to comprise the United States of

North America, Spain, Portugal, Greece, and the free states of South America. This idea of a league, although proposed by Portugal, was very probably suggested by England, in order that she might put herself at its head. Spain knows that she cannot save herself from invasion by the Alliance unless she secures the aid of all the free peoples of Europe and America. England knows that, were Spain to recover sovereignty in Perú, she would continue her petty practices of exclusion; she realizes further that, even if Spain should be unsuccessful in accomplishing this, it would be more to her advantage to support Perú's independence than Spain's rights to that country.

Thus, reassured of peace and of the recognition of the independence of the free American states, His Excellency does not believe that now is the time to attempt anything in Perú that would depend upon the fortunes of war. He believes, on the contrary, that at present we should await further developments in Europe, the while Perú continues to maintain her present threatening attitude. So confident is His Excellency of the realization of his hopes that he is prepared to support and maintain Colombia's auxiliary army in Perú with 30,000 *pesos* monthly, in money and provisions, until the expected developments occur in Europe.

Should the government of Chile be in a position to provide for the maintenance of 2,000 men in Perú, that Republic would add a new and significant service to the many she has performed for her neighbor state.

The Liberator believes that the instant he has received word that peace negotiations have been opened between representatives of the King of Spain and the government of Colombia, he should proceed to Perú with an additional 3,000 men. This plan will be followed without fail.

As the basis for any peace negotiations must be the suspension of hostilities, His Excellency will, at the first opportunity, proceed with this new contingent to Perú. Should the government of Chile then exert itself in behalf of Perú, where the Spaniards have the largest forces and where, therefore, they will most vigorously contest the recognition of Peruvian independence, massed allied power could thus not only counterbalance Spanish power united there, but it could also give Perú greater strength than her enemies and provide more reasons to be recognized and more justification for English intervention in her behalf.

These, Sir, are the considerations which His Excellency instructs me to communicate, for you kindly to place before the supreme government of Chile. His Excellency has every confidence that your government is favorably disposed toward Perú and that Your Excellency will exert your influence with that government to obtain these further services for that country.

Accept, Your Excellency, the expression of my respects. God keep you, etc.

J. GABRIEL PÉREZ

---

165. To José Rafael Arboleda

[*Copy*]

Guayaquil, June 15, 1823.

My dear friend:

I have desired to write you for some time, and I deeply regret that I did not do so before now. I saw an article on the moral power[1] in *El Fósforo* which has prompted me to write you these few lines and to thank you, if you are the author of that article, and, if not, to ask you to convey my thanks to the author. I presume, however, that you are the one who has defended the moral power with such skill and tact.

El Fósforo, No. 16, justly states that there is no taint of inquisition in that plan, since opprobrium would be the accuser; and, as opprobrium is the expression of public outrage against crime, there can be no inquisition. Continue, dear friend, to defend my moral power. I myself, its author, ask for nothing more, in order to preserve the good, than a tribunal to condemn what the laws cannot prevent. I mean to say that my own weaknesses can only be corrected by a tribunal that will make me ashamed. This sense of shame is the purgatory of the enlightened and of those who call themselves philosophers and men of the world. Religion has lost much of its power, which, perhaps, it will not regain for a long time, since customs now differ from the sacred doctrines; hence, unless society establishes a new system of penalties and chastisements, of sins and transgressions, to improve our moral behavior, we shall doubtless move head-

---

[1] See Doc. 70 (ed.).

long toward universal dissolution. All the world knows that religion
and philosophy restrain men; the former by punishment, the latter
by patience and persuasion. Religion has her thousand indulgences
for the wicked, and philosophy offers many diverse systems, each
favoring some particular vice. The one has binding laws and fixed
tribunals; the other has only exponents with no codes or enforcement agencies empowered by political institutions. From this I conclude that we must seek a mean between these two extremes and
create an institution authorized both by fundamental laws and by the
overwhelming force of public opinion.

On another occasion I shall have more to tell you about this. At
present, I have no time for more, and what I have said is of little
value. Meanwhile, I am sending you a letter from De Pradt to me,
together with my reply, which must not be printed on any account.

Be so kind as to present my compliments to the Arboleda and the
Mosquera families. I am your most devoted

BOLÍVAR

---

166. To GENERAL ANTONIO JOSÉ DE SUCRE

[Paz Soldán, *Historia del Perú Independiente*, I, 329]

Garzal, June 21, 1823.

My dear General:

Last night I received a dispatch from Colonel Aguirre, dated the
17th, in which he tells me that Major Pachano has just arrived at
Quito with the news that Colonel Flores was completely routed in
Pasto by over 600 *pastusos*. Flores commanded 500 riflemen and 70
seasoned cavalrymen. Unfortunately, General Salom had come to
confer with me and to obtain muskets and munitions, of which the
department of Quito has none; but these are now on the way.

The *pastusos*, with their mountains and streams, are going to
embarrass us again, as they did at the outset and as they did you in
the last campaign. They will immediately cut off our communications with Bogotá, and for two months I shall not know the decision
of the Congress respecting my going to Perú. Moreover, the Pasto

campaign will be lengthy, as that country cannot be taken without at least 1,000 of the best men. You know that at present we do not have such men available, unless we take them from Guayaquil, where they are fully occupied with garrison and recruiting duties, which are of equal importance. The rebels keep us occupied in Barbacoas and Esmeraldas, and we must dispose of them before anything goes wrong in Perú; this is plain common sense, but it is more easily said than done, as experience in similar cases has always proved. This means that I must go to Quito to expedite matters and to endeavor to raise troops to send against Pasto. Consequently, it will be impossible for me to reach Perú for another two months, and I shall be fortunate if I can be there by then. As I cannot at this time take part in those operations, you are therefore authorized, after you have reached an agreement with the government of Perú, to take such measures as the course of events may necessitate.

I assume that you, keeping in mind my instructions not to attempt anything that might jeopardize the destiny of Perú, will seek those advantages that good judgment would counsel in such critical and momentous circumstances.

Kindly communicate this unpleasant news to the President of Perú for his information.

I previously ordered General Castillo to prepare an expedition of 2,000 men for Perú. I have now instructed him that nothing is to be done at present except to maintain the security of our territory, which is seriously threatened with a general conflagration—all of which I advise you in order that you may inform the government of Perú. I am your devoted

BOLÍVAR

167. Credential of Bernardo Monteagudo, Peruvian Envoy to Guatemala

[*Original*]

Guayaquil, August 4, 1823.

To whom it may concern: Greetings

The liberating armies of Colombia, Chile, and Buenos Aires have been crowned with victory, and, as the day now approaches when the independence of Spanish America must be permanently assured, we find those armies making one final effort to drive the Spanish power from its last footholds in Perú. The allied forces of these four states constitute today the United Army of Liberation of the Republic of Perú, whose Congress, in accordance with the wishes of the people of that nation and of the allies who are defending her, has charged us with the direction of the war. The Congress has granted us supreme military power and unlimited authority to do all that is necessary to make an irresistible effort to end the war quickly. Desirous of having the brave men of all the free areas of America make a united effort to accomplish their wish to save the continent from the evils that threaten it and thereby end the war in a noble and decisive manner, we do therefore hereby specially commission Colonel Bernardo Monteagudo, in his capacity as Envoy Extraordinary to the Most Excellent Supreme Government of Guatemala, to confer with such person or persons as that government may authorize and to request funds and a contingent of troops for the assistance of Perú, under the guarantee of the Republic of Colombia. We authorize him to draft and conclude a treaty to this effect, with the same authority with which we ourselves might act. We promise the most scrupulous compliance with the convention or treaty so entered into, following the exchange, in proper form, of the necessary ratifications.

In witness whereof we have set our hand to this letter of credence and ordered the seal of the Republic to be affixed.

Given at General Headquarters of the Armies of Liberation, Guayaquil, this 4th day of August, 1823. The 13th [year].[1]

SIMÓN BOLÍVAR

---

168. J [osé] Gabriel Pérez, Secretary-General, to Miguel Santamaría, Colombian Minister to Mexico

[Original]

General Headquarters, Guayaquil, August 4, 1823.

His Excellency the Liberator, President of the Republic of Colombia, being as deeply concerned as ever for the independence of America, and acceding to the repeated invitations of the Constituent

---

[1] This commission was subsequently revoked. See Doc. 171 (ed.).

Congress of Perú, has agreed to take charge of the direction of the war in that state, which finds itself in a critical position as a result of the rout of its army at Moquegua. The enemy's gains, however, are insecure, for His Excellency the Liberator has rushed to Perú's assistance the victorious armies that subdued southern Colombia. Tomorrow, moreover, he shall depart to direct personally, as General in Chief of the Allied Forces, the United Army of Liberation of Perú. The Congress of Perú has granted His Excellency supreme powers concerning matters of war and in all related departments, in order that he may carry out the task with his characteristic energy.

His Excellency the Liberator, foreseeing the most remote contingencies and being especially anxious to have the new American powers win the respect of the older nations, especially Spain, either by reason or by force, has deemed it proper to invite the Supreme Government of Mexico to take part in the destruction of the enemy forces that needlessly prolong the war in Perú. To this end, he has given plenary authority to Colonel Bernardo Monteagudo, as Envoy Extraordinary and Minister Plenipotentiary to the Supreme Government of Mexico, to request military aid of that government for Perú. It seems probable that these hopes are not in vain, for their realization will be the surest guarantee of the projected general league, which is the cardinal object of Your Excellency's mission to that great country.

Colonel Monteagudo is further authorized, after he has reached a complete agreement with Your Excellency, thereby forming a single delegation to that end, to encourage Mexico to take part in the proposed general federation, by participating in a general congress of envoys plenipotentiary from the states which were once part of Spanish America. The brilliance and devotion that have ever distinguished the public career of Colonel Monteagudo in behalf of independence lead His Excellency the Liberator to expect that this mission will produce the most excellent results, and he is confident that, performed in conjunction with Your Excellency, it will prove most helpful in advancing the policy of our government and in promoting the general and common interests of the New World.

In complying with His Excellency the Liberator's express orders to send you this credential, I hold it an honor and a pleasure to introduce an envoy worthy of these noble objectives, the attainment of which the Republic of Colombia has ever commended to Your Excellency.

God keep you, etc.

J. GABRIEL PÉREZ

169. J [osé] Gabriel Pérez, Secretary-General, to [Pedro Gual], Minister of Foreign Affairs

[Letterbook]

Guayaquil, August 5, 1823.

To the Minister of Foreign Affairs:

I have the honor of submitting herewith the credential whereby His Excellency the Liberator has authorized Colonel Bernardo Monteagudo, as Envoy Extraordinary to the government of Mexico, to request funds and a contingent of troops to assist in terminating the campaign in Perú; repairing our losses, should we be defeated in the initial encounters; and, above all, providing needed assistance and reserves. As the royalists in Perú are strong and powerful, adequate precautionary measures must be taken, just as if an unfavorable turn of events had already occurred. His Excellency has also authorized him to make representations, in accord with the Minister Extraordinary of our government in Mexico, for the acceptance and ratification of the treaty of American federation proposed by our government.

The Liberator, in proceeding to Perú, desires to set in motion every means within his power and to utilize all available resources, because the danger threatening that state, and therefore South America, is acute.

I am also enclosing a copy of his instructions and letters of introduction to the Mexican government. These copies will fully apprise that government of the object of Monteagudo's mission, the scope of his authority, and the powers with which he is invested.

The Liberator has chosen Colonel Monteagudo for this important mission because of the strength and loyalty of his character and his unfaltering devotion to the cause of the government which he serves; moreover, he possesses sufficient understanding, judgment, and knowledge for its performance. The Liberator has assigned him an annual salary of six thousand *pesos*, as provided by the executive power for envoys and diplomatic agents to foreign lands, and, further, he has promised to have his traveling expenses, transportation, and conveyance paid out of the public funds, in view of the high cost of living in the country to which he is accredited and the long voyage that he must make. Consequently, His Excellency has given orders that twelve thousand *pesos* be paid him from this treasury for his salary and expenses there and back. As the communications between

Guayaquil and the Pacific ports of Mexico are fairly frequent, His Excellency will avail himself of Colonel Monteagudo's mission not only to obtain the funds and contingent of troops that he is to request, but also to procure reliable reports on the true political and military situation in Mexico, as these may also be of great help to our government.

God keep you, etc.

J. GABRIEL PÉREZ

---

170. To [BERNARDO MONTEAGUDO]

[Draft]

Guayaquil [August 5, 1823].

My dear friend:

Dr. Foley has been good enough to place in my hands your favor of the 14th. Yours is a grand thought and one very appropriate to relieve the tedium of a cruel inaction, namely, to devote your valuable time to urging the nations of America to convoke their federal congress. Your talents in that field will be of immense value to the cause of liberty, and I wish to thank you in advance for the benefits Colombia will thereby derive. But you must know that the government of your country[1] has refused to join the federation on the pretext that it is weak with respect to its federal powers and imperfect in its organization. Your government has also stated that Colombia should not have addressed herself to each state individually, but collectively to all. She asks why North America has not been invited, and she points out that Mexico vacillates. She wonders why we have proposed that the headquarters of the Congress be located in Colombian territory. Finally, we have been told by Rivadavia, in a superior manner, as befits his vast learning, that we must not exhibit our *ineptitude* to Europe, but that, on the contrary, we must exert ourselves to impress Europe, demonstrating our abilities by well-conceived and skilfully executed projects. This, in substance, was his reply to Mosquera. It was his intention to spare Buenos Aires the necessity

---

[1] Buenos Aires (ed.).

of admitting that she could not join the federation either as a state, a national government, or as a province; for we do not admit provinces, as they are constituent parts of a state and not independent states which recognize each other as such. This, then, is a case of sour grapes:[1] we are inept because they are anarchic. Such logic is remarkable, and even more remarkable is the *pampa* wind that titillates that minister's brains.

Forgive me, my friend, if I offend the vanity of any of your friends by what I say. I suppose that you have also been offended, but I take this liberty because of the customary frankness that must exist among those united by the same destiny.

Before learning of the outcome of the Mosquera mission,[2] the editor of the paper here, at my insistence, printed the accompanying article in reply to *La Abeja Argentina*, in which the shortcomings of our plan of confederation were enumerated and attacked.

You must have learned, with pleasure and surprise, that this same government of Buenos Aires presented Mosquera with a new plan of confederation which had been received from Lisbon. This plan proposes to convene a congress of plenipotentiaries at Washington for the purpose of organizing an armed confederation against the Holy Alliance, to consist of Spain, Portugal, Greece, the United States, Mexico, Colombia, Haiti, Buenos Aires, Chile, and Perú.

You may note that the plan speaks of us as *the new Hispano-American states*, naming, as you can see, no one state in particular but linking us together and including Haiti. The plan was sent by the Minister of State in Lisbon to the [Portuguese] Minister in Buenos Aires, who gave it to Mosquera without a word of comment. Mosquera states that he knows—for Rivadavia so informed him—that the government of Buenos Aires replied that it was prepared to enter into a pact of peace and amity with Portugal alone. Only God knows what this will mean.

To give my opinion of this plan would entail an *opus magnum*, as the phrase goes. At first sight, and for the immediate future, it has advantages, but later, in the shadowy and dark abyss of the future, there loom some fearful spectres. I shall explain briefly. We shall soon have peace, independence, and some guarantee of international status and domestic strength. These benefits will cost us a part of our national independence, certain financial sacrifices, and a modicum of national humiliation. After England places herself at the

---

[1] De suerte que, como las uvas están altas, están agrias . . . (ed.).

[2] See Docs. 175, 180 (ed.).

head of such a league, we shall be her humble servants; for, in making a pact with the strong, the weak assume an eternal obligation. All things considered, we shall have guardians during our youth, masters during our maturity, and freedom in our old age. But I feel that it is presumptuous for a man to be able to see so far, and, by the same token, I hope that these prophecies will turn out like the others, if you understand me.

I believe that Portugal is merely the tool of England, who prefers not to appear as the prime mover, so that the others will not tremble at her name. To give an appearance of disinterestedness, and to encourage the guests to attend the banquet, the United States has been invited. Once we have assembled, there will be a feast of the Lapithae, and the Lion will come and consume the merrymakers.

The plan of confederation in question embraces all the *casa foederis*. Its assemblies are so divided that one or more terms of the pact can be modified or altered. First, war will be declared on Turkey, as she is fighting Greece; and, lo, we shall witness a war between our Chimborazo and the Caucasus! God forbid that we should be subjected to a cannonading from these two redoubts! Their shot might cross the sea and set fire to the defense that you intend to make of the plan of confederation, which would be so much the worse both for you and for Quito. Later you will see more about this plan in a critique from Jamaica.

I presume that you have received the letter carried by Demarquet, in which I made a few trifling remarks about your manifesto. I shall always approve of it for two reasons: now for its performance, and later for its principles. Within another ten or twelve years every legislator will declare that Monteagudo was right. Today, however, you are guilty of sinning against the liberal ideas of the rabid republicans.

I am, with the highest regard,

171. J [osé] GABRIEL PÉREZ, SECRETARY-GENERAL,
    TO BERNARDO MONTEAGUDO

[*Letterbook*]

Lima, September 2, 1823.

To Colonel Bernardo Monteagudo:

I have the honor of informing you that His Excellency the Liberator desires to warn and instruct you not to make use of the credentials and powers that he granted you before the Mexican government until you are further instructed by him. This decision has been made by His Excellency the Liberator in view of the present situation in the states of the south and the preliminary convention celebrated between the government of Buenos Aires and the envoys of His Catholic Majesty. Bearing still more particularly on this decision of the Liberator is the fact that the mission entrusted to you before the government of Mexico can be carried out to better advantage and upon a more secure foundation after the Constituent Congress of Perú has been consulted, after the outcome of the Buenos Aires convention is known, and after observing the course to be adopted by Chile and Perú, who have been invited by the La Plata government to adhere to that convention.

God keep you, etc.

J. GABRIEL PÉREZ

---

172. J [osé] GABRIEL PÉREZ, SECRETARY-GENERAL, TO [MARIANO DE
    EGAÑA], CHILEAN MINISTER OF FOREIGN AFFAIRS

[*Letterbook*]

Lima, September 11, 1823.

I have the honor of enclosing for Your Excellency the decree of the Sovereign Constituent Congress, in which you will see defined the authority His Excellency the Liberator is to exercise in Perú.

The Liberator, upon setting foot on this soil, has devoted himself seriously to organizing the military department for the purpose of undertaking operations that will expand the territory of this nation, the principal and most productive parts of which are occupied by the enemy. To this end an expedition of 6,000 men is being readied to occupy the sierra of Huamanga, which is so important to this country in every way. His Excellency himself will march at its head. The procurement of funds, in order to equip this army, is another aspect that has occupied His Excellency's attention. He has, with difficulty, obtained a loan of 80,000 *pesos* from the merchants of this capital, upon his personal responsibility. His Excellency has obligated himself to these gentlemen, confident that the loan authorized by this Congress, to be negotiated by Colonel Juan Salazar, who has been appointed minister plenipotentiary to your government, will be obtained. The Liberator urges the government of Chile to take special interest in seeing that this loan is granted, and that the notes which he will issue for the aforementioned 80,000 *pesos* are met, for, as I have been pleased to mention to Your Excellency, this matter has been undertaken on his personal responsibility.

Over and above the negotiation for the two million *pesos*, which is the object of Salazar's mission, the Colonel is also to make representations to the government of Chile for the dispatch of the contingent of troops which that government has so generously offered for the liberation of Perú. That contingent should proceed to Intermedios to join forces with either General Sucre or General Santa Cruz, or else it should come directly to Callao.

Permit me, Sir, to remind Your Excellency of the pitiful situation to which Perú has been reduced and the fate that awaits her if the government of Chile should not take a vital interest in assisting her promptly with men and money. Perú is reduced, so to speak, to her capital, which merely consumes, while it produces nothing. Her rich provinces are occupied by a strong, battle-hardened, and ably commanded enemy. Her free provinces are in the hands of rebels. Peace negotiations with Spain are about to begin, and, if an arrangement is reached between that power and the nations of America, the part of Perú which is today free cannot survive. Thus the time for action is brief and immediate. Unless great speed and effort are exerted, this state is doomed.

The Liberator, however, is reluctant to accept these tragic prospects, for he sees a positive remedy in the coöperation of the Chilean nation, the first state to promote the rebirth and independence of this state.

The Liberator commends Colonel Salazar's mission to the generosity of the government of Chile, in the confidence that no sooner will he have had the opportunity of laying it before that government than the people of Perú will begin to reap its beneficent results.

God keep you, etc.

J. GABRIEL PÉREZ

---

173. To General José Ramón Freire, Supreme Director of Chile

[*Facsimile:* Museo Boliviano; Caracas]

Lima, September 12, 1823.

Very Excellent Sir:

Called by the Congress, government, and people of Perú to direct the military operations in that great and wonderful section of America, I have come, with permission of the Congress of Colombia, to continue my services to America.

The Constituent Congress of Perú has chosen to believe me more capable than I actually am; hence, it has charged me with the difficult task of destroying Perú's enemies and improving her prospects. I have made no glowing promises to this deliberative body, but, if I dare to hope for any success as a reward for our endless sacrifices, it is because I can rely upon Your Excellency and the people of Chile. The Chilean nation initiated Perú's freedom, and surely she will not fail to complete this labor of wisdom and valor. Fortunately, Your Excellency is the magistrate presiding over the destinies of that Republic; I, therefore, cannot believe that the fate of Perú is in doubt, insofar as it depends upon the generosity of her brothers to the south and more especially upon Your Excellency's exalted talents.

Colonel Juan Salazar will have the honor of presenting this dispatch to Your Excellency and of conveying the sincere expression of the high regard and respect in which I have always held Your Excellency. I presume to commend to Your Excellency the vital mission of the Peruvian envoy to the government of Chile, and I take this auspicious opportunity to proffer the distinguished consideration with which I am Your Excellency's devoted servant.

Bolívar

174. J [osé] Gabriel Pérez, Secretary-General, to [Miguel Santamaría], Colombian Minister to Mexico

[*Letterbook*]

Lima, October 6, 1823.

To the Minister Plenipotentiary:

His Excellency the Liberator, having been urged by the Congress and government of Perú to come and assume direction of the war, has accordingly accepted. He arrived in this capital on September 1. The Constituent Congress has invested His Excellency with supreme directorial powers, both military and political, with a view to completing the liberation of that state. His Excellency has undertaken this arduous and difficult task in order to safeguard not only Perú but also the south of Colombia, and, indeed, all the states of South America heretofore Spanish.

Ever since His Excellency liberated the southern departments of our country, he has recognized the need for a powerful, active, and simultaneous coöperation among Chile, Buenos Aires, Perú, and Colombia in order to destroy the only royalist army remaining in South America. This army is a menace to all of these powers, as it is located in the very midst of these states.

As long ago as September of last year, he made overtures to this effect to these governments, stating that he was disposed to contribute all the available forces in southern Colombia for this major enterprise. To date, only Colombia has provided assistance by sending seven thousand Colombians to Perú; and, although the Republic of Chile is preparing an expedition of three thousand men, who, according to the latest reports, were ready to leave Valparaiso this past month, they have not yet arrived. Moreover, should circumstances demand, the Liberator is prepared to bring additional troops to this nation in order to deliver a decisive blow against the royalists and guarantee the security of South America. Perú's situation has been, and still is, critical, not only because of the number and quality of the royalist forces that beset her, but also because of the internal dissension that she has suffered. Her government has passed in turn through three different hands in the space of one year. Certain military factions, forcing their will upon the national representatives, have deprived them of their right to elect a chief-of-state, while President Riva-Agüero has committed the crime of dissolving the Constituent Assembly and of continuing, after he had been divested of the presidency, to exercise presidential powers in a section of the Republic and of openly waging war upon the legitimate government.

The representatives of the nation, before their dissolution, delegated two of their members to His Excellency the Liberator to ask that he come to Perú, as the government itself had repeatedly requested in the past. The Liberator could not view with indifference the distress of that Republic; hence, he went there with the permission of the Constituent Congress of Colombia. Upon arriving in Perú, he found that the representatives of the nation had been newly installed and a President appointed.

Concern for the general interest of America has brought the Liberator of Colombia to Peruvian soil, where he proposes to use every means in his power to establish her freedom. He will oppose not only the common enemy but also any domestic enemies who seek to subvert the order established by the general will of the people.

The military establishment of this Republic is not equal to the type of enemy which it must combat. The war involves innumerable difficulties by reason of the climate and the nature of the terrain, as it is intersected on all sides by the Andes, whose peaks are perpetually frozen, and by stark, sandy deserts without water or life. Yet the Liberator will not abandon this undertaking on which depends the final liberation of this part of America. He has again urged Chile to send the troops that she has promised, and, as I have previously stated, he will employ every means at his command in Colombia to bring about the complete liberation of Perú, whose fate is intimately linked by common cause and interest with that of all America that was formerly Spanish.

The enclosed public papers will give you an idea of the principal events that have occurred in this state.

God keep you, etc.

J. GABRIEL PÉREZ

175. J [OSÉ] GABRIEL PÉREZ, SECRETARY-GENERAL, TO [MIGUEL
SANTAMARÍA], COLOMBIAN MINISTER TO MEXICO

[*Letterbook*]

Lima, October 6, 1823.

To the Minister Plenipotentiary:

I have the honor of enclosing a copy of the preliminary convention celebrated between the government of Buenos Aires and the commissioners of His Catholic Majesty, and also copies of the laws of June 19 and July 4, enacted in that state.

I also enclose the list of appointees named by the said commissioners to communicate and carry out this convention in the United Provinces of La Plata, as set forth in their instructions.

As regards Chile, Perú, and Colombia, a plenipotentiary has been appointed to invite these governments to adhere to the treaty. He has arrived in Chile and is expected in this capital at any moment.

This minister will, perhaps, provide a clearer idea of the negotiations, and he will explain what latitude of powers the Spanish commissioners enjoy. The latter would, indeed, be fools if they persisted in advocating proposals not based upon independence, for such proposals would only result in a repetition of the negative reply that was previously given when they proposed a similar type of convention. It is hoped that, as a result of the conflict now confronting the constitutional government of Spain and because of the unanimous and firm determination existing among the independent nations, the negotiations that she has entrusted to her commissioners in America will, on this occasion, be more just. The Liberator reasons that, although they have not yet made public the basis of the negotiations, it cannot be other than a recognition of independence. Otherwise, Buenos Aires would not have taken the time to entertain any other proposal or to submit it to the other states.

The plan of confederation proposed by the Liberator to the states of America has been prepared throughout in conjunction with the Republic of Perú; preparatory to its ratification, her Congress is currently engaged in discussing it. It is certain to be ratified in all its parts. The Republic of Chile has also accepted it except for a slight modification of some unessential articles, and it is hoped that her Congress, which is now considering the plan, will also ratify it. This league will give us a measure of power that will make the Spaniards more generous, and, at the same time, it will give the cabinets of

Europe a truer picture of the unanimity of our governments and the stability which they have been acquiring from day to day.

The Liberator earnestly desires to have the Republic of Mexico join this American pact. He would like you, in accordance with your mission, to arrange a treaty that will make of America a community of nations, closely allied in war and peace.

The Liberator would like the Republic of Mexico to know how sincerely pleased he is with the restoration of her republican system and the boundless enthusiasm with which she continues to advance on the road to freedom.

God keep you, etc.

J. GABRIEL PÉREZ

---

176. J [OSÉ] GABRIEL PÉREZ, SECRETARY-GENERAL, TO [MIGUEL SANTAMARÍA], COLOMBIAN MINISTER TO MEXICO

[*Letterbook*]

Lima, October 6, 1823.

To the Minister Plenipotentiary:

The present campaign in Perú alone may not decide the fate of that republic, but its favorable or adverse outcome will probably affect the neighboring states. A strong royalist army of war-hardened soldiers occupies the finest and richest provinces of Perú, those which most abound in men and resources and which yield the greater part of the real wealth of that state. In addition to the favorable position which it occupies, this army possesses the greater means of mobility, as it has a large and varied number of domesticated animals. The Peruvian forces and the auxiliary troops of Colombia, Chile, and the La Plata region occupy the entire length of the coastline of this state. Their means of transportation, being maritime, are complicated and costly. General Sucre, with two thousand Colombians and a thousand Chileans, occupied Arequipa last August, and General Santa Cruz, with five thousand Peruvians, occupied the province of La Paz in Upper Perú in June, after he had crossed the Desaguadero River. The Spanish General Valdés and Viceroy La

Serna also succeeded in crossing the Desaguadero. They joined forces with General Olañeta, thereby forming an army superior to that of General Santa Cruz, who found himself obliged to recross the Desaguadero and rejoin General Sucre, who subsequently marched upon Puno from Arequipa.

Meanwhile, the Spanish General Canterac, with one division, has marched from Cuzco toward Puno to rejoin Viceroy La Serna and Valdés. By this time a battle must have taken place between the patriot and royalist armies, with at least sixteen thousand combatants on either side. If victory has gone to the Spaniards, the troops remaining in this capital cannot resist them, as those in Upper Perú will have suffered the loss of at least half their strength. The Liberator, who greatly fears defeat in that quarter, has already taken preparatory measures to save this capital, Callao, and the provinces of the north, in the expectation of receiving assistance from Colombia and Chile. He intends to put into action, in this part of Perú, everything that will be of use in wresting victory from the enemy. The Liberator is convinced that, unless those states render extraordinary coöperation, the enemy will not only dominate Perú but will extend his incursions and aggressions to Colombia, Chile, and Buenos Aires.

In this situation, the Liberator believes it to be his duty to invite the Mexicans, our brothers of the north, to coöperate in the liberation of their southern brothers. That vast and rich republic is now free of the foreign foes who sought to rule her, and, being amply supplied with arms and money, she could render a service of the greatest importance to the Peruvian republic by aiding her with crucial supplies of arms, money, and even troops, which could come by way of the Pacific ports.

His Excellency the Liberator instructs me to charge you with the task of gathering and dispatching this aid, which can be sent either to Callao or to the provinces of Trujillo and Guayaquil. It is understood that Perú will scrupulously discharge the sacred obligations thus assumed and that this whole region of America will always gratefully remember the generous assistance of its Mexican brothers. They alone are missing in this contest of Americans against Spaniards. This contest promises to be the last, for in all likelihood it will decide forever the outcome of the struggle between the former rulers of this continent and their descendants. God grant that the south may yet count Mexico among the number of her liberators.

God keep you, etc.

J. GABRIEL PÉREZ

177. To José Gaspar Rodríguez Francia,
     Dictator of Paraguay

[Original]

Lima, October 22, 1823.

Most Excellent Sir:

Since my earliest youth I have had the honor of cultivating the friendship of Monsieur Bonpland and Baron von Humboldt, who, with their learning, have done more for America than all the *conquistadores*.

I have now learned, to my dismay, that my beloved friend M. Bonpland has been detained in Paraguay, for reasons unknown to me. I suspect that some false reports may have slandered that good and wise man and that the government over which Your Excellency presides has allowed itself to be misled concerning this noble gentleman. Two considerations impel me to plead urgently with Your Excellency for the release of M. Bonpland. The first is that he came to America on my behalf, since it was I who invited him to Colombia, and, after he had decided to undertake his voyage, the events of the war forced him to proceed to Buenos Aires. The second consideration is that this learned man could greatly enlighten my country with his genius, if Your Excellency would graciously allow him to proceed to Colombia, whose government I head by the will of the people.

No doubt Your Excellency is not [un]acquainted with my name or with my services to the American cause; yet if I were to be permitted to pledge all that I value in order to obtain the release of M. Bonpland, I should venture to address this plea to Your Excellency: may it please Your Excellency to hear the cry of four million Americans who have been freed by the army that I command; they all join me in asking Your Excellency to show clemency for the sake of humanity, wisdom, and justice, and out of respect for M. Bonpland.

M. Bonpland can, before leaving your territory, give Your Excellency his word that he will leave the provinces of the Río de la Plata, so that he cannot in any possible manner harm the province of Paraguay. Meanwhile, I shall await him with the anxiety of a friend and the respect of a pupil, for I would be capable of marching as far as Paraguay only to free this best of men and the most celebrated of travelers.

Most Excellent Sir: I trust that Your Excellency will not disregard my urgent entreaty, and I further trust that Your Excellency will count me among the number of your most faithful and grateful friends, if only the innocent man whom I love can be spared further injustice.

I have the honor to be Your Excellency's very obedient servant.

BOLÍVAR

---

178. J[osé] Gabriel Pérez, Secretary-General, to [Pedro Briceño Méndez], Colombian Minister of War and Marine

[Letterbook]

Lima, October 27, 1823.

Mr. Secretary:

I have the honor of informing you that, from official communications of the Peruvian plenipotentiary in Chile, under date of the 15th instant, it has been learned that on that day the Chilean expedition, numbering 2,500 men, set sail for Intermedios. The plenipotentiary further informs us that 600 of the horses ordered purchased in Chile were to follow immediately.

General Sucre, until the 20th instant, had been expecting this expedition at Quilca, but, seeing that it had not arrived and being unable to wait longer, he proceeded to Pisco with his division of Colombians and Chileans. He left General Santa Cruz in Moquegua to assemble his scattered forces, which now number 1,200 men in the infantry and cavalry. The Colombian and Chilean division under the command of Sucre is intact.

The Liberator has decided that the Chilean troops under General Sucre's command are to return to Intermedios to be united with the expedition recently sent from Valparaiso, which by this time should have reached Intermedios. This force, with the troops of General Santa Cruz, will then operate as far south as is possible in that quarter. Should the Chilean expedition fail to find General Sucre at Intermedios and hence go on to Pisco or Callao, it is not certain whether or not the operations that His Excellency has planned for those forces will be carried out. For this reason I cannot as yet advise you of His Excellency the Liberator's final plan of operations until it is known whether the Chilean expedition has reached Intermedios or is on its way to Callao. As soon as this is known, the Liberator will make his decision.

Generals La Serna, Canterac, and Valdés, with nearly all the royalist forces of Perú, are in the south; Brigadier Loriga, with approximately 2,000 men, is in the province of Jauja.

Colonel Morales has departed in order definitely to conclude the treaty with former President Riva Agüero, as I had the honor of advising you three or four days ago. While the outcome is not yet known, it appears that it will be favorable.

His Excellency has dispatched his aide-de-camp Lieutenant Colonel O'Leary to Chile to make further representations for obtaining the two million *pesos* for which Colonel Salazar is negotiating, as there is an acute lack of funds in this capital, and there is no way to speed an operation without money. He is also to propose to the government of Chile that it assume charge of the war in southern Perú by taking over its direction, sending out expeditions, supplying reinforcements, appointing commanders, providing horses, mules, and provisions—in short, to carry on, independent of the operations in the north. Should this proposal be adopted, the Liberator will send all the Chilean troops now in this Republic to work with those of that nation in southern Perú. In addition, he will urge the government of Buenos Aires to send an expedition by way of Salta, where, after uniting with the Chilean troops, it can seize the provinces of Upper Perú, which, being well supplied with manpower and supplies of every variety, afford excellent military positions. Meanwhile, His Excellency the Liberator, with the Colombian and Peruvian troops and the Los Andes division, will wage war in northern Perú. He will request of our government whatever assistance he can obtain, and he will continue to work in this region, independent of the operations in the south. In His Excellency's opinion, this plan may well save Perú and destroy the enemy, who will find his most widely separated flanks attacked by powerful forces, supported and reinforced at need. These forces will operate with hope of a successful combining of widely separated armies—a tactic which always fails. The enemy, however, will have to divide his forces and, whichever flank is broken, the other will be caught between two powerful armies. His Excellency is most anxious that this plan be adopted, but whether it will be or not, he is unable to say.

His Excellency continues to appeal to our government for aid in troops, arms, money, and for whatever else can be sent him, as set forth in my memoranda of the 13th and 14th instants. The Liberator is positive that, unless he has a large and well-directed army, adequately supplied, the royalist forces, whose strength and morale are increasing daily, cannot be destroyed.

God keep you, etc.

J. GABRIEL PÉREZ

---

179. To [José] RAFAEL REVENGA, COLOMBIAN MINISTER TO GREAT BRITAIN

[*Original:* Museo Boliviano, Caracas]

Lima, October 30, 1823.

My dear friend:

The brief occupation of this capital by the Spaniards in the month of July of this year, although it was but a passing incident, has doubtless enabled our enemies to represent it as the result of the inferiority of our forces, or even as proof that Peruvian independence is still exposed to contingencies. But the truth is that this country has gained on the military side and has progressed as far as civic institutions are concerned.

I have repeatedly been asked by the Constituent Congress and the government of this country to take charge of the direction of the war. The leaders of the United Army and the people at large have signified a similar desire. Bowing to the wishes of the people, I have decided to make a new sacrifice in behalf of the independence of America by assuming this weighty obligation. Congress has conferred upon me the supreme military command of the territory of Perú, with directorial political authority over her resources and her domestic and foreign affairs, so that I can procure whatever is needed to save the country.

The Spaniards, numbering about 12,000 men, have maintained

their former positions, occupying the sierra and part of Upper Perú. Between Lima and Pisco, I have 6,000 veteran Colombian troops, 2,000 men from Buenos Aires, and 1,000 from Chile, all under General Pinto. These units are to be reinforced by 2,500 more who sailed from Valparaíso on the 15th and must by now have joined that General in Pisco, or else they are awaiting him in Arica. General Santa Cruz is at Moquegua with 2,000 men from Perú. Between Oruro and Salta, the General left 1,500 men to reinforce Lanza, a former guerrilla fighter who consistently harasses the enemy; as he knows every inch of the terrain, the enemy has as yet been unable to destroy him. Consequently, when the Chilean forces join those of Santa Cruz in Upper Perú, the army will consist of 7,000 men amply provided with horses.

While this is taking place in the south, I shall have united my forces in this northern area with the 3,000 men under Riva Agüero in the department of Trujillo. This operation, however, will be delayed for a few days because that General is in revolt against the present government. I have, nevertheless, arrived in time to act as mediator, and I feel confident that I will win him over completely within a week or more. I shall then have a force of 11,000 men in this area, not counting the 3,000 additional men whom I have requested of Colombia, who should even now be taking ship in Panamá for this city.

From all that I have explained, you can easily estimate that the United Army of Liberation of Perú can count upon a force of 18,000 effectives, aside from the 3,000 that I expect from Panamá.

In spite of the fact that, very soon, I shall have mustered an army far superior to the enemy's, the opportunity has not yet arrived to employ armed force in order to end this conflict. The government of Buenos Aires has just celebrated with the commissioners of His Catholic Majesty a preliminary convention providing for an eighteen-month armistice, which extends to the Spanish army now in Perú. This convention, a copy of which I enclose, is a preliminary to a definite treaty of peace and amity to be concluded with His Catholic Majesty on the basis of the cessation of hostilities in all the new states of the American continent and recognition of their independence. This is in accordance with the law of June 19, therein cited.

If the leaders of the Spanish army now in Perú should be moved by sentiments of peace and therefore recognize the preliminary convention sponsored by the government of Buenos Aires, I should gladly forego the glory of defeating them in order to avoid bloodshed and because Reason will at last have come to console humanity with her healing influence. If, on the other hand, through blind obstinacy, they compel me to continue the war, everything will have been made ready. Although I hate war, I do not fear it. In case of war, a battle worthy to be ranked with Carabobo shall, here in Perú, seal the independence of South America. If we are forced to that extremity, the Spaniards will lose not only possession of these territories but also the benefits to which they would be entitled were they to accept the fact that Reason and Justice demand their recognition of our independence.

The Constituent Congress of Perú is nearing the end of its labors, having published the last section of the plan of a constitution, which is certain to be ratified. This code is only provisional. The permanent Constitution of this Republic must be the work of the representatives of all the people of Perú, who will convene as soon as they are free of Spanish domination.

Meanwhile, large sums are needed to maintain the navy and the army, and the loan now being sought in London is an absolute necessity. If you will point out that our cause here is certain to win, either by reason or by force, I am sure you will find some great [banking] houses that have been unable to invest their money because there is too great an accumulation of capital in London. These bankers can readily be induced to loan us the amount we request. This sum will be securely guaranteed by the first revenues and businesses of this rich country. Busy yourself, therefore; use your influence to establish Perú's credit, so that she may obtain the financial assistance demanded by her present position.

News has reached me here that the Congress of Colombia has failed to confirm your appointment and that Hurtado, a member of the Senate, has been named to relieve you in London. My complete confidence in your discretion and ability for the performance of this delicate assignment, my desire to see Colombia's credit established and the rash and arbitrary actions of Zea redeemed, and the recognition so definitely merited by your distinguished services cause me deeply to regret this action by Congress. I hold it to be the more unjust since you had less reason to expect it after having suffered imprisonment in behalf of the very interests of Colombia which had been entrusted to your care. I find this behavior on the part of Congress most distasteful, and I shall not hesitate to express my displeasure with the force and frankness of which I am capable in attacking whatever is essentially unjust.

Before I close, let me acknowledge the receipt of your letters of April and May, which have given me news from Europe, thereby enabling me to form a proper judgment.

Also, I must not forget to mention the conferences conducted between the Spanish agents and the Mexican government in June of this year. These conferences coincide exactly with the armistice of Buenos Aires, for the Spanish emissaries solemnly and explicitly declared that their government is willing to recognize the freedom and independence of this continent. I presume that the pending negotiations with the Spanish representatives in Colombia must by now have taken place, as the cause of the delay ceased to exist with the rout of the sea and land forces of Morales at Maracaibo.

I am your most affectionate friend,

BOLÍVAR

---

180. To Joaquín Mosquera, Colombian Minister to Chile and Buenos Aires

[*Biblioteca Popular* (Bogotá), No. 102]

Huaraz, November 25, 1823.

My esteemed friend:

I had feared that I would not have time to reply to your kind letter, which I received, together with the copy of *El Liberal* that you enclosed. I thank you most kindly for your thoughtfulness.

I shall give you the same commission I gave Heres; that is, forward me all the news you receive from Europe, together with any information that you can acquire respecting the enemy in the interior. This will enable me to determine what benefits we can expect and what evils we must fear. Nothing, as yet, has convinced me that Riva Agüero will be returned to the path of duty except by force. Until the time when we obtain some results from Minister Novoa's sudden move to Trujillo, I shall endeavor to occupy all the territory formerly garrisoned by the dissidents. The Peruvian battalion *Number 1* marched for the sierra today, to bring the provinces of Huamachuco, Huamalíes, and Huánuco back into the fold of the lawful government. The cavalry should be in Caraz today, and the infantry will depart for Trujillo within four days. The course that has been taken by the army in that area and the one that is to be taken by the three battalions due to arrive from the Isthmus, which will be stationed north of Trujillo, together with the blockade that has been placed on the entire coast, will leave these gentlemen no alternative but to submit to an honorable capitulation or to disperse completely of their own accord, as, indeed, they have begun to do ever since the approach of the Army of Liberation.

I trust that you will successfully conclude your treaty negotiations and that, before your return to Colombia, we may meet in Trujillo or Lima, if you remain there until the end of next month. By that time, should this area be duly organized, I shall be in the capital.

Good-bye, my friend; I am your most affectionate and devoted

BOLÍVAR

---

181. To GENERAL BARTOLOMÉ SALOM

[*Original*]

Pallasca, December 8, 1823.

My dear General:

For some time now I have received no communications from you, nor have I, during this period, written you a personal letter. As you are such an excellent correspondent, and as ships now arrive quite frequently, I ought to be regularly informed on affairs in Quito, Pasto, and Guayaquil. The hostile attitude of this confounded Riva Agüero has confused everything, and I am virtually confined in this Tibet of the Peruvian sierra, which is larger than all the sierras of Colombia combined. General Morales, who is now a general and who is also a poet, will paint you a vivid colored picture of this country, and of the state of affairs throughout Perú as well, so I shall say no more about it.

I am going to write as if this were an official letter, in order that you will execute everything I say just as if it had been ordered by the Secretary-General.

1. Please dispatch to me, in any possible manner and with all speed, but without too much expense, the brig *Guayaquileña* and the sloop *Limeña,* putting on board all the army baggage, munitions, men, and officers that came on the *Monteagudo.* These vessels should come directly to Huanchaco and there unload everything intended for the land forces.

2. I want you to hold the *Monteagudo* in Guayaquil. Dispatch her to me with 900 fully outfitted and equipped recruits, to reinforce uniformly the *Vencedor, Pichincha,* and *Voltíjeros* battalions. Use the uniforms of these battalions as models for those to be made for each group.

3. These recruits are to be gathered between Pasto and Guayaquil and Cuenca and Loja; and, as there is bound to be a surplus, equip and send it to me also. All must be moved to the ports of Huanchaco or Pacasmayo, where landings can be made.

4. The same instructions hold for the expedition that is to come from the Isthmus. You are to send it intact to the aforementioned ports of Trujillo, to join forces with the Colombian army. Do not leave any of these soldiers, except the sick, in Guayaquil.

5. Order one or two thousand additional caps made and as many cartridge cases, and see that a good job is done. At the first opportunity send the caps to me at Trujillo also, since, as you no doubt know, our entire army is now in the north. Until further notice everything is to go to Trujillo.

6. Send no more provisions or anything else to Callao, as that city is now of no concern to us until the Spanish besiege it, and then we will give it all that we have.

7. Instead of provisions, send me large quantities of uniforms, made in Guayaquil and Quito for our entire army, especially for the *Vencedor, Voltíjeros,* and *Pichincha* battalions, and as many more as can be made for the troops from the Isthmus, who will arrive almost naked.

8. Do not send me any more food supplies, as these are plentiful in this department.

9. You are to place the schooner *Macedonia,* which has gone to Guayaquil for repairs, under Captain Drinot or another of our officers, but, as she is a Peruvian vessel, she is still to fly the Peruvian flag. I do not want those gentlemen to appropriate her. The crew

and officers of the *Macedonia* are to sail aboard the *Limeña* to help man her. The *Guayaquileña* is to be as heavily manned as possible but not at too much expense, and the *Limeña,* at even less, for the Spanish privateer has disappeared without a trace, and we do not want to spend needlessly. There is no need to exert ourselves over the *Macedonia* as she is not urgently needed at present.

10. Increase the garrisons at Pasto, Cuenca, Quito, and Guayaquil to the limit, so that we shall have a reserve army in the event of a defeat here. Repeatedly ask the Vice President for troops and more troops for the south, stressing the serious peril which this area faces.

11. Have all our officials and magistrates treat the people of Guayaquil as mildly as possible. But have them ask, beg, and cajole the inhabitants into making more and more sacrifices, lest the Spaniards return and they lose everything beyond redemption. My best regards to Olmedo and the Marquis of San José, as well as to all the other respectable people of that region.

12. Do not trouble with small things, but make every necessary expenditure, even at the risk of obligating yourself for the rest of your life.

13. Write to me frequently by land at Trujillo, where I am going to establish my headquarters for several months, now in the towns, now in the capital.

14. General Morales will take over the general command of Guayaquil, and you will delegate the intendancy to him *pro tempore* in case you are sick, absent, or overworked. General Castillo should be placed in command at Quito; but warn him that, unless he changes his manner, he will make himself as hated there as in Guayaquil, in which case he will have to be sent to Venezuela, to take up a post there.

15. Please write the Marquis of San José in the warmest of terms, telling him that I wish to know whether or not he would care to assume the intendancy of Quito, in case of General Castillo's absence or illness.

16. In Pasto the command should be given to Colonel Flores, or to Major Pallares or Major Obando, if Flores falls sick or dies.

17. If Generals Mires and Barreto are ill, have them go to Piura or Trujillo for treatment until the campaign opens. In any case, they must join me in Perú, as I shall need them when I face the Spaniards. Let General Valdés attend to himself quickly so that he can return to duty, for he bears himself nobly in battle.

18. Pasto demands close watching and many troops.

19. Constantly request the Vice President and the intendant of the Isthmus to send us all the armament that can be spared.

20. Within three or four months at the latest, I must have the other 3,000 men whom I have asked the Vice President to send by way of the Isthmus. Make preparations to send for them.

I am, my dear General, your devoted

BOLÍVAR

1824

182. To the Marquis of Torre Tagle, President of Perú

[O'Leary, XXIX, 361] [1]

Pativilca, January 7, 1824.

My dear President:

Last night I had the pleasure of receiving your letter and official communication, congratulating me and at the same time expressing your regret for my indisposition. Grateful as I am for your sincere expression of friendship and concern, I beg to return my thanks to so valued a friend. I greatly deplore the uprising of the Río de la Plata grenadiers, as it points to a continued and perennial state of anarchy. Be so kind as to tell General Martínez for me that I should be greatly pleased if, for the honor of his country's soldiers, he were to make an example of those implicated in this affair. Had they been Colombians, he would have seen how I would have dealt with them. I have, in fact, ordered that the ringleaders of an armed clash that broke out in Trujillo between General La Fuente's cuirassiers and the hussars of my escort, a few hours after I had departed, be severely punished. This incident was a result of the unrelenting hatred that the Riva Agüero group bear toward us. They continue to accuse us falsely and on baseless suspicions. They still regard us as usurpers, as they did when they controlled the government. Thus it is, my friend, that only General Martínez and his division are on good terms with us and do their duty as faithful allies. I am deeply obliged to General Martínez for his excellent example. Respecting the others, you have seen how the Chileans have acted.

In this connection I have a complaint to make to you, which I believe is well founded: Director Freire, upon my arrival in Perú wrote me in a very complimentary manner, promising that Chile would provide additional aid. He congratulated me upon the fact

---

[1] At least three versions of this letter are extant: that in O'Leary; the Archivo de Pérez y Soto in the Archivo del Libertador; and that published by Arístides Rojas in the *Opinión Nacional*, Caracas, August 17, 1878. All three abound in errors. The two last mentioned have been used to correct O'Leary, by checking obvious mistakes in transcription (comp.).

that I had been given the supreme command by Perú, which placed the troops in question under my orders. In the past, Perú has always disposed of the supreme command of the allied armies as it so desired. I am, consequently, the lawful head of the allied army, for I was appointed by the [Peruvian] Congress. It therefore follows that the Chileans who were in Callao should not have left without my consent, and it would appear that you failed me in permitting them to go without my approval.

The fact is that the Congress, also, should not have made decisions respecting military matters without consulting me: if it issues one order and I another, to the same army, we shall conjure up a monster that will devour Perú. For example, Congress has issued a decree that justice, liberty, and good policy will forever disapprove. Is it not outrageous that free soldiers, in reward for their faithfulness to my banners, should again be consigned to chains? Is it possible or politic that, at a time when every ally is making great sacrifices for Perú, she should order the freedmen to be withdrawn from service?—Everything else is the same way.

I have still another criticism, namely, the manner in which the Delgado affair in Cajatambo has been managed. There is no authority, however lowly, that is not consulted before a decision is reached upon matters within its sphere. This courtesy, which even the meanest *alcalde* merits, has been denied me.

Further, it was extremely disconcerting to learn that the *Vargas* battalion did not receive the muskets I had requested; that the very horses that had been brought by General Sucre from the south were not delivered; that, in spite of my orders, this same battalion did not leave. Only now do I have the satisfaction of seeing that my orders are beginning to be obeyed, and I trust that from now on they will always be carried out, at least by the government, considering that so many dissidents and non-residents ignore and discount my commands.

My dear General, you know that this country cannot be saved in this fashion. Mine was freed because there was unity and obedience; it was not always voluntary, but it was ever present. De Pradt, quoting the masters of the art of war, states, and with much justice, that the soul of this art is despotism; which is to say, unlimited authority and unquestioning obedience. True, the Congress has granted me adequate power, but the same Congress now ties my hands with provisos. The government should consult me even in the exercise of its

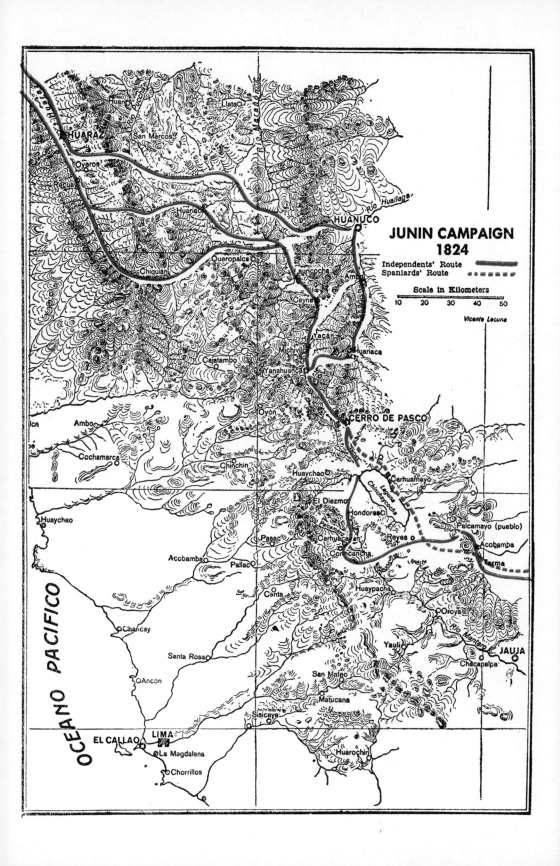

JUNIN CAMPAIGN
1824

Independents' Route
Spaniards' Route

Scale in Kilometers
10   20   30   40   50

Vicente Lecuna

OCEANO PACIFICO

HUARAZ
San Marcos
Huari
Llata
Oyeros
Recuay
Huarin
HUANUCO
Queropalca
Chiquián
Aurocacha
Ambo
Cayna
Cajatambo
Michivilca
Yanahuanca
Yacan
Huariaca
Oyon
Ambo
CERRO DE PASCO
Cochamarca
Chinchin
Huaychao
Carhuamayo
El Diezmo
Laguna Chinchaycocha
Hondores
Huaychao
Pasac
Carhuacayan
Reyes
Palcamayo (pueblo)
Acobamba
Acobambo
Pallac
Coriocancha
Tarma
Centa
Huaypacha
Oroya
Rio Mantaro
Chancay
Santa Rosa
Yauli
JAUJA
Ancon
San Mateo
Chacapalpa
Matucana
Sisicaya
LIMA
EL CALLAO
La Magdalena
Huarochin
Chorrillos

Rio Huallaga

JUNIN CAMPAIGN
1824

normal duties, but it fails to do so. As a result, I can do nothing to achieve what Perú desires—her freedom.

If matters continue in this fashion, I shall rid myself of the burden of responsibility, which I so willingly assumed in order to contribute to the happiness of this country. But first I shall make public an itemized list of the causes that have forced me to take such action. In departing, I shall weep, not only for the fate of Perú, but for that of my good friends and, most especially, for that of her distinguished President, whom I love as dearly as my best friend, and to whom I do not hesitate to say these things without evasion, because his friendship inspires me with boundless confidence. In short, dear President, read with indulgence these lines which spring from my heart and from the strength of my character.

I have forgotten to mention that my secretary is writing to the secretariat of the Congress to plead urgently for positive measures that will enable the army to be supplied. This is a *sine qua non.* Half of Perú is free; the other half is held by the *godos.* We have a congress; they have none. Yet everything on their side spells abundance while we suffer a scarcity which must be seen to be believed. Venezuela experienced a war of extermination for fourteen years, and at no time did we number 400,000 free souls, as Venezuela was the poorest country in all America; but her people did nothing to impede those who were endeavoring to save her. You have had four years of merely playing at war. Here you have had no war of extermination, and this is the second richest country in America.

I want to place a large army near Huánuco to prevent the enemy from moving down to Lima. I therefore want the *Vargas* battalion to be ready to march quickly to the sierra to reinforce our troops in that area. The troops of Perú and of the Río de la Plata are entirely sufficient to defend Callao, and they can obtain fresh recruits in the department of Lima and on the coast to augment the *Pardo de Zela* battalion, which is to remain at Callao to handle the recruits. This battalion must not fall below a strength of 1,000 effectives, since, without fear of contradiction, I can say that it has the best commander in the world, according to what everyone tells me. Further, the recruits should be taken from the coast only; otherwise, they would perish. Furthermore, cadres can be sent to this department and to that of Lima to recruit troops that can be used in the defense of Callao.

Let me say in passing that all the Peruvian troops that are not kept within a fort are certain to desert, thereby constituting a waste of effort and expense. You cannot imagine how difficult it is to retain the troops in the north. As a result, the battalions have new men daily, and all are now raw recruits. No sooner are they left to sleep in the open or taken on long marches than they desert to a man. Such troops are not worth straw. Their own commanders have begged me to send them to Callao, but, as they are from the mountains, I feel they would all die off if they were taken to the coast. I prefer to send them to Cajamarca where their food will cost nothing and the climate is temperate. Even their guns are of little value. In brief, I can tell you frankly that I no longer rely upon any but the Colombian troops. I therefore find myself compelled to withdraw the remaining Colombian units from Callao and Lima if I am to accomplish anything of importance.

Good-bye, my dear President. I am your most affectionate friend and very obedient servant.

BOLÍVAR

---

183. To COLONEL TOMÁS DE HERES

[Draft][1]

Pativilca, January 9, 1824.

My dear Colonel:

I am about to entrust you with a mission which you must discharge with promptness and great tact.

You are to attempt to make President Tagle understand the present state of affairs so that he will recognize the necessity for arranging negotiations for an armistice with La Serna and the other Spaniards in Perú. Tell him the following:

1. That our army cannot meet the enemy in battle until our forces

---

[1] This rough draft is to be found in the section of the Archivo del Libertador preserved by O'Leary, while the last sheet of the original of same is in the Pérez y Soto section of that archive. The two agree except for slight variations in the copying (comp.).

have been increased by at least 6,000 or 8,000 Colombians. Otherwise, we would risk losing Perú and giving the Spaniards added strength in America.

2. That these 8,000 Colombians cannot arrive here for another six months, owing to the incredibly slow pace at which these reinforcements have been coming; this situation exists because I am not in Colombia, and no one is interested in his neighbor's problems.

3. That, if the Spaniards come in the meantime, we shall inevitably lose our entire army, either in a pitched battle or in a prolonged retreat toward Colombia, because the Spaniards by forced marches could not fail to overtake and destroy us.

4. That the Spaniard will make no move upon Lima, but, instead, he will descend with all his forces upon Huánuco; he will then move on to Huaylas, and later he will search for us in Trujillo. His path will be entirely through sierra country, a terrain congenial to the habits of his Indians. He will then face us with 10,000 or 12,000 men, against our 6,000 or 7,000, of whom 2,000 or 3,000 are recruits.

5. That I see no way to obviate these dangers and difficulties other than to negotiate with the Spaniards for an armistice, in order to let time do its work and to see whether or not we can unite the entire Colombian army that I am expecting.

6. That the President should send a message to the Congress on this subject, saying merely: *That he knows that the Spaniards are prepared to engage in peace negotiations with us; that La Serna has asked permission of his government to treat with us on the basis of independence; that it is an opportune time to confer with the enemy regarding this matter and that, therefore, nothing would be lost and much would be gained, as peace brings all that is good and war nothing but disaster.* The President should address the Congress in terms of profound conviction, assuring it that *he has this news from numerous reliable sources, to avoid having to tell them the true reason in order to convince them. For, if more than two know of it, the Spaniards will also know, and they will then speed their operations and ruin all my plans.*

The armistice must include a clause: "Whichever side wishes to resume hostilities may do so after 60 days' prior notice," or less if possible. This must be included, first, to indicate our great confidence in our strength and to have it appear that we are not making the armistice out of necessity; second—and this is the great secret—to be free, having given the required notice, to reopen hostilities when the army from Colombia arrives, unless the enemy should accede to just and truly reasonable principles, which is probable, once he learns of the superiority of our forces.

The President should write rather frankly to the commander of the Spanish advance guard and to Viceroy La Serna, saying *that it has come to his attention that La Serna, inspired by exalted sentiments of humanity, is desirous of ending the war in America by means of pacific negotiation; that there has been enough bloodshed; that the civilized world is horrified by our fratricidal struggle; that the cannon have roared too long; that American blood has too long been spilt on the hands of brothers; that, as we are all sons of freedom and since we all defend the rights of humanity, this bloody war is monstrous more because of its consequences than the disasters it causes; that we are men and should therefore use reason rather than force; that we have but to agree, and the interest of America will coincide with that of Spain in a sole and single purpose; that the government of the Peninsula, the Cortes, and the King have recognized the independence of all America; that Buenos Aires has already concluded treaties, and Mexico also, while Colombia has begun negotiations in Bogotá with the Spanish agents, respecting the matter of an armistice and the preliminaries of peace; that thus Perú alone as yet knows no peace, for lack of an understanding between the contending parties; that the Spanish government can derive great benefits from the present status of Perú; that it is a matter of common sense for Spain to profit from her last remaining hopes of treating with us to her advantage; that in the Cortes of Spain it has been said that, if Perú were to be reconquered by the valiant Spanish troops, that would be the occasion to negotiate profitably for the independence of all America, as then there would be indemnities to claim, whereas now there are none.* These last are the words of the *Cortes. That it should not be thought we are obliged through weakness to seek negotiations and that there would be no objection on our part if the Spanish government should wish to send officers to inspect our army, provided we are permitted a like privilege, whereby each side can be convinced of the strength of the other; that within the next four or five months they will not be able to descend toward the coast without exposing their troops to annihilation; and that, accordingly, they can, at this time, lose nothing by a cessation of hostilities until we can reach an agreement or at least effect an exchange of views.*

All this must be stated word for word as I have written it here. You should make a copy of these opinions and give it to Tagle, should he favor the project. One of you may think of something more to be added; but nothing should be excluded, as this would alter my intention and perhaps cause its defeat.

I shall re-state my secret design: to gain, if possible, four to six months' time for the troops from Colombia to arrive, after which everything will be assured.

The officer who goes to Jauja must be extremely clever. He should be selected from among all the available officers in the capital. Have him insist that he must see General La Serna himself, *that he has matters of great interest to communicate to him by word of mouth.* If he does not succeed in this, then let him inform the commander of the advance guard that, *were the Spaniards to agree to an armistice of eight, ten, or twelve months, the Colombian troops would become demoralized and would eventually leave Perú, as they are not being paid and are suffering a thousand privations; that the government and people of Perú would then have no choice but to seek reconciliation with their brothers, the Spaniards.* Emphasis should be placed on the misery the country is suffering and the insolent bearing of the allies. This officer should say *that the entire population wants peace, even if the devil himself were to lead them. He is to say that he would like to remain but cannot do so out of consideration for his relatives, for I would wreak vengeance upon his family.* This man should be selected like a choice sprig of rosemary.

This ruse may appear to be prejudicial. Such is not the case. The enemy is not to be moved except by flattery. If we succeed in obtaining an armistice of at least six months, we shall have gained our object. Should the officer be questioned as to Tagle's views, or whether or not he has been heard to say anything favoring the Spaniards, he must say *No,* that Tagle is too patriotic to attempt anything, by reason of his previous commitments; but that in the Congress there is no lack of pro-Spanish sentiment, and the same feeling exists among the people; and, if the President were to find himself without the assistance of the allies, with what forces could he oppose the Spaniards? And that, therefore, it would be wise for them to establish communication with us, thereby prolonging the war until the time when the allies become disgusted and depart; which, by the best of logic, must inevitably take place. He should cite as an example the return of the Chileans, adding, however, that he has heard that O'Higgins has gone to Chile to seek them, as they had departed without permission of their government out of disgust with Guise and Santa Cruz.

Respecting this latter proposal, I wish you would visit O'Higgins to see if he would care to accept a commission that I am thinking of offering him, to return to Chile and bring back the expedition. Were he to ask, they would probably grant it to him. Matters have come to such a pass that it is necessary to employ very strong measures in order to obtain an advantage. Make every effort to impress upon him how highly I esteem and respect his person and his talents; spare neither phrases nor praises. Tell him that I expect everything of him, and nothing from the others.

Read to the President the parts of this letter that refer to negotiations with the *godos*. Do it with a great show of secrecy so that he will sense that I do not want even his own ministers to suspect the true purpose of this negotiation; and further relate that I have avoided writing him personally about this matter, for fear that, through one of those mishaps which so often occur, the secrecy of this matter might be uncovered if the letter were to be seen by someone. The *godos*, if they have any sense at all and if they learn that I expect large forces within four to six months, will strike now and put an end to all my planning; hence, it will take extraordinary art and consummate skill to carry out this scheme. Go over it carefully with him, to see if either of you can improve upon it in any way.

That Quito matter has not inconvenienced me at all, and I continue to improve, though slowly.

I almost forgot to add that the President should refer to the forces under my command, to my character and abilities, in a tone of such confidence and assurance as to make at least some slight impression upon the Spaniards. This should be brought up in connection with the offer to let them inspect our army; nor will I experience any inconvenience on that account, for I shall show them the valiant troops of Colombia, heroic and battle-scarred. On this score, you will, of course, do as the two of you think best.

After writing the above, it has occurred to me that the scheme involving the peace emissary may endanger everything unless he acts his part superbly. Consequently, you will determine with the President whether it would be wiser to have the officer go in line of duty or to have him act his part as I have outlined it.

It has also occurred to me that the arrival of Alzaga and his commission[1] offers the most plausible occasion to initiate these negotiations with the enemy.

I am your affectionate and devoted

---

[1] See Doc. 179 (ed.).

184. J [osé] Gabriel Pérez, Secretary-General, to [Juan
de Berindoaga], Peruvian Minister of War

[*Letterbook*]

Pativilca, January 9, 1824.

To the Secretary of War of Perú:

By your communications of the 2d and 4th instant and the documents accompanying them, His Excellency the Liberator is informed that the Congress of Chile has ratified the treaties of friendship and alliance that were concluded in the name of Perú by the Honorable Minister José Cavero.

His Excellency is further advised of the claims that are now being lodged in Chile by the Honorable Minister Juan Salazar, to detain in Valparaíso the brig *Nancy,* which brought Colonel Iturregui.

The present situation of the government of Chile and the financial position of that republic, as described in the memorandum that was addressed to you by the Minister Plenipotentiary of Perú in Chile, a copy of which your Excellency was kind enough to enclose, presents virtually insuperable difficulties to Chile's continuing to render the assistance that she so generously offered to Perú. The Liberator is convinced of this fact, yet he is confident that, should Chile's situation be changed by subsequent favorable developments, the negotiations that were initiated by the Peruvian Minister to Chile may yet produce results.

God keep you, etc.

J. GABRIEL PÉREZ

---

185. J [osé] Gabriel Pérez, Secretary-General,
to General Bartolomé Salom

[*Letterbook*]

Pativilca, January 10, 1824.

Through information that was supplied by the intendant of Guayaquil, His Excellency the Liberator has learned that in Quito, on the night of December 7, a conspiracy was discovered that was directed against the government in favor of the Spaniards; and that some of the conspirators were arrested and are now being interrogated in an attempt to uncover the ramifications of this deplorable plot.

His Excellency has not been disturbed on this account, since, first, he is confident of the patriotism of the people of Quito; second, the conspiracy was discovered in good time; third, only the *godos* were involved; and fourth, you are at the head of that department and in a position to deal with all possible contingencies.

His Excellency instructs me to request that you employ the most efficacious means to seek out the authors of this crime and subject them to the penalty prescribed by law.

None of the suspects must remain at large, particularly those who are disaffected with the regime. Every measure of precaution and security must be taken. The safety and tranquility of the community is the supreme law.

God keep you, etc.

J. GABRIEL PÉREZ

186. J[osé] Gabriel Pérez, Secretary-General,
     to General Bartolomé Salom

[*Letterbook*]

Pativilca, January 10, 1824.

The enemy grows stronger daily in the Pacific where he has four privateers that respect neither flag nor property. In Chile he is adding new forces. The resources of Chile are not what they were thought to be; but even though she had them, Perú's cause is of small concern to her. The south of that republic is today threatened on one side by the enemy in Chiloé, and on the other by savage Indians. In the north the government is little respected. Troops were asked of Coquimbo, but that province refused them. Commerce is disrupted. The Congress is split by faction.

Still less is to be expected of Buenos Aires, for all the political symptoms show that unfortunate country to be on the verge of fearful anarchy.

The Spanish army in Perú continues its hostile preparations against the capital, and its forces become more numerous daily. Free Perú is utterly devastated: the authority of her government is weak in the extreme; the nation's representatives are powerless; the public funds have dwindled to nothing; and the national credit is non-existent. The notes that were drawn against the London loan have very little market value, and commerce is completely paralyzed. All Perú is a spectre of calamity and misery.

Meantime, the army suffers all the privations resulting from the condition of the country. Unpaid and unclothed, it is reduced to bare rations and an occasional gift. The officers receive half-pay when circumstances permit.

This state of affairs would point toward the early collapse of Perú, which would, in turn, threaten the Colombian army, were it not for the fact that His Excellency the Liberator stands at its head and is taking the necessary measures to save it from disaster.

God keep you, etc.

J. GABRIEL PÉREZ

---

187. To GENERAL ANTONIO JOSÉ DE SUCRE

[Blanco y Azpurúa, IX, 417]

Pativilca, January 16, 1824.

My dear General:

I have received your letters and official communications of the 5th and 7th instant, and I have carefully noted their contents. First, I must say that I do not consider it advisable for you to move far from the line of the advance guard, and, in particular, you should not go beyond Caraz. If those miserable places weary you, as is to be expected, advise me beforehand so that I can go and relieve you. I think it extremely important that one of us be near at hand to keep a close watch on the enemy, the better to time our operations and carry them out swiftly.

I came here ill, but I feel better now, though I am still weak. I shall be here two weeks to convalesce and to seek funds from the government in Lima. I shall not go to Lima to lose time and patience. At the end of the month, I shall leave for Trujillo to direct the troops that are arriving from Colombia and to give them any needed assistance. Then I shall proceed to the sierra, after I have collected, along the coast, all the horses and mules that the army needs. In that region there is no shortage of horses or of pasture.

I have ordered General Martínez to enlarge his division; also General La Mar, who is going to Trujillo for this purpose. General Alvarado has taken command at Callao, which has four months' provisions for a siege, and he will make a requisition for additional supplies. Inside the town there are some 500 artillerymen, the *Pardo de Zela* battalion, which has been ordered increased to a strength of 1,000, and over 200 Peruvian cavalry. The Andes Division is also garrisoned in Callao, but, in case of a general advance against us, it will rejoin us by sea.

I have threatened the government that I will leave Perú if, within the month, they have not supplied me with money to maintain the army. I have expressed dissatisfaction with the government and disgust concerning the general state of affairs. I have written Congress in strong terms, demanding sacrifices for the army. All this will produce something, but not much. I have asked Colombia to equip the troops that are coming by way of the Isthmus. I have ordered everything to be brought to Trujillo, convoyed by two or three ships of war so that the privateers, who are doing great damage, will not capture our supplies. As all this will result in many delays, you may be sure that our troops will not arrive for at least four months; that is, the sum total of what we are expecting from the first two divisions that I requested so long ago: to be exact, the 3,600 men of whom over 1,000 have left for Guayaquil and Perú, while the remainder should now be either at the Isthmus or on their way here; and the other 3,000 that I requested when I learned of Santa Cruz' defeat, over three months ago. The Vice President has promised me everything except money. Colonel Ibarra went to fetch another 6,000 men, and I reason that, by the time you receive this letter, he should be in Bogotá.

The operations in Pasto under General Mires have begun favorably. He gave the *pastusos* a thrashing at Taindala and has since reached Yacuanquer.

Pineda and Ante tempted fate in an uprising: Pineda was sent to me as a prisoner, and Ante was left in Quito. They say that the whole matter is of no consequence. I am returning Pineda and giving orders for the conspirators to be punished, so that one example may discourage possible future victims. Guayaquil, Cuenca, and Loja are doing well.

An absurd rumor has been circulating on the northern coasts that Morales is returning from Havana. This story was told in Jamaica by some fool or knave to that imbecile Amador, and he has spread it to the winds. This, I predict, will somewhat delay the expeditionary forces. Of course, in Cartagena and on the Isthmus they pretend to believe the story, since it provides them with a pretext for holding up the reinforcements. Yet the report obviously makes no sense. Havana has experienced a revolution, and the Spanish government there has to maintain itself at the point of the bayonet, so as to provide a haven for its Constitution, which, in any case, will shortly be eliminated throughout the entire Peninsula, since the French are marching in double-quick time from victory to victory, while the Spanish [constitutionalists] suffer a reverse every twenty-four hours. Havana could, in fact, serve as a *rendez-vous* for all the liberals of Spain. To hold Havana, however, they must have plenty of European bayonets, for revolutionary contagion is rife in that city. In addition, the Spanish government is doing everything possible to make peace with us, as the King's ministers and the *Cortes* have announced; hence, they are in no mood for expeditions and extravagant expenditures.

Mosquera has left for Bogotá, commissioned by me to notify the government and people that I am resolved to return to that city and to forget the war in the south unless they send me the 12,000 men I have requested. What is more, I have sent Congress my resignation, expressing my disgust with the ingratitude of the people. This step should not fail to produce some results, just as it did in Lima. Otherwise, I shall simply resign from the service outright. I am determined not to have Colombia lost at my expense, much less to have to liberate her a second time. That is a task that cannot be done twice. I am ready to fight the Spaniards to end the war in America, but no more. I am tired and old, and I now have nothing more to expect from fortune. On the contrary, I am like a rich miser, in constant fear that I will be robbed of my savings: all is fear and anxiety with me. It seems to me as if, at any moment, I am about to lose my reputation, which is all the reward and wealth that I have amassed at such great cost. You no doubt will feel the same way; nevertheless, I must remind you that you are still very young, and you have much to live for. If only I were in your place and had no need to tremble for my own fate; at least I should have desires, at least I should have hopes to cheer me.

Pérez and General Alvarado have been here and have informed me of conditions in Lima, which are neither better nor worse than might be expected in these circumstances. They strongly urged me to go to the capital, but I refused. Pérez has been assigned to take charge of our affairs there, and Alvarado has gone to Callao to assume command, in the hope of leaving, once operations have begun. He has assured me of the good will of General Pinto, who has promised to return to the south to work in that area. Spread this news and let it be known, so that the *godos* will retain part of their forces there. If those gentlemen do no more than keep one or more corps busy in the south, they will do us a great service. General Freire promises me towns and castles in that area. We are expecting O'Leary with wonderful news. He writes in an excellent mood—but no money.

Sarratea lost sixty thousand *pesos* in a vessel; other merchants lost with him. The privateers are three—a brig, a schooner, and a sloop; but they sail individually, each on its own. They stop at nothing. The ships that they have seized are British, so now the sons of Neptune will surely pursue them.

I do not know what else to tell you, save that I am extremely impatient to receive better and more definite news of the early arrival of our troops. I am certain that with another 6,000 Colombians, which will leave us with a reserve of an additional 6,000 in the south, the war in Perú will be ended.

I understand that the President of Perú, in agreement with the envoy from Buenos Aires, will approach the Spaniards [in Upper Perú] to have them declare their stand on the armistice—an affair as broad as it is long. Of course the Spaniards will derive considerable advantage as they will receive war supplies and will have ample opportunity to trade and communicate with Spain [by way of Buenos Aires]. We, on the other hand, will despair, eat our hearts out, and mark time until peace comes. For my part, I shall do nothing to aid these negotiations. In this way I shall assume no responsibility; hence, the Spaniards will know that we are not afraid.

Good-bye, my dear General. I am your devoted

BOLÍVAR

188. To [GENERAL RAMÓN FREIRE], DIRECTOR OF CHILE

[Draft]

Pativilca, January 18, 1824.

Very Excellent Sir:

Yesterday I had the singular pleasure of receiving your memorandum, dated December 23, at Santiago.

I have never been able to convince myself that a government, headed by a congress of free men and by a great general holding the executive power, could commit the political and moral crime of abandoning its own cause and that of its brothers.

In due time General Pinto received strict orders, which had been signed by General Alvarado and delivered by Colonel Sánchez, to return to Callao. Thus, in withdrawing to Chile, Pinto acted wholly of his own volition.

Perú, with no strength of her own, is now at the mercy of her enemies and her allies. Her enemies now fight against her with a zeal and enthusiasm that is truly admirable. We, therefore, must excel the enemy in daring, if we are to preserve and liberate Perú. Otherwise, the war for America will rise again from her very ashes, and our newborn nations will be confronted with a false foundation and imminent dangers; in the end we will be surrounded by our age-old oppressors.

In the light of all these considerations, I do not doubt but that Your Excellency will make a special effort to aid Perú with as many troops as General Pinto took away with him. These, I believe, amounted to no less than 3,000 men. With 3,000 Chileans and the reinforcements that I am expecting from Colombia, Perú will be free this very year, 1824. I pledge this to Your Excellency and to all America.

I very earnestly beg Your Excellency to do everything possible to speed the arrival of this expedition on the coasts north of Callao, where I will personally be on hand to welcome these troops and to see that they are taken to the sierra of Huaylas, where the climate and resources will afford a fitting reception for our generous allies.

May it please Your Excellency to accept in advance the sincere expression of my gratitude and the high esteem with which I have the honor to regard you.

189. To Simón Rodríguez

[*Contemporary Copy*]

Pativilca, January 19, 1824.

To Don Simón Rodríguez:

Oh, my teacher! Oh, my friend! Oh, my Robinson, you in Colombia! You are in Bogotá and you have neither written nor told me. You are without doubt the most extraordinary man in all the world. You may deserve other descriptions which I do not wish to make, for I would not be discourteous in greeting a guest who comes from the Old World to visit the New; yes, to visit his own country, which he no longer knows, forgotten not only in his heart but also in his memory. None better than I knows how you once loved our adored Colombia. Do you recall how we went together to the Monte Sacro at Rome, to pledge upon that holy ground the freedom of our country? Surely you have not forgotten that day of eternal glory for the two of us—a day when, prematurely, I might say, we swore a prophetic oath to a hope we could not expect to see fulfilled.

You, my teacher, how closely you must have observed me, though great distances have separated us. With what elation you must have followed my steps—steps laid out long before by your very self. You molded my heart for liberty, justice, greatness, and beauty. I have followed the path you traced for me. You were my pilot, though you remained upon the shores of Europe. You cannot imagine how deeply engraved upon my heart are the lessons you taught me. Never could I delete so much as a comma from the great precepts that you set before me. They have been ever present in my mind's eye: I have followed them as infallible guides. In short, you have seen what I have done. You have seen my thoughts in print, my soul on paper, and you must have said to yourself: All that is mine; I sowed this plant, I watered it, I strengthened it when it was weak. Now it is vigorous, strong, and productive. Behold, here are its fruits! They are mine; I shall savor them in the garden that I have planted. I shall enjoy the shade of its friendly branches, for that is my inalienable right and mine alone.

Yes, my dear friend, you are with us. A thousand times blessed is the day on which you walked the shores of Colombia. One more just and learned man adorns the brow of proud Colombia. I am desperate to know your plans and intentions. Above all, I burn with impatience to clasp you in my arms. As I cannot go to you, please come quickly to me. You will lose nothing. You will contemplate with enchantment this immense country of yours, which has been hewed from the rock of despotism with the sharp blade of victory by the liberators, your brothers. No, you will never gaze your fill upon the panoramas, the colossi, the treasures, the secrets, the prodigies in which this superb Colombia so greatly abounds. Come to Chimborazo—profane with your bold tread the stairway of the Titans, the crown of the earth, the impregnable battlements of the New World. From that height you will have an unobstructed view. And there, observing earth and sky, admiring the grandeur of this terrestrial creation, you will say: Two eternities are before me: one is past and the other is yet to come; and this throne of Nature, like its Creator, shall be enduring, indestructible, and eternal, even as is the Father of the Universe.

Where else, indeed, could you say so much, so proudly? Friend of Nature, come and discover her age, her life, and her primeval essence. In that tired Old World of yours you have seen only the remains and the refuse of overprovident Mother Earth. There, she is bent with the weight of years, by infirmities and the pestilent breath of men; here, she is a maiden, immaculate, lovely, adorned by the very hand of the Creator. No, the profane touch of man has not yet withered her divine charms, her enchanting graces, her unspoiled virtues.

Friend, if these irresistible fascinations do not tempt you to come here with all speed, I must appeal to a yet stronger appetite:[1] I invoke our friendship.

Show this letter to the Vice President, ask him for money in my name, and come and join me.

BOLÍVAR

---

[1] *apetito* in the original copy in the hand of Diego Ibarra, who acted as amanuensis in the secretariat. It is used here in the sense of a strong spiritual urge. The published versions read *epíteto* (epithet), which is not in context (comp.).

190. To General Antonio José de Sucre

[Blanco y Azpurúa, IX, 419]

Pativilca, January 26, 1824.

My dear General:

I have had indirect news of you from Huánuco, up to the 17th instant, and I have received your very interesting letters and official communications of the 11th and 13th. It is said here that the enemy was headed toward Jauja on the 20th or 21st of this month. I know nothing for certain and, indeed, this news is, perhaps, improbable, because it may be assumed that the enemy came in order to collect a large number of cattle, which he lacks in quantity, and this task cannot be accomplished in a day. I fear that he, by making repeated trips, will collect all the livestock in patriot territory, until not a head is left for us. Accordingly, we must take all available livestock and move it with the troops from this side of the Cordillera to Recuay and beyond, and from the other side, as far as Huari or farther. Let the troops live off the sheep, reserving the cattle until we resume operations. Otherwise, when summer comes, we shall be immobilized for lack of victuals, while the enemy will be well-provisioned.

For this and many other reasons, I feel that we should collect all the provisions possible and take them and the troops beyond Huaraz and Huari. Consequently, all the infantry, including the *Number 1* and the *Vargas* [battalions], should set up cantonments from Huari and Huaraz northward, to guard the livestock and animals and to be ready to join the rearguard with all the supplies at the first report of any move by the enemy. I regard this as a matter of the first importance in the present state of affairs.

Part of the Peruvian cavalry will remain at Huánuco and another part at Cajatambo, in order to observe enemy movements. The *Granaderos de la Guardia*, which is well-mounted and equipped, should maintain cantonments at some central point such as Baños, or at some other location that is better suited for pasturing the horses and for observing enemy operations to the best possible advantage. These grenadiers are to be responsible for informing the troops encamped at Huari and Huaraz of the actions or attempted moves of the enemy. This information should be carried by reliable officers who must not rest, day or night, until they have reached the cantonments. You must give detailed and clear instructions to Major Galindo, who should encamp at Huari with his battalion. You must also instruct the commander of the *Granaderos* to keep close watch on the enemy, to make prompt and accurate reports, and to withdraw quickly along whatever route you designate and, during any such withdrawal, to abide by your instructions. On no account should he risk his splendid detachment, which, I repeat, must be particularly well-mounted, equipped, and armed. Major O'Connor should be detached from his battalion to oversee the carrying out of your instructions to the *Granaderos,* as I think he is the best officer to use at the advance posts.

The *Vargas* battalion, under Major Guerra, should march in small self-sustaining units to Huaraz, but thereafter it should follow the general movement of the troops. This order applies also to the picket of Hussars under Captain Molina, who must follow, driving before him anything that he finds in Cajatambo. We must at all times keep in mind the fact that livestock from one climate will die in another; hence, an effort should be made to separate them and to place them in areas similar to their original habitats.

I might add that, as a general precautionary measure, all impedimenta, hospital equipment, surplus munitions of the units, heavy baggage, in short, all army material, including horses and cattle, must positively be stationed two or three days' march to the rear of all principal headquarters, so that the army can march unimpeded. Furthermore, when it is known that the enemy is receiving reinforcements of troops, we must advance these baggage and supply trains, so that we will not be suddenly exposed to risks and delays. We must constantly keep in mind that the enemy will march at least ten leagues a day, and, if we do not do as well, we shall be promptly overtaken. Because of this fact, our soldiers must make two marches of ten leagues every week, either from one town to another or setting out and returning the same day to the encampment from which they started. The point is that we must have them march ten leagues in one day. We must, at the same time, see that they are provided with every possible facility and that the convalescing, the weak, and the injured are properly cared for, so that they will not get worse. We should also have the men cross the large cordillera from time to time to accustom them to *soroche*[1] and to the arid table-lands. Occasionally they should be made to climb and descend a rocky ridge; at other times have them run for half an hour, or an hour, because,

---

[1] Sickness caused by the rarefaction of the air at high altitudes (ed.).

as Guibert[1] has stated, the key to tactics is in the feet, a secret which the enemy has mastered to perfection.

I have ordered General Lara to send Major Paredes from Cajamarca to Loja, so that the Major can evaluate the resources of that region, prepare a formal report on it, and supply us with a detailed guide. Have some qualified, intelligent officer do the same thing as far as Cajamarca. You were previously instructed to effect the withdrawal of all troops toward Trujillo, which was to have been the general point of assembly. Upon further reflection, I find that Huamachuco is more centrally located and better suited for assembling our troops and establishing our general headquarters. Huamachuco offers everything: pasture, climate, food, and level ground, as well as ravines and elevations, so that we can select, depending on circumstances and the condition of our forces, the terrain best suited to our purpose. Huamachuco, therefore, should be mentioned to all the commanders as the point of juncture and assembly for the army. General Lara is there now, and the troops from Cajamarca will arrive shortly.

The Hussars now located in Moro can move to the town of Otuzco, and the Peruvian cavalry in Trujillo can reach Huamachuco in six days by very easy marches. Bear in mind that the orders for the Peruvian cavalry in Trujillo, now under La Fuente, and probably to be commanded by General Gamarra, as well as those for the *Húsares de Colombia*—these orders, I repeat, should be sent to Santa by way of Huaylas, from Santa to Trujillo, and from Trujillo with all speed to Otuzco, which is located near the road to Huamachuco. If our Hussars are found to be encamped there, let the orders be delivered to whatever officer happens to be in charge. From Santa our Hussars can reach Huamachuco in ten days, and from Otuzco in four; but the horses cannot be kept long at Otuzco as there is no pasture. Thus, the Hussars must go to Otuzco only if danger threatens.

I say to you that Huamachuco, as a location, is preferable to Trujillo because the latter provides no avenue of retreat. It is easy to enter, but to depart by way of the north is impossible. Only if we were to receive heavy reinforcements in Trujillo, should we return there and join them. But, if such reinforcements can reach Huamachuco in time, it will be better for them to proceed there at once, rather than wait for us to seek them out. It is better for a detachment to go in search of the army than vice versa.

---

[1] Jacques Antonio Guibert (1743-1790), French military author (ed.). Blanco and Azpurúa have Pibert for Guibert. Here, as in other letters, errors in names of persons and in geographical names have been corrected (comp.).

Furthermore, Huamachuco affords us the opportunity of employing each branch of the army according to its strength and quality. That city has fine, high plains toward the south, and, from Cajabamba to Cajamarca, other plains reach to the north. These are crossed by a large river with heights on either side, which may also prove to our advantage. For example, we can operate in the following ways: first, if the enemy comes upon us with forces equal to our own, but with cavalry inferior, we can take to the plains; second, if the enemy brings 1,000 or 2,000 more men than we have, and if we have reason to believe that the expected reinforcements cannot arrive in time and that any attempted withdrawal on our part would prove to be disastrous and destructive to the army—in that event, I say, we must select a strong position where we can make a firm stand and where our cavalry can go vigorously and rapidly into action at the slightest setback to the enemy; third, the same strategy will apply if the enemy is equal to us in numbers but greatly superior in cavalry, that is to say, in such a case we must also take up a strong position; fourth, should the enemy come with 3,000 or 4,000 more men than we possess, we must keep retreating beyond Cajamarca in the direction of Jaén, until we have reached a position that is so strong and advantageous that we can defend it, come what may, and perhaps even defeat the enemy. If we find no such position, we will continue our march toward Colombia, after we have first destroyed everything that might impede our march. In this last and most extreme alternative we can receive in Loja, through the ports of that province and of Cuenca, all the troops that we are expecting from the Isthmus, Guayaquil, and Quito, and there we can await and destroy the enemy. To carry out all these instructions you must devise and put into effect such preparatory measures as your good judgment and foresight suggest. Of course, the first measures are those that I have indicated above: to collect all the provisions and horses and other army equipment, placing them from Corongo to the north, and to speed these measures as the information that you receive about the enemy may suggest, depending on the immediacy of his threat and the composition of his forces. Everything might be placed between Atunhuaylas and Corongo but for the lack of pasture for the stock and the cold climate of that country. The horses, mules, and the cattle with Major Galindo can be taken below Conchuco, from Piscobambo northward toward Huamachuco. I should like you to go to Cajatambo after you have issued all your orders and instructions in Huánuco, Huamalíes, and Conchucos. You should go to Cajatambo:

first, to survey that country and its resources; second, to give directions to the *Vargas* unit; third, to get from it everything you can; and, fourth, to be closer to me without getting too far from the enemy. If you will wait for me in Cajatambo, I will go there to meet and confer with you on all these points. And, should I not be able to reach you, you can come to see me here in Pativilca.

The *Number 1* [battalion] can remain in Recuay, living off that country and whatever may be had from Cajatambo and the other border areas. This battalion should be increased as much as possible, and it should make frequent sallies and excursions in all directions, so as to become more mobile than the rest, as it must bring up the rearguard of our infantry.

Major Aldao and a few other good cavalry officers will report to you for assignments to advance posts only, among the troops under Carreño. The surplus muskets in Huaraz can be used to arm the recruits for the *Number 1*.

I had reached this point in this letter when, at ten in the morning, I received your letter and official communication dated the 19th at Huánuco. I have taken note of all that you tell me respecting the forces and movements of the enemy. Accordingly, I authorize you, in the event the enemy should seek us out with forces inferior to ours, though by only a single man, to combine all the forces of Colombia and those of Perú that are available and await or seek out the enemy as you see fit. But you must not fail to bring close to your General Headquarters the regiment of Hussars now stationed at Moro, eight leagues from Nepeña, at the foot of the mountains. Without this regiment you are not to begin any action whatsoever, since you would surely lose for want of cavalry. I shall also send you the excellent squadron of Peruvian lancers that is now at Huaraz. They will march immediately for Cajatambo. This authorization to attack or await the enemy holds for the whole campaign, provided that the following conditions are found to exist: first, that the enemy seeks us on our own ground and second, that we are superior to the enemy in numbers and quality. By quality I mean the proportion of arms, men, and horses, which proportions must not be to our disadvantage; but our forces should, rather, be superior to those of our adversaries.

I am glad you have sent for the Peruvian squadron that was at Huamachuco, though the horses will probably arrive in Caraz more dead than alive, where they are supposed to rest. You may also ask General Lara for some of the munitions that he obtained from Riva

Agüero. I should also like Lara's column to move, since, generally speaking, it is best to keep the infantry constantly on the march— but by no means the cavalry, since horses that are ill-shod and in a weakened and battered condition soon go to pieces, what with rocks, saddles, and lack of pasture.

The Hussars now at Moro can reach Yungay in four days by taking the road from Pamparomas, which leads straight to Caraz. But alert the Colonel in advance to be ready for the order to move. The distance from Moro to Huaraz is twenty-six leagues by way of Huata, Caraz, and Yungay.

I am delighted with your letter and official report of the 19th, because your remarks are both apt and true, but even more because in them I can sense your courageous spirit and your determination to destroy the *godos* at once, without waiting for anything further. Your desires also move me deeply, and they often cause me to vacillate in my decisions. Despite the weakened condition in which my illness has left me, you almost tempt me to rush into a battle, which, in fact, we cannot possibly lose, if it is pitched against equal or only slightly superior forces.

In the enclosed papers you will note some curious things. First of all, the fall of Spain is of particular interest, as it may either confirm our independence or delay it slightly. I incline to the former view, since everything is set in our favor and since the English now desire our independence more than ever. I am sending you a reprint of a private letter of mine to the Toros, which has reached me from Mexico. In it, you will see the terms in which I have always spoken of you.

Have these reprints distributed among the *godos,* particularly the special issue.

Good-bye, my dear General. I am your devoted

BOLÍVAR

Forgive the *brevity*. We shall soon meet again.

191. To F[rancisco] de P[aula] Santander, Vice President of Colombia

[*Original*]

Pativilca, February 25, 1824.

My dear General:

New troubles for you, new troubles for me. You have had the satisfaction of managing the affairs of Colombia so well that she has been able to face the world as a free and tranquil nation. I have not had the same good fortune. Pasto fights with fury, and Perú is a chamber of horrors. My ill-fated proclamation will give you an idea of some of these horrors. Crime, under numerous guises and representing every passion, has opened an immense abyss of corruption beneath my feet that envelops me on all sides and leaves me isolated in the middle of Perú. Can you believe that this is the most trying situation of my life? Yet it is, without a doubt. If I come out of this predicament in good fashion, I shall rightly be entitled to take the name of Faustus, as did Sila.

Every ally is guilty of defection or of treachery. Recently an act of betrayal, by the very government of Perú that we have befriended, was discovered. You can read of this in Canterac's letter, addressed to a friend of Torre Tagle, in which he specifically mentions the latter's plan to deliver the country into the hands of her enemies. He is referred to by the initials T.T. I have ordered the arrest of the members of this faction, whose identity is known. This arrest will be the first act of justice that I shall have performed in Perú. So far I have only acted the part of a grumbler. I cannot continue in this rôle longer, as a loftier interest compels me to take severe measures for the sake of both Colombia and Perú. Our destinies are linked together, and we cannot abandon this country without grave risk of losing everything. The taking of Puerto Cabello encourages me to hope for the reinforcements from Colombia. If they arrive in time, we can triumph; if they do not, be prepared for the worst.

Note what Canterac states at the end of his letter: No matter what the outcome, they will always be Spaniards. The attitude of these *godos* has always favored war. Like all Spaniards, they are consistent in maintaining tyranny and injustice, but they do not possess the character to be consistent in supporting liberal principles. War, then, is the one door they leave open to us. Now that Puerto Cabello has been taken, I believe the hour has come for us to use our army to wage war at the expense of others. Later we shall send in combat-hardened troops, comprising such units as our political situation will permit. At least we can say that our every misfortune has been followed by some good. You know that every one of our successes came after we had first tasted the dregs of misfortune. We must therefore take heart and prepare for new sacrifices, in the hope of better things to come; but such improvements are not to be had except at the cost of blood and money. For my part, I am resolved to go through with it all, and God grant that you will be moved to do the same.

Canterac's letter was written before the Callao victory, but, as a result of this success, Canterac is marching to Lima where he is expected between the 26th and the 28th. In my opinion he has delayed too long, and thus he has helped us to save some of our troops and equipment, that is, if we do not lose everything on leaving Lima.

I believe it would be superfluous for me to describe again the lamentable straits to which we have been reduced by lack of supplies. Callao was lost for lack of provisions and money for the troops; Perú will also be lost for the same reason. Southern Colombia cannot provide the 12,000 or 14,000 men that are needed to withstand the enemy. In God's name, put yourself in my position!

The Colombian and Peruvian navies cost us more than we are worth, because the officers and seamen are English, and the lowest in rank is paid eighteen to twenty *pesos*. They are maintained in the English manner, which costs three times as much as it would in England. In addition to this, three or four provinces of Colombia and Perú alone cannot sustain the war and at the same time maintain governments, armies, and a navy. The war in Pasto consumes more than the department of Quito can provide. This means that Guayaquil and Trujillo must perform miracles. The miserable expense that each Colombian province incurred in sending 3,000 or 4,000 men to Panamá appeared to have astonished you. I wonder what it will cost to bring 16,000 or 18,000 men to Perú. As most of them are from the Isthmus, the expense must be borne by two provinces only, and there is this difference: crossing this sea takes as many months as it does days to reach Chagres in the northern sea. And there is this further difference: because of the excruciating delay of those troops, we are losing provisions and accumulating demurrage on the char-

tered transports. The intendant of the Isthmus does nothing and
continues to ask for money, which has been sent to him. He retains
the best muskets and sends the poor ones, and he does the same respecting the men, for he is most generous at other people's expense.
Let every one act in a similar fashion and we shall soon see what
becomes of Colombia.

I presume that Colonel Ibarra is now embarking the troops that
were in Valencia and Caracas, and I also presume that those from
the Magdalena and Zulia are by now at the Isthmus. Should these
assumptions prove false, I shall order General Sucre and the army
of Colombia to withdraw, and, as for myself, I shall go to the devil.
What is more, unless we get 1,000 good cavalrymen, we shall have
accomplished nothing, for the godos have 2,500 horse, and we have
next to none, for, although 800 are left, they are from Bochalema.
The Guías are in Pasto, and here we have only the lancers who were
formerly the Hussars of Rondón and Silva. All are in excellent condition; they are capable of routing twice their number but not five
times their number, as you can readily imagine, unless, that is, we
should repeat our earlier miracles of Maturín, San Mateo, and
Boyacá. In that event we will need no help whatsoever, for we have
sufficient troops to perform any miracle of miracles.

I remain here, awaiting the fall of Lima, after which I shall proceed to Trujillo and there set up, as I did in Guayana, my peripatetic
government, although there will be no Orinoco River. For, if we had
an Orinoco or an Apure overflowing its banks, I could sleep soundly
until news arrived from Colombia that the 10,000 men, the two
million pesos, and the equipment for the squadron that I have requested had come. I mention this only in the event that my letters
have gone astray, for I do not think you are either deaf or blind, as
you would have to be, not to have seen my five hundred letters on this
subject.

You will have already heard that I did not send a mission to
Mexico to request assistance, as I previously told you I planned
to do, but I am now sending one to Guatemala to ask for 200,000
pesos and 2,000 or 3,000 reinforcements.[1] If they send them, good;
if not, we shall have lost only our effort, which does not amount to
much.

I am sending you some letters selected at random, so that you may
note the news, good and bad, which would be boresome and even

---

[1] See Docs. 167-172, 174-176 (ed.).

difficult for me to repeat, for one does not retain all that one reads. See if anything can be done against Havana.

Pay no attention to any optimistic exaggerations that you might find in these letters, as they were written more to create an impression than anything else. You must believe only me, for I am a reliable oracle on whatever concerns Colombia.

I have heard of the appointment of British commissioners and consuls to Colombia and to all America. This action is a fine performance for a drawing room or a council chamber, but I fear the benefits will not penetrate inland unless there is a complete change. Neither have I any fear of our allies. We shall all mark time as we have been doing until some effective diplomacy other than that of the bayonet and the lance can do its work. It would seem that everywhere men have abandoned the cause of America to the *judgment of God*— the most mandatory of all judgments, for it generally does not permit appeal.

I must not close this letter without telling you that Pasto needs 3,000 men from Antioquia, Chocó, Mariquita, and Cauca. They should come by way of Almaguer and be ably commanded, so that the gentlemen of Pasto will not defeat them, a habit that those gentlemen have developed. Since this is the case, I shall be satisfied if you send me 7,000 men by way of the Isthmus, consisting of 1,000 horse and 6,000 foot. Send them armed and equipped, or send their equipment separately, if this will speed their arrival.

You could order the purchase of clothing, armaments, and other items in Cartagena, Santa Marta, or Jamaica, to be paid for out of duties or some other way. Have it all sent to the Isthmus for our army in the south. Remember that all this material can be had there for half what it costs here. Here we have only debts and more debts, crimes and more crimes, treason and more treason. And with this, I bid you farewell.

Your devoted

BOLÍVAR

P.S. Soon the *godos* will have a better navy than ours, and then goodbye to the south.

192. J [OSÉ] GABRIEL PÉREZ, SECRETARY-GENERAL, TO MIGUEL
SANTAMARÍA, COLOMBIAN MINISTER TO MEXICO

[Letterbook]

Pativilca, February 25, 1824.

The outlook for Perú has become infinitely gloomier because of the loss of the fortresses of Callao and the fall of Lima, the capital, which will necessarily follow. This is inevitable, for we have no troops with which to oppose the enemy, who is marching upon the capital. Our entire army is encamped in the sierra, facing Canterac's men. The Río de la Plata regiment that had been garrisoning Callao mutinied on the 5th instant. It seized its officers, freed all the Spanish prisoners held in the dungeons, declared itself for the King of Spain, and raised his flag.

The Constituent Congress of Perú has invested His Excellency the Liberator with dictatorial power over this nation, and he has accepted this fearful responsibility, hoping that by exerting superhuman efforts and by rallying the remnants of this country, he may yet save her from the slavery that threatens her, rescue the army of Colombia, and spare our own southern region an invasion by an enemy who would be powerfully reinforced by the possession of all Perú.

His Excellency the Liberator, firmly resolved to dispute every inch of ground and to yield no territory to the enemy, has asked for 12,000 or 16,000 men from Colombia and 3,000 from Chile. His Excellency confidently awaits these troops in the northern provinces of Perú.

What makes His Excellency the Liberator's position especially critical is the shortage of funds, for the treasury here is nearly depleted. Accordingly, His Excellency instructs me to inform you to make every effort to obtain a loan of 200,000 or 300,000 *pesos* from the Mexican government or from private subscribers, to be guaranteed by the government of Colombia. You are authorized to negotiate this loan with the government or with private lenders. If you obtain a loan, you are to forward these funds to Guayaquil by whatever means you deem fastest, always remembering that this matter is as pressing as His Excellency's situation is extreme, for he is without funds for even the most indispensable items. I therefore hardly know how to impress upon you the promptness and dispatch with which you must acquire and forward this money.

You are authorized by His Excellency the Liberator to negotiate this loan and to stipulate the manner, time, and terms of payment, under guarantee of the government of Colombia.

The immense resources of Perú, given a few days of peace, are incalculable. Her rich and abundant mines need only laborers, who are now either at war or in hiding, to escape conscription. Yet one single battle will decide the fate of this country, and all the odds favor the liberators, if only they receive the help that is requested. Then the benefactors of Perú will be repaid, and they will enjoy her eternal gratitude.

God keep you, etc.

J. GABRIEL PÉREZ

193. J [osé] GABRIEL PÉREZ, SECRETARY-GENERAL, TO [GENERAL JOSÉ CARREÑO], INTENDANT, COMMANDANT GENERAL OF THE ISTHMUS OF PANAMÁ

[*Letterbook*]

Pativilca, February 25, 1824.

I enclose a blank letter of credence and instructions for you to fill out in Panamá. You are to select some person of unquestioned patriotism, one who has judgment, intelligence, good personality, and sagacity and send him immediately to Guatemala to ask that government for assistance in men and money and to execute the commission that is described in the letter of credence and the instructions. I also enclose a note and a letter of introduction, addressed to the Secretary of State and Foreign Affairs of the Guatemalan government, to be closed and sealed by you after you have filled in the blanks with the name of the person you select. Having done all this, you will make a special effort to see that he departs as quickly as possible to discharge this urgent and extremely important mission. You must not lose a minute, for the condition of this country is such that the loss of a single minute may result in serious consequences.

In commending to you the delicate task of selecting the person who is to undertake this mission, His Excellency places great reliance upon your judgment and intuition. By way of example, His Excellency would suggest the citizens Talla, Ferro, and Argote; but, if none of these is available, you are to select the man who is to be sent.[1]

God keep you, etc.

J. GABRIEL PÉREZ

---

194. J [osé] Gabriel Pérez, Secretary-General, to [Juan Francisco de Sosa], Guatemalan Minister of Foreign Affairs

[*Copy*]

Pativilca, February 23, 1824.

Mr. Secretary:

Throughout the year 1823, military developments in Perú have consistently gone against us, thereby favoring the Spaniards. When, in September of last year, His Excellency the Liberator of Colombia moved to Lima, he found this unhappy country enveloped in fearful anarchy. He discovered that the chief executive, Riva Agüero, who had been divested of his office by the Constituent Congress, was waging open war upon the legitimate government, with 3,000 men of the Peruvian army who had remained under his command in the northern provinces. Riva Agüero carried his unlawful behavior to the point of inviting the Spaniards to occupy the country and to avail themselves of his army. The Liberator, who, at that time, had 4,000 Colombians at his disposal, proceeded north and was able to prevent Riva Agüero from carrying out his perfidious and contemptible betrayal. Colonel La Fuente, who was in charge of Riva Agüero's cuirassiers, encouraged by the approach of our troops, seized and imprisoned his chief and thus avoided a clash between our forces and those dissident troops. Such a clash, even if it had ended in our favor, would always have been highly regrettable as a battle between Americans. The Liberator, although fully authorized by the Constituent Congress to end the sedition of Riva Agüero, granted him and his

---

[1] Manuel María Ayala was appointed but failed in his mission (ed.).

SELECTED WRITINGS OF BOLIVAR 439

army a complete and unconditional amnesty. Late in January, Riva Agüero and General Herrera embarked at Guayaquil on an English vessel bound for Gibraltar.

Since that time, the Liberator has been ceaselessly occupied in perfecting the military organization of Perú and in rehabilitating its few existing units. In this country, which is torn by factions, progress has been slow, and the setbacks have been many, notwithstanding the great energy with which the Liberator has proceeded.

A new misfortune has further aggravated the critical situation of this state. The troops of the Río de la Plata, which had garrisoned the forts of Callao, revolted on the 5th instant. Seizing their commanders and officers, they freed and placed in command the Spanish prisoners held in the dungeons of the fortresses and raised the flag of the King of Spain above the ramparts. This revolt, which lost us the strategic point of Callao, will inevitably lead to the enemy's possession of Lima, the capital, upon which he is marching with a strong column that should reach that city by the 26th. The handful of troops that are garrisoning Lima will have no choice but to withdraw. The fall of the strongholds of Callao and Lima will result in the loss of the enormous stores that are housed in the port arsenal, of the only fortified military post in Perú, and of the increased morale which the possession of the capital and the fortresses has given us. From the moment when His Excellency the Liberator arrived at Callao, he realized the weakness of Perú, and forthwith he requested reinforcements of 12,000 men from Colombia and 2,000 or 3,000 from Chile. He also immediately invited the states of South America to participate actively and promptly in the salvation of Perú, for the future of all the American states is linked with that of Perú.

The royalist army in Perú numbers no less than from 14,000 to 16,000 men, and it occupies all of Upper Perú and the cordillera. We scarcely hold a part of the northern coast, which we shall probably have to abandon. We also hold a very small section of the sierra, and the province of Trujillo as far as Tumbez, the most sterile and arid part of the whole country. The Spaniards, with a strong, battle-scarred, and victorious army, will very probably move against the Liberator, who, today, cannot place in the field more than 4,000 first class Colombian troops and 3,000 Peruvians who, new to soldiering, have been corrupted by bad example and by the factions into which they have been divided. In spite of this fearful prospect, the Liberator is determined not to leave the territory, but, rather, to remain in order to keep the Spaniards from occupying the entire state and to await the assistance that he has asked of Colombia and Chile.

If the Spaniards gain complete possession, they will obtain enormous advantages. The degree of power and armed might that they will then have will be incalculable, and it will constitute a menace to the neighboring states. The possession of Callao will give them a navy. They will then be strong, and they will make their strength felt on both land and sea. But if the troops that His Excellency has requested arrive in good time, a single battle will suffice to wrest from the enemy every advantage that he has gained and to annihilate the Spanish power in America. Freedom and independence for all America will thereby be assured.

His Excellency the Liberator instructs me to submit this account for the consideration of the Supreme Executive Power of the United Provinces of Central America and to ask our brothers in Guatemala, whose generous qualities are renowned and whose concern for the American cause is so deep, to take cognizance of the deplorable position of this state. It is one that demands the assistance of all those who are committed to a common purpose in the struggle against the King of Spain. Your Republic, free of foes, is able to extend a helping hand to her brothers in Perú, who are imminently threatened with new and heavier chains of slavery and death.

If the Supreme Government of your Republic would be so generous as to equip, as quickly as possible, an expedition of 3,000 men to proceed to Guayaquil, where they could receive instructions on their further movements, Perú would recall this generous act in the days of her glory. Or, if your government is unable to undertake a military contribution of this size yet could aid us with 200,000 or 300,000 *pesos,* the position of this country would be enormously improved and the Spaniards would no longer be able to boast that they hold her in their power.

His Excellency the Liberator, in addressing your Supreme Government, is confident that he has not made a fruitless and unsuccessful appeal, for he knows full well that our generous brothers of the north will realize that our good or bad fortune is a measure of their own.

The government of the Republic of Colombia guarantees the repayment of the costs of any expedition or of any loan of money with which your government may see fit to help us.

God keep you, etc.

J. GABRIEL PÉREZ

195. J [osé] Gabriel Pérez, Secretary-General, to Colonel Francisco Salazar, Peruvian Minister to Chile

[*Letterbook*]

Trujillo, March 26, 1824.

I have the honor of enclosing copies of the communications that were sent yesterday by His Excellency the Dictator of Perú to the government of Chile. Their content will serve you as a guide in order to keep before that government a constant and persistent request for the 500 trained cavalrymen that were asked of that government, and for one or two ships of war to coöperate with the forces of Vice Admiral Guisse in the blockade of Callao.

I do not know how to impress upon you the importance of your succeeding in both of these objects and of your making certain that the rest of the expedition that is intended for Perú continues to be equipped.

Perú's situation, since the perfidious betrayal of the Marquis of Torre Tagle, has deteriorated greatly. The loss of Lima and Callao has deprived us of enormous stores, which have fallen to the enemy. The royalist army, having left a small garrison at Callao under Rodil, marched to Jauja, where it is re-forming in order to attack us. It is superior to ours in number but, come what may, we shall not abandon Perú. We will fight a battle that shall guarantee peace to the independent states of the south. As the fate of Perú and the destinies of her allies are jointly threatened, the interest of all, and particularly that of Perú, demands of each of her representatives an indefatigable zeal in his efforts to secure assistance from the government to which he is accredited.

Neither the treason of the majority of those who govern Perú, nor the superiority of the enemy, nor the intrigues of the friends of Spanish serfdom shall for one moment deter His Excellency the Liberator, who is vested with the dictatorial power in Perú because of his irrevocable determination never to allow Perú to become a colony of Spain again or to fall under the yoke of that nation, as this would conflict with the general interest of all independent America.

God keep you, etc.

J. GABRIEL PÉREZ

196. J[OSÉ] GABRIEL PÉREZ, SECRETARY-GENERAL, TO [MARIANO DE
EGAÑA], CHILEAN MINISTER OF FOREIGN AFFAIRS

[*Letterbook*]

[Trujillo], March 27, 1824.

I have just received the duplicate of a most important communication from the Commandant General of the Isthmus of Panamá, and I have the honor of enclosing the original for your pleasure.

This communication will acquaint you with the fears of a European invasion that possess Mexico and Colombia. On this account, we can no longer hope for supplies or reinforcements from Colombia. The 2,000 veteran soldiers who took ship at Maracaibo for Portobelo have been disembarked by order of our government, which is preparing to resist any possible invasion. Consequently, in Perú His Excellency the Liberator is reduced to only his present Colombian troops together with those of Perú, which are greatly inferior to the enemy's forces.

The independent states of the south, such as Chile and Buenos Aires, are, due to their geographical locations, more distant from the point of any attack that threatens Colombia and Mexico. Their situation is such, therefore, that they are obligated to take part, with their troops, supplies, and money, in the destruction of the royalist army of Perú. Otherwise, the royalist forces, through their recent victories, will gather additional forces and with them new means for subduing all Perú. Subsequently, they will extend their control, which even now is far-reaching, to Chile and Buenos Aires. The Liberator, being the leader of Colombia and the commander of Perú, feels that, as an ally and an American, he must immediately acquaint his compatriots, his brothers of Chile, and all the patriots and patriot governments of America with this situation and with these fears, in order that a united and simultaneous effort can be made to hurl back the forces of Spain and France, should they join hands against us.

The Liberator believes, indeed, he is fully convinced, that, if the government of Chile were quickly to send an expedition of 3,000 men to Huanchaco, there would yet be time completely to destroy the royalist army in Perú, leaving to the enemy not a single foothold on the Pacific. This action would form a powerful body of patriot forces in the south. But if the government of Chile does not speedily dispatch a strong contingent, the Liberator will be faced with the painful necessity of yielding Perú's priceless freedom and independence to the Spanish yoke and of withdrawing to Colombia. There he will occupy impregnable positions, such as at Juanambú, and prepare to resist the avalanche that the enemy will hurl against us, unless, contrary to all probability, America's guardian angel should help us defeat the Spanish army before this communication reaches you. This can only happen if the Spanish attack us in our present positions.

In placing these facts before you, His Excellency dares to hope that they will convey to the Chilean government the full gravity of the situation. Accordingly, he trusts that your government will unstintingly lend a helping hand to those who are engaged in a struggle that involves the interests of all America.

God keep you, etc.

J. GABRIEL PÉREZ

197. POWER OF ATTORNEY ON THE AROA MINES

[*Copy*]

March 31, 1824.

I hereby fully authorize my sister, María Antonia Bolívar, for the purpose set forth herein:

1. To take possession, in my name, of the Aroa Valley and the Cocorote mines.

2. To claim by law all my rights as owner of these properties, against those trespassers who have unwarrantably enjoyed the usufruct of my property these many years.

3. To enter into an express and proper contract with whatever party can offer the most advantageous return for the lease of the said mines and valley of Aroa.

4. Finally, I authorize the said María Antonia Bolívar to lease the Aroa Valley and the mines therein for a stipulated period; but on the express condition that I shall in no way be responsible for the cost of the improvements and benefits to the said Aroa Valley upon the expiration of the lease and upon the reversion of the properties to me for my immediate possession and personal use. There shall also

be a clause included in the contract, withholding its validity until the contract has been approved by me and ordered executed by and in accordance with my subsequent consent and approval.

By virtue of this power of attorney, which I hereby grant in proper form, the citizen María Antonia Bolívar is fully authorized to carry out the purposes herein set forth, for which object I do execute the proper instrument in conformity with the law, and as may be found most suited in the set phrases to be added by the notary, by whom the same is to be drawn. Trujillo, this thirty-first day of March, eighteen hundred and twenty-four.

BOLÍVAR

---

198. To GENERAL ANTONIO JOSÉ DE SUCRE

[Blanco y Azpurúa, IX, 431]

Trujillo, April 9, 1824.

My dear General:

I have received your latest communication, dated at the close of last month. It reassures me regarding the condition of the army and the inaction of the enemy. I shall set down briefly what comes to my mind.

On the 12th I am leaving for Otuzco. On that same day the column that came with Córdova will march, though it has been considerably reduced by sickness. It possesses ordnance and equipment for several units, but not half what is needed, as the arsenal cannot work miracles. Nevertheless, a great deal of work is being accomplished.

The remainder of the cavalry will go along, including the *Granaderos de los Andes* and ninety more, to be provided by our forces in Caraz.

Money is being collected from churches and individuals; but silver bullion cannot be sold, for want of specie, which is sadly lacking. Draw against this prefecture for whatever you can obtain in order to pay the troops, as all drafts will be met promptly. Endeavor to obtain the money needed for this month's payroll for the troops encamped there from the inhabitants of your area. Tomorrow the 10,000 *pesos* in silver from the amount held by Romero will be on the way and will arrive by way of Huamachuco, within two weeks at the earliest. From Huamachuco I shall send whatever is available.

The *Vencedor* battalion will be magnificent, with 900 men all well equipped. The *Rifles* is to receive 100 very fine men. The Hussars must now have very nearly 400 and the Grenadiers 200. The pickets that came from Guayaquil will rejoin their units. Ruiz will take as many men as he needs, up to 200 for the *Granaderos de los Andes*.

The Hussars are with Silva near Mollepata, and the number that is lacking to make a complement of 400 will be sent there.

Colonel Paredes has returned with the itinerary that he went to prepare, and he reports favorably on everything.

We shall not lack money for two or three months, during which time we shall probably have decided the country's fate.

General La Mar may have left Cajamarca with the infantry that was stationed there. He has written me in an optimistic vein, for those gentlemen have accomplished a great deal these days. General La Mar and his column will go to Cajabamba.

Lara is in Huamachuco, making all arrangements and collecting money: thirty thousand *pesos* from Huamachuco and twenty thousand from Pataz. This city has given sixty thousand; Cajamarca will provide fifty thousand, as will Lambayeque. Piura will supply twenty thousand *pesos,* and the churches two hundred thousand. From all this must be deducted thirty or forty thousand *pesos* which cannot be collected. We have already spent more than one hundred thousand *pesos;* hence, only three hundred thousand remain for the months to come. The general tax will bring in fifty thousand a month, whereas expenses will not be less than one hundred thousand. I have, however, ordered the sale of state properties, and we shall not hesitate to confiscate all the funds of the congregations and brotherhoods. With a few forced loans we shall have enough to cover expenses for some months more. This means that, as long as we remain on the defensive, we can live for four or five months until we receive reinforcements from Colombia, Chile, Mexico, and Guatemala, which have promised substantial assistance. Another 2,000 or 3,000 men will more than suffice for what is ahead. At the moment, the positions of Corongo and Mollepata are sufficiently strong to support us and even to aid us in destroying the Spaniards. Mollepata must be fortified. Corongo must serve as a trap. The enemy will have to pursue us, and we shall let them follow on our heels, as though we could not help ourselves. In this way only can they be led into the defile of Corongo, which is a veritable mouth of Hell.

The British envoys who have arrived at Santa Marta have assured us that we shall soon be recognized and that we shall receive aid against France in the event of an attack. The [North] Americans promise the same. Spain can do nothing. She has no navy, no army, no money for anything. Any move that she attempts will be attributed to France, and France will therefore be fought as a foreign usurper and as an enemy of England and freedom. Every move of the Holy Alliance will be opposed by England and North America.

We have a report that a frigate and two transports with troops have reached us from San Blas. Seven or eight months past I asked Mexico for troops and money, and I suppose this is the answer. I hear from Monteagudo that Guatemala desires to aid us. Some time ago I requested a similar force from that country, which I am confident of securing. Guatemala wants our protection, and, as she has as yet made no sacrifices for liberty, she is intact. You can rest assured, my dear General, that we shall not want for reinforcements.

Twenty thousand *pesos* have been sent to the Admiral.[1] This amount will keep his men satisfied. The *Macedonia* is to join him. I have purchased a very fine frigate, which is to be outfitted at Guayaquil. She is to belong to Colombia and will bear the name of *General Santander*. Spry will command her.

News of Venezuela was brought me by an officer of the Grenadiers who has just arrived from that country. He reports that Páez is very popular, and he mentions a thousand things that are of interest to one who has not been there for some time. In general, everything is going nicely. The Congress at Bogotá had not met by January 20, because the Venezuelans and *quiteños* did not take part. *Every day makes it more apparent that Colombia will remain united only as long as the liberators stand by me. When this ceases to be the case, civil wars will follow.* But then, the La Plata River might change its course and flow right through our territories—that is, unless some African stream, like the Senegal, should decide to empty into the Apure.

They tell me that the Venezuelan soldiers are desperate to join

---

[1] Martin Georges Guisse (ed.).

me. The *Guardia* is superb, in excellent condition, and of full complement and strength. May God keep it so.

Good-bye, my dear General, I am your devoted

BOLÍVAR

---

199. To F[RANCISCO] DE P[AULA] SANTANDER,
 VICE PRESIDENT OF COLOMBIA

[*Original*]

Huamachuco, May 6, 1824.

My dear General:

Last night I received your letter of February 6, in reply to the letter delivered to you by my aide-de-camp Ibarra. I have always supposed that your decision would depend on the information that would be brought by the British envoys; but this intelligence arrived too late to put an end to your indecision. I well realize that the political status of Colombia perplexes you, for you cannot know the true intentions of Europe. I, who have the misfortune of knowing in advance what each country logically desires, suffer more than anyone. I am also more mortified than anyone, as I am like one who, without shelter, is exposed to the ravages of an unchained tempest. If you found yourself surrounded by enemies and traitors, by envy and resentments, and by atrocious conspiracies against the state and against your person, you would not calmly ponder the question of whether or not you should dispatch reinforcements to Perú. If you order reinforcements to Guayaquil, you will be sending them in defense of Colombian soil, which is gravely threatened.

But it is futile to stir up tempests in the midst of a calm. However much breath Homer may expend in portraying the wrath of Achilles, the reader remains as unmoved as ever. *Cosi va il mondo.*

Affairs in the south are peaceful, for the Spaniards have also been affected by the Peruvian star of dissension. The Pizarros' and Almagros' once quarreled; La Serna has now quarreled with Pezuela, Riva Agüero with the Congress, Torre Tagle with Riva Agüero and with the nation. Currently, Olañeta is at odds with La Serna. This disagreement has given us a breathing spell in which to recover and return to the arena, armed from head to foot.

Of the men that you have sent, not 1,000 have yet arrived, and only a few more of the recruits from Quito are expected to arrive. With all these reinforcements, we may have 6,000 Colombians. At present we have no more than 4,500 available; yet the *godos* tremble before us. For this reason I do not hesitate to write you so frankly in this letter. Even if it should fall into their hands, or if they should learn all the facts about our army, they would not be inclined to attack us. They will definitely give us time to receive the additional 4,000 men that you have promised me in that calm, staid manner that is so typical of cabinets which are situated in capitals, far from the clash of arms and the cries of the wounded.

In order that you may see that more is known of [world] events in Huamachuco than in Bogotá, I am sending you this army *newspaper*. It is very poorly printed, but its news is correct and recent.

I do not know what to tell you respecting the Peruvian situation. During this year of 1824, it has greatly improved, for I have employed the same energy I used in the year 1813, heedless of redeemers and complainers. There is no better argument than a *free republic*. The man who can produce one is in a favored position, and I have set myself to be a producer of hand-wrought republics. This is a full-time job, but a glorious one.

Doubtless you have heard many new things from Ibarra. If you should hear an account from one of the rumor-carrying refugees from Lima, you will hear a patch of lies. The devil is abroad in this land. I had thought that in Perú revolutionary recruits were timid; that is, I had believed that they were the same here as in any other place, but, in spite of this preconception, I have had to convince myself to the contrary. This world is the other world. There is not one good man in the place, except if he be good for nothing. Those who are capable behave like a legion of demons. This places us in the position of jugglers standing on the points of sabres and bayonets, except that we stand upon our guns and are made strong because we are feared by friend and foe alike. I call this *de facto living*, and the Spaniards also experience it. They are supported by principles and attitudes just as we are. Whichever party is beaten will be crushed completely and forever. I do not paint this picture from sheer vanity, since it also holds for the enemy. I give it only for your guidance.

The Chileans have sent nothing, nor will they. Buenos Aires will do the same. That puny republic resembles Thersites, as it can do nothing but abuse, insult, and confound.

Perú's squadron cannot be trusted. I cannot rely on it to do anything. The commanders of the advance posts, following in the footsteps of the government and most of the Congress, have deserted to the enemy, taking their regulars and guerrillas with them. Fifteen or twenty individual officials in all Perú are with us; the rest have joined the enemy, more out of despair than love for the *godos*. Few believe in our prophecies, for disasters not miracles have accompanied them. They may be right. These Peruvians—Such men! Such behavior! I have needed all my army experience in order not to succumb under the tremendous shock of these people and events. I am surprised at my own strength, which I owe to the lessons I was taught in Colombia, where I learned my trade.

Send the 4,000 men whom Ibarra has gone to seek. The day that you hear they have arrived in Perú, you may turn prophet and exclaim: Colombians, not a Spaniard remains on American soil! I promised this, you will recall, in my remarks to the Congress in Lima.

The Spaniards say they have 20,000 men. The day that I have 10,000, I shall destroy them and perform no miracle, notwithstanding the fact that their advance guard has a record of over ten years of victories.

General Córdova is on the General Staff, but he will command the second Colombian division.

Within two weeks I expect 800 to 1,000 men from Quito.

The army has received orders to move toward the enemy and to make contact with him. If he wishes to give battle, we shall not refuse him, as we have great confidence in our troops. Otherwise, we shall have time to await the reinforcements from the Isthmus, and then no Spanish power whatsoever will be able to prevent the defeat of the New World *godos*.

So you see that, though I ask for help, I am not discouraged. Give my regards to everyone—to Ibarra, Briceño, Gual, Urdaneta, París, and Doña Bernarda, who are my favorite friends.

Give Simón Rodríguez money, drawn against my account, and I will repay you, in order that he may come and see me. I have an affection for this man that approaches madness. He was my teacher and traveling companion, and he is a genius, a prodigy of wit and ability for any who can discover and appreciate him. Anything I say about Rodríguez is nothing in comparison to what remains to be said. I should be happy if he were at my side, for everyone has his weak point. See to it that he comes, and you will thereby render me a great service, for this man's company is my delight. Moreover, he can be very helpful to me. With him I could even write my memoirs. He is a master who teaches with laughter and a secretary who gives meaning to dictation. For me he is everything. When I first knew him he was worth his weight in gold. Should I be mistaken in him, he must have changed greatly. Draw upon me for the money you give him, and send him to me. I must satisfy the demands of maturity now that the illusions of my youth have faded. Instead of a mistress, I want to have a philosopher beside me, as now I prefer Socrates to the seductive Aspasia.

Good-bye, my dear General, and forgive me if this letter is somewhat disjointed. I am your devoted

BOLÍVAR

---

200. PROCLAMATION TO THE ARMY

[Yanes y Mendoza, IV, 93]

Pasco, July 29, 1824. The 14th [year]

SIMON BOLIVAR, Liberator of Colombia, Charged with Dictatorial Power in Perú, etc.

Soldiers!
You are about to complete the greatest task that Heaven has ever asked of men—the freeing of a whole world from slavery.

Soldiers! The enemy you must destroy boasts of fourteen years of victories. You are, therefore, about to meet men who are worthy of pitting their arms against yours, which have flashed in a thousand brilliant battles.

Soldiers! Perú and all America look to you to bring them Peace, the daughter of Victory. Fastened upon you, entranced, is the gaze of liberal Europe—because freedom in the New World will give hope for freedom everywhere. Will you thwart that hope? No, no, no; you are invincible!

General Headquarters of the Liberator.

BOLÍVAR

201. Tomás de Heres, Secretary-General, to General
Antonio José de Sucre

[Paz Soldán, *Historia del Perú Independiente*, I, 271]

Chancay, November 9, 1824.

Last night your communications of October 18 and 24, brought by Lieutenant Naranjo, were received. His Excellency the Liberator, vested with the dictatorial power, has been informed of their contents and instructs me to reply as follows:

I am returning to you Captain Machuca's petition and also an official letter in which Lara speaks of 2d Lieutenant Izquierdo, for you to act on as you think best. I have previously advised you that His Excellency is at present cut off from all knowledge of the affairs of that Republic. In Tarma orders have been issued that all casual officers in transit should report immediately to the army. Today, the large number of casuals hereabouts were ordered to do the same. They will therefore report for duty, accompanying the materials that have gone forward.

Whatever His Excellency told you in the private letter that you mention in your official communication of the 24th, regarding the plans for the campaign, should be taken as His Excellency's personal views. To date he has not altered, restricted, or otherwise modified the broad powers that he officially gave you at Sañaica. On the contrary, every day he relies more and more upon the skill, the judgment and energy, the knowledge, and the other remarkable traits that distinguish you. His Excellency's only and exclusive desire is to accomplish the destruction of the enemy with the least possible loss to ourselves. To that end, you must direct all the operations of the campaign. With this in mind, you may either encamp the army or continue active operations. In short, you will do whatever you consider most useful to the public interest.

Respecting the other matters which should be brought to your attention, His Excellency instructs me to state that two Spanish sloops of war are reported to have arrived at Chiloé; further, that 3,500 men were expected to leave Cádiz to reinforce the Spanish forces here; that the Holy Alliance stops at nothing, whether it be by fair means or foul, or even if it be forbidden as criminal, to disrupt America's orderly progress, to sow discord, to stir up dissension, and to create division—all for the purpose of undermining the work that has cost the friends of freedom and independence so much blood and such great sacrifices. To return America to her former ignominious state as a land of Spanish colonies, or at least to erect thrones here to be occupied by persons who are to be chosen by the Alliance, are the fixed and persistent aims of that Holy League.

On the other hand, we have received word that on September 24 two ships sailed from La Puná, bringing from Panamá the 4,400 men whom I previously mentioned to you. The rest of the troops that will make up the complement of 8,000 men are expected momentarily. On the first day of the month, 200 infantrymen, the squadron of Venezuelan Lancers, and 200 cavalrymen supplied by the Prefect of Trujillo left Huanchaco to come here. Government and private communications from Chile indicate that her squadron will leave shortly. Since Vice Admiral Blanco has been relieved by Captain Foster, there is reason to expect the early arrival of the Chilean squadron.

Orders in duplicate have been issued to Colonel Estomba to the effect that he is to provide you with 200 good recruits, material for outfitting them, and all the mules and horses that he can obtain. You may, if you so desire, speed this matter by sending him a reminder.

Large quantities of iron are being requisitioned, which will all go to the army.

In two or three months without fail you will receive a large reinforcement of 5,000 infantrymen, consisting of the troops from Colombia, 4,000 recruits asked of the individual departments, 200 requested of each of the provinces of Santa, Cajatambo, Canta, and Huarochiri, and all the available men from the column that is now operating on this coast, after it has been relieved by the Colombian troops. And to this add 400 or 500 horses.

His Excellency has devoted considerable thought to General Miller's letter, dated October 22, at Mamara. His Excellency instructs me to repeat what I told you in the beginning of this official communication, namely, that you are to operate with absolute freedom and in accordance with the position of your army in relation to that of the enemy. What His Excellency wants is victory. His Excellency commends to you the two following considerations: first, the fate of Perú rests with the fate of your unit, perhaps forever, certainly the fate of all America for years to come; second, because of these factors, you must, when engaged in battle, constantly realize that many and great interests, such as those that I have indicated, are at stake—from principles, prudence, and even love itself to the enormous benefits of which a defeat would deprive us—all this calls for extreme caution and the greatest skill in the planning of operations in order to avoid leaving them to the uncertain fate of arms, without a plan and an absolute guarantee of success.

With sentiments of the highest and most distinguished consideration, I am your humble and obedient servant,[1]

TOMÁS DE HERES

202. To GENERAL ANTONIO JOSÉ DE SUCRE

[Blanco y Azpurúa, IX, 441]

Chancay, November 26, 1824.

My dear General:

Yesterday I received from the aide-de-camp Negreiros your dispatches and letters of the 13th instant, from Andahuaylas. The enemy's behavior is indeed extraordinary, though I believe it is understandable. The position occupied by the enemy necessitated his taking either the road to Callao or the one to Arequipa. Arequipa is not suited to his purpose, as it lacks a fortress to serve as a point of refuge and a base of operations. All this appears quite natural considering the difficult position in which those gentlemen found themselves. If they gave battle, they would be defeated; if they refrained from battle, their persons were in danger. Defeat would have been very unpleasant for them, especially if they had been captured, as they most certainly would have been. In other words, were they to move toward the coast they would lose their army, but they would thereby assure the safety of their own persons. They can, at best, prolong the war a while longer by using Callao as their base of operations and perhaps by attempting one or two naval expeditions, which in the end will be doomed.

You must always keep your army compact and united. With it you

---

[1] This remarkable official communication is a model exposition of the military art. It sums up the essential points and gives only the broadest of instructions to the subordinate, while leaving him perfect freedom to act as the situation may demand (comp.).

must closely follow the enemy, no matter what direction he takes, yet always keep your forces together. One Peruvian battalion, augmented to a strength of one thousand recruits from Jauja, will be sufficient to guard the interior of the provinces. A few guerrilla cavalry can assist this battalion in its duties. For this purpose choose a handful of pickets from the Junín Hussars to serve as the nucleus for these guerrillas. Furthermore, the hospitals to the rear can readily supply men for our forces in the sierra, and a new battalion might be formed from the great number of men that we expect to recruit in all regions.

Therefore, I can tell you right now and in plain words that the operation which you suggested in your official letter, in cipher, of the 13th instant, does not appeal to me. Of all things certain, the most certain is doubt. If you have executed your plan, you have acted contrary to what I have so often told you: *in union there is strength.* Here on the coast we have 3,000 men. Of these, 500 form a guerrilla patrol around Lima, 500 guard Ica with General La Fuente, and 2,000 are here at the General Headquarters. Those here consist of 500 men in three squadrons of cavalry, of whom the best without question are the Venezuelan Lancers; a column of Colombian Chasseurs composed of 500 men and ably commanded by excellent officers; and the *Perú No. 4,* with over 1,000 men. All these troops are trained, equipped, supplied with ammunition, and ready for combat duty. We also expect the expedition from the Isthmus, which will not number less than 4,500 men, for whom I have horses, baggage, and provisions waiting.

If the enemy moves upon Ica, I believe you should follow him in the direction of Huarochiri; but do not cross the cordillera at Viñac, for it is said to be horribly desolate. Choose any roundabout route that you desire, in order to keep the army compact and in good condition. This is a primary demand in all our operations, because only as long as our army is kept united and in good form are we invincible.

As you know, the Spanish squadron has sailed for Quilca. Undoubtedly their intention is to pick up their dispersed forces, should they be defeated, or to help them emigrate, in such an event. For this reason, I expect that within a month the squadron will be back at Callao. It will then be sure to attempt something unless the Chilean squadron, which is expected, has arrived. The enemy may march toward Ica in order to be in a position to take the sierra, or he may return to Arequipa or take refuge in Callao. It follows that the greatest of care must also be exercised in the event the enemy

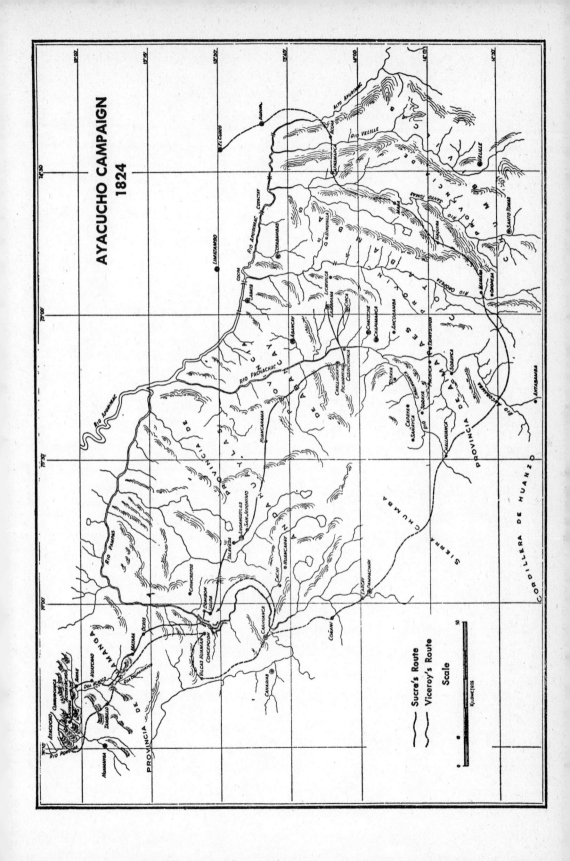

moves on Ica, to avoid any misstep. If such is the case, the best thing would be, if possible, to go by way of Córdoba, in order to follow in his tracks along the sierra, toward Arequipa.

I believe that the situation may force us to form two armies, one for the south and the other for the north. Your army would be in the south. I would have one in the north approximately, if not quite, equal in strength. It would include the reinforcements from Colombia, which are about to arrive, and the thousands of recruits that I have ordered raised and for whom I have arms, equipment, etc.

It appears to be the wisest and surest plan that we can adopt. Accordingly, you must at no time cross the cordillera. Leave the coast to me. Here I shall settle accounts with La Serna. It would be best if you never crossed the cordillera, except in case of absolute *emergency and necessity*.

General Santa Cruz has over 1,000 foot and 400 horse in Jauja. These will enable him to accomplish something, especially as he also has clothing and money for his men.

This very day 200 men are leaving to garrison Tarma, in order to prevent a revolt in that town. They are under Peñalosa, and among them are some fine soldiers from Junín.

If the enemy takes the Lima road, I feel that you should stay in the Jauja Valley until you have received further orders. The Spanish used Jauja as their base of operations, and so must we. From there we can attend to both the sierra and the coast.

In short, dear General, you are authorized to do what seems best to you; this is an authorization without reservations or restrictions.

It appears to me that the situation demands that we divide the territory and occupy it with two armies. Your army must on no account come to the coast. My troops are quite sufficient to besiege Callao and defend the coast proper. The troops from Venezuela and from the coast are more inured to this climate, while your men have now accustomed themselves to the sierra. Our respective zones are thus marked off for us by the peaks of the cordilleras.

I regard it as certain that Olañeta can never be a friend to these Spaniards, but a conjecture is not a fact; hence, you must always have eyes in the back of your head.

The enemy cannot operate actively on the coast for a thousand reasons—his troops are not accustomed to this climate, his horses will arrive practically dead, and the pasture lands will have been laid to waste by our guerrillas. Because of these difficulties I am convinced that the enemy will not attempt to reach the coast, unless, out of sheer desperation, he is compelled to concentrate at Callao. Ica offers him the advantage of being a *godo* town, but I doubt if there is any other place on the coast that is friendly to the Spaniards. Lima is more patriotic every day. By the same token, I believe the *godos* themselves must look to Ica as their first objective, with a view to moving south or north, depending on the fate of their armies.

I must tell you frankly that I do not know what to think or what to conjecture respecting the madness of Valdés, because a man who has committed so many follies during his life will not fail to commit one final one. I can only say that the maxim of the Marshal de Saxe applies here perfectly: "Perú held on by its feet, Perú saved itself by its feet, but Perú can yet lose its footing, for the price of folly is high." Since, unlike the enemy, we are not able to run away, let us maintain ourselves through prudence and circumspection. In the end he must come to a stop, and then we shall fight him. My aide-de-camp Medina will bring you this letter, and he will be able to inform you in detail of anything you wish to know. If what he tells you conflicts with the above, remember that he may be misinformed. What I tell you is the real truth. Give my kindest regards to Generals La Mar, Lara, Córdoba, Miller, *et al.*

I am your devoted

BOLÍVAR

CIRCULAR

His Excellency The Liberator of Colombia and Supreme Commander of the Republic of Perú, extending an invitation to the Governments of the other Republics of America, to send Representatives to Panamá for the purpose of holding a General Assembly there.

[Yanes y Mendoza, IV, 175]

Lima, December 7, 1824.

Great and good friend:

After fifteen years of sacrifices devoted to the struggle for American freedom in order to secure a system of guaranties that will be the shield of our new destiny in peace and war, it is time the interests and ties uniting the American republics, formerly Spanish colonies, possessed a fundamental basis to perpetuate, if possible, those governments.

To initiate that system and to concentrate the power of this great political body calls for the exercise of a sublime authority, one capable of directing the policy of our governments, whose influence should maintain a uniformity of principles and whose very name alone should put an end to our quarrels.

Such a respected authority can exist only in an assembly of plenipotentiaries appointed by each of our Republics and convened under the auspices of the victory obtained by our arms over the Spanish power.

In 1822, profoundly imbued with these ideas, I, as President of the Republic of Colombia, invited the governments of Mexico, Perú, Chile, and Buenos Aires to form a confederation and to hold at the Isthmus of Panamá, or at some other point agreed upon by the majority, a congress of plenipotentiaries from each state "that should act as a council during periods of great conflicts, to be appealed to in the event of common danger, and to be a faithful interpreter of public treaties when difficulties arise, in brief, to conciliate all our differences."

On June 6 of that year, the government of Perú concluded a treaty of alliance and confederation with the Colombian plenipotentiary. By said treaty both parties bound themselves to interpose their good offices with the governments of America formerly Spanish, so that, after all had entered into the same agreement, the General Congress of the confederates could be held. A similar treaty was concluded with Mexico on October 3, 1823, by the Colombian envoy to that country, and there are strong reasons for hoping that other governments, following the dictates of their higher interests, will adopt a similar policy.

To defer any longer the meeting of the General Congress of the plenipotentiaries of the Republics that, in fact, are already allied, in order to await the decision of the others would be to deprive ourselves of the advantages which that assembly will afford from its very beginning.

The number of these advantages is considerably increased when we but contemplate the spectacle that the political world, in particular the European continent, presents to us.

A gathering of the plenipotentiaries of Mexico, Colombia, and Perú will be indefinitely delayed, unless it is instigated by one of these contracting parties, or unless the time and place for the carrying out of this great plan are determined in a preliminary convention.

In view of the difficulties and delays that are presented by the distance separating us, together with other grave motives that general interests suggest, I have decided to take this step with a view toward bringing about an immediate meeting of our plenipotentiaries, while the other governments are completing the necessary preliminaries, already concluded by us, concerning the appointment and commissioning of their representatives.

With respect to the opening date of the Congress, I make so bold as to suggest that no obstacle can oppose its convening within six months from this very date; and I shall also go so far as to flatter myself that the ardent desire which stirs every American to exalt the power of the world of Columbus will obviate the obstacles and delays demanded by ministerial preparations and the distance separating the capital of each State from the central point of the meeting. It seems that, if the whole world should have to choose its capital, the Isthmus of Panamá, located as it is in the center of the globe, with Asia on one side and Africa and Europe on the other, would be the site chosen for this grand design. The Isthmus of Panamá has been offered for this purpose in the existing treaties by the Colombian government. The Isthmus is equidistant from the extremities of the continent, and for this reason it ought to be the provisional location for the first meeting of the confederates.

I myself have yielded to these considerations, and I am seriously disposed toward sending to Panamá the delegates from this Republic immediately upon my being honored with the desired reply to this circular letter. Indeed, nothing can so satisfy the ardent desire of my heart as a general agreement on the part of the confederated governments to accomplish this august American act.

Should Your Excellency not adhere to this plan, I foresee major delays and injuries, at a time when the movement of the world speeds everything on, and when this acceleration may be to our harm.

Once the first conferences between the plenipotentiaries are held, the permanent seat of the Congress, as well as its powers, can be solemnly agreed upon by the majority, and then all our hopes will have been realized.

The day when our plenipotentiaries exchange their credentials will mark an immortal epoch in the diplomatic history of the world.

A hundred centuries hence, posterity, searching for the origin of our public law and recalling the compacts that solidified its destiny, will finger with respect the protocols of the Isthmus. In them will be found the plan of the first alliances that will have marked the beginning of our relations with the universe. What, then, will be the Isthmus of Corinth compared with that of Panamá?

, God preserve Your Excellency.

Your great and good friend,
SIMÓN BOLÍVAR

José Sánchez Carrión
Minister of Foreign Relations

1825

204. To F[rancisco] de P[aula] Santander,
   Vice President of Colombia

[*Original*]

Lima, January 6-7, 1825.

My dear General:

Three days ago I began a long letter to you, and after the better part of it had been written it disappeared. This accident has worried me as I do not know to what use the letter may be put and because I cannot remember all that I wrote.

What most captures my attention at present is the domestic peace that prevails in America.[1] On this I have written you at great length. You will agree that the subject is a fertile one and that it has many ramifications. Every day I am more convinced that it is necessary to provide a guarantee for our existence. I foresee civil war and disorder breaking out in all directions and spreading from country to country. I see my native gods consumed by domestic fire. I refer to Venezuela, my own dear country. These thoughts prey on my mind night and day. I can foresee that the first outbreak in Venezuela will begin the destruction of all hope, forever. There the malady will be deep-rooted, and it will penetrate to the blood. I return, therefore, to my original plan, as the only remedy—federation. Federation seems to me to be a temple of sanctuary from criminal trends. Consequently, I am determined to send delegates from Perú to the Isthmus immediately upon learning that Colombia intends to send her delegates, in order to initiate the union [of states]. I am sure that Mexico and Guatemala will do the same, and, later, Buenos Aires and Chile as well, for this is the universal specific. Let me urge you, my dear General, to hasten to take this important step. Only the expectation of this federation will keep me in America a while longer, that is, until the American Congress becomes a reality. This Congress must serve us at least for the first ten or twelve years of our infancy, even though

---

[1] The long-awaited and decisive battle between the Spaniards and Patriots was fought at Ayacucho on December 9, 1824, resulting in victory for the Patriot forces commanded by Sucre (ed.).

it should dissolve forever following that period. It is my feeling that we will live on for centuries if we can only survive the first dozen years of childhood. First impressions last forever. Moreover, the relations that will be established during those years will serve us for years to come. The great sovereigns of Europe themselves have been obliged to gather in congresses in order to establish cordial and friendly relations among their respective states. As long as they relied on diplomatic negotiations only, discord kept them apart. They formed a congress and composed their differences; now they are invincible. It would seem that we, being nothing, as we are only in the process of being born, should not hesitate for a moment to follow their example. In short, I trust that the government of Colombia will not be deterred from taking the final step that will sanctify her glory.

The fortress of Callao is holding out with a blind obstinacy. I have declared the city outlawed, which I am entitled to do. We can look forward to a few months of siege and blockade.

The Spanish fleet appears to be preparing to leave these waters for the Philippines or for Chiloé. One report has it that the fleet will divide and go in both directions.

You have no doubt heard that, to carry on the siege, I have sent for 2,000 or so of those Colombians who are coming from Panamá. I have ordered the remainder to be placed at the disposal of General Castillo.

The Congress of Perú will meet next month. These gentlemen state that they do not want me to leave or to resign my command, but I shall do both in spite of them. Nevertheless, I shall remain as long as is necessary to subdue Olañeta and Callao and to withdraw our troops to the satisfaction of all concerned. Otherwise, there would be arguments, and everything would go wrong. Moreover, my heart is set on the Isthmian Congress. If I were to leave, it would never be held—or, at best, who knows what it would be like? The one thing that keeps me in America, and particularly in Perú, is this very Congress. If I achieve it, fine; if not, I shall lose all hope of being of further use to my country. I am thoroughly convinced that, if this federation is not formed, there will be nothing to look forward to.

General Sucre has written me various letters reporting the progress of the troops in occupying the country, enforcing the capitulation, and insuring the end of hostilities. Everything goes very well in the interior. The Spaniards have lost all hope of accomplishing anything more in the sierra. Those in Callao, however, pin their hopes on Olañeta, and they have established communication with him through the squadron. These hopes may produce results, but they will be very poor results. We have all the means for preventing any benefits that the Spaniards may expect from either chance or battle. They now have little to hope for in America; Ayacucho marked the final judgment.

Yesterday a French vessel arrived from Quilca bringing news of reports that the Spanish commanders, regardless of whether or not they had capitulated, were boarding French vessels that were lying in port, bound for Europe. The truth is that they are all thinking only of how they can escape from their present predicament. The capitulation has dispelled from their minds the desperation that might have carried them to fresh military adventures. Had we been able to do the same at Carabobo, we should have been much farther along.

You can depend upon my being in Perú for the rest of this year —not as head of the country but as head of the United Army, or, at best, by virtue of the authority that was vested in me upon my arrival.

I have heard many here say that, even after I have returned to Colombia, they hope to retain part of our Colombian troops for some time, to maintain order and strengthen the government. Frankly, this is a just and necessary wish, and it can do us no harm. The troops that we would have stationed in the south can be left here, where their maintenance will not cost us a *real*. Colombia, moreover, needs more of her southern troops in the north. In this way there would be an additional reserve supply which could assist any department that should need reliable and disciplined troops. In an emergency, we might even borrow some Peruvian troops. I might also say, in support of this plan, that it is entirely within the meaning of the treaties between Perú and Colombia and of the proposed federation. So I return to my theme: America is an electrical machine, every part of which is set in motion when any one of its parts receives a shock. Above all, the Mexicans and Peruvians are our only neighbors. We must be ready to come to their aid especially, as any disorders in those nations will doubtless spread to ours.

We have not yet received the mail, which should have arrived by now. I shall answer it when it comes.

I neglected to tell you that the matter of retaining Colombian troops in Perú may come up for discussion at the Isthmian Congress. I therefore want your answer on this point so that I will know whether or not to count upon this plan for the future. You must never forget that the tranquility of southern Colombia will always depend upon that of Perú. We look to the north, where all our interests are concentrated; consequently, we must look to the south for support but not for trouble. I repeat that this is a vital matter, one to which I have given much thought. I believe that I have pointed this out to you many times previously.

The 7th:

We have received the mail from Colombia, which includes nothing of particular importance. The mail from Mexico has also arrived today. This consists of a communication from Acapulco confirming the death of Iturbide and the appointment of . . . [Victoria][1] to the presidency. All this is very good, the best thing that could have happened.

You have no doubt heard what Castillo has to say regarding the troops and the navy. I will not comment on this, since the battle of Ayacucho makes comment superfluous. This very day I have stated that no more troops will come from Colombia. The Minister reports that there are fears of a [Spanish] expedition being attempted there. If you and the others must have troops returned from Perú, ask for them and advise me as to what route they should take. I believe that the Isthmus continues to be the best route, but vessels will have to arrive there in good time from Chagres. A great deal of money has been spent upon this project. These expenditures, according to Castillo, serve no purpose and will do us little good. The same will probably be true of the naval squadron, which has eaten us out of house and home yet cannot even defeat the *Asia*. Apparently, that which is the most costly produces the smallest results. I have received confirmation of the news that the *Asia* is off for the Philippines, which makes me very happy.

According to the newspapers, Victoria appears to be a great man. It is a point in his favor that he took no part at all in the Iturbide régime. It shows that he holds moderate principles.

Iturbide's death completes the third chapter in the history of American princes. Dessalines, Christophe, and he all met with the same end. The Emperor of Brazil may yet follow suit, and the ambitious may yet take heed. This Iturbide had a rather meteoric career—brilliant, swift, and blinding as an explosion. If fortune favors the audacious, I do not know why Iturbide was not so favored, since he was an adventurer through and through. I always expected him to end like Murat. In short, this man had a remarkable career—his life

---

[1] Iturbide's name is repeated here through error (comp.).

brought Mexico freedom; his death brought her peace. I must confess frankly that I never tire of pondering how so ordinary a mortal as Iturbide could have accomplished such extraordinary things. Bonaparte was fated by destiny to perform wonders. Not Iturbide. Yet Iturbide performed greater wonders than did Bonaparte. May God spare us his fate, as He has spared us his manner of life. But we shall never be spared a like ingratitude. The officer's report ends on a rather pathetic note: he expresses his grief but explains that duty and love of country demanded that the sentence of the Congress be executed.

Good-bye, my dear General. I should like very much to withdraw from public life, but first I want to insure our country's happiness. Please send the enclosed to Santana in Caracas.

I am your devoted

BOLÍVAR

---

205. To F[RANCISCO] DE P[AULA] SANTANDER,
     VICE PRESIDENT OF COLOMBIA

[Original]

Lima, January 23, 1825.

My dear General:

The mails have been arriving, but I have not received any letters from you. This does not surprise me, for I did not write you during the campaign. At present there is nothing new. General Sucre was in Cuzco at the close of December. Our peace envoys have taken possession of Arequipa, and the capitulation is being complied with in all regions except Callao. The Spanish generals are fleeing and the Asia also.

I have no news as yet to indicate that the fleet has left Guayaquil, despite all our sacrifices and efforts.

I am still without news of Olañeta. I fear that he may attempt to outwit us by collaborating with the Emperor of Brazil. I have learned that the Spaniards have reached an agreement with that prince to unite their interests under the banner of legitimacy. Moreover, I know that 2,000 Germans have arrived in Brazil and 6,000 Russians are on their way, to support the monarchists. It also appears to be true that the King of Portugal has settled his differences with his son, the Prince of Brazil—all for the purpose of strengthening legitimacy in South America. Brazil, unfortunately, borders upon all our states. She is thus in an excellent position to wage a successful war against us, which the Holy Alliance desires. In fact, I am convinced that it would be most agreeable to the aristocracy of Europe if the power of the Prince of Brazil could be so extended as to destroy the very germ of the revolution [on this continent]. He would, of course, begin with Buenos Aires and end with us. In all South America only Colombia is strong; the other states could easily be destroyed. South America becomes weaker every day. The moment I depart, Perú will again be lost, as there are no men here who are capable of governing. What is more, if I do not put an end to Olañeta, that gentleman, aided by the Prince of Brazil and all the *godos* in this world, will destroy all the other states in America. I therefore believe that the convocation of the General Congress at the Isthmus becomes more urgent daily. I also believe that I should go to Upper Perú to break up that hotbed of tyranny; then I shall return to Colombia for a few months of peace and repose until I can leave for Europe.

I am of the opinion that you should write me as to what you want me to do with this army. Once I am in southern Colombia, I shall have no more authority over it. As I am resolved not to take the command in Colombia, you must instruct both Sucre and me exactly what you want us to do.

In the newspapers from Colombia, I note a number of trivial items. I see that Páez is at odds with the municipality of Porto Cabello; that the *Gaceta de Cartegena* is apparently making atrocious charges against the government—I say apparently, for I have not seen the accusations, only the reply. These public grumblings are the best antidotes to overweening ambitions. Yet it is precisely such attacks that will prematurely force me out of the government.

Good-bye, my dear General. I hope that all is well with you, and that you feel free to command your devoted friend,

BOLÍVAR

206. To F[rancisco] de P[aula] Santander,
    Vice President of Colombia

[*Original*]

Lima, February 9, 1825.

My dear General:

I am most happy to report that the capitulation of Ayacucho has been fully complied with as far as the Desaguadero River. Our troops have moved to its immediate vicinity amidst the rejoicing and the expressions of gratitude of the populace. The day after tomorrow Congress will convene to accept my resignation of the dictatorial power, which I shall make at that time. Immediately thereafter I shall leave for Upper Perú to see what Olañeta is doing in the provinces that he holds. That gentleman is playing a game with both the patriots and the *godos*. No one knows for certain which party he will choose. Meanwhile, General Sucre is marching our troops against La Paz. Our army in that region exceeds 10,000 men, while Olañeta has scarcely 3,000. In one fashion or another we will soon terminate this affair. Its conclusion will be a great relief to me, for I shall then be rid of some of the cares that burden me.

Callao is holding out strongly, because the troops from Guayaquil have not yet arrived. Fortunately, however, the place is blockaded. All in all, I do not believe that the city can remain in the hands of the Spaniards for another two months.

These past two days we have experienced a sinister event here in the murder of Monteagudo, a crime that must have wide ramifications which reach into high circles. The murderers were caught, and their confession implicated two members of the local *godo* faction. I suspect that it may have had its beginnings with the agents of the Holy Alliance who are all around us. Their intention must have been to kill not only Monteagudo but myself and the other leaders as well.

I have ordered a French agent who was here, a Count de Moges, to leave the country.

We have noted in the gazettes that France is sending subversive agents all over America. The French government is becoming the personification of discord, armed with firebrands and attended by the Furies. What baseness! What crime! The members of the Holy Alliance are like shipwrecked sailors—they stop at nothing in hopes of saving themselves. It will be surprising if they do not resort to some desperate measure when they learn how the campaign in Perú has ended.

Mons. Chasseriau seems to be the French spy in northern Colombia and in Mexico. He reported Iturbide's death to his government as bad news.

The year 1824 was not a bad one for America, although its beginning was heavy with stormclouds.

I have not had any dispatches from you recently, or any mail by the post.

I expect O'Leary from Chile momentarily. That country, it seems, is in great trouble, and its people are clamoring for me. The Río de la Plata Congress has met in Buenos Aires. What that Congress will do, I do not know. I imagine, however, that it will concern itself with the affairs of Upper Perú, in which we will have to take part in order not to leave these provinces to that *godo*, the very monarchistic Olañeta, who would be quick to coöperate with the Holy Alliance, as he has openly revealed in his published statements. The provinces of the Río de la Plata do not have a single army to blockade Montevideo, while the Prince of Brazil is fully equipped to conquer them. The Emperor of Brazil and the Holy Alliance are one. If we, the free nations, do not form a similar union we are lost. Although I repeatedly speak of this union, I can never mention it often enough. My current *obsession* is to send representatives to the Isthmus to establish one great Federal Congress. I therefore again urge you to dispatch representatives, because of the urgency and usefulness of this action. This fact is so obvious that every American must be convinced of the need for a general assembly. I believe this to be the last service that we shall be able to render America, and upon its realization I shall relinquish all my authority.

I might tell you, in passing, that I am weary of serving and of having my mind in a constant turmoil. Not even success can induce me to bear the burden any longer. Every day I feel more strongly that I must lay it down, out of sheer mental and physical exhaustion. You cannot imagine how I long for rest, for a profound and extended lethargy. I could almost wish to cease existing for months on end if only I could rest, as I feel I must, both mentally and physically. Everything tires me, and I am exhausted by the slightest effort.

I suppose your Congress occupies all your time. God grant that they manage somehow, like the others. The more I think of your administration the more I am convinced that you are the hero of American government. It is a miracle that a newly created government should be eminently free and well conducted and, moreover, eminently strong. Like a giant, it walks at birth and goes forth to fight and conquer. That giant is yourself. It is a great honor for me that two of my friends and aides have developed as prodigies under my hands. Your achievements and those of Sucre are tremendous. If I could envy, I should envy them. I am the man of troubles; you are the man of law, and Sucre is the warrior. I think each of us should be satisfied with his lot, and Colombia with the three of us. Happy the mother who has always one son to lean on even though the eldest should abandon her because ingratitude demands it—the son's ingratitude, you understand.

Good-bye, my dear General, I am your devoted

BOLÍVAR

P. S. They say Castillo has arrested Guise for his outrageous demands and follies. I am very much pleased that this has happened.

I imagine that the Congress of Perú will make General La Mar president; and if it does not, I shall suggest it. It appears that the Congress does not want me to relinquish the dictatorship. I, however, wish to do so. I desire nothing more than to resign and to lay down the burden of so many distressing duties. Let me add that the people here are contented, united, and at peace. Here they liken me to the staff of Mercury, which could bring the serpents together without their devouring each other. The comparison seems very apt, because not one of them tolerates the other, but they all tolerate me.

Good-bye again.

––––––––––

207. To GENERAL ANTONIO JOSÉ DE SUCRE

[*Draft*]

Lima, February 21, 1825.

My dear General:

I was pleased to receive your letter from Puno, dated February 1, as it informed me about you and about the state of affairs in general.

It seems to me that the matter of Upper Perú offers no problem from a military standpoint, and in regard to the political aspect it is a very simple matter for you. You and the army that you command are under my orders, and you have only to follow my instructions. The army of Colombia, which has come here, is under my command; therefore, I, as the leader of Perú, can direct it and employ it in the war against the Spaniards. You command the army as a Colombian general but not as a chief of state. I, though not as a general, also command the Colombian army, which is an auxiliary of the country over which I preside. I say this in reference to the commitments that you mention. I do not give you orders as the head of Colombia, for I am not her leader. I issue them, rather, as head of the territory that is at war with Upper Perú, as there are no boundaries between enemies.

Neither you, nor I, nor the Congresses of Perú and Colombia can violate or disregard what has come to be recognized as a principle of international law in America, namely: that the republican governments are founded within the boundaries of the former viceroyalties, captaincies general, or presidencies, such as Chile. Upper Perú was a dependency of the viceroyalty of Buenos Aires—an immediate dependency, as Quito was of Santa Fe. Chile, though it was formerly a dependency of Perú, had been separated from Perú for some years prior to the revolution, as was Guatemala from New Spain. Both these presidencies, therefore, could rightfully claim independence of their former viceroyalties.[1] Neither Quito nor Charcas, however, can lawfully be independent unless a treaty is arranged between the parties concerned, either as the result of a war or by the resolution of a congress. I understand you to say that you plan to convoke an assembly of these provinces. But convocation is itself an act of sovereignty. Moreover, in calling upon these provinces to exercise their sovereignty, you will be separating them *de facto* from the other provinces of the Río de la Plata, and by this action you will at once incur the disapproval of the Río de la Plata, of Perú, and of Colombia herself. Colombia could not be indifferent should you violate the very rights that she herself exercised in claiming the presidency of Quito by virtue of the boundaries of the former viceroyalty. Buenos Aires, of course, would demand justice, while Perú would not consent to having her troops take part in a political move without having been consulted.

You possess a rare type of prudence: you are reluctant to exercise the military authority that is properly yours as *de facto* ruler of the country that is occupied by your troops; yet you wish to pursue a

---

[1] The *uti possidetis* of 1810 is the phrase most frequently used to express this reasoning (ed.).

course of action that is legislative in character. I shall deeply regret it if you find this comparison odious, but the situation is similar to that of San Martín in Perú. He was of the opinion that his authority as liberating general was too great; hence, he undertook to promulgate a provisional body of laws, which he lacked the authority to do. I shall tell you, with a candor for which you must forgive me, that you have a strong liking for niceties; this weakness will injure you, as it did in Callao. There, everyone was dissatisfied with you for being soft, and now the same thing will be repeated.

Believe me, General, no one honors your good name more than I. Never has a commander paid greater tribute to a subordinate. An account of your life, written by me, is now in press. In it I give you all the credit that is due you, as my conscience dictates. I say this so that you will see that I am fair, for I object to what I think is wrong and admire what I think is sublime.

I have told you officially what you are to do, and now I repeat: simply occupy the country in a military sense, and await the orders of the [Peruvian] government. The Congress is at this moment deliberating upon what instructions to give me concerning Upper Perú. I do not yet know what its decision will be. But, whatever it is, I shall do no more than my duty, without interfering where I have no authority.

Within a very few days I shall be with you, and I shall bring the aforementioned orders from the Congress.

What you tell me about the troops appears to me to be very satisfactory.

You will see by the *Gaceta* that the Congress has rewarded me lavishly. I do not therefore take to your suggestion that I be given the title of Liberator, which was given to me once before when I did not deserve it. Please accept my thanks, however, for your generous thought.

Within three or four days I shall begin the blockade and siege of Callao. We have now over 3,000 men here to take part in that operation.

I have just at this moment learned that Upper Perú has good friends in the Congress. I call those good who do not favor its annexation to Perú, as this is the basis of our international law. Respecting the others, they prefer to let the country be occupied by the army until its status has been legally and lawfully determined. I believe that this opinion is in full accord with justice . . . I should be very happy indeed, if neither Colombia nor Perú should have to suffer for their sacrifices in liberating that country, as it would be most unpleasant to be no sooner redeemed than martyred. I also hope that you will be spared so unjust a fate.

I am, my dear General, your devoted

BOLÍVAR

P.S. Many greetings to Lara, to Córdoba, and to the other generals.

———————

208. To F[RANCISCO] DE P[AULA] SANTANDER,
    VICE PRESIDENT OF COLOMBIA

[Original]

Lima, February 23, 1825.

My dear General:

As you must have learned, the Congress of Perú was inaugurated on the 10th. The papers will tell you something of what occurred, but they do not give the full story because of the poor reporting of our newspapermen. The fact is that the Congress has insisted upon keeping me in command and I have accepted temporarily—that is, until the government of Colombia recalls me.

The Congress voted to send a delegation to convey its appreciation to the government and Congress of Colombia for their help and support. Furthermore, the delegation is expressly charged to request permission for me to remain in command here for another year, which is the least I can do for Perú. By that time we shall have taken Callao and Upper Perú, and we can then withdraw our troops whenever you wish. It appears to me, however, that, as long as there is no need for them in Colombia, we should be in no hurry to withdraw them, for the following reasons: first, they can be better kept together here, as they are far from home; second, we will save the enormous sum of money that it would cost to maintain such a large body of troops; third, order can be maintained in the entire southern part of the continent; fourth, it will fulfill the objectives of the federation; fifth, we can maintain peace and tranquility in southern Colombia; sixth, at a moment's notice we will be able to transport to the north

6,000 of the best troops in the world, Colombian to the core, uncorrupted, and fully worthy of maintaining the glory of Colombia.

These advantages would find their counterpart in as many disadvantages, should we withdraw our troops too soon. In all sincerity, I believe that such a move would be a serious error. Please believe that the welfare of America depends in large part upon this army. It is a magnificent army, more so than you may think. Its mere preservation benefits everyone. The anarchy in the Río de la Plata menaces all America. That area is controlled by five different states, each an enemy of the other. Brazil would like to swallow the whole. Olañeta's army is monarchist, *godo,* and it supports the Holy Alliance. This army will be kept intact for some time partly by his influence and partly by force. Paraguay is under the sway of the Brazilian Emperor, and the other provinces are openly hostile to each other. Chile, which is in a stage of passive anarchy, is in accord with the government of Buenos Aires, and both states are opposed to the federation of the new nations. The Banda Oriental [1] can devour Buenos Aires any day that it pleases, and then you will witness the Holy Alliance campaigning on the plains of the La Plata [area].

To tell you that popular revolts are extremely contagious is to state a platitude. From Buenos Aires the revolution would spread in triumph to Perú and it would pass on, amidst acclaim, to Juanambú. There is no need to tell you about Venezuela and what may be expected of her. I therefore believe that we should emulate the Holy Alliance in everything that relates to political security. The only difference must be in the principles of justice. In Europe everything operates through tyranny; here, through freedom. This difference surely renders us enormously superior to the Alliance. For example, they support thrones and kings; we, peoples and republics. They seek dependence; we seek independence. Therefore, if we are to raise ourselves to similar heights of power, if we are to be able to sustain a conflict, we must be no less able to adopt comparable measures. Oppression is massed under a single standard; if, then, Liberty disperses herself, she will not be capable of resisting attack. This absurd, outrageous, and criminal weakness among nations has enabled a thousand tyrants in modern Europe to subjugate the very ends of the earth. The European armies of occupation are a novel, ingenious innovation. They conserve the independence of nations and establish order therein; thus, by obviating the need for conquest, they thereby avert war. For

---

[1] Now the Republic of Uruguay, which was then under Brazilian domination (ed.).

this reason we must keep our army in Upper and Lower Perú until the assembly of American states has determined in what manner and by what means peace is to be maintained among the confederated members.

The troops in the south of Colombia are now adequate. If some companies are needed in the north, tell me the branch and the type desired, and they will march without endangering the domestic peace of the south. The Venezuelans now in Guayaquil might serve in the Isthmus, if you should care to send them there, but not those from the Magdalena, as they would all desert. If you want 2,000 or 3,000 Peruvians for Venezuela, we can incorporate them in our battalions and send them along, for we have them in our ranks. These men were either taken from the enemy or recruited in this country to replace our casualties.

I think it would be advisable for you to send a plenipotentiary with powers and instructions to settle the matters pending between Colombia and Perú. Let him bring an account of expenditures in order to arrange for payment, which can be effected in England, if you wish. He should also discuss the matter of boundaries and the question of which troops are to leave and which are to remain for a time. Someone should be here to discuss with us the problem of this army and to attend to the interests of Colombia, which are many. Armero is a merchant who has neither personality nor knowledge of anything. Moreover, he has few personal connections, and he has made an enemy of Pérez, who speaks scornfully of him in public; I cannot prevent this, for Pérez is more uncontrollable than ever. You would not believe how badly he speaks of my ministers, out of sheer jealousy. If Mosquera should agree to come, he would be the best man for the task. He understands the problems of the south and is an admirable person.

Let me urge you to send the delegates to the Isthmus. The moment I am advised of their departure, I shall dispatch those from Perú. I shall never tire of praising this assembly.

The people of Chile, according to O'Leary, who has just arrived, are decidedly with us, but the government is very envious. The people desire the recall of O'Higgins, which is expected to take place. General O'Higgins and Admiral Blanco are also definitely with me, and both are gentlemen. O'Higgins has been placed in the most difficult of situations, from which he could not easily extricate himself, for he has been surrounded by despicable aides.

I am told that there are a great many votes for you for the presidency. If so, it is proof of the wisdom of Colombia, and, moreover, it is evidence that you have managed wisely and well. Nothing has afforded me greater pleasure in these times than the knowledge that the future of Colombia is to be assured by so splendid and wise a choice. Colombians must forget about me for the office of president and think only of you, for you have given proof of your high statesmanship. Many will aspire to the presidency, but the people should confer it upon you only, at least for the present, and until the establishment of that order of things that will be our future salvation. I repeat, I shall remain in office only until I can convoke the Federal Congress [at Panamá], and then I shall retire, worn out from so many cares.

The Congress of Perú has been most generous. General Sucre has been given the name of [Marshal of] Ayacucho, and honors have been conferred on all of us. Two million *pesos* have been set aside for me and the army. Valuable lands have been given to the generals and commanders. Heres has been made a brigadier general; and the chaplain of our army, a canon. I beg you, if you can, to approve all these awards except mine, which I do not want. Above all, the honor that has been conferred upon Sucre is so fitting that it would be a shame if you and the government could not approve it. It was an idea that I suggested to the Congress. My gratitude to Sucre knows no bounds: first, as a matter of justice, and, second, as a matter of generosity. At Ayacucho he took from me the finest sprig of all my laurels: he is the liberator of the Empire of the Incas from Juanambú to Charcas. He therefore will definitely rival me in military glory. For this I refuse to envy him, in order that I may the better deserve the glory that is still mine. If I permitted myself to be envious, I should not merit so much as one leaf of laurel. I might say the same respecting you yourself. No one loves you or praises you more than I, both in heart and in mind, for I believe the finest crown is that which is justly earned. I should be despicable if I thought otherwise. Were I envious, I should scarcely deserve the name of man, for envy is a petty and contemptible passion that belongs to woman. Unfortunately, it is a feeling that is not uncommon among persons of standing, and it tarnishes the very qualities that make them distinguished. I have the conceit to consider myself above such pitiable weakness.

I intend to leave for Upper Perú[1] within the next ten or twelve

---

[1] Present-day Bolivia (ed.).

days to unravel that chaos of confused interests that absolutely requires my presence. Upper Perú belongs *de jure* to the Río de la Plata—*de facto* to Spain. By choice of its sons, who want a country of their own, it would be independent, and by priority it belongs to Perú, who owned it before and who claims it now. This problem is being discussed in Congress this very day, and I do not know which way it will be decided. I have announced my opinion in the same terms that I have used above, distributing it for the edification of the entire world. Sucre has orders to take the country, in the name of independence and the liberating army; however, I believe that the legal right to do this must be examined in the assembly of the Isthmus. To turn Upper Perú over to the Río de la Plata would be to deliver her into the hands of anarchy and to abandon her inhabitants to the troops of Olañeta, who now hold it and might agree to some peaceful settlement. To give it to Perú would be to violate the international law that we have established. To create a new republic, as the inhabitants of Upper Perú desire, would constitute an innovation that I do not care to undertake, for that is a matter that only an American assembly can decide. The country has resources that are equal to those of Guatemala or Chile. It is far from Buenos Aires, and nearly as distant from Lima. Its center is 500 leagues, more or less, from either of these cities, but it is further from Buenos Aires than from Lima. The country is said to be beautiful and very rich. Well, I shall soon see it, and I shall write you what I think best and right.

General Valero arrived today with a fine battalion. I had the battalion take the name of *Caracas*, which the other of that name relinquished at Ayacucho, as it is important that the cradle of independence be always represented in the army. General Sucre is anxious to visit Colombia because of his father's death. Lara and Córdoba desire to do the same. If you should care to give General Salom the rank of major general, he could command the army, as he is the best of men in every way. I ask this favor of you as if it were for myself. Yesterday Salom fought brilliantly at Callao and made an excellent showing. He has served faithfully all his life and in the south better than before. In valor he yields to no one. The government of Perú will soon be giving him that rank, which you could easily anticipate. His comrades have left him far behind, and he must surely feel ignored, for all his modesty. I am leaving him in command of the army of the coast, which numbers over 3,500 men. By the time the commission of major general reaches him, he will be master of Callao at no little cost in blood.

I am leaving the affairs of Perú in the hands of a governing council, with General La Mar as president and the ministers as voting members. These are the best men in Perú, and they are truly deserving of respect and consideration. Each in his own manner possesses great merit. General La Mar is an able officer, a gentleman, one most distinguished in every way. Carrión is capable, honest, and patriotic without stint. Unanúe has all these qualities, and, in addition, he has a greater general knowledge than any other man in Perú.

Heres, the Minister of War, will accompany me, as that minister always stays by my side. This officer has splendid traits of character, but he has no lack of enemies because of his stern manner. I commend him to you lest they make light of him because of the general's commission which the Congress gave him quite spontaneously and freely, without having been the least bit influenced.

General Valero I have only met, but from what I hear and see of him he appears to be an excellent officer. I have placed him under General Salom, in command of the division that is besieging Callao.

My absence from this capital will probably last to the end of the year.

If the Congress [of Colombia] should resent my going to Upper Perú, tell them that I am now under the orders of this country, and, with the Army of Liberation in Upper Perú, I neither could nor should abandon it. Moreover, that territory is at present in dispute; and, as it is now Spanish, it is my duty to occupy it because there are no boundaries for the enemy and the country that he occupies is not foreign territory. Such territory openly becomes the objective of the opposing army, and it must be taken if the war is to be ended. Disputed areas should not be regarded as foreign, and, if we are to go by definitions, what is properly called Perú extends from Cuzco to Potosí, as everyone in this country well knows. Thus they say, "I come from Perú, I am going to Perú," when they mean Upper Perú. All this concerns only the use of words. As for the reasons in the case, I have stated them.

It would be a good thing if the General of the Army of Colombia had the authority to make promotions. A general a thousand leagues from home should have this authority. Sucre, to keep his army happy, was forced to exceed his power on this point. The army here merits this consideration, as it is the savior of America and may in time be the instrument for maintaining peace among us. Moreover, it is an extremely fine army, with no equal in America—indeed, it is composed of *ten thousand immortals.*

This letter is long enough, and I must now conclude it, commending to your attention the deputies of Perú. Make them welcome and you will make them grateful, for between nations such trifles result in greater things. In politics nothing is of greater value or less costly than demonstrations of respect and consideration, especially when the superiority is evident and the courtesy cannot be attributed to fear. Perú can become an excellent sister nation to Colombia. We are worshiped here. There is such a thing as a national sentiment toward another country that is not readily appreciated from afar; in fact, it must be experienced to be appreciated.

I have seen what you wrote to Pérez about the difficulties in Colombia over the expedition to the south. Considering the circumstances, I am not surprised.

I am your devoted

BOLÍVAR

---

209. To F[rancisco] de P[aula] Santander,
VICE PRESIDENT OF COLOMBIA

[*Original*]

Lima, March 8, 1825.

My dear General:

What concerns me most at this time is the note from the French minister published in the *Morning Chronicle* and presumably addressed to Chasseriau. This document, on the surface, appears to be quite candid and innocuous, but, of course, this attitude may have been feigned. Yet I think not, since the French aims are clearly set forth. It is certain, however, that the Europeans are employing every manner of intrigue against us, while we, like the Spaniards toward their Constitution, react most apathetically. Our enemies, meanwhile, apply themselves with indefatigable zeal. France is reported to have sent more than 20,000 men to her islands; some have confirmed this report, and others have denied it. I think we should send intelligence agents to determine its veracity and to note what troops those gentlemen have in their colonies. Further, I think it would be most desirable if we could investigate the exact intentions of the French government. You know that the Prince de Polignac has stated that France wishes us to have monarchic or at least aristocratic governments. That prince has also told the Peruvian envoys *that it matters little to France whether those who are to be crowned in America are European princes or revolutionary generals.* From this it appears that France desires an order of things that will be analogous to that of Europe, but that she has no clearly defined intention of subordinating us to the continent.

In Spain, the French insisted that the Spanish Constitution be amended to conform to their own. The Spaniards resisted the order, but to no avail. If we were to pursue the same course, I cannot see what we would gain. The fact that all Europe is against us and that all America is devastated makes quite an appalling picture. The English and the [North] Americans are only possible future allies, and they have their own selfish interests. It seems politic, therefore, for us to enter into friendly relations with the gentlemen of the Alliance, using dulcet and persuasive words, in order to discover their latest decisions and to gain time. With this end in view, I believe that Colombia, which has taken the lead in foreign affairs, should be able to undertake some move through her agents in Europe. While this is being done, the rest of America, meeting at the Isthmus, can present itself in a more imposing manner.

If the Americans would put their trust in me, I would give them the means with which to avoid war and preserve their liberty absolute and complete. Meanwhile, I again most urgently plead for a meeting of the assembly at the Isthmus. This step, among others, is indispensable in the present circumstances.

I desire nothing for myself, absolutely nothing. You who know me, and others who ought to know me, will be considerate enough to do nothing for me. You and the others should, therefore, place every confidence in me and allow me to deal with the Alliance. I shall state here and now that I will never exercise any manner of executive power either here or in Colombia, although I may be of some service in the Congress or as an envoy to Europe. I shall not assume these duties unless the situation should become hopeless and extremely precarious, for I have resolved to give up everything this very year (unless the French come) and to take over the pleasant post of a plain citizen. Then I can give advice, speak freely, and all the world will be able to see that I have no personal ambitions. Believe me, my dear General, that will be the day when I shall serve my country well; for

I shall serve her freely, without hypocrisy, and in a manner that is truly deserving of gratitude, because I shall sacrifice even my popularity for my country.

I have not heard from General Sucre for quite a few days. I presume that he has crossed the Desaguadero River and taken some of the provinces that were held by Olañeta. I am staying here to direct the siege of Callao, which is certain to cost us a heavy toll in blood and hard labor, as we have next to nothing for carrying on a siege. I have sent to Guayaquil, Panamá, and Chile for heavy artillery, munitions, and even lumber, but I have no idea when they will arrive.

I repeat that you can count on 10,000 men from among those who are here. Of these, over 4,000 are Peruvians who have enlisted under Colombian banners to replace our losses. You have only to say the word for them to be placed at your disposal. You must, however, provide for their transportation north of the Isthmus, and, I repeat, if a large number of troops is not needed in Colombia, 2,000 or 3,000 men might well remain here until the government has been organized.

At the end of this month I plan to go to Upper Perú. I shall leave General Salom in command of the army here, as I have said before, and General La Mar in charge of the government.

At the slightest hint from you or the Congress that I should return to Colombia, I will march. Indeed, I should like to know what you and the others in Bogotá think about this matter. I yearn for a vacation from politics of several months or years, while here I have more to do than in Colombia, since, thanks be to God and to heavenly guidance, I have found a friend there who has relieved me of the problems of government. Here, however, there is no one, for poor General La Mar has neither sufficient will nor character.

The post from Colombia has not yet arrived. It is expected today or tomorrow, but, regardless of when it may arrive, I am writing to you with no letter of yours to answer, for I know that the mail is not likely to contain any letter for me.

The Congress here is in session. It has accomplished some good work and will adjourn the 10th of this month. You will see by the papers how generous they were respecting the matter of the million [*pesos*].[1] Their final decision was truly noble. They awarded two hundred thousand *pesos* to Sucre, either in money or in property. In place of the two hundred thousand *pesos* I have given him an

---

[1] This amount was awarded Bolívar by the Peruvian Congress. He rejected it as a personal gift but accepted it in behalf of the city of Caracas (ed.).

estate that is hardly worth less. It is a very fine place that formerly belonged to the Jesuits. The others will receive a proportionate compensation. Fortune has favored my comrades in the army of the south; yet, human nature being what it is, they are not content. They all long to return to Colombia, or, I should say, to get out of the army. Everyone, it seems, feels as I do. In Perú, I have experienced the rich fulfillment of my highest hopes; nevertheless, I, too, am discontented. I would abandon everything for a change.

Be so good, my dear General, as to give my warmest regards to Briceño, Gual, and Restrepo. Tell Paris to write me about Guatavita, the Zipaquirá salt works, and the diamond mines. Tell him he is a poor one for not writing me, and I might say the same of the others, except for poor Gual.

If Ibarra is about, tell him to come here, unless his wife or his health does not permit it.

I am your devoted

                                                                    BOLÍVAR

---

210. To F[rancisco] de P[aula] Santander,
      Vice President of Colombia

[*Original*]

                                                    Lima, March 11, 1825.

My dear General:

We have just received from General Páez, at Maracay, the communications of January 6 and November 27 and 28, in which he advises us that French naval forces are approaching Venezuela. This move is altogether credible considering the circumstances, especially if the instructions that were given Chasseriau by the French Minister, wherein he spoke of using force in case of resistance, were genuine. If the battle of Ayacucho does not stop the French, we must prepare for a brilliant war. I say brilliant, for without doubt we will make it such in the end, although at very heavy cost.

You may count immediately upon 10,000 or 12,000 men, who can march wherever you say and as soon as you have given the order and arranged for their transportation from the Isthmus to the northern coasts. Our battalions are about half composed of Peruvian troops, who have replaced our losses. Later, if it should prove necessary, we shall send corps made up of Peruvian reinforcements only. In short, as long as I am here, Perú will aid Colombia. She will, in keeping with the demands of gratitude and reciprocity, do as much for Colombia as that country has done for her. When I return to Colombia, I can leave behind an energetic government to take my place, with a few Colombian troops to maintain it. I shall do everything possible in order to render Colombia large scale assistance.

I think you can count upon from 3,000 to 4,000 men from the south of Quito, with cadres from the north and full battalions from the south. Endeavor always to leave the dangerous element in the south. I believe that France should be given to understand that I am not altogether unwilling to adapt our views to those of the Holy Alliance and that, through my influence, a change might be brought about in our government without the sacrifice of a war which would involve the whole world. In fact, at this moment I have not the slightest objection to heading a mission to attempt to exorcise the wrath of the French, even at the cost of my popularity and honor, for I am anxious to spare Colombia the havoc of a new war. If I succeed, I shall be happy; if not, well and good, for I shall have done everything possible to save my country.

I believe America can be saved through these four instruments: first, a great army to make us feared and to enable us to defend ourselves; second, a European policy to delay the first blows; third, England; and fourth, the United States. All these factors must be well managed and coördinated, for without capable direction nothing beneficial will result. In addition, I insist upon the Congress of all the American states at the Isthmus; this will be a fifth instrument.

I shall further add that untiring energy must govern our deliberations, if we are to avoid being caught between the people and the enemy.

Believe me, my dear General, we can save the New World if we come to an agreement with England on matters *political and military*. This simple statement should tell you more than any two volumes. I feel that you should immediately endeavor to determine the views of the British Cabinet respecting the governments in America. These few lines require an elaborate explanation that I cannot give because of distance and the hazards of written communications. In short, from the above and from what I told you the day before yesterday, you can understand my ideas as to how to head off the French invasion.

I believe that to offer any major resistance to these gentlemen on their arrival would be detrimental to us. Puerto Cabello and Cartagena must be defended at all costs. Each should have 6,000 or 8,000 men, and no difficulties should be experienced in provisioning them if we curry the favor of the English and the Americans, so that, come what may, they will protect our ocean convoys. The territory that we evacuate should be covered with guerrilla bands commanded by resolute officers. We should not begin a major war until a year or two after the French army has virtually been destroyed. The so-called warfare of position would be of no use against them, as they are extremely resourceful and can do wonders with their artillery. The wars in Russia and in Haiti should be our model on some points, but without the terrible type of self-destruction that those countries adopted. This policy was helpful there but would serve no purpose here, for things once destroyed become useless to all parties. The French would receive supplies from the outside, while we would have only those available at home. Moreover, when the land has been laid waste, the foe evacuates, while the friend remains to perish. Russia had its snow and ice, Santo Domingo its hot winds, which caused fevers. Here we shall have great deserts in which to seek safety from disaster. In fine, we would only destroy what is ours, and very little is now left for us to destroy.

Believe me, my dear General, we must practice the art of losing at the outset, if we are to win in the end. Let us leave the coastal regions to the enemy, for those areas are pestilential, and there the French are bound to be harassed by the English and the Americans. We must make our defense far inland: first, in order to draw our foes farther from their base of operations along the coast; second, because food is more plentiful inland, the climate is more healthy, and after the enemy has traveled so great a distance his forces will have been greatly reduced. Moreover, we must give our allies, should we have any, time to arm and to join us in the attack.

I may add in passing, and in support of what I have said, that the French are easily beaten by delays, privations, obstacles, climate, tedium, and everything else that goes with a long war. But, on the other hand, they are invincible in attack and assault and in whatever requires speed. All this is well known, but we must never overlook the obvious.

Until we know definitely what the French are planning respecting Colombia, I shall not march south; instead, I shall await your instructions here. If the situation is not acute, I shall not leave until I have sent 12,000 men ahead; this should be accomplished during the course of this year. Nevertheless, if it should be necessary, I will go along, the minute I am advised that my presence is required. In that case, Generals Sucre, La Mar, Salom, and Lara can carry out my wishes.

Do not forget to declare a crusade against the French heretics and atheists—destroyers of their priests, temples, images, and all that is sacred throughout the world. The Bishop of Mérida and all the fanatics can aid in this crusade in the pulpits of the churches and in the streets.

I have neglected to point out to you the principal factor: namely, if, after Europe has learned of the victory at Ayacucho and of the termination of the war in America, the French should undertake or continue operations against us, we must prepare ourselves to face the most significant, the hardest, and the greatest war that mankind has ever seen or experienced. It will be a *world* war. These are my reasons: France, having Brazil as a major auxiliary power and believing that we are occupied in Perú, may intend to distract us either with feints or with actual operations, while, at the same time, she relies upon Iturbide[1] in Mexico, anarchy in Buenos Aires, and the complete lack of government in Chile. Hence, if the threat is unilateral and purely French, Ayacucho has already parried and defeated it. But if, after this decisive turn in American affairs, the Alliance persists in its hostile plan and refuses to heed our overtures, we shall have positive proof that it has determined to launch a general conflict to effect the triumph of monarchy over freedom. A struggle like this cannot possibly be localized, because the interests involved will be too great and widespread, enveloping the world. The entire New World, therefore, will become involved *de facto*; also England with her colonies and interests that cover three-quarters of the globe. For aid in the struggle we shall have the constitutionally-minded populations of Portugal, Spain, Italy, Greece, Holland, and Sweden. We shall also have the Turkish Empire, which is anxious to escape from Russia's claws. The Alliance will have the support of all the continental European governments and, consequently, their armies. Thus, the end of this political and military conflict will be determined by events and combinations so numerous that no human calculation or foresight can hope to predict the outcome. This leads

---

[1] The reference here is to the monarchists in Mexico, for he had been informed of Iturbide's death. See Doc. 204 (ed.).

us to my recommendation that we prepare ourselves for a *long, arduous, and tremendous* struggle. The palliative remedy for all this—if it should come to pass—will be the great Congress of plenipotentiary delegates on the Isthmus, which must adopt a vigorous, extensive, and intensive program. The Congress must have an army of at least 100,000 men at its command, maintained by the Confederation itself and independent of the constituent nations. To this should be added a shrewd policy, in the European manner, a federal navy, and the closest possible alliance with England and North America. After this cruel war, which will leave our countries in ruins, our only gains will be strong, well-organized governments, and American nations united in heart and firmly linked by their political affinity. Indeed, unless our new Greece, like that of ancient times at the close of the Peloponnesian War, should be ripe for conquest by a new Alexander, which is also something that cannot be foreseen or divined.

At this very moment I have received communications from Sucre. According to what he writes, he must by now be beyond La Paz since about February 7 last he was on the point of entering that city. In Upper Perú the outlook is bright, for Olañeta, who would not listen to reason, has been abandoned by his troops, who are deserting to us. Moreover, public opinion in that country is so much in our favor that we have nothing to fear from Olañeta; on the contrary, we can expect that everything will be over at any moment.

I forgot to tell you that the General Congress of the provinces of the Río de la Plata has been inaugurated. It has issued a decree authorizing the executive power to represent that union and to treat with foreign nations until it has voted upon its Constitution, which will determine the form and principles of the government. The British envoy is following these developments with the greatest of interest. He states that he has instructions from his government to deal with and recognize the government of Buenos Aires. All this news is fact.

I am your devoted

BOLÍVAR

211. To Manuel José Hurtado. Colombian Minister
    to Great Britain

[*Draft*] [1]

Lima, March 12, 1825.

Very esteemed friend and Sir:

I profit from the happy opportunity afforded me by Mr. Rennie, to have this letter delivered into your hands and to write you for the first time news of the state of affairs in this country. Since the battle of Ayacucho everything has progressed under the aegis of victory and achievement. Our army is in possession of Upper Perú, and Callao is under close siege.

I presume that you have read in the public prints of the reinstallation of the Constituent Congress of Perú on the anniversary of my assumption of the dictatorship to save that country. This Congress has been extremely grateful in all its acts, and it has behaved generously indeed toward the army that gave this noble Republic its life and freedom. In spite of the distaste that I have always had for governing, I have been compelled, for the good of these people, and, indeed, of Colombia herself, to accept the supreme command of this Republic, subject always to the approval of the Colombian Congress. It is my belief that we shall have done nothing for Perú if we fail to leave her with a government that will insure her existence and prosperity.

The post from Bogotá, of January 6, brought us the alarming news that a French squadron, which must have left from Martinique, was headed for the coasts of Venezuela. As the French have recently been pursuing such a dubious policy, we could not disregard what at first sight would seem to be highly improbable. We are, therefore, waiting for a confirmation of this rumor; if it is found to be true, I am prepared to rush 13,000 Colombians and Peruvians to Colombia to defend that country against the French invasion. I beg you to communicate to me frequently and directly all the news that you obtain concerning the French and the situation in Europe generally. Send your letters by way of Jamaica to Panamá, avoiding Bogotá, as letters that are sent by way of that city take an incredibly circuitous route before they reach me.

I am taking the liberty of charging you with a matter of the ut-

---

[1] This letter, signed and revised in Bolívar's own hand, remained in the office of the Secretary-General as a draft (comp.).

most gravity, and one that is worthy, moreover, of the greatest tact.

It would appear that France has adopted, as a pretext for making war upon us, the democratic system of government that we have chosen. The French ambassador, in one of his conferences with Mr. Canning, suggested that England should join the rest of Europe and use her good offices to persuade us at least to adopt aristocratic systems. You know, as well as all the world, because of my speech to the Congress of Venezuela, that my opinion at that time was that we should emulate the *British Parliament in our legislative branch*. You are, therefore, expressly authorized by me to acquaint the British ministry with my ideas on matters of government, which are very clearly set forth in my address mentioned above. These ideas, vigorously presented, may enable the British ministry to encourage France to *hope* for a change in our Constitution. None of this must take place until it is finally and definitely known that France and the Holy Alliance have determined to make war upon us because of our democratic system of government. The British government might find it expedient, in order to spare us a war, to explain my political ideas to the Alliance as a means of averting an outbreak of hostilities and of providing a basis for negotiations intended to assure the freedom and independence of America, under mixed governments comprising the elements of both aristocracy and democracy. If so, I authorize you to inform the British government of my determination to exert *all my influence in America to obtain a reform that may win us recognition by Europe and safeguard world peace.*

All this is based on the hypothesis that the British government considers war to be inevitable; otherwise, do nothing, nothing at all.

I am, Sir, with the highest consideration, your devoted servant,

BOLÍVAR

---

212. To F[rancisco] de P[aula] Santander,
     Vice President of Colombia

[*Original*]

Lima, April 7, 1825.

My dear General:

Yesterday I had the great pleasure of receiving the mail of February 6, which brought your reply to my circular letter concerning the assembly of the General Congress of the Federated Powers[1] and also a reply from the President of the Senate on the subject of my resignation. Your felicitations upon the Peruvian campaign were brilliant, and your personal letter was even more so; my thanks for everything.

Unfortunately, I did not receive the dispatch that you mention having sent me by an officer, in which you wrote at length on all matters, both past and pending. I am entirely satisfied, as I have always been, regarding your friendship, your absolute devotion to the general welfare and the honor of my name. Believe me, my dear General, my feelings toward you have not suffered the slightest change during any period or moment of my life. You have been and always will be the friend who is the object of my particular esteem and admiration.

Affairs in Perú are proceeding admirably. General Sucre is now either in Potosí or beyond. Olañeta's troops have dispersed, and, like those of Bonaparte, they seek refuge with their most implacable foes: what I actually mean to say is that only Olañeta has sought refuge in the Buenos Aires region, for his troops have joined us. In short, the war in Perú gives us nothing more to fear. Only Callao continues to fight, but its obstinacy will not prevent its inevitable fall within two or three months. For these reasons, I again propose that you immediately order the return of 3,000 or 4,000 of the Colombians in Perú. General Lara's division can embark for the Colombian ports the moment the order is received. This division can provide fine southern troops for the north, as it is composed of reliable men capable of checking the disorders there. You should therefore issue the necessary orders to the Isthmus, so that they may be directed wherever you desire. I again repeat: the moment that I receive your order these troops will leave. They are not departing immediately because I am certain that you have not made preparations for them at the Isthmus. If they were to linger there, they would die, and in any case it would be very costly to maintain them in a place where prices are so high. I rely upon you to issue your orders so that, within ninety days from today, there will be transports at the Isthmus capable of carrying 3,000 or 4,000 men. Let me hasten to advise you that, if the men are intended for Cartagena, assign them to Turbaco; and if for Zulia, to Mérida; and if for Venezuela, to Valencia or Caracas, because every man of them is from a cold, or at least a temperate, climate. If they are taken to the coasts, they will surely die, and the

[1] No. 203 (ed.).

result will be a sacrifice of both men and money. The remainder of the Colombian troops will leave whenever you wish, with the exception, for the present, of 3,000 Colombians who are needed here to maintain union and order.

I have established a Council of Government here, as you will see by the decrees that are being sent you in this post. The Council is a fairly good one and possesses all the executive power in Perú, particularly that which concerns foreign affairs; hence, this government enjoys all the independence that is necessary to deal freely with Colombia. What you state in your reply to this government respecting the Congress at the Isthmus appears very well to me, as it provides a firmer and less nebulous basis for that Congress, which will therefore convene more promptly. The Isthmus is an unhealthy, wretched place; for this reason I believe the Congress should move to Quito, which is a very healthy city and is situated in the very heart of America, only thirty-two leagues from the sea. I have given this much thought, and I can find no more desirable place for that assembly to be held.

I expect Buenos Aires and Chile to enter the Confederation, out of respect for us and for the good or harm that we could do them. I might say to you, however, that confederation with Buenos Aires would be disadvantageous to us at present, as it would compromise us with Brazil and perhaps with the Holy Alliance. Federation with the United States would compromise us with England, as the [North] Americans are the only rivals of the English in America. After you have examined this matter carefully, I should like to know your opinion, as thus you and I might rid ourselves of some of our misgivings.

The government of Buenos Aires has been recognized *de facto* in a treaty of amity and commerce with England: this is proof that we will all be recognized.

By this premature and preferential move, England hopes to have the states of the Río de la Plata unite and form a nation. Nevertheless, I think that Colombia will continue to be in the vanguard.

I am sending you one of two letters that I have received from Padilla concerning his publication. From it you can see his attitude toward the government and the system. Please make no use of it, as it is a personal letter for your private information. I believe this matter definitely deserves the government's attention, not in order to make reprisals, but to take measures to prevent those future horrors and disasters which Padilla prophesies. Equality under the law is not enough in view of the people's current mood. They want absolute equality on both public and social levels. After that they will demand that the darker-skinned elements should rule [*pardocracia*]. This is a very natural obsession that will ultimately lead to the extermination of the privileged class. This, I say, requires considerable thought, which I shall never tire of recommending.

I wrote to you by the last post stating that the fears of France were diminishing by the hour and that I, therefore, had decided to go to Upper Perú to settle the affairs of that country with Perú and Buenos Aires. Upper Perú wishes to be independent, while her neighbors want to rule her. Buenos Aires has legal arguments on her side; Perú, expediency. But Nature, mocking both, has ordained the creation of a new state, because a capital 500 or 700 leagues away would be of little practical use to a province.

The resignation that I submitted to the Congress and the remarks made by Santa María have alarmed everyone, according to what correspondents have written me. You know all that I have had to say on this subject, and I have nothing new to add.

Within the next three days I will leave this capital for the south; hence, I am completely occupied and have no time for long letters. This journey has obliged me to reëngage Pérez as my Secretary-General. There are, in fact, only two persons who can discharge that office, Pérez and Heres. Pérez' capriciousness has won him a consulate and deprived me of his services; but, as he has now resigned, I am using this fact as an argument to say that he has rejoined the Army of Liberation and therefore I can assign him to duty in the service of this country. I know perfectly well that this is not so and that it is all highly irregular, but necessity knows no law. Pérez has reluctantly conceded, and I, too, have been reluctant to take this action. But I can employ no one else. Heres must stay in the Council of Government so that my spirit can remain a part of it, for I would not want to be in the position in which San Martín found himself with respect to Monteagudo and his deputy Tagle. General La Mar is away, and minister Carrión is very ill. The government would, therefore, be poorly constituted were there not someone whom I can trust implicitly and who is in full sympathy with my ideas to represent me in the Council. In a word, my dear General, this matter has been so arranged because it could not be otherwise. Please do not look for rules to cover it. I have felt that I could rely on your indulgence, as has Pérez; if we had not, we should not have gone so far.

The government here has instructions to consult with that of

Colombia on everything pertaining to foreign affairs, more particularly as regards the American federation. The Peruvian envoys will doubtless be at the Isthmus in May. They will discuss whether the assembly is to be held there or elsewhere. Everytime I think of this project I am enchanted, for the creation of a colossus is not a common occurrence. You must order that everything must be overlooked, so that we may have federation. Consideration must be given to any request from whatever quarter, though it may mean tolerating a certain amount of foolishness for some time. What I mean is that the federal union, or the outward appearance of that body politic, must be preserved at all costs. Its mere shadow saves us from the abyss, or at least prolongs our existence. I plan to go wherever the Congress convenes as soon as it decides to meet, as I wish to lay before it some ideas that I have in the back of my mind.

Guatemala has been recognized by Mexico and must be admitted to the Confederation. Guatemala is the most federally-disposed country in all America by virtue of her position and inclinations. We should therefore throw wide the doors to admit her.

General Alvarez, an agent of Buenos Aires, is expected to arrive in this capital at any moment. I do not know the object of his visit, but it will give us an opportunity to discuss the federation with him.

I take the liberty of enclosing a letter for my sister. It is of the utmost importance.

I have drawn no pay from Guayaquil since I was named Dictator of Perú. I have seen a letter from Castillo in which he says that this pay should be charged to Perú; I believe this to be entirely wrong. It has never been my intention to be in the pay of Perú, for I have been serving Colombia. I therefore ask you not to have my pay charged to Perú. It would be quite improper for me to have refused an offer of payment here, as I have done, only later to present a bill demanding payment.

The troops will not arrive at the Isthmus before the month of June. They will go in detachments of some 1,000 men, as a larger number would not be safe. Please give orders to the intendants at Cartagena and at the Isthmus to arrange with me regarding transportation and to prepare the necessary ships in advance at the proper time and place. I will not order the departure of any troops until I have received word that everything has been made ready.

I am your devoted

BOLÍVAR

P.S. My best respects to the ministers and all my friends.

213. To P[EDRO] MOLINA, MINISTER OF THE UNITED PROVINCES
OF CENTRAL AMERICA TO COLOMBIA

[Copy]¹

Magdalena, April 8, 1825.

Most Honored Sir:

I have had the honor of reading your esteemed letter, dated January 20, at Bogotá, in which you kindly acknowledge receipt of mine of December 18.

It would be most gratifying to me, both for the honor it would bring you and for the good of America, if the mission which your government has seen fit to entrust to you were to be completely and brilliantly successful. Upon it may depend, perhaps, the very happiness and strength of America, to which I am devoted heart and soul. The pact of confederation, which is our common bond, must link our fate in perpetuity. I take great satisfaction from the thought that the Congress of the American nations is shortly to convene at the Isthmus, and I am certain that Guatemala, of all the nations that compose our truly sacred league, will ever be the nation that is most disposed toward federation.

I look forward with the keenest anticipation to meeting you there, where you will do your part in the glorious task of uniting all our nations under one common law of prosperity and freedom.

Kindly remember me to your esteemed secretary González.

I take this opportunity to renew the expressions of my highest regard and esteem.

BOLÍVAR

---

214. To GENERAL ANTONIO JOSÉ DE SUCRE,
GRAND MARSHAL OF AYACUCHO

[Original]

Arequipa, May 15, 1825.

My dear General:

Yesterday, upon my arrival here, I received your two letters, dated the 27th at Chuquisaca, together with an official communication from

¹ *Anales de la Sociedad de Historia y Geografía* [Guatemala], September, 1932.

Apotheosis of Bolivar

General Arenales. The General states that his government has ordered him to make it possible for the provinces of [Upper Perú] to determine their own interests and government. This representation on the part of General Arenales has impelled me to issue the accompanying decree, to be executed and put into effect immediately. You will note therein that I seek to reconcile whatever is reconcilable between contrary extremes and interests. I do not think that those who claim Upper Perú can possibly reproach me in any fashion, for, on the one hand, I cite the decree of the Peruvian Congress, and, on the other, I recognize the expressed will of the government of Buenos Aires. Naturally, I grant Upper Perú the right of expressing her own wishes freely. Nevertheless, I am convinced that everyone will be displeased, for I have done nothing more than palliate, or rather neutralize, the different measures that each party could hope to adopt. Among contending groups, the judgments that result from equity are the ones that please the least, since they give satisfaction to neither party. I shall confess to you that I would never have issued this decree if matters had not reached their present stage. But, as my powers are not retroactive, I could not act in any other fashion. Your sentiments and mine are so remarkably in accord that, I must admit, I wanted you to take the very step that you did take in order to leave those provinces, whose chains you had just broken, completely free. I have also wanted to fulfill my duty by doing nothing but obey those who have given me the authority I exercise—an authority that I must never betray, even though its rulings should be counter to the most accepted precepts of liberal policy. I must tell you frankly that I do not believe I am authorized to issue this decree; only the power of circumstances has forced it from me in order to sanction your conduct, to placate Upper Perú, to please the Río de la Plata, to prove the liberal sentiments of the Congress of Perú, and to defend my reputation as a supporter of popular sovereignty and of free institutions. In short, the decree was born of candor, good faith, and impartiality. May it be received in the same spirit of virtuous intentions that inspired it!

In order to allow those provinces to act in complete freedom with no sign of compulsion, I have decided not to go to Upper Perú for at least two months. Meanwhile, I shall visit Cuzco to arrange matters there, and I shall also spend some time here for the same purpose. Thus, by the time that I arrive in Upper Perú, the assembly will have settled any questions that they themselves raise concerning their *interests and government,* to use the words of General Arenales.

This must be the basis for their deliberations so that the Río de la Plata will have no grounds for imputing to us any usurpation of rights or any intervention in her domestic affairs. For, frankly speaking, we have no right to inject into that assembly any issue that might result in a fundamental principle for their institutions. You will, therefore, execute today's decree and order the General Assembly to convene immediately at an appointed place of your choice. The meeting place of the assembly must be cleared of troops of the Army of Liberation within a radius of twenty leagues. No soldier is to remain within the area so defined. A civilian judge must govern the area, and you, of course, will remain as far away as possible. But you must on no account abandon the territory of Upper Perú, as command of that region is entirely in your hands. You will issue a proclamation to the people stating plainly: "I will not visit those provinces until the assembly has concluded its sessions; these sessions are no more than strictly deliberative; they will have no immediate effect until after the Congress of Perú has determined what the Liberator and the United Army are to do with respect to the said provinces; within a radius of twenty leagues of wherever the assembly is to meet, not a single member of the Army of Liberation will be allowed to remain, in order to avoid any possible charges that the military influenced the acts of the delegates." You must put all this in the brisk military style of a soldier addressing civilians. I also believe that you should deliver an inaugural *address* at the opening of the assembly's sessions. In it you have only to mention the reasons that prompted your entry into the territory of Upper Perú, my submission to the Peruvian Congress and the wishes of the government of the Río de la Plata as expressed by General Arenales—all with due propriety and exactness. I think it would be a good thing if you were to make a draft and send it to me in Cuzco so that I can see it and offer an opinion on its appropriateness. This address should be sent to the President of the Assembly.

Use your time, meanwhile, in making the administration of the finances as efficient as possible, eliminating the superfluous and the less vital positions. This is indispensable and in accordance with my decrees and dispositions. Remember that there is a frightful inefficiency—expenses are great, and our needs are greater still. Here, within three months, five hundred thousand *pesos* have been expended. This is terrible and ruinous in the extreme; but I shall remedy all this—at Cuzco, too, where conditions are similar.

I was relying on the money that Cochrane had in his possession here in order to pay a portion of the amount that I had promised the army, but I did not find a penny, for all the funds had been spent. That is how things go, but they must go no further. You must, therefore, introduce a complete change there, and I shall do the same on this side of the Desaguadero.

The General Staff must have forwarded you my order not to regard as being on campaign status any troops that arrive for garrison duty from the date of their arrival at the garrisons. Consequently, the amount for rations and uniforms issued to the troops is to be deducted from whatever is allowed them for the month; that is to say, they are to receive their monthly pay in full after deducting, first, the ration which was allowed them in currency, and, second, a sixth of the cost of the clothing issued to them. I am assuming that an issue of clothing lasts six months and that every six months a new outfit must be provided. An ordinary, cheap uniform might cost fifteen *pesos;* hence, twenty *reales* could be deducted monthly for the outfit. But if the uniform is ornate, like that which General Lara issued his division, its price is so high that it must be charged against past-due settlements. The same order applies to any situation at your end, whatever it may be, and for every corps of the United Army.

My dear General, you must realize that the army of Perú now exceeds 20,000 men, that its payroll runs into millions, and that the transportation of our men to Colombia will cost a fortune, as will the special awards that have been decreed by the Congress; meanwhile, the civil service has scarcely less personnel than the military. The fleet, foreign affairs, and the public debt, therefore, have me desperate. I presume, moreover, that you are no less concerned than I about economies and savings, so that we may not find ourselves still harder pressed. I intend to send 3,000 men to Colombia—1,500 with a Lara battalion and as many more with a Córdoba battalion. But these battalions must be made up of Peruvians and of Colombians from Southern Colombia. Take steps there so that this movement can be effected within two months at the latest. The *Córdoba* battalion will leave by the port of Arica, the *Lara* battalion by the port of Quilca. No Venezuelan or Granadan is to go with those battalions, except commanders and officers or an occasional urgently needed sergeant, who may be from wherever you please.

Please be informed that there is not the remotest fear of an expedition from Spain, or of any hostile moves from the Holy Alliance. It is, therefore, my intention and desire that the Army of Liberation shall be considerably reduced, that the Colombian units shall retain only Colombians, and that the units in Upper and Lower Perú shall be limited to a handful of men so as to reduce expenses and to make it possible to pay generously those who serve the state. In Upper Perú, 4,000 men should suffice as a garrison. Two thousand here, two thousand in Lima, and a thousand between Cuzco and Huamanga would be more than sufficient to garrison a country at peace. As long as we maintain skeleton units, we could, in two months' time, form a fine army capable of combatting all America (should that become necessary). Otherwise, if we attempt to maintain large armies, we shall become insufferable and tyrannical.

Merge the poorly organized units with the better ones to produce complete and perfect units. Squadrons should remain at a strength of 100 effectives and battalions at 400, in eight companies. All should be organized into regiments, in accordance with the decree that was published in the *Gaceta de Gobierno*, which you have no doubt seen, as the Minister of War sent it to you. This reorganization must be effected speedily, yet with great tact and circumspection so as not to create anger or distrust. Let honorably discharged soldiers be assigned to civilian posts.

Within fifteen or twenty days I shall be leaving for Cuzco, taking eight or ten days to make the journey. This means that I should be in Cuzco by the middle of June. I shall leave there July 1, for Puno and, during July, I shall travel leisurely until I have reached La Paz, which should be after the assembly has been held. The assembly cannot take more than a week or two as the only question to be settled is that which has been posed by Arenales. I believe that the celebrated and worthy patriot, Olañeta, should confer with you so that he may present to the assembly ideas that are in conformity both with the decree of the Peruvian Congress and with my decree of this day, so as to avoid delays and unpleasantness. I shall not deviate so much as a line from the decree of the Congress, as I absolutely cannot do so. Tell those gentlemen as much, for their information and guidance. I am as much a slave to the law as is any soldier to discipline or any convict to his keeper.

General Santa Cruz should be made prefect of the department of La Paz in place of General Lanza; and General Alvarado should be prefect in place of Colonel Ortega or any other prefect with less experience and ability than he. As regards General Santa Cruz, you will act immediately. General Alvarado will be leaving your territory shortly. These two, men of the highest integrity, are fully deserving and capable of such high offices. Be so kind as to talk to General

Santa Cruz on my behalf about my ideas respecting his country, so that he may add his voice to mine. I believe that this General and General Alvarado will admirably serve the cause of Upper and Lower Perú.

I may say in passing that the appointment of a Colombian as prefect in those provinces does not appeal to me at all. Least of all Ortega, who, although he may be a martyr, is both a fool and a liar.

I suggest that you read this letter more than once, for I regard it as most important.

The government of Colombia has appointed you and all the others, in accordance with your recommendations and mine, as of December 9. The Congress has voted us triumphal honors—a sword for you and a coat of arms for the army. I am bringing you a uniform of a Colombian general in chief and the sword which the government of Perú has awarded you. I want to be the one to invest the Marshal of Ayacucho with his uniform and to gird him with the sword of Pichincha in the territory of Upper Perú, which he liberated by the sword of Ayacucho. The ceremony will be a most gratifying one, and one of great distinction; it will do honor to the avenger of the Incas, the restorer of their sons, the liberator of Perú.

Here I must conclude, as I can say nothing more that is worthy of you, except that I am your very affectionate and devoted friend,

BOLÍVAR

---

215. To F[rancisco] de P[aula] Santander,
     Vice President of Colombia

[*Original*]

Arequipa, May 20, 1825.

My dear General:

Lieutenant Colonel Elizalde, a nephew of General La Mar and a Colombian officer, as he is a son of Guayaquil, is commissioned to bring you the banners that were taken from the enemy by the Army of Liberation and which are being sent you by General Sucre.

General Sucre tells me that he is writing you at length concerning all the affairs of the army. I am greatly pleased by this, for you will then be informed of its present and true condition.

I assume that you have found it quite distressing to have been deprived of those dispatches and reports that should be sent a government by its armed forces. This lack of news should not be surprising if you keep in mind that I, who am nearer, know nothing more than what I learn through personal letters. The reason is that neither General Sucre nor I has a General Staff, as there is absolutely no one who can manage one. The country in which we are operating is over a thousand leagues long, and you can count on your fingers the number of men who are able to fill really important positions. We are creating two republics at once, conquering and organizing them. We are hampered by political difficulties, for justice and our own sense of tact demand a constant regard for considerations that must not be ignored. Upper Perú is a former dependency of the viceroyalty of Buenos Aires, and yet the Congress of that Republic has reached no definite clear-cut decision [respecting Upper Perú]. We should not leave the country a prey to the enemy or to anarchy. These provinces desire to be neither Peruvian nor Argentine; they prefer to be independent. We are, therefore, surrounded by difficulties in attempting to extricate ourselves unscathed from a situation as complicated as it is difficult. My policy is based on principles of good faith, and I therefore hope for an honorable solution.

I have ordered the Peruvian Congress to convene February 10 next so that the representatives of Perú can settle their differences with their neighbors. As soon as this has been accomplished, I shall go to Colombia, and I shall stay there for several months, free from the cares of state. Then I shall move on to some country other than Colombia. If the government should be willing to use my services as a diplomatic envoy to Mexico, I should be happy indeed, as it is a pleasant country, with a healthy climate, and independent.

Regarding Mexico: a friend of Victoria has written me a forceful letter in support of the Confederation. I have therefore urged the government of Perú to dispatch its delegates at once to the Isthmus. This same friend tells me that Mexico will propose my name as Generalissimo of the Union. I do not desire such a generalcy, much as it may flatter me; but I am very grateful to the Mexicans for their high opinion of me. I beg you to warn the [Colombian] delegates to the Isthmus that they must by no means give their support to the selection of a Colombian general, particularly myself, as military head of the federation. Such a course would not be honorable and would . . . [only invite] rivalry and dissatisfaction.[1]

Never forget the three political admonitions that I have ventured to give you: first, it will not be to our advantage to admit La Plata to the league; second, or the United States of America; third, do not attempt to liberate Havana. These three points seem to me to be of the greatest importance. I believe our league can maintain itself perfectly well without embracing the extremes of the south and north and without creating another Republic of Haiti [in Cuba]. The Spaniards are no longer a danger to us, but the English are very much so, as they, being nearly omnipotent, are therefore to be feared. Respecting Havana, we should tell Spain that, if she does not make peace, she will soon lose her two large islands. I have told you this before, but I repeat it in case that letter failed to reach you. General Sucre is most eager that the expedition [against Cuba] be launched, but I have not yet been able to see him to tell him my thoughts on the subject.

As soon as Callao has been taken, which will be some time in August, I shall send to the Isthmus 3,000 of the Colombian soldiers from the south. I am not doing so sooner because I do not know whether or not you will have everything prepared at the Isthmus and also because the fleet that is to transport them is blockading Callao. Nevertheless, if you want them you have only to ask, although I imagine that you do not need them right away. I do not know definitely, as yet, who will accompany these troops or which battalions will go, as everything will depend upon the decision of the moment and the position of the armies. In any case, you shall have them—and more if you wish—at that time, for you to assign wherever you think they will do the most good. You realize that they will be men who are *whole* in body and mind; they will be especially useful in areas threatened by revolutionary ills. I must repeat: They should, of course, first be stationed in Turbaco, Ocaña, Valencia, or Caracas until they have accustomed themselves to the climate and can garrison the fortified towns. Respecting this matter, you should make arrangements in advance not only for these 3,000 but for the 3,000 more who can leave as soon as you want them—all *southern* Colombians. After that, do not depend greatly upon any more of them going, except veterans of Cundinamarca and Venezuela, who can be of the most use in the south or in Cundinamarca, where the spirit of the people is

[1] The text reads: "Such a course would not be honorable, and would not bring us rivalry and dissatisfactions" (comp.).

so fine and honorable that, indeed, it might serve as a model for all Colombia.

I arrived in this city a week ago. The country is quite attractive, and the people are congenial. Our Colombians were previously so well treated here and were so impressed that they led me to believe that the place would rival Lima, which it does not. The ruins of Lima are to be preferred to the splendor of Arequipa. This city is a gentle shepherdess, and Lima a handsome matron, despoiled by thieves and somewhat maltreated by time. Arequipa, however, is the second city in Perú, though the city of the Incas is larger. I shall remain here for fifteen or twenty more days settling domestic affairs, which are in a state of considerable confusion. I shall then go on to Cuzco for the purpose of visiting the Temple of the Sun and the ruins of the Incas and also to organize that department, which, I imagine, is in none too good an order. In August, I shall visit Upper Perú.

Here, I have seen Lara's division, which is composed of 3,500 men and is the most dazzling in the world; the same can also be said of Córdoba's division. These troops are extremely well uniformed, well paid, and well fed. The Colombian division has cost more than half a million in three months, or possibly an even larger sum. In Arequipa alone over four hundred thousand *duros* have been spent. The entire army of Colombia may, therefore, have cost a million *pesos* so far this year, not counting rations, which have almost all been supplied by the population. This fine army is well deserving, and I await two million *pesos* from England in order to pay them to date, without any arrears.

You will see the decree that I am sending you herewith regarding Upper Perú. Buenos Aires is of one mind with these provinces—all wish the will of the people to be consulted, to which I have no objection. On the contrary, no one has desired it more than I, but, as I was not expressly authorized by Congress, I did not arrange it beforehand. I have now issued this decree to manifest my friendliness toward the Río de la Plata, as I am certain that no harm can come to Perú from this act of generosity.

Please be so kind as to make your arrangements with the government of Lima regarding the 3,000 men who are to go to the Isthmus as I shall probably be in Upper Perú when your decision arrives. The vessels must come from Callao; there are very few on this coast, as commerce, until recently, has amounted to little, for the Spaniards did not permit these ports to be opened.

I have noted with great pleasure an article in the *Morning*

Chronicle relating to the [English] recognition of Colombia and Mexico, and to the promise that recognition of Buenos Aires is to follow. The article states that the British government does not have favorable reports regarding Chile, but it says nothing of Perú and Guatemala. But, as a result of Ayacucho, which is an excellent nego- tiator and the initiator of a new political order, something will be said about Perú. I was also immensely pleased to see what M. de Mollien had to say about you. Praise from a deceitful monarchist and *godo* for a patriot who governs a republic can only be especially gratifying. He stated that you have *talents that are rarely to be found*. This is from a European with pretensions to cleverness, and who is paid to discredit the new states. I took particular pleasure in the acclaim that you have won from this gentleman. What he stated about me is vague, false, and unjust. It is vague because he does not define my capacity; false because he attributed to me a disinterestedness that I do not possess; and unjust because it is not true that my education was badly neglected, since my mother and family made every possible effort in order that I might have proper instruction. They secured for me the foremost teachers in my country. Robinson,[1] whom you know, taught me reading and writing. Our celebrated [Andrés] Bello taught me the art of composition and geography: Father Andu- jar, of whom the Baron von Humboldt had a high opinion, created an academy of mathematics especially for me. I was sent to Europe to continue my study of mathematics at the Academy of San Fernando. I studied foreign languages with selected teachers in Madrid—all under the direction of the learned Marquis of Uztaris, in whose home I lived. While I was still very young, perhaps too young for such arts, I took lessons in fencing, dancing, and horsemanship. It is true that I learned neither the philosophy of Aristotle nor the codes of crime and error. But it may be that M. de Mollien has not gone as deeply as I into Locke, Condillac, Buffon, Dalambert, Hel- vetius, Montesquieu, Mably, Filangieri, Lalande, Rousseau, Voltaire, Rollin, Herthot, and the classicists of antiquity, whether they be philosophers, historians, orators, or poets, as well as the modern classics of Spain, France, and Italy, and not a few of the English. All this I tell you confidentially, so that you may not think that your poor President is as unlettered as M. de Mollien states. Although I possess very little learning, the fact remains that I was educated as well as any child of good family in America could possibly have been under Spanish rule.

[1] Simón Rodríguez. See Doc. 189 (ed.).

He stated that I am wordy. He could with more reason have said that I am inaccurate, for actually I am careless through impetuosity, negligence, and impatience. I do not quite see how an impatient and impetuous man can be wordy. I develop a multiplicity of ideas in very few words, though without much order or coherence.

I am, my dear General, your devoted

BOLÍVAR

---

216. To F[rancisco] de P[aula] Santander,
    Vice President of Colombia

[Original]

Arequipa, May 30 and June 7, 1825.

My dear General:

I have ordered the office of the Secretary-General to advise you of the incident of the Portuguese invasion of Chiquitos in Upper Perú and to send you a copy of the barbarous and insolent demands of the Portuguese commander.[1] General Sucre replied in similar terms, impelled, no doubt, by the indignation that such an abominable atrocity must have aroused in him. Nevertheless, I do not approve of the use of such rejoinders. The outbreak of a new war would benefit no one, and it would wipe out the remnants of our depleted fortunes. I imagine that the Portuguese commander acted without the authority of his government. If the Emperor did grant him such authority, it may have been merely one of the many acts of folly to which he is given in these days. This affair must be studied in all its various aspects.

The invasion may be a move that is being taken by the Emperor of his own accord; if such is the case, it may be of no consequence whatsoever. But if the Emperor has acted with the approval of the Holy Alliance, then the incident is of grave importance, because the Allies are strong indeed, and they have a very great interest in destroying the new American republics. This organized aggression against

---

[1] Portuguese—i.e., Brazilian (ed.).

our republics will be opposed by England and all the liberal governments of the New World. It may therefore be assumed that our destruction can be brought about only by a major war. The outbreak of so vast a war must necessarily be accompanied by many preparations, but as yet we have observed no such preparations under way in Europe. Public expenditures are increasing. England, France, and Russia are concerned with safeguarding the liberation of the Greeks. Russia views this matter with the greatest interest, and France finds herself involved in the problems relative to the indemnification of her emigrés. All of this predisposes the aristocrats toward peace, as they hope to collect compensation for their properties, which were confiscated during the revolution. If, in these circumstances, which appear so greatly to favor us, the Emperor of Brazil should actually undertake to molest us and to invade our territory, so absurd an action could only redound to his harm. The Holy Alliance, therefore, could not have advised his hostile acts, which can only destroy their commerce and injure their cause. By his actions, therefore, he actually risks losing his throne. Hence, I conclude that the invasion of Chiquitos is an absurd and rash act that was committed by the commander Araujo. If it originated with the Emperor, without counsel from the Holy Alliance, the matter is a piece of folly and of no consequence. But if it was prompted by the Holy Alliance, then it is of the utmost gravity and importance. If the latter is true, we must prepare ourselves for a long conflict with the greater part of Europe. I believe that the first thing we must do, if the Holy Alliance mixes in our affairs, is to have Perú and Buenos Aires occupy Brazil immediately; have Chile occupy [the island of] Chiloé; and let Colombia, Guatemala, and Mexico look only to their own defense. All America must unite in the common cause and together attend to all points that are under attack or threatened by attack.

For the development of such a league and pact, the meeting of the federated states at the Isthmus becomes more urgent than ever. There such advance and preparatory measures as circumstances may demand can be planned. If the Congress were to serve as no more than the general headquarters for this sacred league, its usefulness and importance would be immense. We must, therefore, hasten to establish it. There is one more point to be considered, namely, England is certain to make every effort to prevent any hostilities among ourselves and also between us and Europe, since England has no interest in America other than the prospects of a valuable commerce, and commerce lives only on the fruits of peace. Because of this factor, I am of the opinion that we should consult the British representatives and the British government itself respecting their views as to the nature, origin, and consequences of this incident. I further believe that no hostile move should be made against Brazil except after careful study.

I have written to the Council of Government of Perú, urging it to make representations to the government of Brazil and to demand an explanation of this invasion by their troops; and at the same time to inquire of the British ministers and agents as to their views respecting this affair. I also think it would be useful if you were to give similar instructions to our representative in Europe, as we must be very cautious in a matter of such transcendent importance. I have also written to the Peruvian Council of Government suggesting the advisability of their urging the government of Chile to hasten its expedition against Chiloé and warning them that this Island might come into the hands of some foreign power that could do us harm. England herself would not refuse it, as Chiloé, being the first port of call for those who round the Cape, could make England's commerce preponderant in the Pacific.

I began this letter without having as yet received the post from your city, which is scheduled to arrive tomorrow and to depart the day after. Nothing occurs to me at the moment except the affair with Brazil and the peace and quiet that prevails here in Perú, where everything is being done as well as circumstances permit, until such time as the new Constituent Congress and the constitutional government shall have been definitely established.

On June 10, I am going to Cuzco to survey the situation and to set up a provisional administration, which is sorely needed. In July, I shall go to Upper Perú to establish a provisional government in that country, in accordance with the decision of the Congress in Lima.

The provinces of Upper Perú were formerly under the rule of the presidency and the *audiencia* of Charcas. They have a million inhabitants and about two million *pesos* in government revenue. Upper Perú consists of six provinces and is seven hundred leagues from Buenos Aires, which is its only port and was, until recently, its only capital. Public opinion favors the establishment of an independent state like the states of Chile and Guatemala, which in all respects resemble Upper Perú—that is, the people want an independent state that will be subject only to the American federation. I believe this to be right and even necessary for the prosperity of these provinces, as otherwise they would be engulfed by the anarchy that now rules Buenos Aires, where the situation is as follows: The Banda Oriental of the province of Buenos Aires is occupied by the Portuguese; the Pampas Indians infest the territory about the city; and a small town called Santa Fe has declared itself independent of the capital. Buenos Aires is, therefore, no more than a Hanseatic city without territory. Only the provinces of Salta and Mendoza have sent deputies to the Congress in Buenos Aires. But these provinces are themselves subdivided into four or six [parts]. As a result, the entire state of the Río de la Plata actually consists of only two provinces and the city of Buenos Aires. The province of Paraguay is occupied by a certain Francia, who has kept it in complete isolation these past fourteen years. It belongs to no nation, and it has no government. Its head is a tyrant who is a virtual enemy to the world at large, for he deals with no one and persecutes everyone. Those who enter never return. Thus poor Bonpland, Humboldt's companion, is kept there in captivity. Paraguay is nearer to Charcas than to Buenos Aires; therefore, it can more readily be conquered by the troops of Upper Perú than by those of Buenos Aires. The latter city wants war with no one and holds to the principle that each province should govern itself as it desires. This is the opinion of General Alvarez, the Buenos Aires envoy, and General Arenales, a representative of that government who is in command in Salta. The government of Buenos Aires does not seek to govern the provinces of Upper Perú, since it realizes that it has neither the means to do so nor the men capable of governing a great state. The government of the Río de la Plata will be satisfied to rule the provinces that are now represented in the Congress of Buenos Aires, for it believes that they can be the more easily controlled without being hampered by Upper Perú, which would always oppose that government and attempt to secede from a union which would in no way benefit her.

All this means that we shall have a new state in the American Confederation which will be devoted to us because it will owe its existence and freedom to our efforts. On the other hand, the Río de la Plata will be our enemy, but this enmity will spring from envy rather than from rivalry, since rivalry is unthinkable between such dissimilar entities. Perú will be content with the provinces that she now controls. That Republic is great and rich, and she abounds in the resources that make for prosperity. God grant that she will have the men she needs to govern her.

The Congress will meet on February 10 next. I shall then be released from all commitments in this country and can dispose of my time as I deem best.

June 7:

This letter was retained until today with the intention of completing it on the arrival of the post.

Today I have the pleasure of acknowledging the arrival of your very gratifying and encouraging communications. The first is the article in *La Estrella* on the independence of Colombia and Mexico, with that paper's comments relative to the guarantees that England possesses of having nothing to fear from Europe; second, your remarks to the effect that France, Holland, Sweden, and Denmark will recognize us shortly are also highly gratifying. I have been certain of this for some time, as you have doubtless seen in my message, and I have seen it confirmed in a report concerning the recognition of all our states by Holland.

I am also delighted with the authorization you give me to promote our unhappy comrades of Ayacucho. They all deserve some reward, and many have received none. There is no one who does not warrant some consideration, and with good reason indeed.

The assurances you give me of peace and security in Colombia are the most interesting parts of all your letters. For, without doubt, it is a great consolation to know that, in spite of everything, the Republic is safe after so much floundering. Yet among those bright prospects I see a gaping precipice: you speak of retiring from public life because of illness. No, my friend, you must not, you cannot retire. You are the *indispensable man* in the life of the Republic. You must die in the forum as I am destined to die upon the battlefield. Without you, what would become of our army and my fame? I tell you frankly that, if I had not had you to safeguard my life's work, with your talents and your energy, it would long since have fallen to pieces. Moreover, I believe that without you—or if left to me alone—it would not have succeeded as it has. I am no administrator, and I lack the patience to be tied to a desk. I should therefore have undone the work of my comrades-in-arms, for want of your character and capacity for administering public affairs. I repeat: you are the *indispensable man* for Colombia.

I find the mission that you plan to give General Sucre to be admirable, but at the same time it seems to me out of the question, as

I need General Sucre for everything and cannot possibly spare him in the present circumstances.[1]

The matter of boundaries and payment to Colombia will be fully arranged before my departure, no matter who should represent our interests here. If you can persuade him to return, Mosquera could do it to perfection; if he refuses, let anyone come. General Sucre has been assigned to govern the five magnificent departments of Upper Perú; furthermore, I need him in Lima as President of the Council of Government, for General La Mar is most reluctant to take command. Accordingly, General Sucre cannot now be employed in diplomatic negotiations. Pérez could also carry out the assignment you had intended to give Sucre, but not until after he has ceased to be my Secretary-General in Perú. The money and boundary matters will be arranged in accordance with your wishes, since I am well aware that Colombia's claims are wholly justified.

If you do not want the 3,000 men that I offered you, please write to the Minister of State in Lima to the effect that they are not to be sent to you in August, as I have ordered. In this country, for the present, the Colombian troops are no burden at all, but as for later, who can tell what they will be? We have 3,500 men in Upper Perú, and she cherishes them because they serve as a bulwark against the claims of her neighbors. There are 3,000 of our men in this city and 1,500 in Lima, but one out of every four is a Peruvian prisoner from Ayacucho; hence, there remain scarcely 5,000 or 6,000 actual Colombians, whom the country loves because it regards them as well-disciplined soldiers. If you want 2,000 or 3,000 Peruvians to subdue the black factions, ask the Council of Government for them, as I have previously stated; if you do not want them, write immediately, since it is all *arranged* for them to leave at the end of August, as I have already mentioned.

I have seen the draft for the continental federation, which includes the United States and Haiti. I consider it to be ill-advised in its membership but well conceived as to ideas and purpose. Haiti, Buenos Aires, and the United States, each in its own way, offer great disadvantages. Mexico, Guatemala, Colombia, Perú, Chile, and Upper Perú can form a splendid confederation. Guatemala, Chile, and Upper Perú will do what we desire. Perú and Colombia are of one mind; Mexico alone would be isolated amidst this federation,

---

[1] Santander wished to appoint Sucre Colombian Minister to Perú (ed.).

which has the advantages of homogeneity, compactness, and solidity. The North Americans and the Haitians are foreigners to us, if only because they are heterogeneous in character. I shall therefore never agree to our inviting them into our American accord. While I am on the subject, I have read the January 19 issue of *El Colombiano,* of Caracas, which speaks of presidential candidates. I am thoroughly aroused by the ingratitude with which these gentlemen have repaid you for the miracles that you have performed in creating law in a land of slaves and establishing freedom in the midst of war, revolution, and chains. We shall see if another can do as much. For my part, I am determined, first, not to accept the presidency on any terms, but least of all if a new vice president is elected, because I know very well that, however great the ability, talents, and virtues of any other citizen, what is, is, and what is not, is not. By this I mean that you are an excellent vice president, and I have known no other. Consequently, much as I cherish Briceño—and you know I idolize him—I would not want to have to meet any new lifeguards in the Orinoco to pull me to safety, when you have done so well in rescuing me from its turbulent waters. These people want everything to be done by sleight of hand, as the phrase goes. Good luck to them, if they can succeed. For my part, I have done all that I could, and, if they no longer want me, very well; I can then wash my hands of everything, like Pilate. I have made up my mind and, believe me, I shall not change it.

I trust that they will do you full justice in New Granada, unless the envious there have also increased in number.

I am telling Castillo to reduce his battalions in the south to cadres. I am doing the same here with the Peruvian troops in order to reduce expenses and yet preserve the army's morale and maintain a nucleus against eventualities. I commend this method to you, should it occur to you to adopt it.

I am your devoted

BOLÍVAR

P.S. Chile is in a state of frightful anarchy. Freire has gone to Concepción, and Pinto to Coquimbo. The province of Santiago is governed by its intendant. Reports have it that the Chilean Congress will send a deputation to recall O'Higgins. In Chile, it appears, there is a large group for me and another, but smaller, against me.

Upon re-reading your letter, I note that you are delegating Father Rebollo to attend the great American Congress. I know him, and I realize that he is very able. But what will the delegates from the other countries say on seeing a man of the cloth?—they will say that we have no full-fledged statesmen.

---

217. To José Joaquín Olmedo

[Copy]

Cuzco, June 27, 1825.

Dear friend:

A few days ago, while on the road, I received from you two letters and a poem.[1] The letters are those of a statesman and a poet, but the poem is that of an Apollo. The heat of the torrid zone, the fires of Junín and Ayacucho, the rays of the father of Manco Capac, never have these stirred a flame so intense in the mind of any mortal. You fly high . . . higher than any shot that was ever fired. You sear the earth with sparks from the wheel and axle of an Achilles' chariot, such as Junín never knew. You evoke characters of your own creation: of me you make a Jupiter, of Sucre a Mars, of La Mar an Agamemnon and a Menelaus, of Córdoba an Achilles, of Necochea a Patroclus and an Ajax, of Miller a Diomedes, and of Lara a Ulysses. You give to each of us a divine and heroic haze that covers us like the protecting wings of a guardian angel. You mold us in your poetic and fanciful manner; and, to project the fiction of the fable into the land of poesy, you elevate us to a false deity, after the manner of Jupiter's eagle which bore the tortoise to the skies only to let it fall upon a rock, crushing it and dismembering its body. Indeed, you have raised us to such heights that you have cast us into the abyss of nothingness, eclipsing in an immensity of brilliance the pallid splendor of our dim virtues. Thus, my friend, you have pulverized us with the bolts of your Jupiter, with the sword of your Mars, with the sceptre of your Agamemnon, with the lance of your Achilles, and with the wisdom of your Ulysses. Were I less charitable or were you a lesser poet, I might choose to believe that you had intended to use the heroes of our poor comedy in order to make a parody of the

---

[1] *La Victoria de Junín* "Canto a Bolívar" (ed.).

Iliad. But no, that I do not believe. You are a poet and you fully comprehend, as did Bonaparte, that from the heroic to the ridiculous it is but a step, and that Manolo and the Cid, though sons of different fathers, are blood brothers. To an American your poem will read like a canto of Homer; to a Spaniard, like a canto from the *Facistol* of Boileau.

I thank you for it with infinite gratitude.

I am sure that you will worthily perform your mission to England. Indeed, so confident am I that, after scanning all the Empire of the Sun, I could find no diplomat more capable of representing Perú and of negotiating for her to better advantage. You are to be accompanied by a mathematician, lest you should avail yourself of poetic license and choose to believe that two and two are four thousand. Therefore, our Euclid goes along to open the eyes of our Homer, to make certain that he sees not with his imagination but with his eyes, and that he is not entranced with harmonics and meters but keeps his ears attuned only to the rude, harsh, and rasping prose of publicans and politicians.

Yesterday I came to the classic Land of the Sun, of the Incas, of fable, and of history. Here gold is the true sun. The Incas are his viceroys or prefects; fable is the story of Garcilaso [de la Vega]; history is Las Casas' account of the destruction of the Indians. But poetry aside, your every word evokes exalted ideas and profound thoughts within me. My soul is enthralled by the presence of Nature unfolding herself, creating from her own elements a model drawn from the image of her innermost inspirations, with no need of other works or counsel to guide her; nor is she influenced by the whims of humanity or contaminated by the chronicles of the crimes and follies of our species. Manco Capac, the Adam of the Indians, left his Titicacan paradise to found a historic society, unmixed with fable, either sacred or profane.

God made him into a man, and he created a kingdom. History speaks truthfully, for stone monuments, wide and straight roads, simple customs, and authentic traditions bear witness to a social organization of which we have no conception, no prototype, no imitation anywhere else. Perú is unique in the annals of man. This is how it appears to me now that I am here, and all that I have just told you, in more or less poetic vein, seems perfectly obvious.

Be so kind as to show this letter to Paredes, and, as for yourself, kindly accept the sincere assurances of my friendship.

BOLÍVAR

218. To F[rancisco] de P[aula] Santander,
   Vice President of Colombia

[Original]

Cuzco, June 28, 1825.

My dear General:

I arrived at this capital three days ago, after passing through happy, contented, and grateful towns, filled with the memories and the monuments of this innocent empire before it was destroyed by the Spaniards. I tell you frankly that, even if I had not read the *Ruins of Palmyra*, I should still be able to appreciate the memory of greatness in things and events that antedate the present era. This country is the handiwork of Nature remolded by the hands of men, who, though savage, were guided by an instinct that may be termed the wisdom of primitive nature. In its creations this country had no models to follow, nor for its precepts did it have any examples or masters. Its entire creation has been original, pure, like an inspiration from above.

The poor Indians are truly in a state of lamentable depression. I intend to help them all I can: first, as a matter of humanity; second, because it is their right; and finally, because doing good costs nothing and is worth much.

While writing this letter I received the decree of the Congress of Buenos Aires that I enclose. It pleases me greatly since, as you will see, it honors me and opens the way to a settlement of the affairs of this region. The situation in Upper Perú is quite exceptional: The people desire to be independent, and the whole world is anxious for them to have their freedom. Sucre and I, on our part, have done what is right as have the Congresses of Perú and of Buenos Aires. I am greatly pleased about all this as it will enable me to remain on the best of terms with everyone.

Pérez is now free to be employed in any capacity by the government of Colombia. Heres is free, too, as I have released him from the ministry of government in order that he might undertake his mission to Chile. I am badly in need of both of them, but Pérez is ill while Heres is no longer urgently required in the ministry; moreover, I want the Council of Government to remain wholly and exclusively Peruvian, so that none can find fault with me or say that Perú has been injured by actions that were taken either under the influence of the Colombians or in their interest.

Today I have received letters from General Sucre in which he speaks at length on the importance of sending 4,000 men from the south to Colombia. I also think it would be advisable and expedient to send these 4,000 men to Venezuela because my sister, who is quite capable, writes me that Caracas is uninhabitable because of the excesses and threats of domination by the people of color. She, who is poor, tells me that she wants to go to the United States. Consequently, you had best instruct the Isthmus to the effect that we will be sending troops through in September or October. On this particular, please write the Council of Government, which is resident at Lima, so that it will issue orders in conformity with your wishes. I need not repeat what I have so often told you: If the men are to survive, this division must be stationed in a healthy and temperate climate.

I have convoked the Congress of Perú to meet February 10 next. I do not intend to go to Lima at that time, for I do not want it said later that I influenced the deliberations of the Congress. I may not go to Lima until after the constitutional government has been established; then I shall bid them farewell and leave for Colombia. Meanwhile, I shall set up the type of government in Upper Perú that I deem to be suited for that country's welfare. Already the inhabitants call me the father of three republics—meaning that I am also to be the founder of theirs. The temptation is great and exalted, and I do not propose to resist it.

Yesterday I received newspapers from France and from Buenos Aires in which I noted encouraging developments in Europe affecting us, that is, affecting universal peace. The Spanish government has irritated the French government; hence, there is nothing to fear and every reason to hope. We face no further dangers but those of our own making, and these can be held in check with the 12,000 Colombians that I have in Perú. Order the greater part of them to be sent wherever you wish. Any that are not needed in Colombia will be extremely useful here, as this country needs some forces of occupation.

I have intended to write to you a thousand times concerning a very delicate matter, namely, that our American Confederation cannot survive unless England takes it under her protection, and yet I really do not know how desirable it would be for us to invite her to join in a defensive and offensive alliance. Such an alliance would have but one drawback—the entanglements in which British policy might involve us. But this disadvantage is problematic and undoubtedly re-

mote. Offsetting this disadvantage I offer this thought: Existence is
the primary concern, and the manner of existence is only secondary.
If we league ourselves with England we can exist—if we do not, we
shall inevitably be doomed. The first alternative is therefore the more
preferable. Meanwhile, we can grow and become strong, and, by the
time when we might be seriously compromised by our ally, we shall
truly be nations. Our own strength and the relationships that we
shall have established with other European nations will then place
us beyond the pale of our tutors and allies. Let us assume further that
we would suffer from England's superiority. This suffering itself
would be proof of our existence, and, as long as we continued to exist,
we could hope to undo the injury. Whereas, if we remain in our
present state of pernicious isolation, we shall destroy ourselves
through our own efforts to pursue an illusive freedom.

Note that it is I who propose this plan; that is, I offer myself as
a victim to the liberal opposition and even to political censure. For
I am destined to be the head of this American federation, and it is
I who renounce the hope of so high a station for the sake of America's stability. England would never recognize me as the head of the
federation, for this leadership would virtually rest with the British
government. Consequently, nothing can be more truly disinterested,
nothing more generous, than this proposal, as no personal hope or
ambition could possibly have prompted it. So, my dear General, if
this meets with your approval, consult Congress or the Council of
Government that is your cabinet in difficult cases. If these gentlemen approve of my idea, it will become urgent for us to sound out
the British government and to consult the assembly of the Isthmus.
For my part, I shall persist in the idea though none should support
it. Of course, the gentlemen of [North] America will be its greatest
opponents, on alleged grounds of independence and freedom, but
their real reasons will be selfish ones, for they have nothing to fear
at home. I earnestly commend this plan to you. Please do not dismiss
it, however unsound it may appear to you. It may be that, after
everything has been lost, we will wish we could adopt it. The glorious and opportune time is the present. Remember also that the occasion is ripe.

Give my best regards to Don Perucho, to the ministers, and very
particularly to Ibarra, and tell him that I hold him especially dear.

I am your devoted

BOLÍVAR

219. To Esteban Palacios

[*Original*]

Cuzco, July 10, 1825.

My dear Uncle Esteban and Godfather:

Yesterday you were resurrected for me, and how happy that made me!

Yesterday I learned that you were alive and living in our dear fatherland. How many recollections crowded my mind at that instant! My mother, my gentle mother, who so resembled you, arose from the dead and stood before me. My earliest childhood, my confirmation, and my godfather at that event were focused into one as I realized that you were my second father. All my uncles, my brothers and sisters, my grandfather, my childish games, the gifts you gave me when I had behaved—all rushed back to reawaken my earliest emotions, in an overflow of the tenderest recollections.

Everything human in me was touched yesterday. I call that human which is deepest in nature and closest to first impressions. You, my dear uncle, have given me the keenest of pleasures in returning to your hearth, to your family, to your nephew, and to your country. Take pleasure then, as I do, in this genuine joy, and spend the rest of the days that Providence has given you with your own; let a fraternal hand close your eyelids and bear your remains to join your brothers and forebears in the soil that gave us birth.

My dear uncle, you have seen the dream of Epimenides come true. You have returned from the dead to observe the ravages of inexorable time, cruel war, and savage men. In Caracas you are like a ghost that has come back from another world only to find that nothing remains of that which once existed.

You left behind a large and happy family. It has since been cut down by a bloody scythe. You left a country that, newborn, was still nurturing the first fruits of its creation, the first elements of a nascent society, and now you find it all in ruins—all a memory. The living have disappeared. The works of man, the houses of God, the very fields of the earth have suffered the terrible havoc wrought by the quaking force of Nature. You will ask, "Where are my parents, my brothers and sisters, my nieces and nephews?" The most fortunate have been buried within the sanctuary of their own homes; as for the less fortunate, the fields of Venezuela have been watered with their blood and littered with their bones; their only crime was their love of justice.

The fields that were watered by the sweat of three centuries have become parched as the result of a fatal combination of crime and the elements. "Where is Caracas?" you will ask. Caracas no longer exists. But her ashes, her monuments, the ground on which she stood, have been lighted by the lamp of liberty and covered with the glory of martyrdom. This consolation has healed all wounds; at least this is my consolation, and I trust it will be yours.

I have commended to the Vice President the virtues and talents that I know you possess. My recommendation has been as ardent as is my affection for my dear uncle. Make your wishes known to the executive power, and you will be heard. I have asked the government to place five thousand *pesos* at your disposal in Caracas, to enable you to live until we see each other, which will be this coming year. My order was addressed to the Minister of Finance, for him to have a draft for this amount sent to you from Bogotá.

Good-bye, dear uncle. Take consolation in your native land from those kin who are still alive. They have suffered greatly, but they have earned glory from having been ever faithful to their duty. Our family has proved itself to be a worthy one, and its blood has been avenged by one of its members. That privilege has been mine. I have reaped the fruit of all the efforts of my countrymen, relatives, and friends. I have been their representative before mankind, and I shall continue to represent them before posterity. This has been my extraordinary lot. Fortune has frowned upon all the others; upon me alone has she lavished her favors. I offer them to you from the bottom of my heart.

BOLÍVAR

---

220. To F[rancisco] de P[aula] Santander,
     Vice President of Colombia

[*Original*]

Cuzco, July 10, 1825.

My dear General:

Yesterday I received your kind letter of April 6, in which you have discussed various matters of no little importance. What interests me most is the English mission. Briceño tells me that, in exchange for their recognizing us, they have asked us to sacrifice some of our political principles. This is a serious matter. I know not how you and the others propose to deal with it. If we sacrifice our political principles, those of us who will be responsible will lose our popularity. If we do not sacrifice them, England will dissolve us like so much vapor, for, I repeat, her hegemony is sovereign and absolute. Our situation is such that an insignificant French squadron is blockading and taunting us with impunity. What a power we are! What resistance we offer! We must take advantage of this annoyance and bind ourselves body and soul to the English, to preserve at least the forms and advantages of a legal and civil government, for to be governed by the Holy Alliance would mean a rule by conquerors and a military government. To find actual proof that we cannot exist, either alone or in federation, without England's benediction, witness the fall of Napoleon's great empire at the hands of the English, consider Russia's desire to throw herself upon Turkey, and France's upon us, and how they dare not do so in deference to England. The entire Holy Alliance quails before Great Britain. How are we to exist if we do not bind ourselves to her? She is another Roman Empire at the end of her republican period and on the threshold of becoming an empire. England is rapidly advancing, and woe to him who opposes her. Woe to him, also, who is not her ally and who does not link his future with hers. All America combined is not worth one British fleet. The entire Holy Alliance cannot restrain the combined force of her liberal principles and tremendous wealth. Both of these forces are employed in a shrewd and invincible policy that achieves everything it sets out to obtain. Remember that Hannibal, Mithridates, the Gauls, the Parthians, and the entire world opposed Rome, but all succumbed to the policy of the Roman Senate, as long as that body existed. The British Senate now exists in its greatest vigor; that is, its aristocracy is immortal, indestructible, tenacious, and as durable as platinum. Recall what De Pradt has to say of aristocracy in general, and remember that the British aristocracy is multiplied by a thousand, as it embraces all the elements that rule and dominate the earth: valor, riches, science, and [civic] virtue. These are the four faculties that prevail over the temporal world; these are the queens of the universe, and we must either league ourselves with them or perish. For my part, I plead for this policy loudly and wholeheartedly. I shall repeat this to the ministers of Perú so that they will know what is best for them.

I have no doubt but that most of New Granada and southern Colombia will cast their vote for you for the vice presidency.

Respecting your statement about the payment due me for my military service, I cannot deny that you are basically right, but my ancient pride and my scruples force me to reject it unalterably. However, I have no money, and I wish to repay Ibarra the five thousand *pesos* I obtained from him in Angostura. After he had secured a house, he sold it for a thousand and odd *pesos* to pay for my sister's trip to Guayana. I must now repay this amount so that he and his family can move wherever he wants to go. Kindly order this amount paid from my account in the public treasury. I shall be greatly obliged to you. Poor Ibarra has served a great deal. He has nearly gone mad; he is married and has stepchildren. I therefore trust you will assign him a good post, one that he will like. The captaincy of the port of Guayaquil is an excellent post, and its present occupant wishes to relinquish it so that he can do better in business. It pays five or six thousand *pesos* a year and can be satisfactorily handled by Ibarra with the help of the competent naval aide who has regularly been under his orders. Give this post to Ibarra, since Luzarraga is about to resign it at once. If Ibarra does not want the position, make him governor of one of the provinces in the south, a region with which he is well acquainted and where he is highly regarded because of his character and services. I would advise him to go south, as that is the best and most peaceful part of all Colombia.

Everyone writes me from Venezuela that things are very bad and that I should go there accompanied by troops. Consequently, I shall go there with 6,000 men from this excellent army. On the other hand, I shall not go to Bogotá, for I fear Colombia more than Spain herself. I have accordingly issued orders for 4,000 men to be sent to the Isthmus, pursuant to the following schedule; early in September, 1,500 men will leave Arica under Sandes; at the beginning of October, the *Vargas* battalion with 1,400 men will leave from the port of Quilca, also for the Isthmus; and the *Araure* battalion with 1,200 men will embark at Callao for the same place early in December. All these troops will form a single division of 4,000 men under the orders of Sandes; and later, in January or February, General Lara will follow with the *Rifles* and *Vencedor* battalions and the regiment of Hussars, bringing a total of 2,500 or 3,000 men. I am most anxious for Sandes' division to proceed to Caracas and Valencia. Lara's division can go to Cartagena; moreover, Lara would make an excellent intendant for that department—you may be sure he would not let it go to pieces under his hands. The men idolize him, and he is the most reliable man in the world and also the most friendly to Padilla. Montilla can be of use in a thousand other ways. But none can prevent outbreaks in a Cartagena that worships her leader as the soldiers do Lara, for he cares for them as though they were his children. In command of Venezuela we could place the Grand Marshal of Ayacucho, who is every inch a man and all sugar, like his French name. If this country wants a Colombian division, the Córdoba will remain. General Salom can command the department of Barinas or that of Maracaibo. In case of necessity, remember the one-handed Carreño, who is popular everywhere. The troops in Venezuela and Cartagena could be sent on a naval expedition, or be reduced to small groups. Santa María writes me from Mexico suggesting that I head an expedition to Havana. He states that Mexico will contribute 6,000 men and ships if I so desire. Next year we shall consider this, but bear in mind what I have previously said about such an expedition.

The 26th of this month, I am leaving for Upper Perú to settle matters there; after I have organized that country, I shall return to Lima to return to the Congress its authority. In the month of March I shall proceed to the Congress of the Confederation at the Isthmus to see what it is doing and how it is progressing. I shall then go to Bogotá to see how matters stand, and, after that, to Venezuela, with, of course, large forces and full authority. The south will remain perfectly safe with the Córdoba division stationed either in Lima or in the southern departments. I shall never exercise the presidency in Bogotá, even if they should give it to me. My only objective now is to put Venezuela in order, leave my general ideas with my friends, and go somewhere to rest a while, because my body no longer responds. Every day I feel older, weaker, and generally worn out.

Good-bye, my dear General, you should find this letter not wholly devoid of interest. Please reflect upon it carefully.

An uncle of mine has arrived in Caracas, an admirable and very honest man, who was my godfather. He is familiar with revenue matters as he was employed in the treasury at Madrid and in the Council of the Treasury Board, some twenty-five or thirty years ago. He has traveled, and he has lived in the Spanish capital, always as an alternate for Venezuela, of course. He has sound judgment and has done some reading. He is a man very much like Peñalver in every way, but he has seen more of the world, as he has spent forty years in Europe. Please see where you can use him, for he lost everything with the loss of his fortune. If you would be so kind, you might ask him what sort of post would suit him. I also beg that you give instructions for him to be paid five thousand *pesos* against my account at the public treasury in Caracas, so that he may proceed wherever he is assigned. I enclose also some letters regarding men whom I recommend. Torres is an excellent man, and Martínez Pérez is a true patriot.

I enclose, my dear General, two official communications for the Minister of Finance, written with my customary directness, wherein I try to explain myself as best I can. Please give instructions for the five thousand *pesos* to be paid to Ibarra, and the same amount to my uncle. But do not let my communications leave the minister's office, as I do not want anybody in the treasury department to see them. I am recommending my uncle officially so that you will have grounds on which to act.

I am your devoted

BOLÍVAR

P.S. I am recommending Madrid to you.

---

221. To José Joaquín Olmedo

[*Copy*]

Cuzco, July 12, 1825.

My dear friend:

The day before yesterday I received your letter of May 15, which I can only term extraordinary, for, without my knowledge and without asking my consent, you have taken the liberty of making a poet out of me. As every poet is obstinate, you have persisted in imputing to me your tastes and talents. Since you have paid your money and taken your choice, I shall do as did the peasant in the play, who, on being made king, said: "Now that I am King, I shall dispense justice." You must not complain, therefore, of my judgments, for, as I am not trained for the office, I shall blindly imitate the King in the comedy who sent to prison everyone he could lay his hands on. But now to our subject.

I have heard it said that one Horace wrote a very sharp letter to the Pisos in which he harshly criticized metrical compositions. His imitator, M. Boileau, has taught me a few precepts whereby a less informed man can cut to pieces anyone who speaks very prudently in a melodic and rhythmic tone.

I shall start by violating the rules of rhetoric, as I do not like to begin by praising only to end by criticizing. I shall leave my pane-gyrics for the end of this effort where, in my opinion, they properly belong. You should prepare yourself to hear profound truths, or rather prosaic truths, for you of course know that a poet measures truth by standards that differ from those that guide us men of prose. I shall only follow my masters.

You should have stricken out many verses that I find dull and com-monplace. Either I have no ear for music, or they are—they are mere oratory. Forgive my boldness, but as you have dedicated this poem to me I can do with it as I see fit.

Next, you should have allowed your ode to stand in order to fer-ment like wine; it could then be drawn cold, and sipped and savored. Haste is a grievous sin in a poet. Racine would have devoted two years to the composing of fewer verses, for which reason he is the purest versifier of modern times. The plan of your poem, though essentially good, has a capital defect in its design.

You have prepared too small a frame in which to place a giant who takes up the whole picture and whose very shadow blots out the other characters. The Inca Huaina-Capac appears to be the theme of the poem: his is the genius and gist of it: he, in brief, is its hero. On the other hand, it hardly seems proper for him to praise indirectly the religion that destroyed him, and it appears even less proper that he does not desire the reëstablishment of his throne, but, instead, gives preference to foreign intruders who, although they are the avengers of his blood, are nonetheless the descendants of the destroyers of his empire. Such disinterestedness is not human. Nature must govern all rules of behavior, and this is contrary to Nature. You will also permit me to observe that this Inca spirit, who should be lighter than air since he comes from Heaven, has too much to say and his part is too involved; that is why the poets have never forgiven *le bon Henri* for his harangue against Queen Isabelle. Hence, you see that, although Voltaire had some claim to indulgence, even he did not escape criti-cism.

The introduction to the ode is bombastic. It is a thunderbolt of Jupiter that splits the earth and deafens the Andes, which must bear it without a performance like that of Junín. In praising the modesty with which Homer begins his divine *Iliad*, Boileau gave us a precept: He promises little and does much. *Los valles y la sierra proclaman a la tierra*—its onomatopoeia is without appeal. And *los soldados proclaman al general*. Indeed, are the valleys and the mountains the most humble servants of the earth?

Line 360 has overtones of prose—I may be mistaken, but, if I am, why did you make me King?

Let us, to avoid dispute, cite for example line 720:[1]

> *Que al Magdalena y al Rimac bullicioso. . . .*

And this other, 750:

> *Del triunfo que prepara glorioso. . . .*

And there are others that I refrain from quoting in order not to appear too harsh and ungrateful toward my poet laureate.

"The tower of St. Paul becomes your Pindo, and the mighty Thames becomes the Helicon;" here your ode grows dull, and, if you will consult the shades of Milton, you can deftly apply his demons to us. There are other eminent poets from whom you could derive greater inspiration than that to be found in the Inca [Huaina-Capac], who in truth could sing nothing but the *yaravís*. Pope, the poet of your school, could teach you how to avoid pitfalls that Homer himself could not escape. You will pardon me for taking refuge in Horace as I pronounce my oracles. That critic was indignant that the author of the *Iliad* had ever nodded, and you well know that Virgil regretted having brought forth so divine a daughter as the *Aeneid* even after she had been some nine or ten years in the making. Thus, my friend, you must file and file again to polish up the works of man. I have struck land; hence, I end my critique, or, rather, my blind efforts.

I humbly confess to you that I find the versification of your poem sublime. A spirit seems to have borne you to celestial heights. Throughout most of the ode you preserve a life-giving, refreshing warmth. Some of the inspired passages are highly original. The thoughts are noble and high-minded. Your hero's lending of a bolt to Sucre is superior to Achilles' giving of his arms to Patroclus. Line 130 is most beautiful: "I hear the whirlwinds rage and see the sparks fly"[2]—it is truly Hellenic, Homeric. In the portrayal of Bolívar at Junín we see, as in profile, the moment that precedes the combat

---

[1] These remarks refer to the first edition of the ode, in which there are many errors (comp.).

[2] Oigo rodar los torbellinos y veo arder los ejes.

between Turnus and Aeneas. The rôle you give Sucre is warlike and grand. And when you speak of La Mar you remind me of Homer singing of his friend Mentor; though the characters differ, the case is similar—but then, is not La Mar a Mentor in arms?

Permit me to ask, dear friend, where you found the inspiration with which to create an ode so well sustained from the beginning to the end? In the end the battle brings victory, and it is you who have won the battle because you close your poem with dulcet verses, elevated thoughts, and philosophic concepts. You return to the Pindaric vein, and it is so much to my liking that I would call it divine.

Pursue, my beloved poet, the happy course upon which the Muses have launched you with your translation of Pope and your *Ode to Bolívar*.

Pardon, pardon, my friend, but you are to blame for calling me a poet.

Your devoted friend,

BOLÍVAR

---

222. To J[osé] Hipólito Unánue, President of the Peruvian Council of Government

[*Obras de Unánue*, II, 414]

Cuzco, July 28, 1825.

My dear President:

Yesterday I received your esteemed letter of the 10th instant, which has caused me the deepest sorrow and regret. Poor, worthy Carrión dead, yourself ill, Heres out of the ministry of government, Pando on his mission to the Isthmus, and La Mar on leave in Guayaquil! All this combined has shocked me; nevertheless, I made my decisions immediately.

The first thing I have ordered is that you are to continue as president *pro tempore*; second, that you be the vice president *ex officio*; third, that you take charge of the Ministry of Government, though you are obliged to exercise the presidency; fourth, that Larrea, Minister of the Court of Justice, take over the Ministry of Finance; fifth, that Colonel Salazar, the new Minister of War, and Larrea, the new Minister of Finance, become members of the Council of Government; and sixth, that the Council of Government appoint someone to the Superior Court to replace Larrea.

My dear President, a mountain of difficulties and responsibilities has accumulated upon your shoulders, but I believe you can overcome them by virtue of the general respect you enjoy, and with the help of General Salom who commands the United Army, and whom I am again instructing to support you with all his heart and strength.

General Heres must go upon his mission to Chile because I do not want any Colombian to have the slightest influence in the affairs of Perú. In Arequipa, your section of the country, they have caricatured me as a monster who seeks to devour the Peruvians, because it is said that I wish to subjugate them. Because of this and many similar misrepresentations, I want the 3,000 men who were to leave after the surrender of Callao to proceed to Colombia. In order that you can make the necessary arrangements, discuss this matter with Heres, who is fully instructed regarding it.

I am ordering immediate suspension of the expedition of Colombians and Peruvians that I had contemplated directing against Chiloé, as I do not want the Peruvians and Chileans to say that I wish to oppress them. You will, therefore, take no further action in the matter of the Chiloé expedition, concerning which I wrote to Heres at great length from Arequipa.

I strongly insist that the Congress meet on February 10, without fail. You may demand of the Congress its decision as to whether or not it wants to undertake an expedition against Chiloé. It can then be done, if the Congress so orders.

At this very moment I have just seen a decree of the Congress of La Plata, giving me a vote of thanks for the freeing of Upper Perú and for the protection that I afforded that area after its liberation. The decree further stipulates that a mission be sent to Upper Perú to treat with me respecting the future of those provinces, leaving them entirely free to determine their destiny, with no thought of having Buenos Aires rule them. This decree is most gratifying to me and very fair to those provinces. It facilitates the peaceful development of the organization of that country. The provinces of Upper Perú are divided into three parties. The first favors independence, and it is the largest; the second favors Perú; and the third, which is the weakest, favors La Plata. Consequently, I do not doubt but that the assembly will decide for independence, regardless of the desires of Perú and the La Plata. Therefore, you and the others should continue to think about this matter so that at the proper time you may place it before the Congress in its true colors.

I do not understand how it is that only ninety thousand *pesos* remain to be supplied by Cochrane. The quartermaster submitted to me, before I left Lima, an account according to which two hundred and sixty thousand remained to be paid by said Mr. Cochrane. I should like you to report to me fully about this matter. What is even stranger is that the department of La Libertad yields only five thousand *pesos* monthly, which is impossible. The department of Ayacucho should contribute twenty-five thousand *pesos* at least, Jauja, a similar amount, and the customs at Pisco no less than twenty thousand.

If you lack revenues, why not levy a special assessment upon Lima to make up for all those that have been left unpaid, so that the shortage will be made up by that department against what it failed to pay before. This seems to me only just. Of course, I do not doubt but that Cochrane has paid in full, but I still wish to know how the quartermaster deduced that Cochrane owed two hundred and sixty thousand *pesos* before I left Lima. You must know that the two hundred thousand *pesos* that Cochrane issued to me in notes on Arequipa were not paid out there, and the amount that he has sent to Upper Perú hardly totals three hundred thousand *pesos*. I beg you, my dear President, to straighten this matter out with Mr. Cochrane, for everything concerning money is of major interest. Be sure to bear in mind. . . .

I am your most affectionate friend,

BOLÍVAR

223. To Manuel Lorenzo Vidaurre, Peruvian
    Delegate to the Congress of Panama

[*Copy*][1]

La Paz, August 30, 1825.

I shall be most happy, my dear friend, to learn that you have begun work on the covenant that is to be preserved in the archives of the alliance. You are indeed fortunate if you have attended the assembly of the American amphictyons, and if the Isthmus of Panamá has become the second setting for the Isthmus of Corinth, where the free ambassadors of glorious republics were assembled. But Heaven forbid that our future history should be that of the Greek nations, which, it appears, could exist only long enough to witness but brief flashes of freedom, followed by fearful tempests of tyranny, instead of surviving to produce upstanding men and happy citizens. I do not fear the reefs of the Aegean Sea on the peaceful shores of our oceans. I place my trust entirely in the wisdom of our lawmakers. The existence of an entire world that desires liberty and glory is relying upon you. This world has broken its chains in order to enjoy peace under a heaven-ordained order of Nature, whose laws it wishes to obey in order to achieve the aims of society. Do you not find yourself lifted by the flame of your imagination and the ardor of your love of country toward these high purposes? I suppose you are so imbued with the enormity of your task that very possibly the electric spark with which you are fired has increased in intensity. But, my friend, wisdom is not in the Sun, and, although she is the daughter of Jupiter, I revere her not for her lightning shafts but for her cold intellect. Therefore, expel from your heart and from your thoughts all the heat of that torrid zone that consumes you, and dwell in the waters of the Pacific and the Atlantic—you have them close by—so as to develop your ideas with a temperament as cool as Washington's while still abiding on the heights of Franklin, who with his hand wrested the lightning from the sky.

My dear friend, accept the assurance of my sincere affection. Do not feel badly if I do not more assiduously cultivate correspondence with you. The reason lies in certain scruples which Pando will make clear to you.

I am, Sir, your most affectionate friend and servant,

Bolívar

---

[1] Taken from *Archivo Diplomático Peruano. El Congreso de Panamá, 1826.* Tomo I. Raúl Porras Barrenechea, ed. (Lima, 1930), p. 451.

224. To F[RANCISCO] DE P[AULA] SANTANDER,
   VICE PRESIDENT OF COLOMBIA

[Original]

La Paz, September 8, 1825.

My dear General:

General Córdoba's brother is going to Bogotá on temporary leave, in connection with family matters, I believe. I am therefore taking the liberty of recommending him to you. He received a wound as a result of valorous action at Ayacucho.

I also avail myself of this opportunity to tell you that, as I have no Colombian secretary, I am not discussing all that concerns this army in official communications. Santana is with me temporarily, and he scarcely has time for the continuous pressure of urgent business. The most important thing is that I have formed a battalion with a strength of 1,400 and named it the *Junín*. It is made up entirely of Peruvians. This battalion is now on the way to the port of Arica where it is to embark for the Isthmus toward the end of this month. A squadron of Grenadiers, 200 strong, is also to leave, and it will embark jointly with this battalion and for the same destination. I have ordered General Salom, once Callao is taken, to embark with a battalion of 1,200, to be named the *Callao* battalion, together with a company of Grenadiers, all to proceed to the Isthmus, as I have so often told you. I believe these forces will be very effective in Venezuela. Remaining here are nine battalions with 6,000 men and five squadrons with 1,000 horses.

I shall now give you the news of the moment. The assembly of Upper Perú, now called Bolívar, has asked me to provide it with a constitutional code and to exert my influence to prevail upon General Sucre to continue for some years at the head of that Republic. The Republic, of course, wants to be recognized by Colombia, by the Isthmian assembly, and by Perú. Buenos Aires has indirectly suggested that the country should be independent; hence, there is not the slightest doubt but that her government will immediately recognize the new Republic.

I shall send you all the documents respecting this matter by the next courier.

I have been told that Gual and General Briceño have reached the Isthmus as plenipotentiaries. This pleases me immensely as they are both fine men. This amounts to sending angels instead of politicians and is like living in the Golden Age, for it has not been the [present] custom to select men for such assignments on the strength of their virtues.

Everything goes poorly in the Buenos Aires region. The Portuguese press harder every day. I very much fear that we shall have to go to the aid of those ungrateful wretches. The demon of glory will yet carry us to Tierra del Fuego—and, indeed, what can we lose? The army here is not needed in Colombia, and the nations of the south have need of some of the victors of Ayacucho to implant peace and freedom. If you and the others will release us, you can give new life to the four republics in the south.

Please ask the Congress in my behalf to let me pursue my destiny and go wherever America's peril and Colombia's glory may call. Sucre, Córdoba, and the entire army join me in this sentiment.

Salud. Your devoted

BOLÍVAR

P.S. I was decidedly pleased to note that you had triumphed over your enemies in the matter of the commissioners for the loan. I have also noted that the southern departments want you for vice president. If you are not reëlected I shall not accept the presidency, as I do not want another who would be the ruination of me. You and Sucre are the men, in all Colombia, to exercise supreme command. I am of no use in such matters, and I say so in all frankness. I am a man for hardships and no more. I can only serve amidst dangers combined with difficulties; but not in the forum or on the rostrum. If they will allow me to follow my own diabolical inclinations, I shall in the end have accomplished all the good of which I am capable. Enough of postcripts. Once more, good-bye.

BOLÍVAR

---

225. To F[rancisco] de P[aula] Santander,
VICE PRESIDENT OF COLOMBIA

[*Original*]

La Paz, September 17, 1825.

My dear Vice President:

Every day I grow more impatient at the absence of mail from Colombia, for I have had no news since early in April, when the last post left Bogotá bringing word of the negotiations then pending with the British envoys. General Briceño spoke to me of this as being a very important and delicate matter, which makes me anxious to know what has come of it.

I have finally decided that Santana should write a full and complete report to the secretariat in Bogotá, since Colonel Espinar, who is my Secretary-General, took sick at Huamanga, and to date has not been able to come. In consequence, everything has been greatly delayed and the service has suffered accordingly. I have therefore decided to appoint Santana secretary *pro tempore* and to have him send the executive a list of all promotions and the announcement of the formation of three battalions—the *Araure*, the *Junín*, and the *Callao*. He will also send my reasons for having the Grand Marshal of Ayacucho take command of these provinces and the army, as there is no one to replace him in so vital a post, whereas General Heres can adequately take care of Colombia's legation in Lima when Congress convenes in February and until a new executive has taken over in Perú, for I cannot represent two contracting parties in the same transaction. Moreover, this new state [Bolivia] has requested that General Sucre be its chief executive, as you will see from the documents to be forwarded to you officially by the secretary's office. You cannot deny that the honor of Colombia lies in protecting and indeed in assisting this new-born republic, which, having adopted the name of two Colombians, calls herself the daughter of Colombia because she was liberated from the enemy by Colombia's army. In short, you will appreciate that polity and justice here combine to give Colombia high prestige in this area, a matter truly worthy of our consideration. Furthermore, all America looks to us to establish order generally, and order cannot, in fact, be preserved unless General Sucre is in supreme command of the army.

All this will be reported to you frankly and at length by the secretary's office. Santana, of course, is not a man who is given to evasion. He states things as he sees them, without the use of phrases that might tend to weaken his more forceful statements. Hence, your pardon is asked beforehand if he should offend you. Be assured, however, that everything will go well both in Perú and in Bolivia if General Heres is at Lima and General Sucre remains here.

The day after tomorrow I shall go to Potosí to meet the Buenos Aires envoys, and then we shall know the purpose of their mission. It appears that Buenos Aires has decided upon a war with Brazil, but it will not take place this year as both parties are pursuing negotiations which will defer the breach several months. There will, without a doubt, be time, meanwhile, for the representatives of Buenos Aires to treat with the Congress of the Isthmus and the other republics that border on Brazil, and which Buenos Aires would want to involve in this conflict, on grounds of general affinity and identity of principles. This matter requires careful reflection and deliberation, so as to determine a policy, as I have previously suggested.

I have decreed here that all neglected and abandoned mines are the rightful property of the government, to be used in paying the national debt. The same thing might be done in Colombia. They could all be sold to an English company for payment of the interest on the national debt. I believe we could realize a few millions by resorting to such devices, as the moment is favorable for mining transactions.

The Buenos Aires mails have just arrived, but at the moment I have nothing new to report. I depend on the Buenos Aires post to bring me the news, because that from Colombia is late in arriving.

I am your devoted

BOLÍVAR

---

226. To F[rancisco] de P[aula] Santander,
 Vice President of Colombia

[*Original*]

Oruro, September 25, 1825.

My dear General:

On the way to Potosí I received mail from Colombia bringing me newspapers up to May 29—but no letter from you or anyone else. I could only surmise that the treaty was concluded with the British representatives, although I have seen no part of it. Those *pastusos!* After they are recognized, they make war upon us.

I heard of the Pasto affair through Castillo's reports and the dispatches from Flores.

You will hear through the Secretary-General's office what I have to say about sending troops to Colombia by way of the Isthmus of

Panamá. If the commandants at Cartagena and the Isthmus are not authorized to make the necessary preparations to facilitate the transportation of these troops, it will all be useless.

I have decided to go to Venezuela next year with 5,000 or 6,000 men of unquestionable reliability, leaving garrisons in Cartagena and Maracaibo, composed of loyal men who are capable of maintaining freedom. It is my intention to have these troops proceed from Perú, by way of the Isthmus, to Caracas. I believe it is there that I am most needed, and not at all in Bogotá. I shall ask you to station the 3,000 men I am now sending to Colombia in the environs of Caracas. To Cartagena I can send troops from the siege of Callao, who are accustomed to that abominable climate. I am giving Soublette full instructions on this matter, repeating them over and over again to him and to Montilla in order that everything at the Isthmus will proceed according to plan.

I shall probably remain in this country a year, attending to the creation of the Republic of Bolivia. But following that there will be nothing more to detain me in the south. I shall go to comfort my relatives and friends in Caracas, to rest a while amidst the pleasures of country life, and to promote a thousand improvements for the glorious land in which, by the grace of God, I was born.

General Sucre ought to remain here a few years to aid in the formation of this Republic. I will tell you a thousand times that, if our troops are to be well paid, we must keep them down to mere cadres, as our army is too large for our pitiful revenues. This procedure is also advisable to enable the Army of Liberation in Perú to return home and not find its country's treasury too exhausted to maintain it. For my part, I am having the army of Perú reduced to a minimum so that it will not consume [the wealth of] this country. In time of war, the units can again be brought up to strength and do their duty.

I presume that, at the same time you receive this letter, or shortly thereafter, you will receive news of the fall of Callao.

The Peruvian delegates reached the Isthmus in June, but I have heard nothing respecting the Colombian delegates. The government of Chile appears willing to send delegates to the Isthmus, and Buenos Aires will send hers as a matter of necessity. Bolivia's representatives will go as soon as they can be admitted. Next year, therefore, the federation will be complete.

I have seen some remarks about expeditions to Havana and threats exchanged between Mexico and Spain, but none of this appears serious to me.

The archipelago of Chiloé awaits only the fall of Callao before surrendering to the first power that wishes to take it.

I wonder if you hear as much from the north as you do from the south. As for me, I have very scant news from Mexico and Guatemala. I should be most happy to hear from our representatives in those places. I plan to write a long letter to Morales about this.

Affairs in Upper Perú are proceeding quite well, so much so that General Sucre and I are on our way to Potosí. After that I shall establish myself in Chuquisaca to draft a plan of reforms for this country and to draw up her new Constitution. I want it to be strong and new, combining the advantages of the American republics with those of the Netherlands. It will have something of a lifelong tenure combined with some of the freedoms of federalism. In short, it will be something that is certain to make both friends and enemies.

I am your affectionate and devoted friend,

BOLÍVAR

---

227. To F[rancisco] de P[aula] Santander,
VICE PRESIDENT OF COLOMBIA

[Original]

Potosí, October 10-11, 1825.

My dear General:

I am very happy to inform you that the day before yesterday General Alvear and Dr. Díaz Vélez, accredited envoys of the government and Congress of the Río de la Plata, arrived in this city. So far I have only met them unofficially, but I have found them extremely pleasant and attentive. In every way they have manifested a profound consideration and regard for me. They have told me frankly and without hesitation that their government has no objection whatever to recognizing the Republic of Bolívar as a political entity, since the Argentine Congress itself has declared what General Arenales has since repeated, that the northern provinces are completely at liberty to assert themselves freely with respect to their interests and government. Thus you can see that the very party that might logically be expected to place obstacles in the way of the recognition of Upper Perú is itself anxious to remove all difficulties and even comes forward in its behalf. Regarding this important affair, I have, in turn, spoken to them with due moderation, in keeping with the interest that I should take in this new state which has taken my name and has chosen to place its destiny in my hands.

I shall also tell you confidentially that these gentlemen spoke to me with astonishing frankness about the present position of Buenos Aires with respect to Brazil. This difficulty, it appears, is the principal object of their mission. They told me, without mincing words, that, because of the current mutual resentment, they believe war between Brazil and Buenos Aires to be inevitable. This was especially true of popular sentiment, which will eventually force the government to take action against the Portuguese. Moreover, they added that the representatives of the province of Banda Oriental have been seated in the General Congress. This is proof that the Congress recognizes them as representatives of an area included in La Plata territory. In brief, these commissioners made it clear, without the slightest pretense, that they expect war with Brazil, that they do not consider themselves sufficiently strong to engage in such a war, and, finally, that they hope I will support them with the resources of Perú and Colombia.

Through the Secretary's office I am sending the government a copy of my reply to the note, addressed to me by these envoys, formally requesting the customary official interview. I was obliged to reply that, as the Ministry of Foreign Relations is subordinate to the Council of Government, I, unfortunately, lacked the authority to treat with the mission officially. I concluded my reply by promising them that I, for my part, would contribute to the successful accomplishment of a mission that is of interest to all America. This reply has placed the gentlemen in a rather embarrassing position. They have discovered that the foreign affairs of Perú are no longer in my hands, since I relinquished them upon leaving Lima. They have also learned that, with respect to Colombian affairs, I am not permitted to make decisions; and, finally, they have found that, as we are federally united at Panamá, our decisions, particularly in matters of war, must be made federally.

Such, my dear General, is the delicate position in which I find myself at the present time, as the commission has learned with considerable regret. They expressed this regret in a conference they have just held with the Secretary, through whom I thought it best to invite them to an interview for the purpose of adjusting, as best we may, the hindrances that naturally endanger the favorable outcome of this affair, which is so vital for all America and so difficult for me. I am awaiting them, and I shall tell you what happens.

The 11th.—I have just had a long conference with Alvear and Díaz Vélez concerning our problems. They repeated, forcefully and positively, that war with Brazil is inevitable, for the reasons that I have previously stated, and that Buenos Aires is not strong enough to win. In conclusion, they asked me to supply aid from Colombia and Perú. They told me definitely that I must assume the rôle of *protector* of America as the only means of saving her from the evils which threaten her, in particular, the hostile attitude that Brazil has taken toward Buenos Aires, which can only increase in proportion to the advantages that Brazil may obtain. I believe that this is not only probable but that it will come about in the very near future. I know the Emperor of Brazil is exceedingly arrogant because of the protection that he receives from England; and, if you have seen the reports on Sir Charles Stewart's negotiations in Lisbon, you will realize that the Emperor has good reason to be arrogant, for he can expect a great deal from England. Moreover, it would not be surprising if the Emperor of Brazil were destined to be the instrument through whom the Holy Alliance will attempt to destroy our liberal institutions, starting with Buenos Aires, our weakest area.

I have just received advices from Santa Cruz de la Sierra to the effect that another general has arrived with troops from the capital of Brazil, bound for the province of Matogrosso which borders upon that of Chiquitos on the Santa Cruz side; and that these troops have made two advances into the territory of Chiquitos, which belongs to Upper Perú, thereby brazenly violating the neutrality which we have made it a point to observe rather than take reprisal for the occupation of Chiquitos by the Portuguese from Matogrosso.

If you will but reflect upon this grave and vital news, you will readily appreciate that not only is Brazil disposed toward opening hostilities against Buenos Aires and ourselves but she is going out of her way to insult and provoke us as well.

Alvear and Vélez have, as one of the primary objects of their mission, proposed to me that I launch an expedition to liberate Paraguay from the tyranny of Francia. These gentlemen say that we are in an especially favorable position to carry out this operation, which would redound to the great advantage of Buenos Aires, particularly in view of the impending war with Brazil.

These are the main objects of the mission of Alvear and Díaz Vélez. They have discussed them with me with a seriousness and directness that have produced an impression upon me which I am anxious for you to share.

As part of the assistance that these envoys requested of me, they mentioned the Colombian navy, or some part of it, as being the most effective, stating that, because of the probable character of a war with Brazil and the superiority of her fleet, our navy would be of great service to them. They spoke admiringly of the marvelous condition of our navy and added that, as its maintenance costs us enormous sums, the Colombian government, should it decide that its interests lie in participating in a war with Brazil, could decrease these expenditures, as Buenos Aires would assume the expense of maintaining our ships of war; thus, they would be doing their part to support our own glorious principles while defending the freedom of the Argentine people. To induce me to give my consent to the participation of our navy, the gentlemen assured me that the government of Buenos Aires has three millions available to meet such expenses.

This is, in substance, what the gentlemen intimated to me in our recently concluded conference. Everything considered, it is of greater significance than any other negotiation ever conducted between South American nations. Imagine, therefore, the dilemma in which I am placed. I am the leader of two states; yet I do not have the power to determine their views, nor even their interests. I, therefore, find myself in the unfortunate position of being able neither to treat openly with the commission nor to give my final consent to its proposals. I told them frankly that I will do for La Plata all that my present position permits, and that I will exert every effort in *recommending*, with all my influence and with all my heart, that we lend assistance and make every sacrifice that they should find necessary to ask of Colombia and Perú, to insure their country's freedom.

I expect, my dear General, that you will realize that this letter can serve a useful purpose, should you see fit to bring to the attention of Congress the pertinent information respecting this difficult, far-reaching, and delicate affair.

You will recall what I said regarding recognition of the Republic of Bolívar by Buenos Aires. But this will not come about without Buenos Aires requesting, in return, certain sacrifices on the part of this Republic, which I would be unable to refuse; first, because, with respect to the Republic of Bolívar, I am free to act without the slightest hindrance; second, because nothing could be more just than to reciprocate the sacrifices that Buenos Aires, in the beginning, made in behalf of these provinces; and, finally, because these provinces have fresh outrages to avenge at the expense of the Portuguese, who have invaded an entire province, carrying off 600 families and pillaging churches, farms, homes, livestock, and everything.

I shall say in passing that, when the Emperor of Brazil learned of the reverse which we had sustained at Matará, he uttered the following words in the hearing of the court: *That he was pleased with the news, as it was a good thing that that scoundrel Bolívar had been put to rout.* Three days later, however, he suffered the mortification of learning of the victory of Ayacucho. If you will ponder these words of the Emperor you can gauge the contempt that he feels toward us. Because of these cogent reasons, which I cannot disregard, I am this day ordering General Salom to suspend the embarkation of the *Callao* battalion and the company of cavalry, who were to have left as soon as Callao had surrendered. I am advising him, however, to send these or any other Colombian troops under his command if the government of Colombia so requests, as our first duty is to obey our government and to defend our country. The Emperor of Brazil is currently moved by two contradictory principles which make strange companions. After the manner of the Holy Alliance, he professes a mortal hatred of our republics, and yet he takes pride in the protection of the English, who, for reasons of expediency, choose to favor him. England hopes to dominate Portugal through Brazil and Brazil through Portugal, and for this reason she courts them both.

If you will, piece these facts together and draw your own conclusions; it is clear that the Holy Alliance favors Brazil by virtue of principle, while England does so for reasons of expediency. Therefore, no matter what the outcome, Brazil will have a protector or a friendly mediator. As for Buenos Aires, they would prefer that I, rather than the United States or England, act as mediator. I have said no, no, no, to everyone, waiting to see what you and the English will say. While on the subject of England, I might well tell you that a certain very reputable person has written me from Buenos Aires that the government there has appointed a brother of his as representative or chargé d'affaires in England, for the purpose of ascertaining the attitude of the British government respecting the war with Brazil. You will recall that I previously suggested that you take this action as a measure preliminary to any other step, and I again recommend it to your good judgment as something that we must not overlook.

In closing this letter I must confess to you that it was not dictated by me and that its contents are badly confused and lacking in clarity. Keep in mind that it has been necessary to report on two five-hour conferences, and I gave Santana the account to be written up for you as quickly as possible. For this reason the Secretary's report on the two conferences is very faulty. On another occasion I shall write you in a more reasoned manner respecting what took place at these conferences and the wishes expressed by these envoys. For my part, I have simply said no to everything, because I have no authority to act. I have, however, shown them the best of good will and expressed the sincerest of best wishes. I have also given them some hope with regard to the forces of the Bolivian Republic. Buenos Aires is in the same position as was Lima when I was summoned from Guayaquil, and, consequently, I am being made a thousand and one offers of the supreme command, etc.

I am your devoted

BOLÍVAR

---

228. To F[RANCISCO] DE P[AULA] SANTANDER,
    VICE PRESIDENT OF COLOMBIA

[*Original*]

Potosí, October 13, 1825.

My dear General:

Yesterday, to my great delight, I received five of your six letters, dated between April and July, and characterized by that enthusiasm with which you used to write me, to our mutual satisfaction and our country's advantage. I was immensely pleased by all this, since you have informed me of all the affairs of Europe and Colombia. The news is indeed heartening, for it indicates that there is little to be feared from the Holy Alliance and that internal conditions in our country are fairly tranquil. This latter fact is, in truth, a great blessing, since, amidst so many problems, it will be a consolation to hand the Republic over to the new administration in a state of complete tranquility, recognized abroad, and victorious not only over all her own enemies but also over those of her neighbors.

Your letters reached me yesterday afternoon after the post had been dispatched. It was therefore necessary for me to recall it in order to reply to you and to issue any orders that might be necessary as a result of the communications that I had just received and was about to read. You will, therefore, please forgive me if I do not go into detail concerning the enormous labyrinth of subjects that you discuss. For the present, I will relate that yesterday I had news from General Carreño at the Isthmus. He informs me that a British frigate which arrived at Chagres reported that 7,000 Spaniards had reached Havana, convoyed by two French vessels carrying a cargo of arms which had been unloaded in Havana. This incident reveals that the French government is *in Buonaparte* with the Spaniards in their usual treacherous fashion.[1] The British captain added, moreover, that the destination of the expedition is the Costa Firme. General Carreño is accordingly asking General Castillo for troops, and, because of this threat, I have this very day ordered General Salom to send to the Isthmus 1,300 foot and 100 horse from the troops besieging Callao, who are now accustomed to a warm climate. General Carreño has already received, or will soon receive, the *Junín* battalion and the squadron of grenadiers; in other words, 1,600 men. These men can serve him in any contingency, but they must not remain at the Isthmus as they are from cold climates and will die of fever. Tell the intendants of the Isthmus and of Cartagena to ask me for any reinforcements that may be needed, and I will send them immediately. They may also request them of General Salom at Lima as he has received orders to supply them.

I believe it probable that the Spanish expedition will be used merely to guard Havana and Puerto Rico and, if an expedition is undertaken, it will be directed against Mexico. Spain fears us, since we have over 50,000 veteran troops with which to oppose her. Furthermore, France has stated that she wishes to act as mediator. Portugal, having just decided for England, appears unafraid of the Holy Alliance. The Alliance rests upon a makeshift foundation. It is therefore fragile and subject to destruction by the whim of public opinion alone. In effect, my dear General, I fear nothing at this moment, for I have the major part of the American forces at my dis-

[1] ". . . lo que manifiestan el gobierno francés Bonaparte con los españoles del modo alevoso que acostumbran" (ed.).

posal, and I can foresee no major European plans that are not being countered by England. It would thus be advisable for you to issue a statement in the *Gaceta de Colombia* concerning our confidence, our strength, and our ability to cope with our domestic and foreign enemies. Remember, my dear General, that, as long as I am in the south, I will be able to order enormous forces to the aid of all America and, in particular, northern Colombia, which needs them, now and always. Be assured also that the day I leave for the north the Devil will take over all the nations of the south, our arsenal of reserves will disappear, and our anxieties and troubles will multiply. In a word, if there is no foreign invasion, I think it is extremely important that I remain here.

I am very sorry that our delegates did not arrive at the Isthmus before the others. The Peruvian representatives have been there since the middle of June. I believe that the assembly is a prime necessity for America. Moreover, the important issue of Havana must come up before it, which, because of its character and possible results, merits the most profound study. I do not know for certain, but I think that France will be certain to intervene in behalf of peace with America. Should she miss this opportunity to make herself important and useful, she will well deserve a dunce cap; but I am inclined to believe that she will not be worthy of this political stigma.

I believe that Venezuela could very well be governed by Páez, with a competent secretary and a good adviser like General Briceño, and with the help of 4,000 men of the [Colombian] army of Perú, of whom 3,000 are on the way, or soon will be. With the 3,000 additional troops that I can send, everything could be arranged. But I want you to ask me for them and to order the transports prepared so that the troops will not spend a single day at the Isthmus, for, as I have said a thousand times, they would die there. I shall write you a small pamphlet by the next post in reply to your other letters.

Respecting [my] back pay, I estimate that this amounts to one hundred thousand *pesos*, which is a round figure that will more or less serve the purpose. I again ask that General Briceño be given whatever sum you see fit, and that Ibarra be paid five thousand *pesos*. I want Briceño to go to Caracas to marry my niece and become adviser to Páez. There are complaints about Escalona and Mérida: both are demagogues—the former a boor, the latter a scoundrel. General Mariño would not do as an intendant, but he can serve well as commanding general, though General Clemente could do better. General Páez, together with Briceño, will rule the region to perfection, as Páez is feared by all the seditious elements, and the others are secondary.

I am satisfied with what you say about my coming to Upper Perú. This new Republic requires my presence for some ten or twelve months, so that she may be established.

I shall do nothing in the matter of Brazil until the general horizon clears up completely; meanwhile, England will mediate and arrange everything.

The two million *pesos* that you seek in London by 1826 appear to me to be difficult to obtain, because of the shortage of time: first, the accounts are not made up and, second, the time is too short even under normal conditions. I think that you previously mentioned the year 1827, and even that is . . . [none] too easy.[1] However, I shall write to the government and to Armero to arrange with Heres for at least a part if not all of this amount, as soon as the Congress meets in February; for it would be bad form for me to appear as both judge and party to such a transaction, and, moreover, it would be *unethical.*

I remain, my dear General, your devoted

BOLÍVAR

---

229. To F[rancisco] de P[aula] Santander,
     Vice President of Colombia

[*Original*]

Potosí, October 21, 1825.

My dear General:

I shall now answer your letters of April 6 to July 6, which is truly a task of some difficulty.

No attempt was made upon my life in Lima; you need have no anxiety for me in these parts.

As for the information you gave me of the congressional decree relating to my back salary, I have replied that, for the moment, I need nothing.

I have not yet seen the Treaty of Commerce and Navigation with

---

[1] . . . *no es muy facil.* The text reads: *"nos" es muy facil* (comp.).

Great Britain, which you tell me is a good one, but I greatly fear that it may prove to be otherwise as the English are shrewd in these things.

Respecting your administration, I shall repeat what I said officially at Arequipa: you have adapted law to the climate of America, and you have flouted the axioms of politics.

Do not have my letters published, whether during my lifetime or after my death, as they have been written in a style far too free and disorganized.

I am thinking of the *Voyage* of M. Mollien,[1] which does you justice in every respect and deals more or less severe blows to all the others. I should like to see this *Voyage*.

Venezuela's tranquil condition pleases me greatly, although a few have written me expressing their fears. I am also pleased that the intendancies are to be separated from the commandancies of the army. You inquired of General Mires, and I will say in passing that he was always very capable but is of little help today, for his eyes and ears, which he formerly kept open, have been closed. The Mosqueras should be in command in Cauca, as they are the best men in the world.

I shall now reply to your letter of May 6, in which you tell me that the ministers do not favor my going to Upper Perú. I am already here and, I believe, with full justice and reason. This territory now belongs to Perú and when it is independent I shall return to Perú and then on to Colombia, or God knows where, for I do not know what I may do from one day to the next.

All that you say about Upper Perú and the Río de la Plata strikes me as being excellent. These matters are progressing very well. The Bolivian Republic will be recognized by her neighbors to the south and north, as we have thereby removed a breeding ground for anarchy, dispute, and dissension. For this they are very grateful to us. Only yesterday the envoys from Buenos Aires, at a reception and banquet, drank toasts to the Bolivian Republic in terms that defy description. We have so managed this affair, or rather refrained from managing it, that everyone is delighted with our sense of justice and our impartiality. They have accordingly looked upon us as patrons, mediators, and friends.

How shall I ever reply to your long letter of May 6? It is written

---

[1] Georges Th. Mollien, *Voyage dans la republique de Colombia en 1823* (Paris, 1823) (ed.).

on three sheets of paper in an undecipherable hand with an ink that has spread and obscured everything.

I deeply regret that the envoys from Perú arrived so late, and even more so that their credentials are addressed to the Congress. I have not meddled in this, as I take no part in anything I can avoid. I thanked you as I must; this was my sole obligation, and I have satisfied it with my customary zeal and interest.

Thank you kindly for your gracious praise of my message, which truly did not merit a single word from you who understand the requirements and criteria of that type of writing. I knew it would not be brilliant, but I put eloquence aside, as I do not care to submit to politicians, whether they be kings or presidents. For this same reason I have never presumed to give my opinion of your messages, which I well know are perfect, but which are not to my taste because they resemble those of the president of the American hucksters [*regatones*]. I detest that lot to such a degree that I would not want it said that a Colombian did anything the same way they do. That, my dear friend, explains my silence, for otherwise no one follows the course and achievements of your presidency with keener interest than I.

I am delighted to have your support in my controversy with the Congress over the million *pesos;* and still more so to read what you go on to say about the nature of our cordial relationship and the continued growth of your friendship for me, for which I am every day more grateful.

I regret that the Peruvian Congress did not express its gratitude to you, but that is because congresses think only of congresses, believing that the executive must do his duty strictly as a matter of course.

The matter of the presidency and vice presidency of Colombia occupies the minds of our citizens and my own as well; not for my sake but for Colombia's and yours, for you are entitled to my every thought. Frankly, I desire the votes of my fellow-citizens, but I would much prefer to relinquish the presidency and be free to do as I please without having to render an accounting to anyone, provided, however, that you are president and not Montilla or even Briceño. Neither would I want Sucre to be president, who, after you, is the foremost of men but who as yet knows nothing of administration or of diplomatic affairs. You must strengthen Colombia, and Sucre must lay the foundation of Bolivia. I am weary of commands, yet never less so than at this time, when flattery overwhelms me with her favors and I at last begin to see the fruit of the seeds that we have planted. But, dear friend, remember that from 1813 to 1826 makes a full fourteen years. The Liberator of North America was not in office that long—nor should I continue in office any longer, lest some should say that I am more ambitious than he.

Thank you for what you have done for Ibarra. General Clemente is in every way preferable to General Mariño for any post, as I wrote you in my last letter.

Before I forget, I think Revenga should be finance minister, and I am so informing him. If he is not given that post, I want him to come and join me in order to establish Bolivia's revenue system, which I am anxious to see in operation.

I wish to thank you for the news you gave me of Anacleto. Please see that he leaves for Caracas at all costs. I know all about his conduct, and, if he does not behave like a gentleman, I am determined to strip him of everything. I shall not give him one penny, and I will abandon him entirely to his fate.

All that you say about the French is very true and was known to me previously. I have told you my thoughts on the subject several times—sometimes my hopes, other times my fears. I regard France and the continent as bearing the same relation to England that Colombia bears to Santo Domingo. Examine this comparison and you will find it very similar. We continental powers could never make war on those islands [of the West Indies], because of their attitudes and the moral power that they exercise over their very opponents. Follow out the analogy and you will find it convincing.

I can tell you definitely that we have 20,000 men in the south, troops equal to those of the French, who would immediately march anywhere to the north where they should be wanted—and they could settle the issue.

What you say of the British government is all very well, but I think better of that government. With each passing day I consider it more capable of deciding everything. It was once unprepared for anything, but now it is every day better prepared to assume its true place in the world, namely, that of its ruler.

I have already told you that Brazil will be protected by England, in order to reduce Portugal to dependency. To that end everything will be peacefully settled in Brazil through Mr. Stewart, the British ambassador who has just arrived there. It was this reasoning that prompted me yesterday to make such a strong reply to the La Plata plenipotentiaries. Brazil has insulted us and has so far failed to give us any satisfaction; hence, I deemed it politic to complain bitterly of her conduct. If we permit ourselves to be insulted even by a weak country, we shall be respected by none, nor shall we deserve to be nations. I have in no way involved Colombia, nor will I ever, in even the slightest degree. I now govern Peruvian countries only; I do not represent so much as a grain of Colombian soil. Should the Brazilians seek further quarrels with us, I shall fight as a Bolivian, a name that was mine before I was born.

The Congress of the Isthmus should have convened months ago. It seems that delegates are going from Chile and Buenos Aires. The Argentines wish to restrict the powers of the Congress, while I think its powers should be unlimited, to give it strength and a truly sovereign authority.

What you tell me of the war for which we should definitely, arduously, and universally prepare ourselves strikes me as being very fair and reasonable, although I cannot believe all of this momentous section of your letter. I certainly would not go to Europe until all of independent America has been recognized by that entire continent.

The English offer to mediate and obtain our recognition is very old and therefore very threadbare.

I was pleased to note what you said about the agent in Paris—it will be very useful.

I do not believe the [North] Americans should be admitted to the Congress of the Isthmus. Such a step would cause us trouble with Albion,[1] even though the entire American administration favored us, which, I do not doubt, would be the case in view of its composition.

What you say about the Emperor of Brazil being well disposed toward Colombia is difficult to believe. The Emperor was an intimate friend of the *godos* of Perú and has as much of a horror of republicans as we have of the citizens of Ethiopia. M. Bonpland's wife is a great friend of mine. She is governess to the Emperor's children, and, though she speaks of me in the most favorable terms to the royal family, it has never had a good word to say about me.

You conclude your letter of May 6 with thoughts that strike in me a responsive chord, for you discuss the diplomatic affairs of Colombia, about which I am most anxious to be informed.

I am sorry to note the misfortunes of Petare, Baruta, and San Lorenzo, for they indicate little vigilance on the part of the leaders of the area.

I now turn to your letter of June 6.

I have seen the communications between the Spanish government

---

[1] England (ed.).

and the British concerning the recognition of America, and I have also noted what you tell me respecting this matter. There are two very remarkable things about it: first, Spain has declared that she will never treat with us; second, the European ambassadors have protested that they will not meet with our representatives. All this is stated strongly and with a note of finality, but now the French minister suddenly offers his mediation. It therefore follows that these gentlemen are either not at all in agreement or that they are very much agreed to make us accept their mediation and, of course, to make us pay for it. The matter appears serious, complex, and worthy of closer study.

You state that my popularity has suffered because the allied [armies] have failed to arrive in Colombia. To this I shall always reply that I will do whatever I can for America, and then, though all America should perish, *no offer in all the universe* for my personal glory will ever tempt me.

Let us speak of your last message. I consider it the best of all, as it contains great beauty and great thoughts.

If a city named Bolívar[1] displeased you, what will you now say to Bolívar, a nation? This is indeed a blow to Colombian gratitude. I imagine that you, at the height of your indignation, must have envied the kindliness of these gentlemen and have wished to serve them properly so they might show themselves, as they have with us, superior to the services rendered.

As for Chiloé, I am determined to send an expedition there next year, if the Chileans have not taken it by then.

I think the blockade of Havana is magnificent. Should it prove necessary, we shall yet go there; but I prefer peace, for reasons already known to you.

Please accept my thanks for the ship *Bolívar* and for the strengthening of our naval forces; this, after the protection of agriculture, is the best use to make of the onerous loans.

I have told you that until Colombia's account with Perú has been fully determined, no payments can be asked, which you must agree is both right and proper.

What you tell me regarding the payments that have been made in Colombia and those that we have yet to make is astonishing. I abhor debts more than Spaniards. I do not see how we can even pay the annual interest on the debt; this problem alone would drive me from Colombia.

---

[1] The former town of Angostura (ed.).

You inform me that you have leased the mines, and I read in the public papers that land has been allotted for colonies, and that part of the benefits that might have accrued to the state have been sold. Here, I have sold the mines for two and a half million *pesos*, and I expect to obtain far more from other sources. I have suggested to the Peruvian government that it sell in England all its mines, lands, properties, and other government assets to cover the national debt of not less than twenty million *pesos*.

Mérida will pay you for every service you have rendered him as will that scoundrel, Escalona, who used the monster. My enemies—every one—will pay you, just as Montilla has done. I deeply regret the calumnies that are being printed about Toro. He is the best man in the world, and I commend him to you most highly.

I shall now reply to your letter of May 21.

The *pastusos* must be annihilated, and their women and children must be removed elsewhere. The territory of Pasto must be made into a military colony. If not, Colombia will have to deal with the *pastusos* every time there is the slightest trouble or disturbance, though it be a hundred years from now, for they will never forget what we have done to them, however richly they have deserved it.

I am glad the French squadron has departed and the Caracas papers have stopped their slanderous attacks for the time being. Conditions will never be radically improved in Venezuela until 4,000 or 5,000 of the victors of Ayacucho are sent there, in charge of a worthy commander, unlike those scoundrels Mérida and Escalona.

Now to answer your letter of June 21.

You state that Castillo has an unconquerable aversion for work. I can well believe that and more. I also believe that Colombia's financial affairs are doing badly. Guayaquil worked miracles, and Perú is endeavoring to do the same, although the latter was formerly the most corrupt country in all America. All this comes as a result of the honesty of a few officials and the rigor of my own measures. I would rather hear complaints of the stringency of my measures than of disorganization in the affairs of the treasury, as in Colombia. I trust that you will pardon this frankness which I think I owe you, for, perhaps, no one else would tell you as much in such good faith. Revenga must serve in the ministry of finance; the plunderers in public office should be exposed by the public press, and a thousand other appropriate measures should be taken.

You ask me what I think of the world political situation. To answer this, one must write at length or not at all. Everything will favor us if the British take our part. If peace follows, commerce and agriculture will benefit; if it is war, we shall gain in soundness and strength. However, I am inclined to believe that war will not come for three or four years, unless some evil genius brings it on.

There is no doubt but that your last message is a very good one, and it will surely be well received in Europe. The reply to Haiti was most politic, although, in my opinion, the secretary phrased it poorly.

It is foolish for us to turn Jacobin much less to rant against kings, except for a good cause and with proper dignity, when they have offended us.

I have seen the correspondence between Spain and England respecting the recognition of our independence. The results of this will be seen in France's intervention, as she hopes to turn Spain's refusal to her own advantage.

I am very pleased that Gual and Briceño are going to the Isthmus, as these are important assignments.

I very much regret Páez' difficulties with the liberals; nevertheless, I want Páez in charge in Venezuela, with Briceño to advise him as his friend and as a man of great ability.

Now for your letter of July 6.

What you tell me about France, England, and the United States, and the growing number of sea and land forces is very important. I do not know what to make of these alarming preparations.

Alarming also is the foolishness of the *cuervos*[1] respecting foreigners. This means that, if we do not take precautions, the *cuervos* will eat us up; if you doubt it, consider the case of Dr. Pérez. But you are at fault, for you did not deal with them as you should have done, out of deference to the nonsense of the Masons and the attacks upon your principles by certain of your own friends. They are always favorably disposed toward me, because I flatter them and keep them within what I believe to be their proper bounds. The Devil take the Masons and all such philosophic charlatans. They seek to reconcile the two good parties of the white *cuervos* with the black: to degrade the former and exalt the latter. The philosophers, Masons, and *cuervos* will keep me from going back to Colombia. There is none of that type here, and if any appear, they will be duly taken in hand.

I am your devoted

BOLÍVAR

---

[1] Literally "crows"—a colloquial term for clerics (ed.).

230. To F[rancisco] de P[aula] Santander,
   Vice President of Colombia

[*Original*]

Potosí, October 27, 1825.

My dear General:

Yesterday I received a letter from you, dated July 21, in which you referred to everything in a placid manner, as if there had been no new developments. Yet in the same post I received word from the Isthmus, from Lima, and from Arequipa that some 10,000 or 12,000 French had disembarked at Havana and Puerto Rico. I truthfully do not know what to make of this. On the one hand the report seems plausible, but, on the other, it appears most unlikely. I have also seen a letter from Jamaica which mentions this expedition as a positive fact, and the English captain of the *Isis* reported at the Isthmus in the month of July that he had seen 6,000 men and muskets unloaded at Havana, convoyed there by French ships of war. This seems to me not only natural but logical, since Spain must garrison Havana. No matter what the truth may be, Colombia can count upon 15,000 or 20,000 men in the south. You will, of course, at once give any orders that you please to General Salom and General Lara, who have some 5,000 or 6,000 Colombians under their command, to place them wherever they may be most wanted and most needed. Today I am ordering General Salom to send to the Isthmus 1,400 men from those under his command at Lima, without waiting for the surrender of Callao. These troops are to serve on the Isthmus or wherever they may be required to defend and garrison Colombia. These 1,400 men complete the first contingent of 3,000 who are to return to Colombia, of whom I spoke to you many months ago. I should be very pleased if you would issue orders to have the required transports at the Isthmus to convoy these 3,000 men. I shall never tire of repeating that the first thing to be done is to station vessels at the Isthmus in good time, as otherwise all troops landing there will perish. Please understand that the *Junín* battalion, which by now will have reached the Isthmus, is to go either to Mérida or to the heights of Caracas, for every man will die if they are stationed along some coast, or in Turbaco or Trujillo. The *Callao* battalion can better resist those hot climates, as it will have come directly from the siege of Callao. It is, moreover, a fine battalion, accustomed to battle fire.

What you tell me respecting the presidency and vice presidency is both good and bad; good in that most people have you in mind, and bad because of the abuse you suffer for the sake of those gentlemen's ambitions. You ask my advice in this matter, and my reply is very simple: you must by all means remain in the vice presidency; otherwise, the country is doomed. I shall not return to Colombia, for I will never, never exercise the presidency of Colombia, much less that of any other country. These words are as irrevocable as those of fate itself.

I am very pleased that the Republic has witnessed such amazing progress during the year—it was to be expected.

I am also very pleased that the United States are not joining the federation, and I deeply regret that you did not send the delegates to the Isthmus during July, after having asked me to send Perú's delegates in June. This will not make a good impression on those who kept their word.

The Secretary-General will send you a confidential letter from Funes in which you will see the difference between the views of the Buenos Aires government and the claims of their plenipotentaries. This contradiction is called politics, and I, too, shall play the game of politics. This remark will tell you all that can be said regarding this and similar instances. The treaty of friendship and commerce between England and Colombia is similar to a scale weighted with gold on the one side and dross on the other. If the two were put up for sale, we should soon determine whether or not they were equal in value. The difference that would appear would be an equality of a type that is necessary between the strong and the weak. Such is the situation and we cannot escape it. The Buenos Aires treaty has made me laugh, and therefore I have nothing to say in its favor.

I have read the French consul's official communication to Gual. This is the height of insolence. I consider this action and the behavior of the French naval officers to be deliberate provocations.

I shall answer your inquiry respecting my salary. During the period following my departure from Bogotá through my stay in Guayaquil, I received twenty-four hundred *pesos* a month, as I left six hundred *pesos* to pay for the Bogotá pension. After I had ordered money given to Paris against my account, I drew only two thousand *pesos* a month, until I was named dictator in Perú. The records kept in Guayaquil will support these transactions. It was not right for the President of Colombia to be in the pay of Perú. If there is any difficulty about those months, have them charged to my back pay. The amount involved is not more than sixteen thousand *pesos,* a small sum not worth troubling even to refuse. I told the Peruvian authorities that my government would pay it, and, therefore, I would not accept the fifty thousand *pesos* which they offered me.

I am delighted with what you tell me of Padilla; he is the outstanding man in Colombia. I admire him greatly for his public service and his attachment to me. God preserve that attachment!

The letter from our agent in Paris was a pleasure to read, but the bad faith of that government leads me to share Hurtado's suspicions; moreover, the movements of the French and what you have told me concerning the obstinacy of the Spanish government tend to confirm these suspicions. My answer to it all is that we have 20,000 men in the south who are capable of destroying the French and the Spaniards together.

I am your devoted

BOLÍVAR

---

231. To F[RANCISCO] DE P[AULA] SANTANDER,
    VICE PRESIDENT OF COLOMBIA

[*Original*]

Chuquisaca,[1] November 11, 1825.

My dear General:

I arrived here a week ago, and I was received with an elegance and grace worthy of ancient Greece. These towns daily show a stronger attachment for their liberators and, in truth, they anticipate what they should expect of us. They believe that wisdom itself should come to them from our hands. Having previously asked for a magistrate and for men to defend their liberty and law, they now ask me for a constitution. The humility with which they make their requests does us great honor and is definite proof of the prudence and discernment of their deliberations.

You will have been officially informed that these people want General Sucre to remain here for a few years, together with a Colom-

---

[1] Present-day Sucre, Bolivia (ed.).

bian division of 2,000 men. I beg you to exert your influence to have this favor granted, as otherwise the very new career of the Bolivian Republic might end at any moment. Gratitude and pride prompt my interest in this country, and, consequently, I shall always exert myself in her behalf.

As I told you yesterday in my official letter, Lara's division of 3,000 men must begin to leave Arequipa for Colombia in February; I should therefore like to know where you want this splendid division sent. Let me say, in passing, that, if this division is sent to the south of Colombia, it will be lost, as most of the men are southerners and Peruvians. This division would serve admirably in Venezuela, as it is composed of excellent personnel and is sincerely devoted to General Lara. For southern Colombia we have the battalions that are now in Lima, consisting of northerners. Furthermore, please believe me that if we lose this opportunity to supply Venezuela with a good division, we shall never have another, unless we obtain it at great expense from Europe or from our allies. If there should be conflict between these troops and those battalions and squadrons already in Venezuela, send the latter to Cundinamarca or even to the south. During the long march they will be reduced to mere cadres, and then they can be easily maintained anywhere at small expense. I repeat, we have never had a division like Lara's, and for this reason we should take it north. In the south it would go to pieces because most of the men are southerners, and those who are not would be so near home that they would desert. Moreover, the officers are a select lot, for all the useless ones have been taken out. Córdoba's division will remain in Upper Perú as long as General Sucre stays here, and we shall always make it available in case help should be needed in Colombia. The divisions of Córdoba and Salom give us 5,000 Colombians in Perú. We can increase this number to 7,000, in order to complete the 13,000 that we brought here.

After I had written you in the last post, I was shocked to see the outrageous stories written about you in Bogotá. Fortunately, they are so extreme that they speak for you rather than against you, for no one can possibly believe them. If only not to be exposed to such abominations, I shall never be president of Colombia. We have removed the gag from their mouths only to have them insult us, and we are witnessing the truth of the fable of the man and the viper, for now that they have felt the first bit of warmth, they use their venom against their benefactors.

The envoys of Buenos Aires are so pleased with the reception I have accorded them that they think only of complimenting and flattering me in the most exaggerated terms. General Alvear, by all accounts their most renowned soldier and a man of real merit, is returning to Buenos Aires immediately. He has wonderful intentions. He would like to be in agreement with me on every point and on every subject, and he has gone so far as to suggest (as his secret thought) the union of the Argentine and Bolivian Republics, the whole to bear my name. He advocates this plan obstinately, and he even insists that I am the man who is fated to determine the destiny of the Río de la Plata. Without me, he declares, his country will experience unrest for a long time to come. With the exception of four individuals in his government, all the people, he says, want me as their country's guardian angel. Chile and Buenos Aires are in similar straits, and both are anxious for my services. You can therefore imagine how attracted I am by the possibility of assisting deserving brother peoples, whose governments, in fear of me, have tried to discredit me. For this reason you must make every effort to prevent Colombia's glory from remaining incomplete, in order that I may become the arbiter [*regulador*] of the destinies of all South America. You can be sure that, without me, Chiloé and Chile herself will be lost forever. You can also be sure that, while I stay in the south, I can aid Colombia with 20,000 picked, incorruptible troops. In brief— if I leave, all is lost. You should, therefore, beg Congress to give me permission to remain for a few years among the nations to the south of Perú. If you use this phrase, it will include everything I want. State that, as this Republic has not yet been proclaimed nor its boundaries fixed, it can neither take a name nor set any terms for me; that the [Colombian] Congress need only indicate a date for me, for, should I desire to go to Buenos Aires, I could reach La Guaira within thirty days, whereas overland by way of Colombia, which is more than a thousand leagues, I could hardly arrive there within three months. The same holds for any troops I might take with me, who would thus arrive faster and in excellent health and spirits.

If there are no pressing dangers in Colombia, tell my friends, who would be the ones interested in recalling me, that, although I have done a great deal for Colombia, I can do infinitely more if I am left free to act as I see fit. Let them not treat me like a small child in need of guardians, for no one has shown greater devotion to my country's cause than I. I cannot take part in the domestic affairs of Colombia, since at any moment I might find myself involved with one faction or another; whereas, on the outside at the head of a great army, I am beyond reach of danger; consequently, I can threaten the seditious elements with a formidable force. No matter what arises, you can always count upon 20,000 men to be ready to fly wherever their country's welfare calls them. Caesar threatened Rome from Gaul. I, from Bolivia, threaten every conspirator in America, and thus I keep every republic alive. If I lose my strategic position in the south, the Congress of Panamá will serve no purpose, and the Emperor of Brazil will take the Río de la Plata and Bolivia.

No courier has yet reached me, and I have no news from the north.

We have had news from England up to the end of July, but nothing that is worth mentioning. Some talk of war, but without foundation. Havana is reported to have 10,000 or 12,000 men, who may sail against Mexico. If only they would commit that folly, they would lose both Mexico and Havana. Should that occur, you can offer 6,000 Colombians from the south and 4,000 Peruvians, whom I should immediately bring up to safeguard any danger point. But please note that I would rather go to Mexico than to Havana, for the same reasons as ever. Only as a last resort should we defy them all and cross the ocean to Spain!

I am your devoted

BOLÍVAR

---

232. To Manuel Lorenzo Vidaurre, Peruvian Delegate
    to the Congress of Panamá

[*Copy*] [1]

Plata, November 11, 1825.

My esteemed friend:

On the eve of Saint Simon, at Potosí, I had the pleasure of receiving your kind letter asking me if I intend to remain in Perú. I shall tell you frankly that my intention is to renounce all authority in Perú in order to leave the General Congress, which is to be con-

---

[1] Taken from *Archivo Diplomático Peruano. El Congreso de Panamá*, 1826. Tomo I. Raúl Porras Barrenechea, ed. (Lima, 1930), p. 446 (comp.).

vened on February 10, completely free in its deliberations, so that it may adopt and promulgate such laws as the deputies deem best for their country and its future. Unquestionably they, better than anyone, can provide for the welfare of their nation, since they represent it completely. These are my sentiments, my esteemed friend, and, believe me, I will carry them out.

I was shocked to learn that you [and Pando] were alone on the Isthmus, and it is especially unfortunate that installation of the great Congress should be delayed because the other appointed delegates have not yet arrived. Nevertheless, you can take consolation in the knowledge that you were the first to tread the happy soil that is destined to become historic.

I have noted the information that you gave me about the French and Spanish in Havana and Puerto Rico.[1] I have made provisions against all eventualities. You must not forget that I have at my disposal twenty thousand men who will march wherever America's safety demands, and I shall lead them myself if the danger is extreme.

Please give my best regards to your esteemed colleague, Pando.

I am your very affectionate friend,

BOLÍVAR

---

233. To GENERAL CARLOS MARÍA DE ALVEAR, SPECIAL AGENT
     OF THE UNITED PROVINCES OF THE RÍO DE LA PLATA

[Draft]

Plata, December 5, 1825.

My dear General:

Yesterday I had the pleasure of receiving your personal and confidential letter concerning the matters about which you wish to consult me. I am perfectly free to give you a frank reply, but it must remain confidential; that is, my letter is addressed not to Alvear the plenipotentiary but to Alvear the citizen. Similarly, it is not the head of Colombia and Perú but the citizen Bolívar who is writing.

Your first point of inquiry is in full accord with my innermost

---

[1] See Doc. 228 (ed.).

wishes, but I would add that the league between this Republic and the Argentine is one that I would like to see enlarged to include all Spanish America, in accordance with the general plan of confederation.

The second point may be regarded as answered in the first, since I cannot believe that Perú and Colombia would conclude separate treaties with the Río de la Plata, in violation of the solemn and prior treaty by which they are now bound.

To the third question, I shall reply that it is difficult to state precisely what instructions the Peruvian government will give its envoy to Río de Janeiro. He is to protest the outrage committed against these provinces; for, respecting foreign affairs, that government is completely independent of my authority. I have privately suggested that it would be well to make some representation favorable to the interests of the Río de la Plata in the conferences to be held with the ministers of Brazil; but I could add nothing more as, in my opinion, the great federation permits nothing more.

The fourth question is the most delicate of all. A partial league forms no part of my project as it is contrary to all that I have advocated. But, should circumstances, brought about by some unforeseen reverse or unexpected action on the part of the Brazilian Emperor, compel this country to make common cause with the Río de la Plata, it seems to me that, basically, the treaty would be limited to a temporary league and military alliance, which would stipulate the number of troops, their maintenance and command, and the appointment of the generals who would direct them—all of which is necessary and essential for insuring the complete success of any military operations. Everything else, as I understand it, would be secondary.

On your fifth and last question, I shall express myself with complete frankness: First, at this writing I have not the authority to order a single soldier to march against the Emperor of Brazil, since, in this respect, Perú and Colombia are subject to the Congress of Panamá; second, if I should be asked for reinforcements for *some other service,* as you have suggested, I should be not only able but willing to release them, and it would be a source of great pleasure to me to be of service in this manner. The maintenance and replacement of these troops would be all that we would require, and I should be most happy to serve the Río de la Plata in an enterprise that would, by sparing us future sacrifices, be conducive to our welfare.

The pleasant and dignified manner which you displayed toward me at the time when I had the honor of treating with you has inspired within me a confidence and true friendship toward you, which I cannot refrain from expressing now that the occasion presents itself and it becomes my duty to place before you the high esteem with which I am your affectionate friend and servant.

---

234. ESSAY ON PUBLIC EDUCATION[1]

[Draft]

Government molds the character of a nation and can set it upon the path to greatness, prosperity, and power. Why? Because it has charge of the basic elements of a society and can thereby organize and direct public education. A people whose principles of education are wisdom, virtue, and discipline will be wise, virtuous, and warlike in character. A nation will be superstitious, effeminate, and fanatical if its educational system develops such attitudes. That is why the illustrious nations have always included education among their fundamental political institutions. For example, Plato's Republic—but why examine theories? Consider Athens, the mother of the sciences and the arts; Rome, the master of the world; virtuous and invincible Sparta; the Republic of the United States, that land of freedom and home of civic virtue. What made them what they have been and what they are at present? In effect, nations move toward the pinnacle of their greatness in proportion to their educational progress. They advance if education advances; if it decays, they decay; and they are engulfed and lost in oblivion once education becomes corrupt or is completely abandoned. This principle, dictated by experience and taught by philosophers and statesmen, ancient and modern, is today so well-established a doctrine that scarcely a man will be found who is not convinced of its truth.

Happily, we live under the sway of an enlightened and paternal government which, amidst the exhaustion and poverty to which the King has reduced us, amidst the trials and turbulence of a war of extermination, although caught in the vortex of its hardships, cast

---

[1] Written for the administration of public education in Bolivia late in 1825 or early in 1826 (comp.).

its benevolent gaze upon the people and beheld their sufferings. This government was deeply moved by what it saw, and, though its resources were few, it endeavored to find such remedies as humane considerations might suggest. Out of necessity its attention was focused upon the point of greatest significance, upon the true cornerstone of any nation's happiness—education.

It is not my intention to discuss curriculums, the founding of schools, the cultivation of the arts and sciences, the encouragement and appreciation of literature, or the promotion of the useful arts. The people have seen this system of moral rebirth in practice with their own eyes, and every man has benefited from its salutary effects.

I shall confine myself solely to the school that was opened here on October 1 of this year. What a difference! Bands of children who were systematically devoted to idleness and formerly the scourge of the streets, the bane of the market place, and a source of anguish for their parents, are today organized into an orderly and decent community. Hear them recite learnedly on the history of religion and the elements of arithmetic, drawing, and geography; see them write with elegance, according to the Carver method; behold them, filled with an unquenchable thirst for knowledge and encouraged by the hope for prizes, ignoring the attractions of indolence. Herein, today, we have the object of happiness, one that has the blessing of the people. If there is any man who, at sight of this transformation, fails to experience similar emotions, he must, indeed, be insensible to all good. But I, who am deeply moved, shall reveal my interest in so useful an institution by venturing a few suggestions, which may, perhaps, be found worthy of adoption.

The director of a school, that man of generous and patriotic impulses who has sacrificed his leisure and freedom to devote himself to the hard task of building citizens for the state—citizens who will defend, enlighten, sanctify, and ennoble it, and who, in time, will give it sons as worthy as themselves; such a man indeed deserves the praise of his country. He is entitled to the veneration of the people and the gratitude of the government, which should encourage him and accord him honors and distinctions.

Of course, I am not speaking of those so-called schoolmasters, those men of ordinary clay who, armed with the rod, a sinister frown, and a perpetual harangue, play the part of a Pluto rather than that of a gentle philosopher.

Such men teach more of prejudice than of truth. Theirs is a school of servile minds, where, among other vices, dissimulation and hypocrisy are learned, and where fear crowds every other emotion from the heart. Away with such tyrants; let them go to Salamanca,[1] where they will find a place.

The government must act as it has done heretofore, selecting from the multitude, not a scholar, but a man distinguished for his education and noted for the purity of his character and the naturalness of his bearing, a man who is pleasant in manner, kindly, friendly, and open-hearted: in short, one in whom there is much to emulate and little to correct.

Words, however excellent the original ideas they may have represented, take on different meanings after long abuse, thereby evoking different images. This seems to me to have happened to the words Teacher and School. Because of the barbarous character that these institutions assumed under the Spanish rule, these words now produce disagreeable images. To say to a child, "We will go to school" or "We will see the teacher," was tantamount to saying, "Let us go to jail" or "Let us visit our enemy," for to place a child in school was to *make of him a vile slave* to fear and boredom. I therefore believe that these terms must make way for others which are free of these fears. Some will say that names have no effect, but experience proves that they have a direct bearing upon our judgments. How many quarrels, disputes, and wars have centered around a word! For a century to come, the name Spaniard will be associated with terror by our descendants! Let the schoolmaster, therefore, be given some other name, perhaps Director, and the school, Community.

To mold the heart and mind of youth will be the work of the director: that will be his mission. When his understanding and ability have engraved upon the character of the children the cardinal principles of virtue and honor; when he has so disposed their hearts, by means of example and simple demonstration, that they respond more quickly to a symbol that spells honor than to one that promises them a pot of gold; when they have become more interested in the acquisition of knowledge than in the winning of prizes and more concerned about having done a disgraceful thing than about the loss of their favorite playthings and games—then he will have laid the firm foundations of our society. For he will have found the spur wherewith to inspire in youth a noble daring, with the strength of mind with which to defy the allurements of idleness and to engage

[1] The Spanish University of Salamanca (ed.).

in hard work. Youth will then make unprecedented progress in the arts and sciences.

Fortunately, our society today is engaged in this progress. Children are concerned with their studies; they speak only of what they have learned, and they are unhappy the day that school closes.

Rewards and moral punishments are the proper motivations for rational beings who are maturing; sternness and the rod should only be used on beasts. The former method develops elevation of mind, heightening of sentiments, and decency in behavior. It contributes greatly to the formation of man's moral standard of values, creating within him this inestimable treasure and enabling him to be just, generous, humane, gentle, modest, in short, a man of principles.

Like the director, the pupil must possess certain qualifications at the time he enters the community; to wit, a physical and moral disposition to receive instruction and at least two suits of clothes, a necktie, a hat, and a schoolbook.

Teaching is nothing more, we might say, than the training of a body of troops, except that soldiers are trained physically, and children both physically and morally. And even as the former are drilled from morning until night, giving regularity, precision, order, and timing to their movements and labors so as to achieve a perfect unity, so, too, must the child be instructed and keep on learning at every hour of the day.

The first habit to be inculcated in children is cleanliness. If the results of the observance of this practice by the community are examined, its importance is obvious. Nothing is more pleasing to the eye than a person with clean teeth, hands, face, and clothing. If unaffected grace of manner is linked with this quality, it is as if heralds had preceded us to prepare a favorable reception in people's minds. It will therefore be the director's first concern to make a daily inspection with a view to constant improvement in this regard. A prize or distinction rewarding this virtue will be sufficient motivation to cause it to be practiced with enthusiasm.

At the same time, practical instruction should be given in manners and in the ceremonies and deference to be accorded all persons, in keeping with their station. This is not a trifling matter. It is of such practical importance that its neglect gives rise to quarrels, enmity, and grief. There are people so precise and sensitive respecting this matter, especially foreigners, that they will not forgive the slightest breach. I have seen a person censured for standing too near the table, for smoking at a gathering, or for having his hat on. This is not surprising; it is the feeling of educated men that they have suffered an offense when a breach of good manners occurs in their presence. What shall we say of our parties [*tertulias*] and banquets? What rudeness! What grossness! They should be called gatherings of swine rather than assemblies of rational men.

In this particular, however, one must avoid the opposite extreme of being over-scrupulous in the practice of the rules of behavior, for this produces an affectation that is as offensive as it is absurd, whereby some men seem rather to be ingrained in principles than to have the principles ingrained in them.

As words are the vehicle of instruction, it should be a primary concern of the director to see that diction is pure, clear, and correct, that barbarisms and solecisms are avoided, that due attention is paid to emphasis, and that things are called by their appropriate names and not by approximations.

Once the school community is assembled, it would be wise to divide it into classes, namely, first, second, and third, composed of the beginners, the intermediate, and the advanced, placing at the head of each class a child capable of directing it, who should be named the monitor. Monitors should be elected and should wear special insignia, so as to excite ambition in all the students. The children should be trained in taking part in orderly and impartial elections, in order to accustom themselves to restraint and justice and to the recognition of merit alone.

Children should address each other in the familiar form of *you* [*tu*] and should use *Sir* in addressing the director.

Quintilian preferred the public school to private instruction, because, in addition to the advantages of meeting and associating with persons of varied abilities, it is in the school, he says, that true friendships are made that endure for life. In following this line of thought, I would have each child freely choose another in his community with whom he would have more to do than with any other. The purpose of such an alliance might be that of mutual defense before the director and of mutual assistance in other ways, such as sharing possessions, correcting each other, and being constant companions.

The director should teach whatever time, his ability, and the capacity of the pupils permit. But the principal subjects should be reading, writing, the principles of religion, arithmetic, and geography. I think the easiest method of teaching reading is first to train children in the alphabet, then in the pronunciation of syllables, but without any spelling, and then go on to the reading of suitable books.

This method should be accompanied by instruction in the rudiments of Castilian grammar.

For penmanship, I consider the Carver system superior to all others in its simplicity, ease, and beauty. Its practice should include the teaching of spelling and the reading of handwriting.

For the elements of religion and its history the catechism of Fleurí and Father Astete can be used to advantage.

In arithmetic, the notebook in which the lessons are kept is sufficient.

For teaching universal geography and the geography of the particular country, a complete outline should be prepared. The lessons in these subjects should have a set hour, be simple in presentation, and should last for as long as the average capacity of the pupils permits. Specific tests and comprehensive examinations should be given at fixed intervals, and, finally, prizes should be awarded.

A man of ability, who understands the human heart and can guide it skilfully, and a simple system, with a clear and natural method, are the effective means by which a community can make extraordinary and brilliant progress in a short time. Lacking these prerequisites, precepts and labors may be multiplied in vain only to produce perplexity and confusion.

Children need play and recreation as well as food. Their physical and moral needs alike demand it. But this release must be channeled to some useful and worthwhile purpose. The director should therefore plan and, if possible, supervise all play. The following are known to be useful and constructive games: ball-playing, tennis, tenpins, kite-flying, balloon-tossing, checkers, and chess.

The winning of a prize or any unusual feat of industry, honor, and high sentiment must never be allowed to fall into oblivion, but should, on the contrary, be remembered forever. Accordingly, a record should be kept of the most outstanding achievements, the names of their authors, and the dates when they were accomplished. This record should be kept by a secretary who, elected by ballot, would enter and attest the facts in a book that should be properly adorned and reverently kept in a visible place. On the principal national holidays, let the school community assemble with distinguished citizens present, and let the most eminent of them read aloud the glories and achievements of youth. Let a record of the ceremony be kept, and let cheers and acclamations be given for those whose names are inscribed in this precious register. This would be the day of the community, a day of fiesta and of rejoicing.

Bolivar in 1826.

1826

235. Views on the Congress of Panamá

[*Draft*]

[Lima, February, 1826]

The Congress of Panamá will bring together all the representatives of America[1] and a diplomat-agent of His Britannic Majesty's government. This Congress seems destined to form a league more extensive, more remarkable, and more powerful than any that has ever existed on the face of the earth. Should Great Britain agree to join it as a constituent member, the Holy Alliance will be less powerful than this confederation. Mankind will a thousand times bless this league for promoting its general welfare, and America, as well as Great Britain, will reap from it untold benefits. A code of public law to regulate the international conduct of political bodies will be one of its products.

1. The New World would consist of independent nations, bound together by a common set of laws which would govern their foreign relations and afford them a right to survival through a general and permanent congress.

2. The existence of these new states would receive fresh guarantees.

3. In deference to England, Spain would make peace, and the Holy Alliance would grant recognition to these infant nations.

4. Domestic control would be preserved untouched among the states and within each of them.

5. No one of them would be weaker than another, nor would any be stronger.

6. A perfect balance would be established by this truly new order of things.

7. The power of all would come to the aid of any one state which might suffer at the hands of a foreign enemy or from internal anarchic factions.

8. Differences of origin and color would lose their influence and power.

---

[1] Whether or not America, in this usage, included the United States is not clear, but that nation had been invited to send a delegate (ed.).

9. America would have nothing more to fear from that tremendous monster[1] who has devoured the island of Santo Domingo, nor would she have cause to fear the numerical preponderance of the aborigines.

10. In short, a social reform would be achieved under the blessed auspices of freedom and peace, but the fulcrum controlling the beam of the scales must necessarily rest in the hands of England.

Great Britain would, of course, derive considerable advantage from this arrangement.

1. Her influence in Europe would progressively increase, and her decisions would be like those of destiny itself.

2. America would serve her as an opulent domain of commerce.

3. America would become the center of England's relations with Asia and Europe.

4. British subjects in America would be considered the equals of American citizens.

5. The relations between England and America would in time become those between equals.

6. British characteristics and customs would be adopted by the Americans as standards for their future way of life.

7. In the course of the centuries, there might, perhaps, come to exist one single nation throughout the world—a federal nation.

These ideas are in the minds of many Americans in positions of importance who impatiently await the inauguration of this project at the Congress of Panamá, which may afford the occasion to consummate the union of the new states and the British Empire.

---

236. To General Antonio José de Sucre

[Draft]

Oruro, January 22, 1826.

My dear General:

I arrived in this city yesterday afternoon, and I am resting today before proceeding tomorrow to Arica, where the *Chimborazo* awaits us.

---
[1] The Negro (ed.).

As I was leaving Cochabamba I received news from Chile and letters from O'Leary, who was about to leave for Lima. It is certain than an expedition against Chiloé has left Valparaíso. It is headed by Freire and consists of 2,500 men, convoyed by several men-of-war commanded by Blanco. The sloop *Chacabuco* went ahead to the archipelago with two Chilean officers who were sent to parley with the islanders. These envoys were not received; one was shot for having made an attempt to distribute some of Freire's proclamations. Chile is governed by a *junta* of ministers, while Freire is preparing his own downfall, for I do not think he will succeed in this, his second attempt. Chiloé is strong because of its position and the attitude of its inhabitants: all in all, it is another Pasto. All of which means that Freire will accomplish nothing. In the end the Chileans will lose patience and ask us for troops to move against Chiloé or against Freire himself.

Last night I received the post of the 15th, which had sought me in Potosí. It brought me very heartening news. I now have letters from Santander up to October 20, the main points of which I will summarize for you.

Politically, alliance with Great Britain would be a greater victory than Ayacucho, and once it is realized you may be certain that our future happiness is assured. The series of blessings that will result for Colombia, if we ally ourselves with that Mistress of the Universe, are incalculable. I am beside myself with joy and happiness at the very thought that our interests and policies may be linked with those of Great Britain. What Mr. Canning said in the House of Commons can give us great satisfaction, as it demonstrates that, in England's failure to receive Rivadavia, Buenos Aires is more to blame than England. France herself begins to seem . . .[1] at least tolerant, and her minister Villèle takes a great deal of interest in us. His efforts to induce Spain to recognize us have been infinitely greater than what we might have expected from a minister of a Holy Alliance nation. I have just received a French paper, the *Journal de Commerce*, which speaks very favorably of our affairs. This paper has always been very liberal, and now it proves to be more so than ever. Add to this France's recognition of the independence of Santo Domingo,[2] which, though purchased at a price, is nevertheless to the purchaser's advantage; the opening of French ports to Colombian vessels; and the

---

[1] Deleted in the draft: "if not friendly" (comp.).
[2] The Republic of Haiti (ed.).

conduct of Villèle and it is apparent that, far from having cause to fear the French, we may, in all probability, hope for their friendship. The only cause for suspicion of these gentlemen is their dispatch of French troops to the island of Cuba and the expedition, also destined for Cuba, that Santander reports as having left La Coruña on *El Guerrero*. It has also been reported that the King of France was about to send 25,000 French troops to Spain for the purpose of establishing some sort of constitution.

It appears that England will not mediate between Buenos Aires and Brazil and that Stewart is going to the Río de la Plata and from there to Chile. If this is so, we may presume that England is not averse to a war between those countries, which is what I have feared. Yet I doubt that the [British] envoy will go to Chile, as I do not see what he could accomplish there.

I am sending you a copy of the election returns that were known in Bogotá on October 21. You will note that the presidential vote is unanimously for me. The majority vote for the vice presidency was for Santander. The remarkable thing is that Baralt received so many votes. It is clear, therefore, that Santander will be elected vice president by a majority of votes, twice as large as for the runner-up.[1] The votes that he should fail to obtain in Venezuela he will secure in the south, and he can always rely on a majority from New Granada. I am therefore quite pleased with the elections, for with all my soul I want Santander to be our vice president. I suppose I shall be elected president, but, as I am resolved not to serve, the administration will remain as it is at present.

It is certainly strange that Santander did not receive the votes of Guayaquil, for he has favored it above the other departments, such as Ecuador and Azuay, whose territory he partitioned instead of increasing; it is stranger still that they should forget the victor of Pichincha and favor Briceño, who has done nothing especial for them— such is the way of the public mind.

Santander has sent me a letter from Yanes, whom you doubtless know, in which the latter describes conditions in Caracas, stating that a conspiracy exists there to seize control under cover of the Constitution and the laws, and that a federation is sought. *El Cometa*, which I enclose, has an article on the candidates and will give you an idea of what these gentlemen are thinking.

---

[1] Reference is made to the congressional elections; the Congress chose the President and Vice President (ed.).

I have some papers from Buenos Aires, and they contain nothing bad; in fact, the news is good. I am not sending these papers to you, nor will I summarize their contents, as you have probably seen them. I cannot, however, help commenting on what they say of Greece. I consider it a very important development that Greece has placed herself under the protection of England, for this move will completely upset the plans of the Holy Alliance, and it sheds glaring light upon the intentions of England.

I can tell you nothing about Colombia except what I have learned from Santander, and I have received only one letter from him which Heres sent me from Arica, where he had gone in search of me after Santander had relieved him of his commission to Chile.

I enclose the copy of a letter that I received from Lafayette, but I have yet to receive the original. You may well imagine the satisfaction and pride that it gives me, as does also the fact that I am to receive a gift from the family of Washington by the hand of the heir to his virtue and glory, the only surviving General of the revolution of that country.[1] I am simply delighted. You will also note what Lafayette has to say concerning the federation of Panamá, which you should compare with what is being said against it in Buenos Aires. I should therefore like you to have this letter published in a paper in your city, stressing what Lafayette says about me and the federation. Have the General praised in glowing terms, and send plenty of copies to Buenos Aires.

Salom's letters are slow in arriving, but he did write that he expected to celebrate the recent anniversary of Ayacucho in Callao, that the rations of the troops were about to be reduced to twelve ounces, and that, as Rodil was seriously ill, Aznar was in command. Salom added that his troops had just enough provisions for the month of November.

Today I made the promotions shown in the accompanying list. I regarded them to be both right and expedient.

I have been informed that the *Cazadores* battalion and the cavalry regiment at Potosí have mutinied, the former one day refusing to drill and the latter to line up and that [Ar]raya leaped to his horse, sword in hand, shouting he had a regiment [in reserve] to make short shift of such vermin. Add to this the knowledge that the prefect does nothing and is drunk all day, that there is no order in the

---

[1] George Washington P. Custis and Eliza Parke Custis, through Lafayette, presented Bolívar with a medallion of Washington which today is preserved in the Casa Natal in Caracas (ed.).

ranks, that the men spend all their time in brawls and disputes, and that the scoundrel of a prefect is perfectly unconcerned. Were anybody else in charge, Potosí would now have a two months' supply of water on hand. For this reason, Samuel and Galindo, too, should speed their departure for Potosí. Ferguson, who spent six days in Potosí, confirmed everything that we had been told and also had a few details of his own to add that were new to me.

---

237. To [FRANCISCO DE PAULA SANTANDER], VICE PRESIDENT OF COLOMBIA

[Draft]

Lima, February 17, 1826.

Very Excellent Sir:

The additional articles which Your Excellency, in your communication of November 5 last to the government of Perú, has proposed for the American assembly at the Isthmus will unquestionably lend greater depth, stability, and firmness to the Confederation. The invitation extended by the government of Colombia to the noble and powerful King of the United Kingdom of Great Britain and Ireland for that nation to become one of the confederated powers, will, if accepted, be of immense immediate benefit to the new republics, which, guided by his example and shielded by the patronage of his friendship, will the more readily solidify their organization and set out firmly upon the course they must pursue.

The penalty of expulsion from the Confederation for failure to conform to the decisions of the assembly, when that body acts as arbitrator between two of its members, is just and expedient. It is reasonable to expect that, since the advantages of membership in the Confederation are to be great, the penalty involving their loss must be still greater in proportion.

Compulsory mediation by the Confederation in any dispute that might unfortunately arise between a confederated and a foreign power, however desirable for the Confederation, would possibly cause difficulties with non-members. This right to mediate would

necessarily invest the Confederation with an indirect power of intervention in the affairs of foreign nations.

To give the assembly authority to make and conclude, in the name
of the Confederation either directly or through duly appointed delegates, purely defensive treaties of alliance designed to preserve the
peace, would enable such plenipotentiaries of the Confederation, independent of the member states of the Confederation, to commit those
states on highly important matters that would involve the entire
nation. Though the plenipotentiaries should have broad powers to
negotiate and agree upon major subjects, treaties of alliance, even
purely defensive ones, should preferably be negotiated only with the
prior knowledge of the respective governments.

Although I am not, at present, charged with the executive power
of this Republic, which is vested in the Council of Government, my
deep concern for America's welfare prompts me to make these observations upon the amendments that you have proposed for consideration by the Isthmian assembly—an organization which I believe to
be a necessary adjunct of continental stability.

The Council of Government has tendered its good offices to the
Republics of Chile and the United Provinces of the Río de la Plata,
with a view toward having them agree to send plenipotentiaries to
the Isthmian assembly and to adopt in its entirety the plan proposed
by the government of the Republic of Colombia. I must say, however,
that I have little hope of their adopting the plan in its present form,
while I believe that I may safely say that the government of this Republic [Perú] is most favorably disposed toward the government of
your Republic and is a good friend and faithful ally of Colombia.

---

238. To José Rafael Revenga, Colombian Minister
    of Foreign Affairs

[Original]

Magdalena, February 17, 1826.

My dear Revenga:

I have before me your letters of October 21, November 6, and
November 21, in which you write at length respecting the Confederation of the Isthmus and the amendments that you have proposed to

its members. I am writing an official letter to the Vice President, giving my opinion of these addenda, and I should like herein to discuss them with you at greater length.

An alliance with Great Britain would give us great prestige and respectability. Under her protection we would grow, and we would later be able to take our place among the stronger civilized nations. Any fears that powerful England might become the arbiter of the counsels and decisions of the assembly, that her voice, her will, and her interests might determine the course of its deliberations are remote fears; and, should they one day materialize, they cannot outweigh the positive, immediate, and tangible benefits that such an alliance would give us at this time. First the Confederation must be born and grow strong, and then the rest will follow. During its infancy we need help so that in manhood we will be able to defend ourselves. At present the alliance can serve our purpose; the future will take care of itself.

For the plenipotentiaries to negotiate, either by themselves or through persons they might authorize, treaties of alliance, even purely defensive ones, would be to confer upon them an extraordinary power to decide matters of the greatest importance that would affect every nation. It is my opinion that their authority should be restricted to negotiating preliminary agreements, subject to subsequent ratification by the governments concerned. In all other respects, however, the amendments appear to me no less wise and fair than the over-all plan itself. I believe as you do that, if the plan were to be adopted by all America and by Great Britain, it would represent an enormous bulwark of power which would inevitably result in stability for the new states.

I must say that I entertain no hopes that Chile and the United Provinces of the Río de la Plata will either join the Confederation or accept, in good faith, the plan in its present form. On the contrary, I expect them to take action against it. Those two countries are in a lamentable state, and are virtually without government. For this reason, I deeply regret that you gentlemen, through our representatives, have sent the proposed amendments to those governments before ascertaining whether or not they would join the Confederation and approve these amendments. On the contrary, they will now proceed to publish them and make them the butt of their ridicule, irony, and satire, however unfounded. I also wish that nothing had been said of the invitation to the King of England until we were quite sure of his consent, for, if it is not obtained, England's refusal will greatly lower the Confederation's standing; whereas, if the negotiations had been conducted secretly, the Confederation's credit would at least have remained unimpaired and it would have acquired greater lustre if the British delegates were to appear at the Isthmus, thus encouraging those who had not previously joined the Confederation to solicit admission.

The government of Perú has employed its good offices with Chile and Buenos Aires, but, I repeat, I think it utterly futile, for the reasons that I have stated. In this connection, I can assure you that this government has the highest regard for Colombia, that it will long continue to be united with her, and that it will view with pleasure any additional move to strengthen the existing bonds and relations.

Compulsory mediation between any confederated power and a foreign power would, I believe, create great obstacles for the latter. The confederated powers, however, would derive tremendous advantages from mediation.

I shall now add a few words regarding Buenos Aires and Chile. The former will never join the Confederation in good faith. She will in every way attempt to hinder and impede it and will place every possible obstacle in the path of the assembly. This is a foregone conclusion, considering her present organization and the temperament and principles of her ungovernable inhabitants. As for Chile, if she sends plenipotentiaries, she will do so in the best of good faith, and she will be more amenable and useful to the Confederation.

I had very recent news from Venezuela, and from trustworthy sources. These have assured me that, although the opposition is less active than previously, this tranquility is highly deceptive and stems from sinister causes. General Páez tells me of the variety of opinions held there, and I mean to send him a constitution that I have drafted for submittance to the Congress of the Republic of Bolivia, as it reconciles the interests of all parties, provides for a government that is firm and stable and endowed with great strength, yet it preserves intact the principles of freedom and equality that we have proclaimed. If public opinion is prepared through the press, this draft may be submitted to the Congress of 1831, at which time the Colombian Constitution may be lawfully revised.

Here they have granted seats in the Constituent Congress to deputies from the provinces of Jaén, Bracamoros, and Mainas, long since claimed as Colombian territory. I have spoken to Armero of this matter, and I assume that you and the others will order our plenipotentiary to this Republic to present and prosecute the claim until restitution to Colombia has been made.

I am pleased to learn that you are preparing material in defense of the government. That is what you should do, because it is right and because these unfair attacks should be answered. I am also glad to know that you now head the Ministry of Government.

With high esteem, I am yours devotedly,

BOLÍVAR

---

239. To F[rancisco] de P[aula] Santander,
     Vice President of Colombia

[*Original*]

Magdalena, February 21, 26, 1826.

My dear General and friend:

I have previously told you that I came here with the intention of returning my command to the Peruvian Congress, but I am resolved to do only one thing, namely, exert my influence for the welfare of these people. The machinery of government is extremely wearisome for me; moreover, my enemies refuse to believe that I abhor authority: in proof of this I shall later tell you a very strange story.

Lima received me divinely. These people vie with the Colombians in the love they have for us, and they would compel me to govern them. General La Mar is ill and does not wish to serve in the government—my position, therefore, is a serious one. The Congress will convene this week to decide on this and other matters, which will be a severe test of their wisdom. I shall tell them that I positively cannot be their constitutional head and that, besides, Colombia expects me. I hold only a military command, one which I shall retain until I leave the country. Many of the members of Congress are considering proclaiming this the Republic of Bolivia, like Upper Perú, after arranging a treaty with that country. Their thought is to hold me here by this honor, to make Sucre the head, and to replace the poor Constitution they now have with the one that I have drafted. If this plan should succeed both countries will need us to straighten out

their affairs. There are others who would have me become the absolute ruler of all the south, as they reason that Chile and Buenos
Aires will need my help this year, because war and anarchy are leading them to destruction.

I shall, of course, ignore this group entirely, as their proposal is
alien to my thoughts.

Regarding your government's proposals concerning the Confederation, I can only state that, as a matter of delicacy, I have refrained
from influencing the decisions of this government in this matter.
I suspect they will not want to become involved in too binding a
confederation, for several reasons. The reasons they give me are
flattering to myself, but there must, of course, be other motives.
They also fear the expense, as they are deeply in debt and quite
impoverished. Here a great deal is owed to everyone. They have no
desire to attack Havana, since they have to attend to Chiloé, which
belongs to them and which they can turn over to Chile in settlement
of what they owe that country. They have a larger navy than they
can use; they therefore do not care to purchase any more vessels.
They are wary of allying themselves with the English, but, as the
population is a submissive one, there is no fear of the darker races
revolting. I make note of all this so that you may the better know the
principal ideas that may be brought up in opposition to Colombia's
mode of thinking.

Strictly confidential.

In the last several days I have received letters from friends in
Venezuela, proposing Napoleonic ideas to me. General Páez is at
the head of this move, urged on by his friends, the demagogues. A
secretary, who is also an editor of *El Argos,* has arrived bringing me
the plan. You will see this plan written between the lines of this
letter, the original of which I enclose, and which you must guard
with great care so that no one else will see it. Carabaño is the author
of this letter. General Briceño has written me, saying that he was
obliged to restrain those who were preparing the coup in Venezuela,
by advising them to consult me. General Mariño has also written me,
as have other lesser but more rabid demagogues. You can, of course,
well imagine what I shall reply. My sister tells me there are three
parties in Caracas, the monarchists, the democrats, and the *pardocratas.* She advises me to be a liberator or die. I intend to follow this
advice though the entire human race should perish as a consequence.
I shall answer General Páez by sending him my projected constitu-

tion for Bolivia,[1] to enable him to reflect upon my ideas respecting the uniting of stability and freedom and the preservation of the principles that we have adopted. I shall also add that he must not drive his friends to despair or they will be forced to another and more cruel extreme, as no alternative is left them except sheer anarchy. You will recall that those men were first federalists, then constitutionalists, and now they have turned Bonapartists; hence, they can look forward to no fresh titles except those of anarchists, *pardocratas,* and hangmen. For the present they call themselves moderates, and they have recanted their former opinions, but Briceño adds that all this constitutes a threat which I must dispel. Having lost the first [political] skirmish, they aim to conquer or die by fighting one final battle.

I shall ask General Páez to create a favorable public opinion respecting my Bolivian constitution which reconciles the extremes and all the benefits; even the federalists will find that their wishes have, in large part, been satisfied. In 1831 the Constitution can be altered to insure the stability and preservation of the Republic. I will remind Páez that he should be wary lest he suffer the fate of Iturbide, who fell because he relied too heavily on his supporters, and, further, that he should also beware the fury of a people justly resentful of any new aristocracy that will destroy equality. I shall mention this and much more in an effort to erase from their minds so fatal, absurd, and inglorious a plan, one which would dishonor me before the world and all posterity and bring down upon us the hatred of free men and the scorn of tyrants—a plan which is abhorrent to me as a matter of principle, prudence, and pride. This proposal hurts me more than all the insults of my enemies, since it presupposes that I am moved by vulgar ambition and that I am capable of descending to the level of an Iturbide and other contemptible usurpers of power. According to these gentlemen, no one can be great unless he adopts the tactics of Alexander, Caesar, and Napoleon. I intend to surpass them all in disinterestedness, since I cannot hope to match their exploits. My example may be of some service to my own country, since moderation on the part of the chief magistrate may reach even the very lowliest, for whom my life may perhaps serve as a guide. The people will revere me, and I shall be as the ark of their covenant.

I am your devoted

BOLÍVAR

---

[1] See Doc. 251 (ed.).

The 26th: I have just received your letter of November 21, and I do not understand why my letters from La Paz have not reached you, since I remained there until the 9th. I liked the article by De Pradt very much. We are indeed fortunate to have such an excellent writer on our side. His *drapeau blanc* made me laugh heartily.

---

240. To [José María Pando], Peruvian Delegate
    to the Congress of Panamá

[*Draft*]

Magdalena, February 26, 1826.

My dear friend:

Following my journey south, I returned to Lima on the 7th instant for the purpose of convoking the Congress on the 10th, but, despite the fact that notice was given far in advance, a sufficient number of delegates has not yet arrived to open the Congress. They are arriving every day, however, and soon we shall be able to proceed.

Even before I reached the capital, I was aware of the incident between the Council of Government and Captain Maxwell of the British frigate *Briton*. Strong words on both sides brought the matter to a disagreeable pass, and the explanations given have not improved the situation. The arrival of Mr. Charles Ricketts, Consul-General of His Britannic Majesty, placed the matter of Captain Maxwell's behavior under his jurisdiction, and recriminations multiplied. Fortunately, a few conferences between the Consul and myself have smoothed the matter over, with the return of three of the most recent notes which the Council of Government sent him. Difficult, troublesome, and delicate situations of great importance will frequently arise that will place the government in other difficult situations, or involve its honor, if the Ministry of Foreign Affairs is not placed in the hands of a man of sound judgment, who possesses extensive knowledge of diplomatic practices, is familiar with their application and procedures, and is versed in the use of the language of civilized nations; further, he should be aware of the nation's interests as well as those of the other nation concerned, and he should be able to balance these so as to derive every possible advantage without betraying greed, ambition, or fear. You fully realize how sensitive a ministry this is, and you no doubt understand that for this reason you were selected for that portfolio.

There is no reason, either just or unjust, for you to suppose that you have been recalled for lack of confidence in you or because of a rumor that a communication addressed to you by the Spanish government was intercepted. This report is absolutely without foundation. It had not yet reached me, and if it had I should have rejected it as an utter impossibility. The evident proof of the falseness of the charge is your appointment as minister of foreign affairs, a post which places you in constant contact with the government and enables you to exercise considerable influence in one of the most important branches of the administration. Such a post can be filled only by a person who can be trusted implicitly, and you have been appointed to occupy it.

In the enclosed issue of the *Gaceta del Gobierno,* a notice of your appointment has been inserted, together with a short statement of your abilities and qualifications. The article is too brief to be to my liking or to yours. I should have wanted it to be longer as there is more than enough material, but that will be arranged when you arrive in Lima.

Pérez Tudela, who will replace you, has had several conferences with me, and I have told him my views on the Confederation. I have also instructed him as to what to say to Vidaurre.

Your sister has obtained an order for your effects to be delivered to her. At first she had some difficulty in arranging this, but as soon as the matter came to my notice I had it attended to.

---

241. To General Pedro Briceño Méndez, Colombian Delegate to the Congress of Panamá

[*Original*]

Lima, February 27, 1826.

My dear Briceño:

Guzmán has delivered a letter from you which I have read with much interest. It is indeed fortunate, especially for me, that you have arrived in Caracas at such an opportune time. Never have you given a more convincing proof of your excellent good judgment than in combatting the ideas which are prevalent in Caracas and in having me consulted respecting a project that would certainly have ruined my reputation and stained my name and memory forever.[1] You can rest assured that I shall have no part of it.

As you may well imagine, your letter has given me much cause for thought, and after prolonged reflection I have decided that the best remedy for this evil, which might easily prove our undoing, is to send Páez my draft of a constitution for Bolivia, in reply to the letter that he wrote me. He can then familiarize himself with my ideas about linking stability with liberty and preserving the principles we have adopted. This was the fundamental aim that I had in view in drawing up the Constitution of Bolivia, which combines the best features of all the extremes, since in it even the federalists will find their demands satisfied to a large extent. I shall further inform Páez that in the year 1831 a reform insuring the stability and preservation of Colombia can be made, but that, under no circumstances, is it advisable to resort to extremes that would irremediably reduce us to the most frightful anarchy. Nothing is more dangerous than reform, especially reform of this kind. I should like you, for your part, to write Páez to the same effect, explaining and amplifying my ideas and sentiments in order to dissuade him from rushing into a project fraught with dangers and difficulties and altogether inglorious.

I have returned to this capital after a trip through the provinces of Upper Perú and after having been accorded the greatest honor to which any mortal can aspire, that of having his name given to a whole country. Had I never been given, or should I never receive, any other public recognition, this alone would suffice to fill my heart and soul.

The General Congress has not yet convened for lack of delegates, but it will surely meet within the fortnight. Truly, I am in a difficult, though flattering, position. Everyone in this country pins his hopes on me. They insist that I remain to guide them along the new path they are about to enter, while everyone in Colombia has given me his vote for the presidency. Reports of the Colombian elections indicate that I shall inevitably be elected and that Congress will then recall me. Such is my situation, and it is indeed a difficult one. In short, I do not know what I shall do except to let the events themselves determine the course that I am to follow.

---

[1] See Doc. 242 (ed.).

I am very impatient for the installation of the general assembly at the Isthmus. Since this is a step of the highest political significance and interest, we are obligated to bring it about as quickly as possible. The eyes of all Europe are fixed upon the Isthmus, eager and curious to know the purpose of our alliance. I therefore urge you and Gual to prevail upon the other delegates, in order that the assembly can meet at the earliest possible date. I need not tell you that the day I hear that the assembly has opened will be a very happy one for me.

It is not improbable that France, together with Spain, may choose to pursue a course similar to that which the former adopted with respect to Haiti, and that they will support such a project with a strong fleet and perhaps an army. For my part, I feel we should all perish rather than purchase our recognition at so vile a price.[1] I think that the delegates at the Congress of the Isthmus should keep this thought in mind and attempt to create a [uniform][2] opinion among the other states concerning the matter of purchasing recognition from Spain.

I am sending you newspapers from Chile in which you will find the details of the surrender of Chiloé, an event of no little significance.

My regards to Gual, Pando, Vidaurre, and the rest, and believe me to be your affectionate

BOLÍVAR

P.S. The Congress of Perú will be inaugurated in the next six or eight days, and we shall then find out who is to rule this country. Because of his illness and because he positively does not want to take command, poor General La Mar is retiring to Guayaquil. Sucre is badly needed in Bolivia, and, moreover, they have asked Colombia to release him to them. I doubt whether General Santander will accept the vice presidency, in which case you or Sucre will be elected. With such alternates we can console ourselves for the loss of Santander.

I think you should have your wife come and join you wherever you decide to go. That would be better for both of you. Otherwise, absence means a loss of time that should be spent in the pure and innocent delights of love. Any other course, I fear, opens the way to grief and sadness. I say this in all sincerity. I have told Santander

---

[1] French recognition of Haiti was obtained at the cost of a large indemnity and a fifty per cent reduction in import duties (ed.).

[2] In the text the word uniform (*uniformar*) is left blank (comp.).

to have a sum of money remitted to you out of my account. I do not know if he has done anything about it because in money matters there are always certain niceties to be considered.

I commend to you most particularly Tudela, who is an extremely well-informed and resourceful person. Also Vidaurre, who is a devoted friend of mine, the kind of man who is led astray by the goodness of his heart and the fire of his imagination. Give him every consideration, and, if the occasion so warrants, your advice as well.

As always, your affectionate uncle,

BOLÍVAR

---

242. To General José Antonio Páez

[*Draft*]

[Magdalena, March 6, 1826]

My dear General and friend:

I have received your very important letter of October 1 last, brought to me by Guzmán, whom I have met and heard with some surprise, for his mission is truly an extraordinary one. You tell me that Colombia is in a position similar to that of France when Napoleon was in Egypt, and that I, like him, should exclaim: "The plotters are wrecking the country; we must fly to her rescue." To be sure, virtually the whole of your letter is penned with the sharp point of truth, but the truth is not enough to make a plan effective. It seems to me that you have not judged the men and the events with sufficient impartiality. Colombia is not France, nor am I Napoleon. In France they think deeply, and their wisdom is deeper still. The population is homogeneous, and war had brought her to the brink of the precipice. No republic was as great as France, which throughout history had always been a kingdom. The republican government, discredited, had become the object of nearly universal execration. The monsters who ruled France were both cruel and incompetent. Napoleon was great and unique but highly ambitious. Here we have none of this. I am not, nor do I care to be, a Napoleon.

I regard these examples as unworthy of the glory that I have achieved. The title of Liberator is superior to any that human pride has ever sought. It cannot, therefore, be degraded. Moreover, our people have nothing, nothing whatever, in common with the French. Our Republic has raised the country to heights of glory and prosperity, endowing it with laws and freedom. No Colombian leader is a Robespierre or a Marat. The danger was over when hope began to appear; accordingly, nothing justifies the course that you propose. Republics surround Colombia on all sides, and Colombia has never been a kingdom. By its elevation as by its splendor, a throne would inspire terror. Equality would end, and the men of color would lose their rights to a new aristocracy. In fine, my friend, I cannot see the wisdom of the plan Guzmán placed before me. I believe, moreover, that those who promoted it are the same type of men who supported Napoleon and Iturbide in order to revel in their leaders' prosperity only to abandon them in their hour of peril. If, however, those men are acting in good faith, you may be sure that they are hotheads or extremists, whatever their principles.

I shall tell you quite frankly that the plan will not benefit you, me, or the country. I believe, nevertheless, that in the next period in which the Constitution can be revised, appropriate amendments favoring sound conservative principles can be introduced without violating any republican doctrines. I shall send you a plan of a constitution that I have devised for the Republic of Bolivia, embodying full guarantees of permanency and freedom, equality and order. If you and your friends should approve this plan it would be highly desirable if you will comment upon it publicly and commend it to the people. We would thus render a service to our country—a service that will win the support of all parties but the extremists; in other words, of all those who seek genuine freedom joined with true stability. On the other hand, I would not advise you to do for yourself what I would not permit to be done for me. But if the people should express their choice by giving you the nation's vote, I should most gladly employ my sword and my authority in sustaining and defending the sovereign will of the people. This assurance I give you with the same sincerity with which I remain your constant friend.

243. To General [the Marquess of] Lafayette

[*Draft*]

[Lima, March 20, 1826]

Dear General:

I have recently had the honor of seeing, for the first time, the noble characters, penned by your hand, which have so greatly benefited the world of Columbus. This good fortune was made possible by Colonel Mercier who delivered to me Your Excellency's esteemed letter, dated October 13 last.

From the public papers I have learned, with inexpressible pleasure, that Your Excellency has been so kind as to honor me with a treasure from Mount Vernon: The image of Washington, some of his mementos, and one of the monuments of his glory are to be bestowed upon me by Your Excellency in memory of that great man, the New World's foremost son. Words cannot express how greatly my heart cherishes so glorious an assembly of thoughts and objects. Washington's family honors me in a manner far exceeding my remotest hopes, as a reward from Washington, given by the hand of Lafayette, is the ultimate in human compensations. He was the outstanding architect of political reform, even as Your Excellency is the outstanding *citizen-hero*, the champion of freedom, who on the one hand has served America and on the other the Old World of Europe. What mortal then is deserving of the high honors which Your Excellency and Mount Vernon propose to confer upon me? My embarrassment is equalled only by the infinite sense of gratitude with which I tender Your Excellency the respect and veneration due the Nestor of human freedom.

I am, Your Excellency, with the highest regard, your respectful admirer.

244. To [PEDRO GUAL], COLOMBIAN DELEGATE TO THE
     CONGRESS OF PANAMÁ

[*Draft*]

[Lima, April, 1826]

Esteemed friend:

A few days ago I had the pleasure of receiving your kind letter of
February 26, from Panamá, advising me of your arrival in that city
and acknowledging receipt of the letter delivered to you by Pando.
It is truly unfortunate that the assembly of the Isthmus has not yet
begun because certain of the envoys have failed to appear, but I
am consoled to see you so firmly resolved to go forward with this
enterprise which is of such importance to all America and such an
honor to you and the other delegates.

Nevertheless, I hope that by now the Congress of Panamá has
been convened and has begun its important tasks. In attending to
these, I think it would be helpful to keep in mind the ideas advanced
by Abbé de Pradt in the little work he has just published, entitled
Congreso de Panamá, as his views are highly enlightening and
significant. I agree with you that the assembly of Panamá is an absolute necessity for the welfare and tranquility of America. I am so
utterly convinced of this that I want the assembly to be a permanent
one, so that, while acting as arbiter of the differences that will daily
arise between the new and neighboring states, it may become the
bond that will unite them forever. Please keep this idea foremost in
your mind, in order that you may make use of it when and if you
see fit.

I hope you will shortly be joined by the delegates from the Republic of Bolivia, that is, as soon as this Republic has been declared
a sovereign and independent state, which is now only a matter of
months.

245. To F[RANCISCO] DE P[AULA] SANTANDER,
    VICE PRESIDENT OF COLOMBIA

[*Original*]

Magdalena, April 7, 1826.

My dear General:

I have your very kind letter of January 21, in which you write at length about many things although you tell me nothing as yet of the elections, which are currently more important to us than any other topic.

I thoroughly approve of the plan for the naval expedition and the armistice, which appear to have been admirably conceived. This is definitely what we need. I consider that an armistice with Spain is preferable to a peace treaty.

I do not think it expedient to withdraw our privateers. They constitute our only offensive weapon against Spain. In the event this step is taken, I should like you to have the non-government press announce that Perú and Bolivia will grant letters of marque to Colombian and other privateers if they will make application for them to these governments.

I was pleased with the appointment of Cockburn, although a report reached me that it was the Admiral Alexander Cochrane.

I am glad you are sending Madrid to France.

I concur in all that you say respecting Brazil and Buenos Aires. Rivadavia seized the government by a ruse, but he will not hold it for long. He is a crafty enemy of ours who would have us fight the Emperor [of Brazil] without so much as a nod in acknowledgment.

I strongly urge you to see that Sucre is permitted to take over in Bolivia.

I have now answered your letter in full.

In the past few days we have had some difficulty convening the first Constitutional Congress. The delegates from Arequipa, who are the *caraqueños* of Perú, would have this be a constituent rather than a constitutional convention, as it should be. They raised this question in a preliminary meeting and many deputies from other provinces followed their lead, some because of misunderstanding and others because they were corrupted. On my advice, the Council of Government supported the Constitution, and, when I saw that my delegates and I were about to be worsted and began to fear that anarchy would raise its head anew in this Constituent Congress, I solemnly repeated what I had been saying day after day—*that I was leaving.* This announcement produced a general uproar. All the civic organizations, the people, and Congress itself united in imploring me to remain. Plans were devised to prevent my departure at all costs and to silence those who had aroused me. I am easily moved by the entreaties of persons who love me, and in Perú everyone loves me, or at least all, with great fervor, say that they do; it is certain that in a thousand there is scarcely one who hates or, rather, fears me. Needless to say, this incident decided the matter in the preliminary meeting, although seventeen votes were heatedly cast in opposition to the government's stand.

The main cause of all this is that a certain Luna Pizarro, a small-time clergyman like Dr. Pérez, sought to change the Constitution or, rather, sought to arrange everything to suit his fancy. It was he who forced San Martín to leave Perú and who wrecked the *junta* that was headed by La Mar. He was the one who insisted that Arequipa grant him unrestricted powers as a delegate, and, when he was refused admission to the Congress because of such powers, all the delegates of Arequipa took his part.

The Council of Government that I left here was composed of fine and honorable men like Roscio, Juan P. Ayala, and Restrepo; on the other hand, however, they are lacking in force and popularity. They are accused only of being weak and indulgent, unfit to govern. People are demanding a new Council, but I can find no better. I am awaiting the return of one Pando, who went to the Isthmus, in order to have him head the Ministry of Foreign Affairs.[1] This gentleman held a similar post in Madrid in the days of the *Cortes.* He has much in common with Revenga, though he is superior to the latter in every way, having spent his time in Europe in the diplomatic service. It is difficult to know which to praise more, his incorruptibility, his energy, or his keen understanding. Although he is the first man in all Perú, he is neither very likable nor much liked. He was born in Lima where his entire family lives, but he is not widely known, because he has always lived abroad. I do not know what to do. This country cannot be established in four years or in six. The Congress and the executive will always be of the same type. The country is now tranquil under the spell of my influence. Carrión has said that I am Mercury's caduceus around which the serpents are coiled in friendship, but if the staff were withdrawn they would tear each

---

[1] See Doc. 240 (ed.).

other limb from limb. I am tired of governing and anxious to leave; truthfully, I would be greatly pleased if I were to receive an order to return to Colombia. All that keeps me here is the matter of the Bolivian Constitution. I have now completed it, and I should like to submit it personally to the Congress of that country. If, therefore, the Colombian Congress has refused me permission to go to Bolivia, or if it has recalled me, please write me an official letter, in strong terms, which will justify and necessitate my departure for Colombia. But at the same time I entreat you not to let the legislative power have any part in my recall, as the Emperor of Brazil may yet defeat the Argentines and place these southern republics in imminent danger. Yet, if Congress recalls me, I shall have to obey, come what may. That is why I want you to recall me, and not Congress. Moreover, I want to add that I will neither go to Bogotá nor head the government. Never, never, never. In this century of philosophy no one acquires or retains honor except by rigid adherence to principles. Our political critics demand many unities in the formation of a modern heroic tragedy. As a result, the *catastrophes* are indeed unfortunate.

Tell Soublette his last letter afforded me great pleasure, though I do not approve of what he said about relinquishing the command; yet I do approve his leaving America to labor in a region offering greater security. Tell him to keep writing to me and I shall always give him good advice, as in this instance.

You have no doubt heard from White and others the story emanating from Venezuela respecting the crown. My enemies and foolish friends have so much to say about this crown that they will drive me from Colombia and America. They refuse to believe that I detest rulership as heartily as I relish glory, and that glory consists not in ruling but in exercising great virtues. I have sought glory and freedom. Having achieved both, there is nothing more that I desire.

I am your devoted

BOLÍVAR

P.S. I have not yet sealed this letter because I am waiting for your letter, which I am certain Heres is bringing. As yet, I have received no reports or newspapers. A sheet sent me by Armero contains the report that the United States is sending an envoy to the Isthmus to attend our conferences, except those that deal with war. This is quite important.

Armero gave me a copy of the proposed armistice with Spain. I have given instructions to say that I feel it should be submitted to this government, which I am sure will accept it. This plan affords us a thousand advantages, and I must therefore remain in the south either until it becomes effective and peace is concluded, or until the war is resumed. The Spaniards keep sending numerous troops to the Islands,[1] four regiments having only recently arrived. This knowledge, in addition to the fact that my continued presence in the south will add weight to Perú's part in the armistice, convinces me that I must remain here until I see whether this important negotiation is to be adverse or favorable. If it should be adverse and if the Spaniards should undertake any operation against us, I can provide 20,000 men from the south. We would not have these, however, should I leave. You can be sure that, if I leave, everything will collapse.

At this point I have still not received your letter.

BOLÍVAR

P.P.S. General Sucre tells me that he has eight thousand *pesos* in Guayaquil which can be used by the government, in return for an equal amount to be paid to his brother in Cumaná. I should be glad if you could render him this service.

---

246. To José Rafael Revenga, Colombian Minister
    of Foreign Affairs

[*Original*]

Magdalena, April 8, 1826.

My dear Revenga:

Yesterday I had the pleasure of receiving two of your letters which, although exceedingly interesting, are neither as long nor as detailed as I might have wished. I beg you not only to write me frequently but to give me all the news, as no one can better keep me informed of Colombia's foreign and domestic affairs than yourself.

The plan for armistice with Spain impressed me as being magnifi-

---

[1] The Antilles (ed.).

cent, and I hope it will materialize. I have long been of the opinion that an armistice with the Spaniards would be of more value than peace. General Santander is fully informed of my reasons for thinking so, as I have had occasion to submit them to him. Our charge d'affaires has given me a copy of your instructions to our envoy in London, which are to serve as a basis for the negotiations to be initiated with the Spanish government. I consider these instructions excellent, like everything else you do. I believe my presence in the south may carry weight in the negotiating of the armistice, since it will considerably increase the influence of Perú, which will no doubt take part in the negotiations. With this in view, I have advised Armero to furnish an exact copy of your instructions to the [Peruvian] Minister of Foreign Affairs. For my part, I shall not fail to advise this government, since the stronger we present ourselves the greater the advantages that we can expect from the negotiations.

I consider the ratification of the treaty with Great Britain to be a matter of great importance and even more so that government's suggestion to us regarding the Emperor of Brazil. I am also pleased that the United States is sending an envoy to the Isthmus, no matter what the terms. I am fully aware of the sad state of our treasury, and for this very reason I have been anxious to have you take it in hand. Again I urge you to do so. It is true that you have worked hard, but no task is finished when more remains to be done.

I am, my dear Revenga, your most affectionate and devoted friend,

BOLÍVAR

---

247. To F[RANCISCO] DE P[AULA] SANTANDER,
VICE PRESIDENT OF COLOMBIA

[*Original*]

Magdalena, May 7, 1826.

My dear General:

I have great things to tell you in this letter, although I have heard nothing from you in the last two mails—that is, the previous one, which brought nothing from you, and the present one, which has yet to arrive. I shall accordingly be expressing myself haphazardly on extremely important matters.

First, I shall tell you that not enough members of the Peruvian Congress could be gathered to open its sessions. The delegates, after waiting here for three months and seeing that the Congress was unable to meet, issued a statement in the *Gaceta del Gobierno,* a copy of which I enclose. As you will see, I rendered my report, which the Council of Government issued together with the decree that appears after it. Consequently, this Congress, of its own volition, has momentarily ceased to exist. This came about as the result of circumstances which demanded unified authority, without any legislative body to stand in the way of action—America's guardian angel must have so willed it.

Pando, who has just arrived from the Isthmus, is the bearer of news of the utmost importance from Gual and Briceño. The sum total of what I have learned through these channels is of paramount interest.

It is definitely reported that, first, Morales, with 14,000 men, is about to launch an expedition against the Costa Firme; second, another 14,000 Spaniards will follow as replacements to the first, with two additional ships; third, they have a fleet that will make short work of ours; fourth, Mexico will make a separate peace for a sum in the millions; fifth, the Holy Alliance is the power behind these operations, and France is standing the expense in order to compel us, by a formidable threat, to accept her terms and conditions; sixth, England is doing nothing to stop it, and on the contrary, she wishes us to change our fundamental laws as the sole means of reconciling Europe with America; seventh, in the circumstances, the Congress of Colombia has summoned General Páez to appear before it, and the General will probably disobey, as he is charged with being the author of a project to establish monarchy in Colombia; and, in either case, whether General Páez obeys or disobeys, the Spaniards are expected to benefit by the general confusion resulting from this quarrel between republicans and monarchists; and, finally, I am told that the situation is hopeless unless I come to Colombia at once, as matters have reached the point where war, domestic or foreign, appears unavoidable.

Consider for a moment how this miscellany of tangled problems has affected me. On the one hand, the Holy Alliance and its armies seek an empire; on the other, my honor, the laws, and Congress, all demand that the Republic be preserved. If we yield to the Alliance we shall have peace with the outside world under Europe's protection and civil war at home with the democrats. If we stand firm for republicanism, we shall have war abroad and anarchy at home, for, with the army taking one side and the people the other, no one can aid us except by undertaking a new conquest and imposing a government of blood and fire that will wipe out both parties.

If I go to Colombia, I can prevent many of the ills that threaten us, but I doubt that I can avert them all. In the first place, the damage already done cannot be remedied and nothing I could attempt would prevent the damage the Spaniards can inflict upon us. Furthermore, my presence will only increase the anger of the factions, as each will claim that I am coming to its aid; each will strive to get the upper hand so that, on my arrival, I will find it dominant and thereby give it my support. Add to this the fact that only in the south do I have an army capable of imposing order by force or respect. But the moment I leave here, all factions, which now stand in awe of me, will throw off all restraint and fight each other, whereupon the very source of all my strength will evaporate. Our army will be able to travel only with great difficulty, and it will be greatly reduced. General Sucre, the one man who could take my place, is thoroughly disgusted with the command and for the present he can attend only to Bolivia and the Córdoba division. General Santa Cruz, who is to become President of Perú's Council of Government, is in need of help rather than being able to render it. He still has enemies but few friends, and by the very use of his authority he will at once call into play against him the self-interest of many. Perú holds a temporary lien upon me until such time as an authority has been created by my influence and has accredited itself by reason of its services.

Paraguay has allied itself with Brazil, an alliance which Bolivia has reason to fear. The Río de la Plata has reason to fear both the Emperor of Brazil and the anarchy which grows steadily as a result of the constant changes in the government of Buenos Aires. Chile's heart is with me, but her government is allied with Rivadavia. Córdoba has invited me to become the protector of a federation composed of Buenos Aires, Chile, and Bolivia. This plan originates with General Alvear, who intends to see it realized at any cost. General O'Higgins and his friends also favor this plan, as do the *pelucones*[1] of Chile, who are rich and numerous. What am I to do amidst all

---

[1] Literally—big wigs, the clerical and landed gentry (ed.).

this? I have thought about it a great deal, but I have come to no conclusion. Some advise me to form an empire around Potosí, reaching as far as the mouth of the Orinoco; others desire a federation of the three sister republics, a true federation in place of the Confederation, which they say is merely nominal and chimerical. I am for the second of these proposals. The two southern republics[1] would readily agree, provided that I become the federation's *protector*. Pando, on the other hand, favors the empire, as do the members of Perú's Council of Government. They argue that they want peace with Europe at any price and that they cannot exist unless I maintain order for them—yet they will consent to the new Confederation. The more that is desired, the less that is obtained. What are we to do with Venezuela and Cartagena? Each of these places has its own ideas and customs. Páez may agree to what I propose, but what do Montilla and the Admiral say? Both appear very loyal to me, personally. The first is capable of nothing, the second of anything.

When the courier has brought your messages and as soon as I have dealt further with the Council of State, I shall send O'Leary to you with my latest comments and resolutions.

I am your devoted

BOLÍVAR

---

248. To General Antonio José de Sucre

[Blanco y Azpurúa, X, 322]

Magdalena, May 12, 1826.

My dear General:

To enable you to better understand the alarming state of affairs, I am enclosing a letter that I have sent to General Santander.

Pando, who has just come from the Isthmus, assures me that Colombia is in a state of complete paralysis and that ruin threatens us on every hand, because of, first, the divergent parties; second, finances; third, the organization of the government, which is com-

---

[1] Bolivia and Perú; Colombia was the third sister republic (ed.).

plicated and costly; and fourth, the many laws that oppress the Republic. The result is that Quito envies the situation in Perú. Demarquet, who has just arrived, has demonstrated this to me with a great mass of evidence and a profusion of facts which have caused me considerable concern. He states that Quito has not revolted against the government out of respect for me and because my arrival is expected momentarily. The municipality of Bogotá complains that it can no longer endure the burden of the laws because they are so numerous and also because they are contrary to the actual state of affairs. In Venezuela everything goes poorly, for the army supports one party and the people another. Páez, as head of the army, is hated by the people, and the *pardocracia* gains ground as fast as the other factions lose it.

Congress is divided: the Chamber of Deputies sides with the people against the government and keeps asking for me. The Senate, on the contrary, supports the government and is willing to have me stay away.

The Cabinet is divided: Castillo has ruined the Republic with his inept administration of the treasury, yet he wishes to become vice president, which, of course, makes him an enemy of Santander. Revenga, saying that Santander does not want him, has submitted his resignation three times in one week, and he exhorts me to *preach virtue*.

Soublette backs Santander against Páez. He has asked me to come and states that I must remain, because *they are destroying everything that I have built up*. He says the Chamber of Deputies is in a continual state of agitation, denouncing Páez, Santander, Hurtado, and the loan.

The Vice President told me in his last letter that he had little to communicate, but the letter itself shows extreme discouragement as he was evidently reluctant to continue in the vice presidency, though at the time he did not yet know of his election. Later, on March 15, he was duly elected by a large majority of votes, and I am still awaiting his letter of the 21st which should have arrived in the post of the 8th of this month.

In short, Colombia presents a most distressing picture, for her super-abundance of liberal strength is being poorly expended; the only remedy for this is absolute sobriety in the government. With this in view, I shall have to proceed to Colombia in the next two or three months. I am delaying my departure only until I have received your reply to this letter and until I have seen the new Council of

State in operation here for some two or three months. I intend to organize this new Council with Santa Cruz as President; Unánue, Vice President; Pando, Minister of Foreign Affairs; Larrea, Finance; and Heres, War. I begin to have more and more confidence in these men of the Council. They want the three republics to be joined in a more closely knit federation than that of the United States, with me as president, and a vice president of my own choice, which would be you.

My Bolivian Constitution is to be published this very day. It is intended to serve the states in particular and the federation in general, with such adaptations as may be found necessary. You, in Bolivia, must point the way to this federation by adopting the Constitution immediately, for it has been revised almost beyond belief. Pando states it is divine, a work of genius that attains the fullest possible measure of protection. Pando is a man incapable of flattery, forthright to a fault, and above all well informed and high principled. Consequently, his approval must be sincere. He thinks the Constitution can be simultaneously adapted to the government of one or of many states because of the variants it provides to fit each case. Everyone will receive this Constitution as the keystone of the alliance, as the bridge between Europe and America, between the army and the people, between democracy and aristocracy, and between monarchy and republic. Everyone tells me that my Constitution will be the great instrument of our social reform.

Endeavor, therefore, to prevail upon your Congress to accept it without any reservations. Tell those gentlemen that their wisdom in the first Congress has saved America and that now they must not destroy her by a disastrous refusal. Tell them, moreover, that the peoples now oppressed by anarchy after having survived the revolution are clamoring for a monarchy, for our reforms have proved incapable of producing the general good and are incompatible with our populations; that the clergy and the military have banded together against our principles, because clergy and military are unduly curbed by our reforms; and that in me lies the hope and very lifeblood of our republics. Have them recall Epaminondas, whose funeral rites Alexander celebrated with the utter destruction of Thebes. Remind them that above my tomb many tyrants will arise, who will be modern Sullas and Mariuses, bringing on bloody civil wars. Tell them that I offer the peoples, whom the army has liberated, a code of prosperity which links stability with freedom in greater measure than was ever known in any government of man and that, by insisting upon perfection, they can only reap disaster.

Perú's Council of State will recognize Bolivia and offer her a pact of union, a pact that can also be made with Colombia, where I shall prepare the way for its acceptance.

The purpose of the pact must be the attainment of the most perfect possible union under a federal system. The government of each state will continue to be vested in the President and Vice President and their Chamber and Senate, respecting all matters affecting religion, justice, civil administration, national economy—in short, everything but foreign affairs, war, and the federal treasury. The federal government will be composed of a president, a vice president, and three chambers to administer respectively the national treasury, war, and foreign affairs. Each department [or province] of the three republics will send a deputy to the greater federal congress, where they will be divided into the three corresponding groups, with each group containing one third of the delegates from each republic. These three chambers, with the Vice President and the Secretaries of State (the latter to be selected from the entire Republic) will govern the federation.

The Liberator, as supreme head, will annually visit the departments of each state. The capital will be located at a central point, such as Quito or Guayaquil. Colombia would be divided into three states: Venezuela, Cundinamarca, and Quito, of which one would take the name of Colombia—probably Cundinamarca. The federation would bear whatever name is decided upon, probably the name Boliviana. There will be only one flag, one army, and one nation. Heres thinks it would be better to form two nations, Bolivia, consisting of Lower and Upper Perú, and Colombia, composed of her constituent parts, and that I should be president of both and rule them as one. As I have said before, the Council of Government [of Perú] desires a union of all three republics, and Pando leans toward both opinions.

We must therefore set an example by joining Bolivia and Perú in a federation, and when I proceed to Colombia I shall see what can best be done. Colombia cannot continue in her present condition, for everyone demands a change, whether on the federal or the monarchic side. The same thing is true here; nor can Bolivia remain as she is, because the Río de la Plata and the Emperor [of Brazil] would eventually bring about the destruction of that Republic. The only alternative for Colombia and Bolivia is one army, one flag, and one nation. Otherwise, dissatisfaction will increase to the point where a monarchy will necessarily be the only solution, which is exactly what the army, the Church, and Europe desire.

Be this as it may, I regard it as vital to give this plan its start in Bolivia and Perú. I think it is no less vital that you carry on the affairs of that country until I return to set up a general administration for the whole federation. Then, there will be no difficulty in finding a friend whom we can consider for replacing you in the presidency. General Santa Cruz will fill the presidency of Perú, unless he loses favor, which I do not expect, as he is quite likable and capable.

My friend, you cannot abandon us at this critical moment when, more than ever, we need men of ability with an aura of glory and popularity about them, like yourself. I was the one who was tired and in need of rest, but the presence of danger and the current difficulties bolstered my fallen spirits. For the brave, danger sharpens the appetite, and, as I am certain that you share my sentiments, I have not doubted for one moment that, once you are apprised of the great danger to which America is exposed, your desire to serve will be rekindled. Be assured that the highest destinies await you. I have been offered a crown for which my head is not suited; yet, in the twilight of future events, I seem to see it hovering above the figure of the victor of Ayacucho. Should it not be this diadem it will be another, a thousand times more glorious—one of laurel in recognition of your virtues. In a word, without you I can do nothing and the world that rests upon your shoulders would fall hopelessly into one vast sea of anarchy.

See that these matters are widely publicised in the press, and do not for a moment doubt but that I will go to Colombia and will return to establish the basic foundations of government.

Chile and the Río de la Plata, as well as Guatemala, can join in our plan as allies.

Write to Córdoba and our friends in the Río de la Plata in order to maintain these friendly relations.

Chile will be with us when you least expect it, and Guatemala too, for she fears Mexico, as does Panamá, also.

To sum up, I ask that

1. You remain in Bolivia until my return.
2. The Constitution be adopted.
3. The union of these two republics be arranged.
4. You maintain the most harmonious relations with Perú's Council of Government.

5. You labor to have the Río de la Plata adopt our own sound principles.

Have no fear of the Emperor of Brazil, as England has an understanding with us in this regard, and she will maintain the peace as a matter of necessity and good politics.

The United States, together with Russia and France, is trying to prevail upon Spain to grant us recognition; so that the strength of the battalions need only be set at 600 regulars instead of the 1,000 I spoke of before. The Emperor of Russia is not Constantine, who was next in line, but his brother Nicholas. The latter holds to the principles of Alexander, while the other is a Cossack. It is reported that the accession to the throne involved a little bloodshed because of the ardor of the troops, but that the brothers dealt nobly with each other, etc., etc.

BOLÍVAR

249. To [MANUEL DE VIDAURRE], PERUVIAN DELEGATE
   TO THE CONGRESS OF PANAMÁ

[Draft]

[Magdalena, May 16, 1826]

I have read, with great pleasure, your kind letter of April 8, in which you enclosed a copy of the principles you have worked out for the Confederation. I had previously seen several of your other writings, and I was greatly pleased to note that you still devote your leisure time to the welfare of your country.

The Council of Government, after receiving your recent communications and hearing the reports rendered by Pando, has decided upon the final instructions that you gentlemen are to receive. I wish to point out that I have had no part whatsoever in framing these instructions; because delegates from Colombia will attend the Confederation, and I, therefore, have thought it a point of duty and delicacy not to influence in any way the orders that the delegates of Perú receive from their governments. Moreover, the instructions given by the Council of Government are dictated by the best interests of the country, which none can hold dearer than the men in this government. Accordingly, my dear friend, I trust that you will redouble your efforts, in harmony with those of your esteemed colleague Tudela, and that together you will leave nothing undone to further the greatest American enterprise ever undertaken, one that will do the greatest honor to all who contribute to it.

Pando has told me a great deal about you and himself, and he has expressed great satisfaction with the harmony that has always prevailed between the two of you. I believe the same will be the case between you and Tudela, whose ability and discretion I highly esteem. Pando has already been appointed Minister of Foreign Relations, and his ability and knowledge of foreign affairs give us excellent reason to expect that he will acquit himself creditably.

In short, my dear friend, I hope you will keep me. . . .

---

250. To General Pedro Briceño Méndez, Colombian Delegate to the Congress of Panamá

[*Original*]

[La Magdalena, May 25, 1826]

My dear nephew:

How your letter of April 12 has set me to thinking! I have been thinking it over ever since, and, as a result, I have made several decisions.

I am writing Gual what I think and know about the Congress, the fleet, and Perú's boundaries. To you I shall simply say, read that letter.

There is no point in discussing the seamen here as there are none. Coastal trading vessels and ships of war are manned by foreigners.

The situation in Colombia, as you describe it to me, has completely engrossed my attention. I believe your description is true and only too painful. I also foresee a terrible crisis in the years to come, and, accordingly, I have resolved to return in August or September. After I have spent the remainder of the year in the south, surveying the situation in the provinces, I shall go to Bogotá, determined not to accept the presidency, as that would forever incapacitate me for service to my country. It will be ill-advised if they force me to serve now, for they will only regret it later, as I am sure there will be some unforeseen developments of great magnitude with respect to the revision of the Constitution. Upon my arrival in Bogotá, I shall see how matters stand there and in Venezuela. I shall probably ask Congress for permission to go to Venezuela for a short rest, with every intention of serving the country if the Congress wants me to do so. In Venezuela I shall try to put an end to the partisan spirit and, at the same time, preach to my friends the gospel of my Bolivian Constitution, as opposed to federalism and monarchy. This Constitution reconciles extremes and provides the means for insuring domestic tranquility combined with freedom for the provinces. In the year 1831 it may be helpful in revising [the Colombian Constitution]. You will observe that my reasoning is quite republican yet philosophical in belief. The republican aspect was necessary in order to silence the charge of monarchical ideas which some attribute to me and which others proclaim as being the means to salvation. In Buenos Aires and in Chile they use this as a pretext to speak of me in horror.

When I come to Colombia we shall discuss the matter of salaries and settle the dispute between my sisters; Juanica is very much in the wrong since Antonia is not to blame for the sudden changes I ordered her to make.

I will settle Páez' affairs as best I can. I am not sending the warships requested by your people, as Colombian vessels are subject to the orders of the intendant of Guayaquil.

The schooner *Guayaquileña*, on which these papers are going, is to return here, and you can write me fully by this vessel whatever you can and whatever you please. The same holds for Gual.

Please forcefully urge upon Santander and the gentlemen at Cartagena the necessity of having the *Pichincha* battalion, which will leave Arica within three months, proceed to Caracas. This is the best body of troops in the army. I also want the *Vargas* battalion stationed in Caracas, as I would rather not go there without these troops.

I am, my dear nephew, your very best friend,

BOLÍVAR

251. MESSAGE TO THE CONGRESS OF BOLIVIA

[Original]

Lima, May 25, 1826.

Legislators:

In submitting to you my draft of a constitution for Bolivia, I am overcome with embarrassment and trepidation, for I am convinced that I am not qualified as a lawgiver. When I reflect that all the wisdom of the ages has not been sufficient for the drafting of a perfect fundamental law, and that the most enlightened legislator has been the direct promoter of human misery, in travesty, as it were, of his divine mission—what can I say of a soldier who, born among slaves and isolated in the wildest section of his country, has known only captives in chains and his comrades-in-arms, pledged to unshackle them? I, a legislator! Your deception and my embarrassment may well argue for preference in this matter. I do not know who suffers most in this terrible dilemma—you, for the evils that may result from the laws you have asked of me, or I, for the opprobrium to which you have condemned me by your confidence.

I have summoned all my powers in order to expound to you my opinions relative to the manner of governing free men, in accordance with the accepted principles of civilized peoples, although the lessons of experience point only to long periods of disaster, interrupted by the briefest intervals of success. What guideposts shall we follow amidst the gloom of such disheartening precedents?

Legislators! Your duty compels you to avoid a struggle with two monstrous enemies, who, although they are themselves ever locked in mortal combat, will attack you at once. *Tyranny* and *anarchy* constitute an immense sea of oppression encircling a tiny island of freedom that is perpetually battered by the forces of the waves and the hurricane that ceaselessly threatens to submerge it. Beware, then, of the sea that you are about to cross in a fragile bark with so inexperienced a pilot at the helm.

My draft of a constitution for Bolivia provides for four branches of government, an additional one having been devised without affecting the time-honored powers of any of the others. The electoral [legislative] branch has been accorded powers not granted it in other reputedly very liberal governments. These powers resemble, in great part, those of the federal system. I have thought it expedient and desirable, and also feasible, to accord to the most direct representatives of the people privileges that the citizens of every department, province, and canton probably desire most. Nothing is more important to a citizen than the right to elect his legislators, governors, judges, and pastors. The electoral college of each province represents its needs and interests and serves as a forum from which to denounce any infractions of the laws or abuses of the magistrates. I might, with some truth, describe this as a form of representation providing the rights enjoyed by individual governments in federal systems. In this manner, additional weight has been placed in the balance to check the executive; the government will acquire greater guarantees, a more popular character, and a greater claim to be numbered among the most democratic of governments.

Every ten citizens will elect one elector, and thus the nation will be represented by a tenth of its citizens. Ability is the only prerequisite for this post. It is not necessary to possess property to have the august right of representing popular sovereignty. The elector must, however, be able to write out his ballots, sign his name, and read the laws. He must be skilled in some trade or useful art that assures him an honest living. The only disqualifications are those of crime, idleness, and utter ignorance. Understanding and honesty, rather than wealth, are the sole requirements for exercising the public trust.

The legislative body is so composed that its parts will necessarily be in harmony. It will not find itself divided for lack of an arbiter, as is the case where there are only two chambers. Since this legislature has three parts, disagreement between two can be settled by the third. The issue is thus examined by two contending parties and decided by an impartial third party. In this way no useful law is without effect; at least it shall have been reviewed once, twice, and a third time before being discarded. In all matters between two contending parties, a third party is named to render the decision. Would it not be absurd, therefore, if, in matters of the deepest concern to the nation, this expedient, dictated by practical necessity, were scorned? The chambers will thus observe toward each other the consideration which is indispensable in preserving the unity of the Congress, which must deliberate without passion and with the calm of wisdom. Our modern congresses, I shall be told, consist of only two houses. This is because England, which has provided the model, was forced to have the nobility and the people represented in two chambers; and, while the same pattern was followed in North America where there is no nobility, it may be presumed that the habits acquired under British rule inspired this imitation. The fact is that two deliberating bodies are always found to be in conflict. It was for this reason that Sieyès insisted on only one—a classic error.

The first body [I propose] is the Chamber of Tribunes. It has the right to initiate laws pertaining to finance, peace, and war. It exercises the immediate supervision of the departments administered by the executive branch with a minimum of interference by the legislative branch.

The Senators enact the codes of law and the ecclesiastical regulations and supervise the courts and public worship. The Senate shall appoint the prefects, district judges, governors, *corregidores,* and all the lesser officials in the department of justice. It shall submit to the Chamber of Censors nominations for members of the Supreme Court, archbishops, bishops, prebendaries, and canons. Everything relating to religion and the laws comes within the province of the Senate.

The Censors exercise a political and moral power not unlike that of the Areopagus of Athens and the censors of Rome. They are the prosecuting attorneys [*fiscales*] against the government in defense of the Constitution and popular rights, to see that these are strictly observed. Under their aegis has been placed the power of national judgment, which is to decide whether or not the administration of the executive is satisfactory.

The Censors are to safeguard morality, the sciences, the arts, education, and the press. The Censors exercise the most fearful yet the most august authority. They can condemn to eternal opprobrium arch criminals and usurpers of the sovereign authority. They can bestow public honors upon citizens who have distinguished themselves by their probity and public service. The sceptre of glory has been placed in their hands, for which reason the Censors must possess integrity and a conduct above reproach. For any trespass on their part, however slight, they shall be prosecuted. To these high priests of the laws I have entrusted the preservation of our sacred tablets, as it is for them to denounce the violators of these laws.

The President of the Republic, in our Constitution, becomes the sun which, fixed in its orbit, imparts life to the universe. This supreme authority must be perpetual, for in non-hierarchical systems, more than in others, a fixed point is needed about which leaders and citizens, men and affairs can revolve. "Give me a point where I may stand," said an ancient sage, "and I will move the earth." For Bolivia this point is the life-term President [*presidente vitalicio*]. Upon him rests our entire order, notwithstanding his lack of powers. Not only has he been rendered headless in order that none may fear his intentions, but his hands have been tied so that he can do no harm.

The President of Bolivia enjoys many of the powers of the [North] American chief executive but with limitations that favor the people. His term of office is that enjoyed by the President of Haiti. For Bolivia, I have borrowed the executive system of the most democratic republic in the world.

The island of Haiti, if you will permit the digression, was in a state of perpetual insurrection. Having experimented with an empire, a kingdom, and a republic, in fact every known type of government and more besides, the people were compelled to call upon the illustrious Pétion to save them. After they had put their trust in him, Haiti's destinies pursued a steady course. Pétion was made President for life, with the right to choose his successor. Thus, neither the death of that great man nor the advent of a new president imperiled that state in the slightest. Under the worthy Boyer, everything has proceeded as tranquilly as in a legitimate monarchy. There you have conclusive proof that *a life-term president, with the power to choose his successor,* is the most sublime inspiration amongst republican regimes.

The President of Bolivia will be less dangerous than the President of Haiti, as the succession is provided for in a manner that better secures the interests of the state. Moreover, the President of Bolivia is deprived of all patronage. He can appoint neither governors, nor judges, nor ecclesiastic dignitaries of any kind. This limitation of powers has never before been imposed in any constituted government. One check after another has thus been placed upon the authority of the head of the government, who will in every way find that the people are ruled directly by those who exercise the significant functions of the commonwealth. The priests will rule in matters of conscience, the judges in matters involving property, honor, and life, and the magistrates or men of state in all major public acts. As they owe their position, their distinction, and their fortune to the people alone, the President cannot hope to entangle them in his personal ambitions. If to this is added the natural growth of opposition which a democratic government experiences throughout the course of its administration, there is reason to believe that, under this form of government, usurpation of the popular sovereignty is less likely to occur than under any other.

Legislators, from this day forth liberty will be indestructible in America. Observe the savage character of our continent, which of itself bars a monarchical order, for the deserts invite independence. Here, there are no great nobles or churchmen. Our wealth has amounted to little, and it is no greater today. The Church, though not without influence, is far from seeking domination as it is satisfied to insure its own preservation. Without these supporting factors, tyrants cannot survive, and, should any ambitious soul aspire to make himself emperor, there are Dessalines, Christophe, and Iturbide to warn him of what he may expect. No power is harder to maintain than that of a newly crowned prince. This truth, which is stronger than empires, defeated Bonaparte, the conqueror of all armies. If the great Napoleon could not maintain himself against an alliance of republicans and aristocrats, who then in America will undertake to establish monarchies upon a soil fired with the bright flames of liberty, which would consume the very pillars intended to support the royalist structure? No, Legislators, fear not the pretenders to a crown which will hang over their heads like the sword of Dionysius. New-found princes who should be so bold as to erect thrones upon the ruins of liberty will instead erect tombs for their own remains, which will proclaim to future ages the fact that they *preferred vain ambition to freedom and glory.*

The constitutional limitations upon the President of Bolivia are the narrowest ever known. He can appoint only the officials of the Ministries of the Treasury, Peace, and War; and he is Commander in Chief of the army. These are his only powers.

Administration is the province of the Cabinet, which is responsible to the Censors and subject to the close vigilance of every legislator, governor, judge, and citizen. The revenue officers and soldiers, who are agents of the Cabinet alone, are hardly the persons calculated to make it the object of public affection, and therefore its influence will be next to nothing.

Of all the higher officials, the Vice President is the one with the most limited power. He must obey both the legislative and the executive branches of a republican government. From the former, he receives the laws, and from the latter his instructions, and he must proceed between these two branches, following the narrowest of paths, with precipices on either side. Despite these disadvantages, this form of government is better than an absolute government. Constitutional limitations increase political consciousness, thereby giving hope of ultimately finding a beacon light which will act as a guide through the ever-present shoals and reefs. These limitations serve as dikes against the violence of our passions, which are prompted by selfish interests.

In the government of the United States it has of late become the practice for the Secretary of State to succeed the President. Nothing could be more expedient, in any republic, than this practice. It has the advantage of placing at the head of the administration a man experienced in the management of a nation. In entering upon his duties, he is fully prepared and brings with him the advantages of popularity and practical experience. I have borrowed this practice [of succession] and embodied it in the law.

The President of the Republic will appoint the Vice President, who will administer the affairs of the state and succeed the President in office. By means of this device we shall avoid elections, which result in that great scourge of republics—anarchy, which is the handmaiden of tyranny, the most imminent and terrible peril of popular government. Compare the tremendous crises in republics when a change of rulers takes place with the equivalent situation in legitimate monarchies.

The Vice President must be a man of the loftiest character, for, should the President not appoint an honorable citizen, he will fear him as an enemy incarnate and be ever suspicious of his secret ambitions. The Vice President will have to exert himself in order to merit, through faithful service, the high esteem necessary to discharge the highest duties and to deserve that great national honor—the supreme command. The legislative body and the people will expect both ability and integrity of this high ranking office as well as a blind obedience to the principles of freedom.

If hereditary succession perpetuates the monarchical system and is all but universal, is not the plan which I have just proposed, wherein the Vice President succeeds to the presidency, much more expedient? What if hereditary princes were chosen for merit and not by fate? What if, instead of wallowing in idleness and ignorance, they were put in charge of government administration? They would unquestionably be more enlightened monarchs, and they would contribute to the happiness of their peoples. Indeed, Legislators, monarchy, which rules the world, has won its claim for approval by means of the hereditary principle, which renders it stable, and by *unity*, which makes it strong. Hence, although a ruling prince is a spoiled child, cloistered in his palace, reared on adulation, and swayed by every passion, this other prince, whom I might venture to call the impossible man, is a ruler of men, for, by virtue of power firmly and constantly applied, he maintains order and willing subordination among the citizens. Do not forget, Gentlemen, that these great advantages are combined in a life-term presidential and vice presidential tenure and a vice presidential succession.

The judicial power that I propose enjoys an absolute independence not to be found in any other nation. The people nominate the candidates, and the legislature chooses the persons who are to serve in the courts. Unless the judicial powers emanate from this source, the judiciary cannot possibly be faithful to its obligation to safeguard individual rights. These rights, Legislators, are those that insure freedom, equality, and security—all guarantees of the social order. The real foundation of liberty resides in the civil and criminal codes, and the worst kind of tyranny is that which is exercised by the courts through that powerful instrument, law. As a rule, the executive is the custodian of public affairs, but the courts are the arbiters of private affairs —of the concerns of individuals. The judicial power determines the happiness or the unhappiness of the citizens. Whatever liberty and justice the Republic enjoys is dispensed by this power. At times, the political structure is of minor importance if the civil organization is perfect, that is, if the laws are rigorously enforced and held to be as inexorable as fate.

It was to be expected that, in keeping with the ideas of our time, we should prohibit the use of torture and confessions, and that we should shorten the procedures by which law suits are made lengthy by the intricate maze of appeals.

The territory of the Republic will be governed by prefects, governors, *corregidores*, justices of the peace, and *alcaldes*. I have been unable to elaborate upon the internal organization and the exact authority of each of these positions. It is my duty, nevertheless, to commend to the Congress rules and regulations governing the administration of departments and provinces. Bear in mind, Legislators, that nations are composed of cities and towns, and that the happiness of a nation stems from their well-being. You can never give too much attention to the proper administration of the provinces. This is the crux of the legislative art, yet it is neglected only too often.

I have divided the armed forces into four parts: regular army, fleet, national militia, and internal revenue patrol. The duty of the army is to protect the border. God grant that it will never have to turn its weapons upon our citizens! The national militia will suffice to preserve order at home. Bolivia has no extensive coastline and therefore has no need of a navy, although the day may come when we will have both.[1] The internal revenue patrol is in every way preferable to a civilian guard, which is not merely superfluous but evil. Accordingly, the Republic must garrison her borders with regular troops, using the revenue patrol to combat fraud at home.

I have felt that the Constitution of Bolivia may have to be amended at intervals, in accordance with the demands of changing world conditions. The amendment procedure has been provided for in terms that I consider best adapted to the subject.

The responsibility of government officials is set forth in the Bolivian Constitution in the most explicit terms. Without responsibility and restraint, the nation becomes a chaos. I should like most forcefully to urge upon you, the legislators, the enactment of strict and well-defined laws on this important matter. Everyone speaks of responsibility, but it receives lip service only. When there is no responsibility, Legislators, the judges and all the other officials, high and low, abuse their powers, as there is no rigid check on government servants. The citizens, consequently, are the victims of this abuse. I recommend a law that will provide for an annual check on every government employee.

The most perfect guarantees have been provided for the individual. *Civil liberty* is the one true freedom; the others are nominal, or they affect the citizens slightly. The inviolability of the individual—the true purpose of society and the source of all other safeguards—is guaranteed. *Property rights* will be covered by a civil code, which you should wisely draft in due time for the good of your fellow-citizens. I have left intact that law of laws—*equality*. Neglect it, and all rights and safeguards will vanish. We must make every sacrifice for it and, at its feet, cast the dishonored and infamous relics of slavery.

Legislators, slavery is the negation of all law, and any law which should perpetuate it would be a sacrilege. What justification can there be for its perpetuation? Examine this crime from every aspect and tell me if there is a single Bolivian so depraved as to wish to sanctify by law this shameless violation of human dignity. One man owned by another! A man reduced to a chattel! An image of God coupled to the yoke like a beast! Where are the legal claims of the enslavers of men? Guinea did not authorize them, for Africa, devastated by fratricidal struggles, spawned nothing but crime. Now that

---

[1] Bolivia, until the 1870's, possessed a coastal strip between Chile and Perú (ed.).

the remnants of those African tribes have been transplanted here, what law or power has jurisdiction to sanction these victims' becoming the slaves of masters? To transmit, to ignore, to perpetuate this criminal breeder of torture would be a most detestable outrage. To establish a principle of ownership based upon a heinous dereliction cannot be conceived unless the very elements of law and right are distorted and all our concepts of men's obligations perverted beyond recognition. No one can violate the sacred doctrine of *equality*. And can slavery exist where equality reigns supreme? Such contradictions impugn our sense of reason even more than our sense of justice. We would be better entitled madmen than tyrants.

If there were no divine Protector of innocence and freedom, I should prefer the life of a great-hearted lion, lording it in the wilderness and the forests, to that of a captive in the keep of an infamous tyrant, a party to his crimes, provoking the wrath of Heaven. But no! God has willed freedom to man, who protects it in order to exercise the divine faculty of *free will*.

Legislators, I shall mention one item which my conscience has compelled me to omit. A political constitution should not prescribe any particular religion, for, according to the best doctrines, fundamental laws guarantee political and civil rights, and, since religion has no bearing upon these rights, it is by nature indefinable in the social organization, because it lies in the moral and intellectual sphere. Religion governs man in his home, within his own walls, within himself. Religion alone is entitled to examine a man's innermost conscience. Laws, on the contrary, deal with surface things; they are applicable outside the home of a citizen. If we apply these criteria, how can a state rule the conscience of its subjects, enforce the observance of religious laws, and mete out rewards and punishments, when the tribunals are in Heaven and God is the judge? Only the Inquisition could presume to do their work on earth. Would you bring back the Inquisition with its burnings at the stake?

Religion is the law of conscience. Any law that imposes it negates it, because to apply compulsion to conscience is to destroy the value of faith, which is the very essence of religion. The sacred precepts and doctrines are useful, enlightening, and spiritually nourishing. We should all avow them, but the obligation is moral rather than political.

On the other hand, what are the religious rights of man on earth? These rights reside in Heaven where there is a tribunal that rewards merit and dispenses justice according to the code laid down by the great Lawgiver. As all this is within divine jurisdiction, it would seem to me, at first sight, to be sacrilegious and profane for us to interfere with the Commandments of the Lord by enactments of our own. Prescribing religion is therefore not the task of the legislator, who, for any infractions, must provide penalties, not mere exhortations. Where there are no temporal punishments or judges to apply them, the law ceases to be law.

The moral development of man is the legislator's first concern. Once such a growth has been attained, man bases his morality upon the truths so revealed and acknowledges religion *de facto* and all the more effectively for having come to it by personal experience. Moreover, heads of families cannot neglect their religious obligations to their children. The spiritual pastors are obliged to teach the Gospel of Heaven. The example of all the true disciples of Christ is the most eloquent teacher of his divine doctrine. But doctrine cannot be commanded, nor is one who commands a teacher, for force can play no part in the giving of spiritual counsel. God and his ministers are the authorities on religion, and religion exerts its influence solely through spiritual means and bodies, never through instruments of the nation's body politic, which serves only to direct public energies toward purely temporal ends.

Legislators, as you now proclaim the new Bolivian nation, what noble, generous, and elevated thoughts must inspire you! The admission of a new state into the community of nations is just cause for man's rejoicing, for it augments the great family of nations. What a joy it is then to its founders, and to me, to see myself likened to the most renowned of the ancients—the father of the Eternal City. This honor rightly belongs to the creators of nations, who, as their very first benefactors, truly deserve the rewards of immortality. Similarly the honor done me is immortal, and it has the added factor of being gratuitous because it is undeserved. Where is the Republic, where is the city that I have founded? Your magnanimity in giving my name to a nation has far outdone any services I may have rendered, for it is infinitely superior to the service of any one man.

My embarrassment increases as I contemplate the magnitude of your reward, for even if I had contributed the talents and virtues, indeed the genius, of the greatest heroes, I should still be unworthy to give the name you have desired to take—my own! Shall I express gratitude, when gratitude alone can never express, however feebly, the emotion stirred within me by your kindness, which, like that of God himself, is infinite! Yes! God alone had sovereign power to call this land Bolivia. And what does Bolivia signify? A boundless love of liberty, and, after you had received it, you, in your enthusiasm, could conceive of nothing equal to it in value. When, carried away by the immensity of your joy, you could find no adequate way to express the sweep of your emotions, you put your own name aside and adopted mine for all time to come. This act, which is without parallel in all history, is especially so in view of the sublime disinterestedness which inspired it. Your deed shall demonstrate to the ages that as yet exist only in the infinite years of the future how strongly you cherished your right—the right to exercise political virtue, to acquire sublime talents, and to know the satisfaction of being men. Your deed, I repeat, shall prove that you were indeed fit to receive that great heavenly benediction—*the Sovereignty of the People*—the sole legitimate authority of any nation.

Legislators, happy are you who preside over the destinies of a republic that at birth was crowned with the laurels of Ayacucho, a republic destined to enduring life under benign laws which, in the calm that has followed the fearful tempest of war, shall be dictated by your wisdom.

BOLÍVAR

---

252. To F[rancisco] de P[aula] Santander, Vice President of Colombia

[*Original*]

Lima, May 30, 1826.

My dear General:

After a great deal of thought concerning the affairs of the day, I have decided to dispatch Colonel O'Leary to bring you these papers, which, though they are of little immediate importance, may prove to be of great value in the future.

My purpose in sending O'Leary is to enable him to tell you at length whatever you care to know about Perú, Bolivia, Chile and Buenos Aires, the army, and myself. As soon as you have been fully and well informed, O'Leary is to continue to Caracas in order to see

General Páez on my behalf and to persuade him to do nothing in violation of his oath respecting the matter now pending in Congress as a result of the Caracas incident.[1] You may give him any message you please for Páez and in whatever manner may seem advisable. I have sensed that this is an affair of major importance, and I have therefore decided to inform you in this fashion. O'Leary will report to you fully concerning the matter.

Your vice presidency and my reëlection constitute two additional reasons that have made me dispatch O'Leary. In the present circumstances your continuance in office is the best thing that we could have hoped for. With you at the head of the government, I can devote myself to the affairs of the south and later I can proceed to Venezuela and remain there a year or two to set those men, or, rather, those complex affairs, in order. But, during the four years to come, I must not act as president. Otherwise, the year 1831 will mark the outbreak of a long-overdue tempest. I should like you to be elected president, so that, on completion of your term, I would be eligible for reëlection to that office. If, in violation of the law, I am reëlected for another term, the respect due the majesty of the law will be impaired, and we will thereby cause a real revolution. If I am not reelected later, I am certain that the question of a new president and the revision of the Constitution will bring on a crisis in the Republic. For this reason, I want our friends to make certain that the resignation which I shall submit to the new legislature is accepted. In this way the public interest will coincide with my private wishes. I am very much in need of a rest so that I can return to work in earnest during the years to come. Otherwise, I shall have no strength left for the future, and my first step will be to leave Colombia in order to breathe more easily. I must on no account hold the command during the next four years, as I intend to remain in the south until I receive permission from Congress to go to Venezuela. Once in Venezuela, I shall have a thousand excuses for not going to Bogotá. As my services will, in any case, not be available, I disqualify myself now for the future. I wish you would use these arguments in a manner most likely to accomplish the purpose I have in mind.

---

[1] Páez, in Venezuela, had called out the militia to put down various roving bands of brigands. The civil governor of Venezuela refused to acknowledge the order and complained to the government in Bogotá that Páez had exceeded his authority in drafting the militia, whereupon the Congress accused him of violating the Constitution and ordered him to Bogotá for trial—such was the beginning of the downfall of the Republic of Colombia (ed.).

As the President of the Senate has summoned me to take the oath on January 2, I intend to obey; hence, I shall leave here in August, to go to Guayaquil. I shall remain there for the rest of the year so that I can tell Congress that I did not remain outside the country after they had summoned me, but that I cannot accept the presidency because I have held command not only for the maximum of eight years that the Constitution provides, but for fifteen—and I shall add many other things as well.

Within the next three months we shall send the *Pichinchà* battalion to the Isthmus, for passage to Venezuela. It will consist of a thousand regulars, and it is the finest battalion in the south. Later, another body of one thousand regulars will follow the same route to the same destination. These troop movements will take place at intervals of three months—I do not intend to go to Venezuela until I have at least three thousand men there from the army of the south. I shall endeavor to see that they are well provided for, since the financial chaos will, in large measure, be remedied if the Congress grants me as much authority in the north as it gave me in the south. You can rest assured that this is an urgent necessity if a thousand abuses and irregularities are to be corrected.

I shall not inform you of the new ecclesiastical program because we have not yet submitted it to the government of Perú for decision. It awaits General Santa Cruz, who is more liberal minded than the President now in office.

The Republic of Bolivia has been recognized by Perú. I have forwarded to the [Bolivian] Congress the draft Constitution that it requested, together with an address in which I explain it.[1] I am also sending a copy to you to have printed in the finest possible format, and I ask you to place it in the hands of a person of some training who will take pains with the style and proofreading. In Caracas they can make another printing for circulation throughout Venezuela. It may serve to eliminate the monarchical ideas that have recently been advanced there. My proposed Constitution reconciles the extremes. In it the federalists will find their aims largely realized, the monarchists will recognize an enduring, sound, and strong government, while the democrats will observe that, more than anything else, equality has been preserved. My address contains some vigorous thoughts, for I felt that the circumstances so required. Those who are intolerant and those who love slavery will read my speech with horror, but I was

---

[1] See Doc. 251 (ed.).

obliged to speak in this manner because I think I am in the right and because good policy, in this instance, is backed by truth. I wish that some of our good friends would publish articles in the newspapers stressing the wisdom they find in my proposed Constitution. Many people have told me it could be adopted in Perú after a few modifications demanded by local conditions have been made. May God grant that some features of my draft Constitution will be incorporated later in our Colombian Constitution!

O'Leary has orders to return to Bogotá to meet me there in January, although I very much doubt that I can be in the capital by that time.

General Sucre will remain in command in Bolivia for two or three years. General Santa Cruz will head the [Peruvian] Council of Government. Here in Perú everything is still extremely insecure, as essential yet hazardous political processes have yet to be experienced. For one thing, a new executive must be chosen by popular vote, and a new constitution must be framed and then submitted to a popular referendum. I do not know how they will meet these tremendous issues, and I greatly fear that serious disturbances will occur.

The negotiations for a new loan being made by Perú's envoys in England are faring badly. The envoys report that they cannot hope to obtain the loan without granting a tremendous discount. The government has told them to contract for only a million pounds sterling to provide for payment to Colombia and to our Colombian army, which has not been paid in full, but they are not to grant a large discount; instead, they should seek a contract with one of the larger banking houses where the discount will be smaller in amount. This news will be very disappointing to you. You could transfer the claim to this million to London as a lien on the new Peruvian loan, so that those charged with its collection can negotiate directly for the said million with the Peruvian representatives. In case there should be some small loss as between the amount actually received and the million contracted for, the difference would probably be paid by the government of Perú or at the worst it would have to be borne by Colombia. It would not amount to much in any case. I shall advise Armero to take this up with the Foreign Minister of Perú, so that the Peruvian envoys [in London] will be authorized to treat with the minister from Colombia respecting this matter. All this must be tentative as anything can happen, for it is not impossible that the new loan will have been obtained by the time the instructions reach London; hence, the funds may be available to pay the million.

On the subject of seamen, it is useless to hope for any from Perú, as there are none. The Peruvian government has had to engage British sailors for its vessels. There is no coastwise traffic because there are no native mariners, and, as a result, foreigners engage in this commerce illegally. The few that might be obtained in Payta would desert on the Isthmus before taking ship at Portobelo. To keep them confined as far as Cartagena would be denounced as an outrage, while by the payment of one ounce per head we can avoid this scandal and engage seamen in the Antilles.

Illingworth is leaving for Colombia. He will take with him several lesser officers whom he trusts implicitly. I repeat that Illingworth is the most capable seafaring man we have.

Gual has written me from Panamá, and his entire letter is concerned with the urgent necessity of our speeding the settlement of the boundaries between Perú and Colombia. He is of the opinion that, to bring the matter to a conclusion, we should cede the province of Loja to Perú. I have answered him that I do not share his views, nor must we relinquish Mojos or Bracamoros, provinces that we should retain because they are ours and because they are not a desolate waste like those in the Marañón River area. I have told him that a line could be drawn from Jaén to the Marañón and that this river could serve as a boundary between the two waste areas. The colonial boundaries between the provinces of Quito and Perú should be taken as our national borders. I believe, therefore, that Colombia should authorize Heres to commence negotiations on this basis, which can and, indeed, should be accepted, since it is in the best interests of both parties. I am certain that Heres will perform his mission successfully, for, in addition to the justice of the claim, his friendship with General Santa Cruz, who is to be the President of the Council of Government, should facilitate matters and enable him to obtain a favorable result that would please Gual, without injuring our interests by the sacrifice of Loja. There is always time enough to take a loss, especially when there is no reason for it.

I am your most affectionate friend and servant,

BOLÍVAR

P.S. Let me commend very especially to you my aide-de-camp O'Leary. His pay is due him, and it will be a favor to me if you could see that he receives it. I want to say the same for poor López Aldana. His son has served us well, very well indeed.

253. To [MANUEL PÉREZ DE TUDELA], PERUVIAN DELEGATE
   TO THE CONGRESS OF PANAMÁ

[Draft]

[Magdalena, May, 1826]

From your letter of April 11, I was very pleased to learn of your safe arrival at the Isthmus of Panamá, and I am indeed glad you were so delighted with the welcome Gual and Briceño extended to you. I am sure that the most perfect cordiality will always exist between you and these gentlemen as you are all animated by the same desire and you can have but a single unified purpose.

Everything you say of the federation appears excellent to me, and I concur in the decision to await the arrival of the Mexican delegates. Regarding commercial treaties and the like, the Council of Government, so I have been informed, is forwarding you its latest instructions, which I am sure will enable you to proceed with less indecision and greater clarity of purpose. Whatever those instructions may be, let me assure you I have had no hand in them whatsoever, since it did not seem proper that I should in any way influence the instructions the government of Perú should choose to give its delegates, inasmuch as delegates of Colombia will also attend the assembly. This is a conviction to which I firmly adhere. I am telling Vidaurre the same thing, and I am certain that the good judgment and understanding of all the delegates will approve a decision that can in no way affect the utility of the plan itself.

I believe that you will find Vidaurre's friendship valuable. He is an exceptional man, but his interest is dependent upon his enthusiasm and patriotism. In addition, he is a hard worker and a fine friend. I should be delighted to hear that you entertain for each other the very sentiments with which I assure you I remain your devoted friend,

254. To General Antonio José de Sucre

[Draft]

Magdalena, June 3, 1826.

My dear General:

I neglected to inform you through Wilson that General Santander, by letter of March 6, told me that the [Colombian] Congress was discussing whether or not to permit you to remain in Bolivia and to place 2,000 men at that country's disposal. Santander added that he believes both requests will be granted so that by the time the envoy Olañeta arrives [in Bogotá] this matter should have been decided. Now, therefore, is the moment for that envoy to depart to attend to this matter, which means so much to Bolivia, as it is essential to her welfare and interests and is, above all, an indispensable act of gratitude. I do not mean that Olañeta is necessarily the person who should go, as you may be able to use him in Bolivia to better purpose, but I want the envoy to Colombia to be a man of character and ability, able to establish the closest and best possible relations with Colombia.

Now that Bolivia has been recognized by the government of Perú, I believe her first duty is to send representatives to the Isthmus of Panamá, where they may represent their country and promote her interests. I am, therefore, of the opinion that Mendizábal should go to Panamá, taking his secretary to assist him in this new assignment, as his secretary appears to be a capable man already familiar in part with the affairs of his government. To enable these gentlemen to leave immediately, you can forward them their credentials and instructions by a mail service officer and send Mendizábal, at the Isthmus, the form in blank for appointing the secretary of the legation, this form to be filled out here, where a good Bolivian can surely be found to fill the post. In this regard, I have two things to recommend to you: First, the most appropriate instruction that can be given the Bolivian delegation to the Isthmus is that they should endeavor to identify their interests with those of the Colombian delegates, as the latter have been given the broadest and most liberal instructions. Tell your delegates to work as closely as possible with the Colombian; second, endeavor to send with the officer who takes the instructions whatever money the delegates may need to carry out their mission. It cannot be provided here because there is none, and the government is hard put to pay its creditors. If good negotiable drafts can be obtained, so much the better. In this, as in everything else, you will do as you think best, as any advice that I give is only intended to help you.

I have arranged for the *Pichincha* battalion to leave for Panamá in the next three months with a complement of about 1,000 regulars, the best to be had. All those entitled to pay will, of course, receive what is due them before they leave. I have written General La Fuente to this effect, and I trust that you for your part will coöperate fully in carrying out my wishes. The *Pichincha* battalion is bound for Venezuela, where it will serve admirably. Within six months, that is, three months after the *Pichincha* has left, the *Bogotá* battalion will follow, also destined for Venezuela. For this reason, I want the *Bogotá* battalion stationed in Cochabamba so that these men can accustom themselves to the hot coastal climate and forget the frosts of Potosí. The *Bogotá* will also have about 1,000 regulars, after the Venezuelans, Magdalenans, and Isthmians have been discharged and replaced with Peruvians from the rest of the division of which it is a part. You will realize, from all that I say, that my intention is to bring to Venezuela a body of troops foreign to all parties and to all troublemaking and to leave in the south only native Colombians who can render fine service here but who might do much harm there. As soon as the *Pichincha* and the *Bogotá* depart, you will be able to use the 1,500 Colombians who will remain at Arequipa under Sandes.

I am sending you my address in a very poorly printed edition, together with copies of the Constitution. I should like you to send many copies to Buenos Aires in order to determine its effect and to have the pleasure of hearing what the press will have to say. I feel sure they will find fault with it. Please put this material in the hands of someone who will have it reprinted in the best possible form and appearance.

O'Leary will definitely leave on Friday, taking my Constitution with him to Colombia. He has orders to see everyone, to talk with Páez, and to meet me in Bogotá to report on conditions in Venezuela.

As I told you in my last letter, I am set upon going to Colombia, not to assume the presidency, which I am fully resolved not to accept, but to sustain, as best I can, an edifice which in the very process of rising is about to collapse.

Before the *Bogotá* battalion leaves it must be paid in full with funds from Upper Perú, because Lower Perú has paid the troops which left Arequipa in full, including the amount that was owed them by Upper Perú; and it is only right that Upper Perú do the same for the *Bogotá* battalion, now that Perú has no funds after paying out such large sums for Bolivia's account, which have not been repaid and cannot be for quite some time.

The *Bogotá* battalion will go accompanied by a battalion of the same division that is to be stationed at Tacna, to replace the *Pichincha*. It will remain, as always, under your orders. The 1,500 men remaining in Arequipa will fully replace those lost by the departure of the two battalions, and you will continue to have a unified, well-organized division.

---

255. To F[rancisco] de P[aula] Santander, Vice President of Colombia

[*Original*]

Magdalena, June 7 and 8, 1826.

My dear General:

I have received with great pleasure the communications, dated March 23 to 28, brought me by Lieutenant Armero, although I was displeased to learn that you have been suffering from your *cólico*. I had already learned, through the mails and earlier still from Pando, of our reëlection. I have ordered the publication of these documents together with my reply to you. I will not accept the presidency. I must not, I cannot, I will not. I am weary of office and of many other things. I was not meant to be a president, but a soldier. I beg you to show this letter to anyone who cares to read it.

If the gentlemen of the Congress want to compel Páez to come to Bogotá and he refuses, his nonsense is no fault of mine.

If the army is resentful because it is badly treated and paid with ingratitude, it is no fault of mine.

If the people of color rise and spread havoc because the government is not strong and the madness of all the others leads them to take matters into their own hands, it is no fault of mine.

If Páez and Padilla are being opposed without the presence of a force capable of subduing them, it is no fault of mine. These two men have the elements of their power in their blood; therefore, it is useless for me to oppose them because my own blood means nothing to the people.

I shall leave here for Colombia in order to resign this office, and

I am fully resolved to accept no other. For governing in conformity with the law, you are a better man than I, and for governing without laws any tyrant will suffice. It is without a doubt glorious to serve one's country and to preserve her existence in battle, but it is altogether odious to hold office when one's own fellow-citizens are his enemies and the people at large appear to be the victims. I have sacrificed everything for my country and her freedom; but I cannot sacrifice the noble rôle of freeman and the exalted title of Liberator. To save my country I have had to be a Brutus, but to restrain her in civil war I should have to be a Sulla. This rôle does not suit me; I should, instead, prefer to lose everything, including life itself.

Your message to the Congress is what it should have been. You have been subjected to too much abuse not to have defended yourself.

You are right, in saying that you wish to see me, to regret the fact that I must leave the south. It is only too true that the entire structure here will collapse when I leave for Colombia.

I want to thank you for the aid accorded Bolivia and for the permission granted Sucre.

We are in a very embarrassing situation as regards the Congress of Panamá. Delegates have arrived from various countries, but the Mexican delegates have yet to appear. The delegates from Bolivia will set out shortly. They are now here awaiting only the credentials and instructions they are to receive from General Sucre.

General Valero is a man not to be trusted either by you or by the government. Here he earned a very bad reputation through his despicable behavior, and lately he has organized a number of lodges that are giving us trouble. He is altogether unscrupulous—a man capable of serving any flag or government. He does not hesitate to recommend any riffraff, as he did recently in the case of a scoundrel who came here posing as a relative of yours, an aide-de-camp of mine, and a native of wherever you please. I have ordered him to leave the country—such is the type of man that Valero has recommended.

The 8th.—I have just received the post of April 6, with a letter from you of the same date, to which I now reply.

What you tell me of Morales and the Havana expedition, we learned some days ago by way of Panamá, and I have already given all the necessary orders for the *Pichincha* battalion to leave Arica in August with about 1,000 picked men, to be followed by the *Bogotá* battalion, similarly composed. These two battalions, together with the *Vargas,* which must by now be at the Isthmus, are the forces that made up the Lara division, which you may use, as you have suggested, for the defense of Venezuela.

I am glad you did not suffer the disappointment to which you refer.

I greatly regret the death of the widow of Camilo Torres, and I have noted what you mention regarding the other three widows. We shall arrange all this when I get to Colombia, bearing in mind that my intention is to give part of the pension to the children of Torres, a distinguished man to whom I am greatly indebted.

At the moment I have no means of assisting Rosario. I pay out annually fifteen thousand *pesos* in pensions to various persons; and, as I no longer expect to receive the President's salary, I greatly fear the pensions must end. The million from Perú will prove a mirage. I am afraid Colombia is going to suffer seriously from the Páez affair and as a result there will be no money for anyone.

I am your devoted

BOLÍVAR

---

256. To General Agustín Gamarra

[Paz Soldán, *Historia del Perú Independiente*, II, 74]

Magdalena, June 30, 1826.

My esteemed General:

Dr. Torres is about to undertake the administration of the diocese in your department, having been appointed by Orihuela to take charge during his absence. Dr. Torres is a churchman especially noted for his high principles and abilities, for he has a broad knowledge of the fine arts and sciences. He is a particular friend of mine, and he earnestly desires to contribute to the welfare of Perú by strengthening her regime and improving her institutions. Imbued with these sentiments, he is bound to be of great help to you in your department. He has my express instructions to coöperate with you in all that has to do with religion and to bring the civil authority into complete harmony with the ecclesiastic, by inducing the curates and other clerics and agents of the church to lend their positive support to the civil establishment, and by establishing a complete understanding between them and yourself, placating also those who may have had their differences with you. Since Dr. Torres is as discreet as he is affable, he is eminently fitted to accomplish these objectives, which I greatly desire to see realized, for, in Perú's present condition, only the closest coöperation among all public officials can create a solid front capable of withstanding the large number who seek to create disorder and anarchy for motives of personal ambition. I recommend that you listen to Dr. Torres' suggestions, for he is thoroughly versed in my ideas as to how to preserve the work which has entailed so many sacrifices. Let us not quarrel with the churchmen, as they can always call religion to their aid and induce others to make common cause with them. Misunderstandings with them are always futile; friendly relations with them are always beneficial. They do their persuading in secret and manage men's consciences; whoever possesses these weapons is certain of victory.

General Santa Cruz is to remain here as President of the Council of Government, surrounded by men of especial merit, by virtue of their integrity, intellect, and excellent reputation. I have been very pleased to note that his selection for this high office has been accorded widespread approval. The prefects, and especially General La Fuente, are greatly pleased; all will work together earnestly to preserve the order that has been established and to further the progress of the government. Santa Cruz has spoken to me at great length about you, in the most cordial manner. He has the best of intentions, and he is relying on your active coöperation to maintain everything, as this is the duty of everyone and it is in the interest of all concerned. I have explicitly instructed Dr. Torres to tell you his personal thoughts and desires pertaining to what he expects of you in administering that important department. I insist, my dear General, and I shall always insist, on the necessity of all authorities working in perfect harmony and in close coördination, while remaining properly subordinated to the head of the government. The slightest vacillation, the smallest dissension in a new-born state, can result in its ruin. There is enchantment in the prospect of a great people being governed by authorities who are properly coördinated, with each attending to his particular functions and all moved by a strong love of their country. Such a nation becomes, in time, as firm and unshakable as a rock. Perú can achieve that happy state without further sacrifices only if the officials will occasionally disregard petty interests and keep their eyes upon the one great goal: the preservation of the Republic.

The Council of Government has ordered reprints made of the proposed constitution of Perú for the purpose of supplying them to the prefects, for the latter to distribute among the electoral colleges. A carefully worded statement, prepared by the Minister of the Interior, is to accompany each reprint. This, my dear General, is a task that must be executed with the greatest skill and understanding, for its outcome is of major importance. It can prove to be of enduring service to the Republic and must, therefore, be managed by you and Dr. Torres in perfect accord, so as to obtain a favorable result. You must so obligate yourselves to the electoral colleges in your department that they will approve the draft of the Constitution in its entirety. If there is any article to which they object, let this objection be reserved for discussion or change at the next Constitutional Congress. If complete approval by all the electoral colleges cannot be obtained, endeavor to procure its adoption by the colleges by leaving only one debatable article or another for the next Congress. Once the draft is approved by the colleges, the fundamental law of the land stands ratified. We thereupon will avoid the turmoil of a constituent assembly, as there will be no further occasion for convening it, as the Constitutional Congresses cannot alter the essentials of the Fundamental Law which the people have ratified in the electoral assemblies. Think back upon all the evils that have been created in new republics by constituent assemblies—the perils to which they have exposed their nations, the clashes of angry passions, the outbursts of hatred, the conflicting interests and the vengeance then taken by an absolute power—and you will realize how right I am in urging you to see that the colleges in your department adopt the Constitution of Perú that is to be submitted for their approval. I am certain that, should this not be accomplished, and should Perú have to pass through the terrible crisis of a second constituent assembly, the Republic will irremediably split asunder and the efforts of all these many years will be destroyed forever.

In order to take no chances in a matter of such importance, I feel that you should begin far in advance to test public opinion and to influence it so adroitly as to be certain of producing the result that we have in view.

Colombia, which appeared beyond the reach of changes that could appreciably alter the course of her government, has just received a severe blow from which she will not easily recover. Congress has upheld an accusation made against General Páez upon trivial grounds and has instructed the executive to relieve him of the military command of Venezuela and to order him to appear in Bogotá. General Páez has disobeyed this order. Moreover, he has retained his military command, and the municipality of Valencia has named him Director of War in Venezuela. This incident, so shameful and disastrous in its implications for Colombia, is a lesson to us all on the dangers of deliberative bodies wherever peace and order are not yet perfectly established. I shall have to proceed to Colombia to determine whether or not I can restore the order which has been disrupted, and to try and save her from the danger that threatens.

Good-bye, my dear General. Accept the expression of the sincere affection with which I am your most devoted friend,

BOLÍVAR

---

257. CIRCULAR OF THE PERUVIAN COUNCIL OF GOVERNMENT
TO THE PREFECTS OF THE DEPARTMENTS

[*Contemporary copy*]

Lima, July 1, 1826.

Mr. Prefect:

The critical and extraordinary situation in which the Republic finds itself has been the constant object of the most serious thought on the part of the Liberator, into whose hands Supreme Power was placed, and of the Council of Government, to whom His Excellency has seen fit to delegate it. It is a fact that Perú is still without a set of fundamental laws to guarantee her future tranquility and to serve as the basis for her desired prosperity. As the Liberator and the Council are animated by a sincere love for this unhappy country, so deserving of a better fate; as they have a deep sense of sanctity for the duties they have assumed; as they fear to leave to the uncertain combinations of fortuitous events surrounding them or to the whims of headstrong and ambitious men the great task of uniting and stabilizing the elements that make up the nation following a period of horrible disorganization; and, finally, as they are impelled by the pressing need to provide for the immediate attainment of these high purposes, since men pass on but institutions remain, they now, therefore, do not hesitate to submit to Perú, after careful consideration, a proposed constitution which, by their order, I now have the honor to forward to you.

The Liberator and the Council of Government ask you, with the least possible delay, to convoke in your department the electoral colleges that recently elected the deputies to the Congress and to submit the proposed constitution for ratification to those bodies, which represent the will of the nation. Their verdict will decide the destiny of the Republic. The government and all who love order, tranquility, and the general good will anxiously await that verdict. We shall then know if we truly have a country; if the bitter days of disruption, of treachery and uncertainties have gone never to return; if we may harvest the fruit of the devastation, sacrifices, and horrors that we bore with such heroic fortitude; and if we may hope that, by presenting to the civilized world a proper appearance of order and dignity, we may be recognized as members of the great family of nations.

Impartial and disinterested Peruvians will admit that the time when our Constituent Congress met was not propitious to the successful completion of the arduous task it had before it. Then, a large part of the territory of the Republic was occupied by enemy hordes, political passions were raised to the height of frenzy, and the nation was divided into rival factions. The legislators, unfortunately, were thus far from enjoying that calm and quiet so indispensable for reflection and the successful accomplishment of their exalted task. Their efforts, which were inspired without question by upright and patriotic intentions, were foredoomed to failure by the difficulties under which they labored, by the inexperience to which the artful policy of our former overlords had condemned us, by their pursuit of the illusion of utter perfection, which is entirely unattainable in human affairs, and by their suspicion of the executive power, which was a natural thing in those who for years had suffered its inevitable abuses and who, by a sort of fatal instinct, were inclined to the opposite and equally pernicious extreme.

The result is only too notorious. The Constitution was enthusiastically adopted, and it can be said that this act was the beginning and the end of its existence. Its single chamber, without counterpoise or check, and without responsibility, constituted, for observant

men and sincere patriots, a dangerous source of the worst possible oppression, disturbances, and upheavals. The fears aroused by this
unwise arrangement, already condemned by the fact that it had resulted in disaster in other countries, were all the more swiftly realized
on viewing the mere shadow of a government which the Constitution
had created, the incapacity of the Senate, the independence of action
granted to the so-called municipal power in imitation of the French
Assembly that had previously sowed that seed of disaster in the heart
of France—these were just so many factors in rendering the Constitution totally impracticable, in exciting disorder, and in discrediting
the noble cause of independence.

The poorly balanced branches of government were soon engaged
in a dismal struggle for supremacy. The vestiges of slavery, which
were in conflict with the illusions of unbridled liberty, led to un-
restrained violence, ambitious aspirations, and criminal betrayals. The
classes that thought themselves mistreated opposed the progress of
the new administration by the force of their inertia or by their well-
concealed machinations. The excesses of local authorities, unchecked
by a strong central power, angered the people, who cared not for
empty theory but for the practical benefits which the laws provide.
Disorder, disobedience, and decay infected every branch of the public administration. And when, as was to be expected, these evils led,
in turn, to sedition and treachery, the Constituent Congress itself,
disgraced by factional disputes, was obliged to veil the profaned
image of freedom, destroy its own handiwork, and create the tremendous power of a dictatorship, under which things and persons alike
are silenced.

Only a miracle of Providence, which watches over our country,
saved us from the abyss to which our errors had brought us. If the
victories of Junín and Ayacucho freed us from the heavy yoke of the
descendants of Pizarro and Almagro, the unparalleled moderation of
the Dictator spared us from what otherwise appeared inevitable. We
have had the fortunate experience, one without parallel in the history of nations, of witnessing the use of absolute power to reëstablish the rule of law and to prepare the way for us to gain a rational
freedom—the goal of our desires and fondest hopes. But can this
precarious situation, this extraordinary order of things, be prolonged
without grave peril and injury? Can we idly trust to the caprices of
chance the task of organizing our ultimate political organization?
Or shall we permit certain unfortunate developments, which perhaps are not far distant, to enable anarchy again to raise its ugly

head? No! The Council of Government will not be driven to this crime for fear of the evil tongues of those who are corrupt and who thrive only in the shadow of discord. The government is aware that the generous heart of the Liberator is oppressed by the unlimited authority vested in him, and, following his example, the government desires to lay down that power delegated to it, as soon as its high aims can be accomplished, namely, the establishment of institutions that will place firm restraints upon despotism and anarchy, the two most cruel scourges known to man.

The political code which the Liberator has presented to the Congress of Bolivia is a work of transcendent genius, destined to mark an epoch in the history of civilized nations. It had hitherto seemed impossible to reconcile the granting of the highest possible degree of freedom and influence to the citizen with the existence of a strong executive power that would be capable of discharging its important duties without damaging restrictions, yet also lacking the ready means for usurping power, while at the same time providing a legislative branch so well constituted in all its parts that its operation would afford not even the slightest possibility of oligarchic tyranny, of inconsiderate haste in the drafting of new laws, or of the paralyzing shocks and conflicts which are the reefs upon which popular assemblies have repeatedly foundered. The Council of Government could not, therefore, refrain from offering, for ratification by the nation, this signal work of mature wisdom, introducing slight modifications that the particular conditions existing in our country would appear to make necessary. Nor could the Council refrain from raising its voice on this solemn occasion, to exhort the people of Perú to accept this beneficent Constitution, which promises them many days of peace and happiness in the future.

The Council does not feel that it can justly be accused of inconsistency in its resolutions, if this order is compared with the decree of May 1 last. The census called for in Article I of that decree can and must be quickly taken by all prefects, by the time when the electoral colleges are convened for the sole purpose of examining the proposed constitution. It can, as provided in Article II, serve as the basis for the election of the representatives of the nation, in the event that the Constitution is ratified, as the Council most earnestly hopes it will be, in fulfillment of the laudable desires expressed in the memorial directed to the government this past April 21 by fifty-two of the deputies elected to the Congress.

The Council of Government offers to the Almighty the most fervent prayers that He may choose to enlighten the minds of the members of the electoral colleges during this most important crisis in Peruvian history. In their hands rests the fate not only of our own generation but of many yet to come. Whatever the outcome, the Council will have performed a sacred duty, and when its members return to the status of private citizens their consciences will be at rest and their hearts at ease in the grateful knowledge that they laid aside all personal ambition, all private interest, all unworthy considerations, in order to shield their country from the disasters that threaten her and to render her the most sublime service within man's gift—that of endowing her with strong and free institutions.

I transmit to you the views and instructions of the government for your information, and for their proper execution. They are to be given all the publicity possible. I have the honor to give you my best respects.

God keep you, etc.

José María Pando

258. To F[rancisco] de P[aula] Santander, Vice President of Colombia

[Original]

Magdalena, July 8, 1826.

My dear General:

Yesterday, I received your letter of May 6, and various newspapers and private communications that have kept me awake all night, not because they add anything to what I already know, but because they confirm my previous conviction that *all is lost*. Neither a general federation nor a local constitution can restrain these unruly slaves: particularly now that every one pursues his own ends.

I regard the Congress of the Isthmus as a theatrical play, and I view our laws as did Solon, who believed that laws only served to burden the weak without restraining the strong. While these thoughts keep passing through my mind, the newspaper writers proclaim that heroes are subject to the laws and that principles take precedence over men. What an ideology! This is to be the celestial land where laws personified will engage in combat in place of *heroes,* while *principles,* like the Fates, will direct affairs and govern man. Virgins and saints, angels and cherubin will be the citizens of this new paradise. *Bravo! Bravíssimo!* Let those legions of Milton march on to stem the course of Páez' insurrection, and, since principles govern rather than men, you and I are no longer needed in any capacity. This is the point I have wished for in this celebrated tragedy, a thousand times repeated through the centuries, yet ever new to the blind and the stupid, who observe nothing until they are themselves affected. What leaders!

General Páez has written me, under date of April 6, and he has sent me other letters which describe the threatening situation that confronts him. All this, it seems, is the work of two or three former slaves of Morillo, who are now their liberators' masters.

I am very much pleased that the Congress has been able to meet to enact measures in the present crisis. It can rely upon all those who are dependent upon me, but not upon me personally. I want no more civil wars. I have experienced four in fourteen years, and censure inevitably falls upon both the vanquished and the victor. I repeat, all is lost if Páez continues upon his path of insurrection, for, when any object is falsely based, the slightest mishap causes its downfall. He who falls is indeed lost. I do not care to be that person. I am weary of exercising this abominable discretionary power when I am convinced, to the very marrow of my bones, that our America can only be ruled through a well-managed; shrewd despotism. We are far from emulating the happy times of Athens and Rome, and we must not compare ourselves in any way to anything European. Our origins have been of the most unwholesome sort: All our antecedents are enveloped in the black cloak of crime. We are the abominable offspring of those raging beasts that came to America to waste her blood and to breed with their victims before sacrificing them. Later, the illegitimate offspring of these unions commingled with the offspring of slaves transplanted from Africa. With such racial mixtures and such a moral history, can we place laws above heroes and principles above men? Very well then, let these ideologically minded gentlemen govern and fight and we shall again witness the beautiful ideal of a Haiti and see a breed of new Robespierres become the worthy magistrates of this fearful liberty. I repeat: all is lost; and, since everything progresses in a manner counter to my ideas and opinions, let them manage without me. Should the government or the Congress summon me, I shall go to Colombia; then, from Guayaquil, I will proclaim, in solemn tones, what I have just stated in this letter.

I think that matters cannot possibly be reconstituted as they were before, as those who know only how to continue in the Spanish fashion will doubtless desire. No possible benefit would result from mere legal reforms. It might be said that we already have too many laws, especially laws modeled after those of the Spanish liberals. So it is, but what does this signify? Where is there an army of occupation to impose order? Africa?—we shall have more and more of Africa. I do not say this lightly, for anyone with a white skin who escapes will be fortunate. The sad part of it all is that the ideologists, who are the vilest and most cowardly of men, will be the last to perish. Long accustomed to the yoke, they will bear it patiently, though imposed by their own slaves. The masterminds of this tempest—Pérez, Michelena, de Francisco, and all those other wretches—will fan the first fires of the pyre that will consume our remains. Their one reward will be that they will go last. Never has the tocsin been sounded in vain; everyone hears it, and all are preparing for combat, friend and foe alike. As the legislators did the trumpeting, their call will not be ignored, as in Caracas, where the voice of the law has gone unheeded by the inhabitants and where, instead, whoever has conscientiously attempted to comply with it has suffered punishment—a crime worthy of that heavenly land!

I am sending you the papers from Bolivia that report what took place at the installation of the Congress. I have told General Sucre that the birth and existence of Bolivia is a hymn to wisdom. Most couples have happy weddings . . . but then . . . ! ! !

I know of the arrival of the French agent.

Revenga tells me that you are anxious for him to become Minister of Finance, a choice that I approve, though I feel that everything we do today is of no value whatsoever. In England the failure of Colombia's bankers is only one out of some six hundred similar bankruptcies.

I am your devoted friend,

BOLÍVAR

259. CIRCULAR LETTER TO PERSONS OF INFLUENCE IN COLOMBIA

[*Original*]

Lima, August 3, 1826.

Every section of Colombia has sounded, as if in unison, the cry for revision of the Constitution. Venezuela and Guayaquil demand it urgently; large numbers of influential and patriotic men have assured me that all Ecuador insists upon a change. Revision of the Fundamental Law, but not its elimination, appears today to be the earnest desire of the people. But after this first step, would not others follow, and still others in search of happiness, until we arrive at the very brink of a precipice? Experience, unfortunately, only confirms this truth. I shudder to think of the enormous quantities of powder that are ready to explode, and I shudder at the thought of the horrors that may envelop our country.

I have seriously reflected upon the situation in Colombia and upon the means of insuring the existence of the Republic, the rights of her citizens, a strongly constituted authority, stable institutions, all with the thought of affording the people a full measure of happiness and freedom and of giving the government the greatest possible vitality and strength, while avoiding disastrous upheavals that can only weaken us at home and discredit us abroad. This mature reflection has resulted in the views which will be made known to you by Citizen Antonio Leocadio Guzmán, who is thoroughly familiar with my way of thinking. Colombia is not alone in wanting reform. All the republics of South America desire it, for they are daily more aware of the weakness of their political structure and of the impossibility of strengthening it and advancing firmly along a road built upon quicksands. Experience has taught them, and at a heavy cost, how easily the inconsistencies to which improperly weighted bodies, having no firm base, are exposed. In vain have they sought salvation in weak institutions equipped with feeble internal parts. They long to see their sacrifices ended by the adoption of a vigorous, stable system that will impart its vitality to the whole of society.

I believe that now is the time to render Colombia a most important service and also to make it available to the republics of the south, who will welcome it with enthusiasm.

I contend that the draft Constitution I have submitted to Bolivia can become the keystone of union and stability for these governments.[1] This charter recognizes the popular will to a greater extent than any other, for it consecrates the sovereignty of the people by conferring upon the electoral bodies the direct exercise of the functions most essential to sovereignty. It renders the government strong and vigorous by means of life-term presidential tenure and vice presidential succession; hence, it avoids the upheavals, the factions, and the ambitions produced by frequent elections, as have recently occurred in Colombia. Its chambers, with their broad yet specific powers, restrain the President and the other members of the government from abusing their powers. These chambers, being the repositories of all that might tempt the ambitions of the citizens, strip the executive of the means of attracting a personal following, yet they keep the executive vigorous and effective in the important departments of war and the treasury. In no representative system of government can I discover so much popular freedom, so much direct participation of citizens in the exercise of sovereignty, or so vigorous an executive, as in this proposed constitution. In it are combined all the advantages of federalism, all the firmness of centralized government, all the stability of monarchical regimes. By means of it all interests are intertwined, and all rights and guarantees are assured.

BOLÍVAR

---

260. To General José Antonio Páez

[*Original*]

Lima, August 8, 1826.

My dear General:

Some months past you sent Guzmán to inform me of the state of affairs in Venezuela, and you yourself wrote me a splendid letter in which you, without reservation, stated what you thought. Since that time everything has progressed with an amazing rapidity, and the forces of evil have visibly increased. Sixteen years' accumulation of powder will produce the explosion that will, perhaps, wipe out our

[1] See Doc. 251 (ed.).

victories, the glory of our name, the happiness of the people, and the freedom of all. I feel that soon we shall be surrounded only by the ashes of all that we have accomplished.

Some members of Congress, paying their debt to freedom with black ingratitude, have endeavored to destroy their liberators. The impersonal zeal with which you have enforced the laws and maintained the public authority has been rewarded with defamation, and perhaps with punishment. The press, that self-appointed tribunal and instrument of calumny, has made light of the views and services of the most deserving patriots. It has, moreover, fostered the spirit of individualism, for, by preaching ill of everyone, it has destroyed the confidence of all.

The executive, guided by this artful tribunal and by the confused deliberations of our legislators, has pursued an illusive perfection. He has overwhelmed us with a welter of laws and institutions, good in themselves but at the moment wholly superfluous. The morale of the army has suffered more from our citizens than from our enemies. They have sought to humble the army, to make it as gentle as a lamb in the presence of its captives and as bloodthirsty as a lion toward its oppressors, thus demanding of it the impossible, the accomplishment of which would itself be disastrous. Amidst this chaos the provinces have drifted apart. Each has taken authority and power unto itself; each desires to be the center of the nation. We shall not speak of the democrats and fanatics, and we shall say nothing of the persons of color, for to enter the bottomless abyss of these problems is to bury reason therein as in the house of death. What can we expect of so violent, so frenzied a clash of passions, rights, demands, and principles? Chaos is less fearful than this terrible scene, and, though we turn our eyes from it, it will neither disappear nor cease to haunt us in all its terror. Believe me, my dear General, a great volcano lies at our feet, and its rumblings are not rhetorical; they are physical and very real. Nothing can persuade me that we will be able to overcome the prodigious number of difficulties that confront us. As if by a miracle, we attained a point of accidental equilibrium, like two wild ocean waves coming together at a given point during a calm that appears fixed though lasting but a moment. Mariners have actually seen this happen many times. I once represented that given point, and Venezuela and Cundinamarca the encountering waves, and the moment has just ended with the constitutional period of the first election. Now there will be no more calm, no waves, no meeting point to produce a miraculous period of peace. Everything will revert to the elements of creation, of primary matter. Yes, matter, I say, because everything will revert to nothing.

Consider, my dear General, who shall reconcile now all minds, who shall restrain the oppressed classes? Slavery will break its yoke, each shade of complexion will seek mastery, and the others will fight on to victory or death. The latent feelings of hatred among the various sections will break out anew, as does every violent force that is repressed. Every philosophy will struggle to dominate, every hand will seek to rule, and the most violent will wear the toga. Cries of sedition will resound in every sector. But what is most horrible of all is that every word I say is *true*. You will ask me, "What part shall we take? In what ark shall we find safety?" My reply is very simple: *Beware of the sea you are about to cross in a fragile bark with such an inexperienced pilot at the helm.* It is not vanity or any inner personal need or conviction that compels me to give this answer. It is nothing more than the lack of a better one. I feel that, were all Europe to try to lull our storms, it would scarcely be able to bring our calamities to a head. The Congress of Panamá, an organization that might have been magnificent if only it had been effective, is no different from that crazy Greek who sought to direct sailing vessels from a rock. Its power will be a shadow, and its decrees mere advice, no more.

They write me that many thinkers favor a prince under a federal constitution. But where is the prince and what political division of our land could produce harmony? All this is visionary and absurd. You will tell me that my poor delirium of a constitution is worth even less, and that it embodies every evil. I know this, but I must say something in the midst of so much conflict if only not to remain silent. Guzmán's memorandum points out a thousand virtues in my draft constitution. You will read it with admiration, and it would be very helpful if you were to be convinced by its eloquence and logic, because a spark of enthusiasm can serve to enliven the body politic. Guzmán will give you my ideas on this subject. I even wish that, with slight modifications, the Bolivian code could be adapted to small states embraced within a vast confederation. By applying the section that concerns the executive to the general government, and by apportioning the electoral power to the individual states, we might, perhaps, obtain more or less lasting benefits, depending on the spirit in which we would direct this labyrinth.

At the moment, the most sensible thing to do is to maintain vigorously the public authority, in order that it can use force to quell passions and check abuses, by means of the press, pulpits, and, if need be, bayonets. Theory and principles are good things in peaceful times, but when agitation is widespread the application of theories would be like trying to govern our passions by the rules of Heaven, which, perfect as they are, often have no relevance in actual practice.

In short, my dear General, Guzmán will tell you all that I have omitted here in my effort to avoid a lengthy statement in a paper that will remain immutable though the facts themselves should change a thousand times over.

One hundred days have passed since the first of the events we now deplore took place in Valencia,[1] and as yet we do not know what you have done or what has happened there. The country seems to be under a spell.

I confess to you frankly that I have very little hope of seeing order restored in Colombia, the more so as I find myself disillusioned with the turn of events and the desires of men. A real horror of rulership, if not of the world, has gripped me. I cannot visualize the remedy for such extensive and complicated evils. In my eyes the fate of Colombia was sealed the day that you were summoned by Congress.

Farewell, dear General. God give you the light to save that poor country from the fate that threatens it.

I am your devoted friend,

BOLÍVAR

P.S. After sealing this letter I had to open it in order to inform you that I have just heard that Urbaneja and Ibarra, commissioned by you to come and see me, have arrived at Payta, but that they have gone to Guayaquil, in the belief that I was there. They have written, informing me of the object of their mission, which is of such a nature that I am preparing to leave promptly for Guayaquil, where I had, in any case, been thinking of going before this communication reached me.

---

[1] See note 1, p. 607 (ed.).

261. J[osé] GABRIEL PÉREZ, SECRETARY-GENERAL,
TO [PEDRO GUAL AND GENERAL PEDRO BRICEÑO
MÉNDEZ], COLOMBIAN DELEGATES TO THE
CONGRESS OF PANAMÁ

[*Original*]

Lima, August 11, 1826.

Gentlemen:

The unusual efforts of Spain, in sending large contingents of
troops to Cuba and Puerto Rico; the draft and other active measures
directed to the same purpose; the vessels of war that she has fitted
out and which now give her a great superiority over our vessels in
the Caribbean, where her ships skirt our coasts and blockade our ports
and fortresses; the preparations that she continues to make in order
to increase her fleet; the well-founded fear that her land and sea
forces, already large, will be heavily reinforced; and the fact that
we may be invaded by expeditions stronger than that headed by
General Morillo—all these factors have caused His Excellency the
Liberator to ponder the means of taking immediate and adequate
measures to unite all our forces, not only to be in a position to offer
vigorous resistance, but to despoil the enemy of what he still holds
in America and even to attack him in Europe, in order, thereby, to
force him to sue for peace or render him incapable of launching fresh
invasions. His Excellency believes that this result can be obtained
if Mexico, Guatemala, and Colombia enter into a close alliance,
pooling their resources and working in concert, pursuant to the plan
I am authorized to place before you. The bases of this alliance would
be as follows:

1. To allow Spain a period of three or four months in which to
decide whether she prefers to continue the war or to make peace.

2. During that interval the fleet and army of the alliance would be
outfitted and assembled.

3. The army would consist of at least 25,000 men and the fleet of
thirty ships; namely, four ships of the line, eight heavy frigates, eight
light frigates, and the remainder, sloops, brigs, and schooners.

4. Each country would pay a stipulated amount for the maintenance of its contingent, making suitable provision to that end.

5. Each government would have command of its own contingent,
but in agreement with the others and within the framework of a
general plan.

6. The purpose of this plan would be, first, to defend any section of our coasts that is attacked by our enemies; second, to send an expedition against Havana and Puerto Rico; third, to attack Spain with a very large force after these islands have been taken provided that the Spanish government has still failed to make peace.

7. In any joint operation of naval and land forces, it may be agreed that the senior officer would be the commander in chief, but should Mexico and Guatemala find this arrangement unacceptable Colombia will freely relinquish command, either on land or on sea.

Guatemala and Colombia would furnish half the total forces of the army and navy and half the expenses, and Mexico the other half, as Mexico has twice the population and wealth of Colombia. Guatemala is less favored than Colombia, so that the advantage weighs on the side of Mexico, whose population exceeds that of the other two contracting republics by more than a million. The advantage, therefore, rests entirely with Mexico.

His Excellency is of the opinion that, although you gentlemen are not authorized by the executive to sign a treaty on these terms, you should at once propose and conclude it, always provided that the envoys of Mexico and Guatemala [to the Panamá Congress] agree. The magnitude of the peril, the threat of an early and powerful invasion, make it necessary that every possible means imaginable be adopted to consolidate our resources for resistance and victory. His Excellency believes that the present friendly attitude of Mexico and Guatemala should be turned to advantage before some circumstance alters or dispels it, leaving Colombia to carry a mighty and unequal struggle alone and unaided. Considering the circumstances, His Excellency is convinced that nothing is more important than the concluding of this pact. It will make us strong, and it will be the salvation of us all. Moreover, His Excellency, on arriving in Bogotá, will lay these and many other considerations before the government and the legislative body, presenting all the reasons that have led him to make these recommendations to you; and he trusts that they will meet with the approval of the nation's representatives and the government.

God keep you, etc.

J. GABRIEL PÉREZ

262. To [GENERAL ANTONIO JOSÉ DE SUCRE][1]

Lima, August 18, 1826.

[Draft]

Just as I was about to board ship, I was forced to postpone my voyage to Colombia for a few days owing to the latest developments that have taken place in this capital during the past two days. From the moment it was known that I planned to depart, the inhabitants of this city began to set in motion every possible design to compel me to change my mind. They begged me in every way imaginable not to abandon them at so critical a moment. I, however, resisted every plea, for the welfare of Colombia means more to me than anything else, despite the fact that the electoral college of the province of Lima, which was to ratify or reject the Constitution and designate the new president, had unanimously adopted the Bolivian Constitution and nominated me for the office of constitutional president. At the same time it appeared that similar sentiments prevailed throughout the Republic, and the other electoral colleges might be expected to follow the example of this province, if they have not already done so, as in the case of Tarma.

This development, which is of inestimable importance because of the good that it portends, has caused me to remain in this capital for several days in order not to lose such excellent prospects and to give these people a final proof of my gratitude for their gracious behavior during the past few days. I shall therefore wait for General Santa Cruz, and, meanwhile, we will know whether or not the Constitution has been ratified throughout the Republic. . . .

After this letter was written, we decided that the word *union* instead of *federation* should be used to describe the nation that is to be formed by the three great states of Bolivia, Perú, and Colombia under a single charter. I say *union*, lest later they demand a federal system, as occurred in Guayaquil. There the word federation was hardly mentioned before they were thinking in terms of the former type of small republic. I believe it will be necessary to make a drastic revision in Venezuela, one that will create a powerful and direct authority capable of restraining the factions and solving the most immediate problems. I am of the opinion, therefore, that the state of

---

[1] These two fragments are judged to be part of the same letter. Sucre's reply of September 20, 1826 (O'Leary, I, 390) indicates that the latter half was dated August 18 (comp. and ed.).

Venezuela should be equal in rank with Bolivia, and the remainder of Colombia with Perú. It would be highly desirable if Bolivia could prepare for such a union, not only with Perú, but also with Colombia. The plan would be somewhat as follows: each state would have a vice president, similar to the one provided for in the Bolivian Constitution; the president-at-large would have a vice president and ministers-at-large. To accomplish this, I think Santa Cruz should be named vice president for Bolivia while you should be the vice president-at-large. There should be no difficulty in finding a capable man for Perú. If you should refuse this office, I will also, and everything will collapse amidst terrifying confusion. All this would have to be settled by agreements between Bolivia and Perú and between Colombia and Perú. Accordingly, it would be well if Bolivia and Perú were to set the example. If, by chance, Perú's representative should have reached Chuquisaca (for he is reported lost at sea), I feel that negotiations on this basis should be initiated with him at once. Each state will meet its own debts and commitments, so that none will bear the burden of the others' obligations. Each state will have its own legislative body and will manage its own internal affairs, in agreement, however, with the other states. If you will propose this plan you will be rendering America a great service, and it will make me happy to know that Bolivia, the model nation, was the one to present it. My dear General, I commend this idea to you as it may well prove to be our path to salvation.

---

263. To GENERAL ANDRÉS DE SANTA CRUZ

[Copy]

Guayaquil, September 14, 1826.

My dear General:

At last I am here, and on the 18th I go to Quito in order to proceed immediately to Bogotá. I have received a great deal of news respecting the course of events in Venezuela, as you will see by the papers that I enclose. The misunderstanding between General Páez and General Santander is now so openly avowed that without my presence there is no hope of an amicable agreement. Fortunately, I am the focal point at which all parties, all interests, and all desires converge, no matter how opposed or however much at odds they may be. This confidence makes me the arbiter and mediator of their differences. I have, therefore, good hopes that everything will be satisfactorily arranged and that matters will revert to their normal course. I have received requests from all quarters of the Republic to return and calm the threatening storm, and all have placed their fate and destiny in my hands.

All the southern departments have acclaimed me Dictator, as you will note in the accompanying documents. Perhaps all of Colombia will do the same, in which case the path will have been cleared much more effectively than I had hoped.

I am writing Pando concerning my reasons for not wanting your government to ratify the treaties that were celebrated in Panamá until I can give you my final opinion. After I have studied the treaties carefully in Bogotá, and after your government has given its views, we can proceed with greater understanding without assuming obligations that may cause us embarrassment or injury. You will see my letter to Pando.

General Santander complains, in his latest communications that I have received here, that one entire post has been lost. I had previously received similar complaints from General Sucre. If the postal administration is not in the hands of persons definitely loyal to the government, incalculable harm can be done. You will fully appreciate what has to be accomplished to insure safety and speed for all government communications. This is always a vital matter and especially so in present circumstances. Accordingly, the administration of the mails in your capital must be placed in trustworthy hands.

My dear General, in Colombia I am about to enter a horrible labyrinth that will occupy all my time; hence, you must not feel slighted if I have little to say of the affairs of Perú except in reply to what you write me. The dictatorship to be entrusted to me will have to effect a complete reform, as our present organization constitutes an excess of power unwisely employed and therefore detrimental. You know that I abhor the details of administration, and that sedentary duties make me very tired. All this will depress me and make it difficult for me to write you and my other good friends as assiduously as I might wish. I trust that you will be so kind as to repeat this to these friends, in particular, Generals La Fuente, Gamarra, Pardo de Zela, Orbegoso, and Echenique, and that, when you write them, you will include a good word for me. The courtesy will please everyone.

I have seen Vidaurre who, as always, was most attentive. He is anxious to go to Perú to arrange the treaties, although he has been informed that the government desires to use his services in Colombia. Yesterday, while dining with a large group, he spoke beautifully on the union of Perú and Colombia. If he continues in this frame of mind he can be very useful. He has changed his tone considerably. I told him that he should work in conjunction with Pando on a treaty of agreement with Colombia. He replied that the idea was greatly to his liking and that he himself had thought of it more than three years ago, for which he called General Castillo to witness, and the General confirmed it. All this leads me to believe that, if Vidaurre is properly approached, he will act in concert with the government. I believe that Pando should be instructed to write him frequently, if he does not leave; and, if he goes to Perú, Pando should see him often in order to impress upon him his own sentiments and views. Vidaurre told me that he has a very high opinion of Pando, and I endeavored to strengthen this opinion, assuring him, among other things, that Pando is his friend.

I am your devoted

BOLÍVAR

---

264. To GENERAL PEDRO BRICEÑO MÉNDEZ, COLOMBIAN
    DELEGATE TO THE CONGRESS OF PANAMÁ

[Draft]

Guayaquil, September 14, 1826.

My dear Briceño:

I have arrived here at last, and I shall proceed promptly to Bogotá with the hope of quieting the disturbances in our country. Fortunately, I serve as a point of union, and all are willing to have me decide their conflicting interests and demands. I go, therefore, to serve them as willingly as ever.

The departments of Guayaquil, Ecuador, and Azuay have acclaimed me dictator, and Cauca and the others will do the same. This support will provide a firm basis for my operations and will afford me the means with which to organize all [the departments]. I have read here the treaties celebrated at Panamá, and I shall give you my frank opinion. The convention respecting troop contingents, in particular as regards the manner, circumstances, and numbers in which they are to be supplied, is futile and ineffective. It enables the enemy to act with a full knowledge of the facts and to invade with double the number of our forces. The convention does not regard an invasion as being serious unless it involves over 5,000 men, and aid will be rendered in such cases only. This condemns certain countries to inevitable occupation. A cavalry strength of one to ten is contrary to all the principles of the art of warfare. The provision dealing with the artillery is equally unsound. The transfer of the assembly to Mexico will bring it under the immediate influence, already disproportionate, of that power, as well as under the influence of the United States of North [America]. These and many other reasons, which I shall tell you verbally, compel me to ask that ratification of the treaties be deferred until I reach Bogotá and examine them calmly and in detail, together with you yourself and others. The Treaty of Union, League, and Confederation contains articles which might hamper the execution of certain projects that I have in mind, which I regard as being to our advantage and of great magnitude. I must, therefore, repeat and emphasize that the aforementioned treaties must not be ratified pending my arrival. I am so advising General Santander, and I want you to tell him also. Throughout the south there is unanimity of opinion, and I hope it will be possible to say the same for Colombia. Please see my proclamation.

---

265. To General Andrés de Santa Cruz, President
of the Peruvian Council of Government

[Original]

Popayán, October 26, 1826.

My dear General:

I have had the pleasure of receiving your letters, brought to me by Colonel Ibarra. The content of these letters is very gratifying, as I can see that the people of Perú honor me to excess, even after my departure. Every public demonstration has been virtually unanimous in my favor, and I am, therefore, inclined to entertain the liveliest hopes for harmony and good feeling. But I must tell you frankly that the Guisse affair[1] has given me the clue to the true spirit behind the apparent motives. As for myself, I find this incident sufficiently noteworthy and significant to again call your attention to the necessity of putting a stop to the enemies of Colombia and of my own person. There is no other way, my friend. Those gentlemen wish to come to power and to rise from their present state of dependency in which, unfortunately, they are placed for their own good and out of necessity. The will of the people is the governing law or force. We must give full sanction to the will of the majority. I might also say in passing that we have no interest whatever in opposing the force of the popular will if it is properly expressed. I have sufficient problems in my native land, which I have long neglected in order to serve other nations of America. Now that I see that the evils have become excessive and that Venezuela is the victim of my very achievements, I have no desire to merit the title of ingrate in the land that gave me birth. Moreover, I also have to consider how to reconcile the happiness of my friends in Perú with my own personal glory. You and the others will suffer the consequences if you undertake to support me against the wishes of the people, and I shall be thought ambitious and even a usurper of power, if I exert myself unduly in the service of countries other than Venezuela. I therefore release you and my good friends the Ministers from any obligation to abide by the opinions which certain well-meaning souls have been harboring. I counsel you and the others to take cognizance of the changes in popular sentiment, and, instead of sacrificing yourselves to the opposition, place yourselves at its head. Substitute a purely Peruvian program for continental American planning, that is, a program designed exclusively to promote the interests of Perú. I have nothing specific in mind for carrying out this thought, yet duty and my reputation compel me to recommend it. Believe me, my dear General, what I have just said is sincere and from the heart. No resentment, no spite has prompted me to make this recommendation—and *certainly not* the slightest shadow of suspicion that you gave Guisse your support. Never, never could

---

[1] Admiral Martin George Guisse of the Peruvian navy was tried and dismissed for political activity and extortion (ed.).

I do you so terrible, so abhorrent an injustice! Were you not worthy of my confidence, you would never for an instant have had it. It is precisely in recompense for your admirable loyalty that I have come to the aforementioned conclusion. I do not want, ever, any of my friends to be victims of their devotion or to suffer the unbearable stigma of being considered enemies of their country. Hence, let the Council of Government have a free hand. Let it follow its conscience, free and unimpeded. Let it hear the people's will and promptly obey it. Thereby the Council will have achieved my fondest hope— the well-being of Perú.

Be assured, General, of the sincerity of my intentions and of the genuineness with which I profess these sentiments. They are in absolute accord with my conscience, my understanding, and my good name. I intend to do all the good that I can for Venezuela without attempting anything further. It is for you and your friends, therefore, to do the same for Perú. Since I cannot be of direct help to them from afar, I should at least like to give them good advice and a good example to follow. One's native land must take preference, as its elements have shaped what we are. Our lives are no more than the essence of our own unhappy country. There we find those who have witnessed our birth, the authors of our being, and those who have given us our very souls in the process of education. There lie the tombs of our fathers, demanding that we provide them security and peace. Everything there recalls us to duty and excites in us tender sentiments and happy memories. Our own country is the scene of our days of innocence, our first loves, our first impressions, and all that has made us what we are today. Are there any greater sacred claims upon love and devotion? Yes, General, let each serve his native land as a paramount duty, and let all other things be secondary. If we do this, you and I shall have nothing to regret.

Colonel O'Leary has returned from Bogotá, after having seen General Páez in Venezuela. His commission did not produce the expected results, because O'Leary went to convey not my wishes but those of Santander, and instead of acting as mediator he turned conspirator. This is unfortunate, but I look to a final settlement that will satisfy every one.

When the Council of Government finds that the Colombian troops are an embarrassment or a hindrance to Perú, they should immediately be returned to Colombia, after every effort has been made to pay them fully or in part. If there is no money, they will have to go unpaid, since we came only to seek brotherhood and glory.

I beg you, my dear General, after you, together with Pando and Larrea, have carefully weighed the contents of this letter and reached a decision, to be so kind as to apprise General Sucre of the beginnings, progress, and outcome of this matter. Speak to him as your brother-in-arms of Pichincha, which is to say plainly and frankly. You are fully aware of the many problems that trouble General Sucre, for he is hemmed in on all sides by enemies. The decision not to recognize Bolivia would prove a boon to Sucre if men were sane and not mad, as this would signify a desire to reduce Bolivia to the level of La Plata and Chile—to anarchy. But you will soon see the effect of this treacherous threat. The ambitious will soon have a platform from which to denounce their liberators, for those demented ingrates choose to believe that our every good deed is inspired by self-interest and love of power. They will see whether or not their country will become that *inferno of mankind which is anarchy*, as a poet has said. In short, tell General Sucre all your thoughts and hopes, so that he can act accordingly.

Please show this letter to Pando and Larrea, the best men in all Perú; I would lay down my life to save them—a sacrifice, my dear General, which I would as willingly make for you in token of the candid and loyal friendship of your sincere and devoted friend,

                                                        BOLÍVAR

———————

266. To F[rancisco] de P[aula] Santander,
    Vice President of Colombia

[*Original*]

                                        Neiva, November 5, 1826.
My dear General:

On arriving here today, I found your letter of October 29, in which you informed me of General Bermúdez' removal and of the eastern provinces' having joined Páez. I cannot understand why such a thing should happen at a time when Páez is in such a difficult position, or why it has all occurred simultaneously under the leadership of three individuals in three different places. No doubt you, being in the capital, know more about it.

What you tell me of the cities of Mompox and Santa Marta does not surprise me, for when the people act they do not work in concert or agreement.

I wrote to you from Guayaquil, Quito, Ibarra, and Pasto. At Popayán I also prepared a letter which I later destroyed. I did the same with a reply that I wrote to the letter brought by O'Leary. I am now replying to the one brought by the officer you sent expressly to bring me news of my nephew Clemente and to advise me of the interception of the insurrectionists' correspondence with the Spaniards. Everything considered, facts and discoveries, incidents and accidents, causes and effects, I am confirmed in the fear that Colombia is lost forever; dictatorship or no dictatorship, Indians will be Indians; *llaneros, llaneros;* and lawyers, connivers. Believe me, my dear General, we cannot save this New World from the anarchy whose jaws are already open to devour it. We should accordingly let the people express their will, enforce it, and so have no one but themselves to blame for whatever ensues. I am not strong enough to rule a world, let alone govern it by metaphysical ideas and moral principles. The English are right in saying that we are incapable of loving liberty or of governing ourselves by laws. But no, what they say is meaningless, for we cannot possibly be Englishmen, who *alone* love liberty and law.

I do not choose, my dear General, to preside over the obsequies of Colombia. For this reason, I abide by my determination to resign the presidency and leave Colombia *without a moment's delay.* The year 1827 will be a thousand times worse than '14 and '15. Despotism harbors the seed of its own destruction, and anarchy contaminates the blood of the body politic for centuries. Páez' insurrection will have repercussions throughout this century, for his empire will be divided among *those that we know only too well.* Do not deceive yourself; this is beyond remedy, palatable or otherwise. This means complete and permanent ruin; and, while the people reach out to me as if by instinct, you gentlemen are trying to shy away from me with that nonsense in the *Gaceta* and insulting official communications addressed to those who have confidence in me. Very well. Try and save the country with a constitution and laws that have reduced Colombia to a Satan's palace which is aflame at every corner. I, for my part, shall attempt no such task. The first of January, I shall yield my power to the people, if the Congress is not going to meet on the second. I shall march to Venezuela and there give final proof of my devotion to my native land. If you and your administration should presume to go on with the Republic under the sanction of your laws, I, from this moment, renounce the presidency of Colombia forever, in order that she can be saved by those who know how to effect this miracle. Discuss this matter carefully with the gentlemen in the government, so that, the day I enter Bogotá, we will know who is to guide the destiny of the Republic, you or I. I repeat, the one use that I shall make of that power will be to return it to the people, that is, to the electoral colleges, for them to do with Colombia what they will. If my native land is to be buried alive, I will not bury her. The blame will fall on you, or on the Congress, which forced her to this extremity by its stupid, unfair treatment of Páez.

My dear General, I am eager to see you and the other gentlemen as soon as possible; we shall meet with tears in our eyes like two grief-stricken brothers at the deathbed of a dearly beloved mother.

A thousand regards to all those gentlemen who are my friends, and for yourself accept the heartfelt greeting of your devoted

BOLÍVAR

---

267. To [GEORGE CANNING], FOREIGN MINISTER OF GREAT BRITAIN

[*Draft*]

Bogotá, November 22, 1826.

Sir:

Mr. Campbell, His Britannic Majesty's chargé d'affaires, has been so kind as to place in my hands the letter which Your Excellency has been pleased to send me through the Minister Plenipotentiary, Mr. Cockburn, whom we, unfortunately, have not been able to greet in our capital. Permit me, Your Excellency, to express to you my signal satisfaction on receiving your esteemed letters and noting the lofty terms in which Your Excellency has chosen to compliment me upon the achievements of the army of my country and the status which Colombia has acquired by His Britannic Majesty's gracious recognition of her independence. Your Excellency is the principal recipient of our eternal gratitude for this salutary measure which is in the interest of both countries. I have fully expressed my views publicly respecting the debt that we owe His Britannic Majesty's government. My words were inspired by my gratitude.

Your Excellency's observations upon the necessity of preserving peace, once we have obtained it, and upon the good relations that we must establish with our neighbors in Brazil and other states are eminently wise. His Britannic Majesty, in maintaining his concilia- tory views respecting the state of belligerency between Brazil and Buenos Aires, has extended his good will to all the peoples of Amer- ica, for internecine warfare in the New World might result in prob- lems difficult of solution. Even before Your Excellency recognized my views, which favored tranquility for the new states, I had taken steps very much in conformity with British policy. I trust Your Ex- cellency has received evidence of these sentiments through Mr. Ricketts, your Consul General at Lima. I expressed myself with con- siderable confidence respecting the affairs of Brazil and Buenos Aires, for I feared that the events in the Río de la Plata might spread to Bolivia and Perú. I assuredly did not fear the type of order that the Imperial Government of Brazil would provide that country, as the tendency of a republic is toward anarchy, which I regard as tyranny gone mad. His Britannic Majesty's government may therefore be well assured that I am entirely in accord with the spirit of Your Excel- lency's esteemed letter of May 20.

Grant me license, Sir, to congratulate myself upon receiving from the guardian of Europe's freedom a document that I shall treasure in the archives of my glory. And should Your Excellency wish to con- tinue to so honor me, I shall look forward thereto with the respect and esteem wherewith I have the honor to be Your Excellency's very obedient servant.

268. To General José Antonio Páez

[Original][1]

San José de Cúcuta, December 11, 1826.

My dear General:

Since entering this city, I have seen the proclamations that were issued in Venezuela, and I have also received a confused report of what took place at Caracas and Puerto Cabello. I cannot but be surprised that these extraordinary events should have occurred after Guzmán arrived at your General Headquarters, and that my name was used to promote the most infamous of intrigues. You know perfectly well that Guzmán came to Lima only to propose to me, in your name, the destruction of the Republic after the manner of Bonaparte, as you yourself have said in your letter, the original of which is in my possession. Through Colonel Ibarra and Urbaneja, you offered me a crown, which I was duty bound to refuse. General Mariño, as well as Carabaño, Rivas, and several other gentlemen of this type wrote me to the same effect, urging me to become a sovereign prince. Everyone in Perú and Colombia knows this. It is stupidity, therefore, to attribute this diabolical plan to me since I scorned it as a fevered concoction born of the contemptible ambition of certain hangers-on.

Following these treasonable attemps there occurred the developments that have placed the Republic in its present predicament. Of course, the gentlemen in the conspiracy spoke of federation, and Guayaquil urged that system upon me when I was in Lima. I answered Guayaquil that my political convictions were embodied in my Bolivian Constitution. By that time, Guzmán had independently examined that Constitution and had earnestly pleaded with me to send him on a mission to Colombia to quiet the general agitation provoked by the revolt of Valencia. I did, in fact, send him to you to give you my views, which were as follows: first, that our country should not perish in the throes of civil war; second, that everything should remain as it was, pending my early return to Colombia; third, that public opinion should be prepared with respect to the powers that

---

[1] Both the original and the rough draft of this letter are extant. The original, together with the collection of letters from Bolívar to Páez, went from Arístides Rojas to Pérez y Soto and then to the Archivo del Libertador. The draft is dated December 12 and begins "Al entrar en este valle . . ." ("Upon entering this valley . . ."); the letter as written is dated the 11th and begins "Al entrar en esta villa . . ." (comp.).

would have to be given me to arrange the affairs of Venezuela, since the Constitution authorizes me to punish only according to the law; and fourth, that my Bolivian Constitution should be defended against its assailants. You are aware that this Constitution is the most liberal and free of any that exists. I do not know what Guzmán did during his mission. In some quarters he did too much, and in Venezuela, to judge from current conditions, he evidently did too little.

In short, General, I have mentioned all this in order to point out my conclusion: I have come to Colombia to save both you and our country from the greatest of all catastrophes. No personal ambition brought me here. Consequently, I do not see how ulterior motives of any type can be ascribed to me. I informed you from Bogotá, over my signature, that I had served Venezuela, Colombia, Perú, and Bolivia in order to save Caracas from the evils that afflict her, and that I do not wish to govern Caracas, Venezuela, or Colombia, or any other section of America. This is precisely what my Bogotá proclamation states, but in still more emphatic terms. I want no throne, no presidency, nothing. Hence, I seek only tranquility for Venezuela so that I may resign my office. But first we must assure the future of our country without bloodshed and battle. This is my most earnest and sincere desire. I offer myself as a victim for this sacrifice; but I will not tolerate anyone's making himself the sovereign in our nation. You have no right to do so, nor I, nor any part of the people; otherwise, all that which is to be done will be void and without effect. Furthermore, the Constitution to be issued next January 15 for the department of Venezuela will have no more value than if it had been issued by a hamlet, for, with respect to the entire nation, any single part is nothing. Recently, I sent General Silva to consult with you at Apure, where, I am told, you are now to be found. The General bears instructions that I deemed expedient in order to arrange with you for the recognition of my authority until the National Assembly meets, at which time I shall relinquish it. Above all, the object of General Silva's mission is to forestall the meeting of the Constituent Assembly of Venezuela and to urge you strongly to come and see me wherever I may be. The same plea is being conveyed to you by General Briceño by way of Puerto Cabello.

I beg you, my dear General, do not turn a deaf ear to these words of harmony, these words of salvation, each one of which is weighted with the blood of our citizens and the destinies of our children. Banish from your side all who advise you to the contrary. With me you have conquered, with me you have won glory and fortune; you must place your every hope and trust in me. On the other hand,[1] General Castillo opposed me and lost; General Piar opposed me and suffered defeat; General Mariño opposed me and went down to defeat; General Riva Agüero opposed me and lost; and General Torre Tagle opposed me and was defeated. It would seem that Providence condemns my personal enemies, whether American or Spanish, to perdition. But see where she has placed Generals Sucre, Santander, and Santa Cruz. For so sincere a friend as yourself these examples and counsels are superfluous. The dictates of your heart will tell you more than the whole record of history. I trust in the goodness of your heart as I trust my sword, which will never be turned against me. My sword and I are both yours.[2] In utmost sincerity, your most devoted friend,

BOLÍVAR

269. To General José Antonio Páez

[Original]

Coro, December 23, 1826.

My dear General:

Upon my arrival here, I had the satisfaction of reading your proclamation of December 15, which came in manuscript form from Curaçao.[3] It expresses my innermost convictions. I am overjoyed that the letter brought you by Colonel Ibarra was responsible for this document, which does honor to us both. God grant that your prophecies be fulfilled even beyond my fondest hopes! My one ambition is to achieve happiness for Venezuela and for all America, if possible. I assure you, in all sincerity, that I am exceedingly weary of public life, and that the happiest moment of all my life shall be the moment when I relinquish my authority to the representatives of the people at

---

[1] The rough draft has also "General Labatut opposed me and lost" (comp.).

[2] Deleted in the original, "to live and die together" (comp.).

[3] Páez announced that Bolívar had come to aid in the reform of the administration, rather than to destroy Páez' authority (ed.).

the great convention. Then all will be convinced of my true motives. Indeed, to what can I aspire? I tremble lest I fall from the heights of glory where my country's fortunes have placed me. I have never coveted office; at present it oppresses me and bows me down. I shall not fight for rule; on the contrary, I should esteem it a favor were a quick death to spare me the chaos in which I find myself. I shudder to think, as I constantly do, of the horrible calamity that threatens Colombia. I distinctly see our handiwork destroyed, and I hear the curse of the centuries ringing about our ears for our being the perverse authors of such lamentable changes. I am indeed anxious to escape the abyss into which we have descended—but only by the path of duty, no other.

Your proclamation states that I come as a citizen. What would I be able to accomplish as a citizen? How can I lay aside my duties as a servant of the state? Who has dissolved Colombia in so far as her laws and I are concerned?

The nation has manifested but one unanimous wish: reforms and *Bolívar*. No one has challenged me, no one has replaced me. Who then shall seize the reins of office from me? Your friends? You?! The ingratitude rather than the treachery of such an act would multiply such infamy a thousandfold. I cannot believe it. I shall never believe that you would permit the ambition of your friends and the ignominy of your name to reach such a point. It is not conceivable, General, for you to want me humiliated for the sake of a band of turncoats whom you and I have never seen in battle. Do not presume to disgrace Caracas by making her appear to be the patron of infamy and the mockery of ingratitude itself. Does not everyone in Venezuela owe everything to me, and are not even you indebted to me for life itself?[1] But for my services, the perils I faced, and the victories that I won by dint of perseverance and hardships without number, the Apure would be a wasteland, the tomb of heroic dead. You, my dear General, and the brave men of your army would not be in command of Venezuela, because the honors that tyranny would have assigned to you and your men would have been the sword rather than the crown of glory that circles your brows.

I have come from Perú to save you from the crime of civil war. I have come so that Caracas and Venezuela might not again be stained with the most precious blood in all the world. And now you wish

---

[1] Páez was a prisoner of the Spaniards in Barinas in December, 1813, and his life was saved by Bolívar's victory at Araure (ed.).

me to be a simple citizen! It cannot be. The title of citizen is one that would honor me a million times over were I to receive it only in recognition of my complete disinterestedness.

There is no other lawful authority in Venezuela today but mine— and my authority is supreme. The Vice President himself no longer has power here, as it is so stated in my decree; hence, there will be no further excuse for recrimination or disobedience. The roots of your power lie in the municipalities and date from an upheaval caused by three assassinations. There is no glory in this, my dear General!

With all my heart I offer you my friendship, my services, and whatever may do you honor; but everything must pursue the path of order, abiding by that true sovereign, the majority of the nation. Cumaná itself has not disowned the government. I sincerely hope General Mariño has been well received, lest Cumaná be transformed into another New Guinea and fail me in reëstablishing the public order.

What is most surprising to me is that you have not said a word either about my supreme authority or about my intended mediation. You asked me to come, but, after such grave developments, you have not written me a single syllable. All this places me in a quandary. Believe me, General, in the shadow of mystery lurks crime. I want to know the facts. I want to know whether you obey me or not, and whether the land of my birth recognizes me as its head. God forbid that my authority be disputed on my own hearth, like Mohammed's, whom the world adored and his compatriots rejected. Nevertheless, he triumphed though his cause was not as great as mine. I will yield everything for glory, but I shall also fight for it. Will this be the sixth civil war that I have had to put down? God spare me! I shudder at the thought.

Dear General, with me you shall be everything, yes, everything. I want nothing for myself; you may have it all, but not at the cost of my glory, which has been founded upon duty and right.

The most convincing proof of my sacrifice for you and for Venezuela is my decree, which I now send you.[1] I ignore duty and law in calling a national convention. This I am not free to do; nevertheless, I offer myself in sacrifice to avoid a civil war. What more can you ask of my devotion?

Believe me, I do not intend to promote victory for one party at the expense of another, either at the convention or anywhere else.

---

[1] A decree of amnesty, calling for a National Convention to consider revision of the Constitution of 1821, was issued on January 1, 1827 (ed.).

I shall not oppose federation; nor do I seek the adoption of the Bolivian Constitution. I only want my fellow-citizens to be united under the law. I want freedom to work for them and wisdom to guide them, so that they will accept my resignation and permit me to go far, far away from Colombia. In proof of this intention, there is the sale of my mines at Aroa and all my goods, which my sister is negotiating.

Farewell, dear General. I leave tomorrow for Puerto Cabello where I shall await your reply. Puerto Cabello is a great monument to your glory. There may it rise ever higher and surpass my own! I say this in all sincerity, for I envy no one.

Accept the assurances of the warm affection of your devoted friend,

BOLÍVAR

[*In margin*] This letter received today, February 15, 1827.

1827

270. Proclamation to the People of Colombia

[*Gaceta de Colombia*, Special Edition, January 25, 1827]

General Headquarters, Puerto Cabello,

January 3, 1827—the 17th [year].

SIMON BOLIVAR, Liberator-President of Colombia, etc.

Colombians:

Order and law have resumed their divine reign in every section of the Republic. The vile and sanguinary serpent of discord has fled in fear before the peace-maker of Colombia. There are no more domestic enemies in the country; kisses, embraces, tears of rejoicing fill the heart of our country. This day marks the triumph of peace.

Granadans! Your brothers of Venezuela, always your fellow-citizens, are your comrades-in-arms, children of the same destiny. They are your brothers of Cúcuta, Niquitao, Tinaquillo, Bárbula, Las Trincheras, San Mateo, La Victoria, Carabobo, Chire, Yagual, Mucuritas, Calabozo, Queseras, Boyacá, Cartagena, Maracaibo, Puerto Cabello, Bomboná, Pichincha, Junín, Ayacucho and your brothers of the Congresses of Guayana, Cúcuta, and Bogotá—you are all brothers together on the fields of glory and in the councils of wisdom.

Men of Venezuela, Apure, Maturín! The reign of evil has ended. One of you bears the olive branch, that, under its shade, we may celebrate the festival of freedom, peace, and glory. Let the year 1826 pass into eternal oblivion; let it disappear into the remote ages, forever to be lost in the dimness of time. I have forgotten the past.

Colombians! Forget the days of sadness that you have endured, and let their memory fade into silence.

BOLÍVAR

271. To George Canning, Foreign Minister
    of Great Britain

[*Contemporary Copy*]

Caracas, January 27, 1827.

Most Excellent Sir:

It is with great satisfaction that I have the honor of informing you that the late disturbances in Colombia have ceased to trouble America and our friends in Europe. Great Britain will also benefit from our constitutional victory, since she herself is concerned with Colombia's existence, by virtue of the services rendered in the form of supplies furnished us by British subjects. I feel that I can reassure Your Excellency that this country has wholeheartedly supported its statesmen and laws. The foreigners living here can testify to this fact, which is, in reality, quite remarkable, for never has there been a people so transported with joy on regaining control of its own institutions. But what has filled our cup of good fortune to the brim is the decisive action of Great Britain, in supporting her old friend Portugal against the perfidy of the Spanish government. His Britannic Majesty's government has thereby assured the existence and welfare of the American hemisphere and has given the constitutional nations the firm hope that they will enjoy the generous protection of your great people. Your Excellency has fulfilled the hopes of the liberal world, and, by this signal contribution, you have earned the veneration of posterity. Your memorable words, spoken in the recent Parliament, would appear to be the decrees of Providence itself, and their prophecy will be fulfilled. This I long for with all my heart, as I also hope that peace in America will be a prerequisite to the termination of the present war with Spain, as the finest tribute to Britain's glory.

I remain your Excellency's devoted servant,

BOLÍVAR

272. To the President of the Senate of Colombia

[*Gaceta de Colombia*, April 22, 1827]

Caracas, February 6, 1827.

Very Excellent Sir:

At no time has the Republic been in such dire need of the august authority of Congress as in this period when internal dissension has divided men's minds and stunned the nation.

Summoned by Your Excellency to come and take the oath of office as President of the Republic, I proceeded to the capital, but I was obliged to depart at once for these departments of Old Venezuela.

On the way from Bogotá to this city, I issued decrees of such importance that I dare to describe them as vital and urgent. Your Excellency will be so kind as to call them to the attention of the Congress, and to urge in my behalf that Congress deliberate upon them in the light of their wisdom. If I have exceeded my authority, the fault is mine; but I gladly sacrifice my innocence for the salvation of the country. This further sacrifice I had yet to make, but I am proud not to have evaded it.

When, in Perú, I received official notice that the people had [again] elected me President of the Republic [of Colombia], I sent word to the executive power that I would not accept the chief magistracy of the nation. For fourteen years I have been supreme civil and military head and President of the Republic, because the threat of danger has compelled me to fulfill this obligation.

The dangers no longer exist, and I may therefore retire to enjoy private life.

I beg the Congress to review the situation of Colombia, of America, and of the entire world. All things favor us. On the American continent not a Spaniard remains. *Domestic peace* has prevailed in Colombia since the first day of this year. Many powerful nations have acknowledged our political existence, and not a few have become our friends. A large number of the American states are allied with Colombia, and Great Britain is threatening Spain. What more can we hope for? Only the arcana of time can tell what store of benefits Providence has prepared for us; she alone is our guardian. As for me, the suspicion that I desire to usurp a tyrannical power hangs over my head, a suspicion that troubles many a Colombian heart. Zealous republicans regard me with a secret fear, for history teaches them that men in my position have always been ambitious. In vain does

Washington's example rise in my defense, for, in truth, an occasional exception cannot stand up against the long history of a world that has always been oppressed by the powerful.

I am torn between the woes of my fellow-citizens and the verdict that posterity will pass upon me. I myself do not feel that I am devoid of ambition. I, therefore, should like to escape from the clutches of that fury, in order to relieve my fellow-citizens of their anxieties and to make sure that, after my death, the memory of my name will be linked with that of freedom. As these are my sentiments, I renounce the presidency now and forever. The Congress and the people must realize that my resignation is irrevocable. Nothing could induce me to continue in public office after having spent an entire lifetime in this service. Now that the triumph of liberty has placed everyone in possession of that sublime right, shall I alone be deprived of this prerogative? No! The Congress and the people of Colombia are just: they will not impose on me the ignominy of *desertion*. My days are numbered: more than two-thirds of my life have been spent. Permit me, then, to await death in the peace and obscurity of my paternal home. My sword and my heart shall none the less always be Colombia's, and my last breath shall be spent in praying to Heaven for her happiness.

I plead with the Congress and the people to grant me the favor of allowing me to be a *plain citizen*.

God keep Your Excellency,

Simón Bolívar

---

273. To Sir Robert Wilson

[*Copy*][1]

Caracas, May 26, 1827.

My esteemed and worthy General:

Your letters, which we received last evening from the latest packet, brought us the most gratifying news. Mr. Canning's Cabinet and your worthy friends are the saviors of lofty principle and of the

---

[1] This copy was transcribed verbatim from the original in the O'Leary collection. Earlier published versions have introduced unwarranted changes in the text (comp.).

American cause. You assure us that the liberal party will triumph forever and that the affairs of England will be conducted by a cabinet composed of men of cosmopolitan vision who are friends of all mankind. Your own joy must be the measure of my own, because you and I share the same sentiments which reach the heights of enthusiasm. We have won, dear friend, and humanity has won with us. Today, we can justly claim that the defense of humanity was an honor, yet a thousand outrages have heaped humiliation upon the noble champions of the good. That such incidents may not be repeated is my most ardent wish. I am convinced that England alone is capable of protecting the world's precious rights, as she is great, glorious, and wise. The power that succeeded in destroying Napoleon has, thereby, made itself responsible for the happiness of all nations, because Bonaparte himself headed a great reform movement that was intended to benefit the human race. England, therefore, must put into effect the promises of that prophetic conqueror.

The shock with which my resignation was received in England has given me a great deal of satisfaction. In resigning, I sought revenge against my detractors, who had flooded the presses with their false accounts. I am also tired of public service. Europe cannot appreciate the efforts I must make to maintain order in some of these areas. My labors, in fact, are similar to those in the fable of that ancient who was condemned to carry his staggering load to the highest peak only to roll back with it into the abyss. I find myself combatting the combined forces of a whole world. I stand alone; the contest, therefore, is very unequal, and so I am bound to suffer defeat. History itself fails to record any example that might encourage me, nor does legend reveal this particular type of prodigy. The deeds attributed to Bacchus and Hercules are nothing compared to what is demanded of me. Can one man alone set half the world in order? A man such as I?! No, my dear General, abandon any such hope. If you knew me today you would not expect me to continue in service, for my legs no longer carry my weight. Superhuman efforts have sapped my energy, and I have fallen into a state of utter discouragement. Nevertheless, I am determined to keep matters in hand until the assembly meets in convention to decide the fate of the nation.

Respecting Perú, I do not know what to say. A heinous crime has destroyed that Republic, which for a while survived as by a charm because of the life I had given it. There are no men left in Perú. Bolivia will do well as long as Sucre is president.

My beloved aide-de-camp attends to his duties with admirable zeal and good sense. A son like him must be a great blessing to you. Since your impress is upon him, he could be no less. The sons of heroes do not always attain their fathers' stature, a rule to which Alexander was an exception, for he excelled his parent. I do not ask as much of your Belford, for he should be content to follow in the footsteps of his distinguished father.

I very much regret your [other] son's illness, which you mention with a natural reluctance. You give us cause to fear for his life, which, being part of your own, must not be lost, especially since his youth entitles him to go on to fulfillment.

Your friends, impressed by the courtesies you have shown me, do me great honor. For this incalculable advantage I am again indebted to your friendship. Kindly convey my appreciation and respectful admiration to Lord Lansdowne and Mr. Brougham.

The portrait that you ordered engraved with so much care—another act of courtesy and kindness—has just arrived in La Guayra; hence, I have yet to receive it.

I have the pleasure of giving you the sincere assurances of my highest esteem and cordial friendship.

BOLÍVAR

P.S. I deeply regret not having previously expressed my most sincere thanks to your esteemed daughter, Miss Jemina, who so generously favored me with the unforgettable gift of the purse that she made herself. Gifts such as these are dearly cherished by a soldier who admires whatever is lovely and gracious.

BOLÍVAR

True copy—Hallowes

---

274. To [GENERAL JOSÉ GABRIEL PÉREZ], SUPREME
    COMMANDER IN THE SOUTH

[Draft]

Caracas, June 8, 1827.

My dear Pérez:

I have learned with great regret that, at the end of March, you were still occupied in suppressing the disorders precipitated by the

Colombian division under Bustamante. I have believed from the first that the result would be favorable to the good cause, and, though we have heard nothing as yet, we are impatiently awaiting definite news at any moment. In my opinion, Perú acted correctly in expelling that division, as I have faith in General Santa Cruz' intentions, which can never be injurious to Colombia. You will have learned by now how we must judge the views of our neighboring government. I suspect, however, that you are more concerned with events here than with what I think about affairs there.

I shall begin without mentioning any unnecessary details. Venezuela is quiet and is flourishing under the reforms that have been made. The public has conformed fairly well, and the ideas that will prevail will depend upon the direction that I give them; which is to say that, in Venezuela, they are anxious to please me in this regard. Everyone wants reform, but no one ventures to state what it should be. The only point of general agreement is that a government should be established in Venezuela to attend to her needs and interests. The classes here have established a satisfactory enough relationship—an improvement brought about by my efforts. Previously all was chaos here, from which an attempt was made to procure the best possible order. Would you believe that the treasury receipts balance with the government expenditures? Yes, it is so. Salaries are paid monthly to government employees, and occasionally even back pay. I understand that in the rest of the Republic the opposite is true, despite the fact that half the Colombian army is stationed here, in complete disproportion with respect to the rest of the country. By the end of the month, I shall have completed the greater part of my reforms. The treasury has been fully rehabilitated; education, agriculture, commerce, police, administration, and the tobacco monopoly have all been improved; the navy and the army have undergone very beneficial changes. During the two days that I was in Bogotá, I saved the state six millions in expenses; and in Venezuela, as well, very extensive savings have been introduced. The public morality has been treated to instructive examples and some severe lessons. These reforms are a major accomplishment, but much more remains to be done. I am resolved, as long as I am able, to serve Venezuela and to do nothing else. This is my country, and here my duty lies.

The enclosed copy of the *Gaceta* will tell you a great deal of my decision to resign forever my command in Colombia, and about the treasury reforms that have been instituted. I do not intend to be like the condemned man in the fable, who constantly had to repeat his work. Perú was in good order when I left, while this country was torn asunder. Would I be right, therefore, again to bring ruin to Venezuela by leaving in order to organize Bogotá? I think not. My decision is irrevocably taken.

I am alarmed over the disorders in the south. Treason on the part of the officers there is more barbarous than the war that we have just ended. Perú is about to go through a cycle of continuous convulsions, and her domestic disturbances will affect her neighbors, Colombia and Bolivia. This agitation is lamentable and, what is worse, I can see no remedy for it. Cundinamarca will also suffer greatly from the dissensions that will be sown there. The great convention of Colombia will be a tournament, or, to put it more plainly, an athletic arena. Passions will hold sway, and Colombia will suffer the consequences. In brief, this New World is a storm-tossed sea that will not be calmed for many a year. Some will attribute a part of this unrest to me; others, all of it. Therefore, to avoid additional blame, I shall go no further. I shall resign myself to the part allotted me in this diabolical partition.

What is to become of all of you in the south? The more I ponder the problems there, the more I sympathize with its leaders, and, when I think of Venezuela, the same feelings overcome me. In short, let me end this letter by telling you that, when you can do no more, you and the others should return to Venezuela to serve the land that gave us birth. This letter is also for Flores, to whom I am not writing separately, as there is nothing more I could add to what I have said herein.

---

275. To the President of the Senate of Colombia

[O'Leary, XXV, 538]

Cáchira, August 24, 1827. The 17th [year].

His Excellency the President of the Senate:

While en route to the capital, with such speed as the rainy season, the poor condition of the roads, and the state of my health would permit, my Secretary-General here received two communications from the Secretary of War. In one of these was enclosed the decree of the 8th instant ordering the reduction of the standing army of the Republic to less than 10,000 men; the other contained several articles relating to the latest insurrection in Guayaquil, which is spreading rapidly, for it has been reported that the department of Ecuador is sending delegates to participate in the uprising and that Asuay is also to take part.

After noting the contents of these communications, I could not refrain from analyzing these developments and comparing them with the present state of our Republic. An army division in Lima has mutinied against its commanders. It has defied the law, and has plotted to partition the Republic in the interests of foreign powers. Having failed to accomplish this with sufficient promptness, it proclaimed a federal government, which has favored the cause of certain ill-advised persons in Guayaquil, who, since last year, have been laboring to remodel our government along federal lines. I had previously endeavored to restrain these persons by making known to them, through my Secretary and through the draft Constitution with which I satisfied the demands of Bolivia, my convictions in favor of a central government that would be more in keeping with our needs. The federation now being proclaimed is nothing more than an open invitation to the traitors who invaded those departments. Lending emphasis to this peril is the news that the enemy is collecting troops in the Canary Islands in order to invade Colombia, that an air of anxiety prevails among us, and that there has been a recent decline in our morale and public spirit; thus, the National Convention itself will not be able to produce the benefits for which we have hoped, as long as the Republic is torn apart and her security placed in the most imminent danger.

At a time when each moment increases the urgent necessity for preparing our defenses against foreign invasions and maintaining political unity, order, and law at home, the army has been ordered reduced to a strength that would not suffice even in a time of guaranteed peace. The Congress has evidently not been informed of the true state of the Republic. It has doubtless deceived itself by picturing the situation that ought to exist, and, although the capital itself is bristling with factions and the very representatives of the people are exposed to bitter uncertainties, our political and economic conditions have probably been represented to the Congress as a veritable model of prosperity. The decree in question is palpable proof of this fact. The sole reason advanced to explain this order is that a larger force is no longer needed.

In communicating this decree, the Secretary of War added, on the authority of the Vice President, that it would be wise to reduce to cadres the two battalions and two squadrons which had been gathered at Cartagena because of the invasion of the south and which I desired to have ordered to the interior. These are the very units that, in these days of factions and crime, have remained faithful to the Constitution and been its shield. These units are especially long-standing, and they are composed of our veterans. It is argued that our depleted treasury makes this measure advisable. Therefore, is it proposed that, because the treasury is exhausted, the Republic should remain defenseless or be placed in the hands of those who have reduced her to her present extremity? Assuming that Spain does not have any aggressive intentions toward us—although as yet there has been nothing to reassure us of this—would not the deplorable state of our Republic be sufficient inducement for her to invade us? Assuming further that Perú had not exhibited ample proof of sinister intent as regards Colombia, would not our unpreparedness incite her to rivalry?

I shall not inquire what end has been sought by inducing Congress to enact a decree that will seal our ruin. Nor shall I comment upon the coincidence of these two communications arriving on the same day, or upon the reasons behind the proposal to dissolve the most loyal, the most tried and proven of all our forces, at a time of mounting danger, in order to entrust the preservation of the nation's rights to raw troops or to those who have sought distinction by indulging in the most signal disobedience during a crisis when the government has scarcely 10,000 soldiers at its disposal. But I must not conceal the fact that the Republic is approaching dissolution, or rather, that it has already been dissolved and that reduction of the army makes any remedy impossible. Every region has clamored for reforms, and, although in some sectors anxieties have given way to hopes inspired by the National Convention, each day presents new obstacles to the convoking of the people's representatives. In view of the enormous backward step which the southern departments have taken, there is little assurance that they will take part in the convention in any but a hostile mood, intending not to reason but to dictate. Indeed, there is reason to fear that the decree ordering the reëstablishment of a constitutional order throughout the Republic and obliging the eastern departments to revert to the paths whereby the political and civil unity of the Republic can peaceably and quietly be resumed, may once again innure their feelings. Who will then join in establishing the state? Congress does not sympathize with those who basely seek to destroy Colombia; nevertheless, I am convinced that the measures that have been recommended to it as being for the good of the country can have no other result.

By all means let the army be reduced in so far as it should be compatible with public needs; but it should not be rendered incapable of repelling a foreign invasion; it should not be rendered incapable of restraining those who would rob the people of the opportunity of erecting a government; it should not be rendered incapable of holding anarchy in check at a time when all the springs of political control have snapped. We must not be deterred by the depletion of the treasury, so deplored by the Secretary of War, if this is actually what prompted the decree. The treasury had been exhausted in the four eastern departments, where, moreover, all sources of income seemed to have evaporated; yet, when a sound economy had been established and order restored, income and expenditures were made to balance. There is nothing to prevent a similar success in the rest of the Republic. Indeed, the wisdom of Congress must accomplish a great deal more. Congress must maintain both the army and national unity, and it must provide for the public needs as well.

The decreed reduction in the armed forces will lead, let me repeat, to inevitable ruin. The army should be increased rather than reduced, and the treasury should be reorganized. If either is refused, if the executive is denied the powers indispensable for the safeguarding of the Republic, I shall not assume the presidency. Is it right that one who has grown old before his time, in order that Colombia might have independence and her own laws, should officiate at her funeral rites or deliver her severed limbs to the enemies whom he has conquered or set free?

I beg Your Excellency to bring the foregoing to the attention of the honorable Senate Chamber and to accept my assurances of the profound respect with which I have the honor to be Your Excellency's very obedient servant.

SIMÓN BOLÍVAR

276. To Joaquín Mosquera

[*Biblioteca Popular* (Bogotá), No. 102]

Bogotá, September 24, 1827.

My dear and good friend:

Your brother Tomás, whom I have appointed Commander in Chief of Cauca, will deliver this letter to you. My purpose in writing is to inform you that I arrived in this capital the 10th of this month, and that I am now at the head of the government, having taken possession on the very day of my arrival. This is surely the most costly sacrifice of any that I have made for Colombia and for my friends, but it is something I could not avoid, for the nation and those friends expected it of me. Imagine what my position and troubles will be now that I will have to overcome, at one and the same time, the frenzy of my enemies and the clamors of my friends, the depletion of the treasury and the nation's impaired credit. Please believe, my dear friend, that, in this trying situation, the great convention is the only glimmer of light that I see, the only beacon that guides my steps. I can tell you that I stake all my hopes, all my past glory, on seeing Colombia reunited in this august sanctuary of the people, where the nation's wishes will be freely expressed and her destiny decided. This is the one opportunity left to this poor country. If we lose it, what will become of her? Consequently, men of good will and enlightened interest like yourself must, on this occasion, exert every effort and bring their influence to bear, so that the deputies who come will truly represent the interests of a trusting people. If only you would come yourself!

[Tomás] Mosquera is perfectly familiar with the past and present situation in this capital and with my views on current affairs. He will therefore be able to tell you all that I leave unsaid. I have asked him to pay my respects to you, your wife, and your family.

He tells me you have retired from politics completely, but, should the great convention call you and were I to plead with you to contribute your ability and high character, would you refuse? No indeed, for if you did I should go myself and seek you out in your place of seclusion. But this will not happen because you will not ignore the call of your country and your friend who holds you in deep and abiding friendship.

BOLÍVAR

277. To GENERAL JOSÉ A[NTONIO] PÁEZ

[*Original*]

Bogotá, September 29, 1827.

My dear General:

I take great pleasure in answering your kind letter which I received the day before yesterday together with the inclosures you sent me respecting the news of Spain and Morales, which I have read with great satisfaction, for rumors have been circulating about an expedition reported seen now at Coro, now at Cartagena. Your letter, therefore, dispels these rumors and worries. In return, I can inform you that the Congress has voted a decree approving my actions in Venezuela and authorizing me to make whatever changes I deem necessary, in particular in the matter of finance. It remains for you, then, to inform me what changes you consider most urgent and necessary to ameliorate the present situation in Venezuela. This matter is the object of my unceasing efforts, as it is of yours. This decree has made me all the happier in that it assures Venezuela's future, at least for the time it is to be in effect, until the meeting of the great convention, which will mark a new epoch in the history of Colombia. Meanwhile, the Congress, by this same decree, has provided that Venezuelan affairs shall remain in *status quo,* as I shall leave them. We shall thereby be spared the problems and dangers that might result from any change.

I have seen, as I have previously stated, the Caracas papers, both pro and con. I am grateful to my friends for the part they have taken in my defense, and, as regards your treatment of Level and Domínguez, I have simply told the government that you had duly reported this matter.

Here all is quiet, but we lack funds. You in Venezuela are more fortunate. Every day I realize more and more how much I have sacrificed in making myself responsible for the destinies of this Republic, which can hardly stand on its own feet. But the great convention is approaching, and we will be relieved of these problems when we place the country's future in its hands.

My health, badly shaken by the journey here, is improving daily.

My best to friends Carabaño, Peña, and Peñalver, and please believe me to be your ever devoted friend,

BOLÍVAR

278. To José Fernández Madrid, Colombian
   Minister to England

[Copy]

Bogotá, October 14, 1827.

My dear friend:

I want to avail myself of the opportunity afforded by today's departure of the post to England, to give you the latest personal news and recent developments. The day before yesterday, we received reports from Guayaquil and the south, where affairs have greatly improved. Guayaquil, which had virtually seceded from the union, is in the process of returning to the fold now that she has learned of my presence in the capital. I have received a thousand messages of congratulations from that city, in addition to the news that the leading fomenters of the recent dissensions are being forced to leave. This development will make it possible for the great convention to meet in a spirit of unity, order, and tranquility.

I have had the election rules printed and distributed, and I can assure you that the people are receiving them satisfactorily. The convention, therefore, is sure to be held in March. Meanwhile, I shall attempt to maintain unity and harmony among the inhabitants who were divided and prepared to fight among themselves because of local factions and conflicting interests. The latest news from Venezuela reveals that everything there is under control. The new tax regulations have produced good results, and it may be expected that, given time, more and more progress will be made, despite the impoverishment of the country and the problems yet to be solved.

I particularly want to commend to your diligence and kindness the matter of my Aroa mines. I have nothing else in the world on which to live or with which to pay my obligations.

Your family is well. I have placed myself at their disposal, and I ask you, my friend, to believe that I am your devoted

BOLÍVAR

279. To Dr. Cristóbal Mendoza, Intendant
    of the Department of Venezuela

[Copy]

Bogotá, October 23, 1827.

My dear friend:

The last mail did not bring me any word from you concerning the state of affairs in Venezuela. General Páez wrote to me, giving me an account of the news of the moment, and, of a certainty, it was not very encouraging. I have accordingly taken the measures that I deem necessary to avert internal dangers and repulse external ones. From various sources comes the report that Morales is planning to pay us a visit with an expeditionary force of no less than 12,000 men, whom we must receive, however reluctantly. I wrote both you and General Páez concerning this important matter by the last mail. Do not forget that, in an invasion, the militia and the men of Apure will be of very great value.

I shall never tire of writing you about the great convention and the election of deputies. Venezuela has men of sterling merit for this purpose—Peñalver, Yanes, you yourself, my dear friend, and Aranda, who has defended Venezuela so gallantly, and Peña, whose perseverance and character could be of immense service to Venezuela. As for myself, I shall proceed to Caracas as soon as the convention meets; you may expect me then.

My friends, and those most devoted to the common cause, write me from all sides that I must not remain away from the convention. But they fail to consider that any interference on my part would be termed by our enemies, and even by those who are impartial, as an assault upon liberty. They would say that I had fomented . . . [division]¹ in the convention not in order to serve the people and their interests but to further myself and my personal interests. No, my dear friend, I have all too often, in serving the general good, exposed myself to attack, to the detriment of my good name. You know that there are those who accuse me of being ambitious. You, who know these things, can judge my position. In the south conditions have shown marked improvement.

Believe me always to be your devoted friend,

BOLÍVAR

---

¹ *Dimisión* in this copy (comp.).

280. To COLONEL PATRICK CAMPBELL, BRITISH
     CHARGÉ D'AFFAIRES, BOGOTÁ

[*Copy*]

Bogotá, October 27, 1827.

Sir:

We were indeed grief-stricken to learn yesterday of the truly shock-ing news of the death of Mr. Canning. England, like America, could not have lost as much in the passing of any other one man. In fact, the whole world will mourn his loss. We were all beginning to reap the benefits of his farsighted and liberal policies. Greece will sorrow for her protector, and America can never forget that it was Mr. Can-ning who made her rights respected. I, personally, feel indebted to him for making triumphant the cause that I have defended. All man-kind found itself interested in the life of this illustrious man who wisely and methodically realized that, what the French revolution had offered as an illusory promise, we in America have successfully put into practice. In short, my dear Colonel, we can never sufficiently mourn the death of the heroic and sublime minister whom England has just lost. And as you, more than any other man, share this general sentiment, I suffer the grief that is common to us both, and I cannot but give expression to it in the hope of lightening, if possible, the burden of our misfortune.

Accept my most heartfelt condolences and the assurances of my particular regard and esteem.

BOLÍVAR

---

281. To GENERAL ROBERT WILSON

[*Copy*]

Bogotá, November 13, 1827.

My dear General:

Why did our Canning, my very dear friend, have to be torn from us? Why did we have to lose the greatest of statesmen? Liberty has been orphaned and hope defeated. Twice in this century mankind has moved toward the achievement of its rights, and twice Fate has intervened. Bonaparte's ambition and the death of our good friend are the two cruelest blows dealt to that good cause. I know not if the world is condemned to servitude, but I do see that destiny does not favor men of good will who seek to restore the happiness of their fellowmen.

In vain do I seek encouragement in the thought that England will continue to pursue Canning's liberal policies. True, I have good reason to believe that the King's closest advisers will not abandon the splendid policies that have enhanced England's prestige. Nevertheless, a secret presentiment warns me that the formidable European oligarchy will speedily readopt its former pretensions [respecting America]. I should like to be free of these depressing forebodings— but, can I brush them aside? No, my dear General.

I know that you, too, are bowed down by the immense loss that we have suffered. For my part, I have felt the keenest pangs of grief, which I have expressed in every possible manner, but my agony goes beyond that. I grieve for the present and for the centuries to come. Can you tell me whether or not I am right in harboring these dark thoughts?

You will be pleased to know that young Belford applies himself with ever increasing zeal and distinction. I fancy that you have transmitted to him your very own heart and soul. He does you honor every day I have occasion to give him evidence of my regard and esteem.

Accept, my dear General, the assurances of my respect and highest regard.

BOLÍVAR

True copy [sic] Hallowes

282. To George IV, King of the United Kingdom of Great Britain and Ireland

[*Draft*]

Bogotá, December 14, 1827.

Great and good friend:

Colombia would not be deserving of all the rewards of self-govern-ment if she, in the very enjoyment of its precious benefits, were to forget the coöperation that she has received from certain wholehearted friends of suffering humanity. It is impossible to record the assistance provided us by foreigners without vividly recalling the determination of many of Your Majesty's subjects who, moved solely by the noblest generosity, came here to share our struggles, our privations, and our lot. They exposed themselves to the severest penalties, standing shoulder-to-shoulder with our patriots, their stout hearts never doubt-ing whether to risk those penalties or to abandon the cause of an entire continent. Their offence,[1] however, now seems obliterated by the friendship which Your Majesty has accorded the new American nations. Those men, nevertheless, still are liable to the penalty which, in 1819, was imposed upon British subjects who took part in foreign wars. Such punishment is all the more keenly felt, inasmuch as with it these men suffer Your Majesty's displeasure.

Sir, on behalf of my comrades-in-arms and in the name of a grate-ful Colombia, I beseech Your Majesty's grace for those men who so generously aided us.

Your Majesty's good friend and devoted servant.

---

[1] Prior to July, 1819, when the Foreign Enlistment Act became effective, recruiting of British subjects was forbidden in England by a royal proclamation of 1817. Many British subjects, however, were recruited and joined the South American armies and navies in violation of the poorly enforced proclamation and act (ed.).

283. To José Fernández Madrid, Colombian
     Minister to England

[Copy]

Bogotá, December 21, 1827.

My esteemed friend:

I take pleasure in replying to your two kind letters of September 21 and August 3, which I received yesterday. From their content I note that you are still confident that our finances are improving, but, dear friend, the very reverse is true. Our troubles and suffering increase more and more every day. In this capital there is hardly enough money to pay the civil employees, and more or less the same situation is true of the rest of the Republic. I am not able to improve matters because it is not within my power to do so. I cannot exceed the limitations imposed by a constitution to which I must conform. I may not change the laws which complicate our system [of government], and, lastly, I cannot act as a god to alter circumstances and change the minds of men. It hurts me deeply to have to give you this dismal picture, but I cannot hide it from you. It is my duty, in my position, to speak the truth, although it breaks my heart.

You will receive the special powers that you mention in your letter, and I should like you to do everything you possibly can to succeed in your objectives.

As for the mines, let me hasten to say that I should like you to see those gentlemen and tell them that they must state immediately and definitely whether or not they intend to comply with the contract, arranged with one of their agents, within the period provided. Tell them that, as they are not a duly constituted firm, I want to conclude this matter once and for all, since I shall be in no position to sue them. Should these gentlemen refuse to buy in accordance with the stipulated terms and time, find some one who will. Perhaps Messrs. Powles [sic] would take over the mines in lieu of the notes issued to them for twenty-two thousand *pesos*. I am sure you will attend to this affair with your customary zeal and energy.

The great convention is about to convene, as elections are now being held. I have no idea what this assembly will lead to. You expect great things from it, whereas I do not know what to expect. In Caracas there is talk of federation, and no one knows whether or not the south will also favor it. The one sure thing is that I regard it impossible to achieve stability for this country. If the country is divided, it is lost. Should the convention vote for vague and weak laws, like all laws of a very liberal government, then this large part of the world will have to endure all the hardships of a land without a government, because it is self-evident that the strength of a government must be in proportion to the size of its territory. In short, Colombia and all America are, in our time, lost nations. Dismiss your illusions, and, if need be, let the British government know the truth, because in the end the deceiver is always the deceived.

Give me some news of Olmedo and Rocafuerte, to whom you will please convey my regards, and tell Paredes that the esteem in which I hold him is unchanging.

I regret that you were told of your brother's being under suspicion, because there is not the least doubt in my mind but that all you tell me is absolutely so; but I must speak frankly, without casting any reflections upon your brother—and what I am about to say is no reflection on anyone—namely, that between you and the next man there is considerable difference.

The other day I called on your wife and met your darling little ones.

I remain your devoted friend,

BOLÍVAR

1828

[*Copy*]

Bogotá, January 22, 1828.

My dear Arboleda:

You can have no idea of the pleasure that your letter gave me, for it serves to confirm more than ever my high opinion of you. Your past intention, now reaffirmed, to attend the great convention for your country's sake, is indeed worthy of yourself and of the best citizen on earth. I, who know the cost of this sacrifice, can appreciate what it is worth. As you are well known for your views, and because you are a rich and honorable man, enlightened and fearless, you are a wonderful victim whom the demagogues would avidly seek to crush. Yes, my dear friend, the great convention may easily prove to be the tomb of our good cause and of our best citizens. Such, at least, is the mission of those selected—bad faith dominates them, and only a miracle will prevent them from complying with the will of their masters.

From Pamplona and Popayán, from Bogotá to Cartagena, all New Granada is leagued against me, and she has sought out my enemies to defeat my views and damage my good name. Santander is the idol of this country, or rather of those who represent it, or at least of those who have appropriated for themselves the people's sovereignty. I do not know of a single friend of mine who has been elected as a delegate. Some, of course, hold me in esteem, but their sentiments are not publicly known. By oversight, as it were, we shall have friends in the great convention, or shall I say that the deputies will change their minds the closer they come to the throne of the law? There they will see anarchy looming above their heads and over the entire nation, and they will shudder to see the snake-like coils of its mangy mane. I hope they do not ensnare me again!

I am very, very sorry, more so than I can tell you in only a few words, that you will not attend. But this disappointment is not the only one, as there have been many others very much like it. My friends have been injured by the contagion which I spread. In the eyes of the connivers, any friend of mine is the transgressor, unworthy of the nation's trust. Oh, for patience and hope, the best antidotes for evil; but, as you and I are not at all well, we need a stronger cure for our maladies than patience and hope—my maxim, therefore, is worth nothing.

I am, a thousand times over, your devoted

BOLÍVAR

---

285. To GENERAL JOSÉ ANTONIO PÁEZ

[Contemporary copy][1]

Bogotá, January 29, 1828.

My dear General:

I have received your esteemed letter of December 17, which begins very optimistically and ends, as is only natural, by complaining of the new troubles that have followed upon the old. You have labored mightily and with success, and your country and I are indebted to you for these latest services; but much remains to be done before order can be restored in Venezuela and a spirit of unity achieved. You have written to me several times, urging me to attend the great convention and exert my influence in order that Venezuela might be permitted to have her own government. I deeply regret that, in reply, I must tell you that what you wish cannot be accomplished for the present. Those who oppose me have undermined my popularity, while the representatives to the convention are my personal enemies, and, having opposed the great convention, they are now to be the judges who determine the reforms. As a matter of conscience, I have pointed out to them that things cannot continue as they are, for many reasons that I have enumerated, and that we must, therefore, strengthen the government so that this vast country can remain intact. I have told them that, if this cannot be done, they had better divide Colombia rather than subject her to a ruinous federation void of every social principle and guarantee. I added that

---

[1] In the collection of Dr. Cristóbal L. Mendoza, Caracas, Venezuela (comp.).

Bolivar in 1830
By Arturo Michelena.

I would not reassume office in Colombia for anything in the world, but I would aid the government if they would make it strong, as I desire, and that otherwise I shall depart peacefully, because I would not care to live here a single day after they have divided the country or created a federation, for war will be the immediate consequence. Yes, my dear General, that is my true confession and the voice of my conscience. That is how I view it, how I sense it, with no reservation that might enable me to change my opinion. I foresee certain destruction, unless the government is given an enormous power, capable of stifling the anarchy which will raise its thousand and one seditious heads. After seventeen years of pitiless war and revolution, our motherland has brought forth a sister more cruel than Megaera, more parricidal than Jupiter, more bloodthirsty than Bellona. Such, dear General, is anarchy. I shudder on contemplating the horrifying picture of what lies ahead. We shall go down amidst the wreckage of our country, for all is evil and growing more so. Force, by its very violence, carries within it the germ of its own destruction. Division itself spells ruin, and federation will be Colombia's grave. Nevertheless, division is to be preferred to other evils, but as a respite rather than a positive good. Well, these are my gloomy views, and I shall be infinitely happy if they prove to be mistaken. Although I have delayed communicating them to you to spare you further grief, I have at last determined to do so, because I feel obligated to reveal to you my inmost thoughts, for them to serve you as guidance in the future.

I earnestly entreat you to apply yourself unremittingly to end the anarchy that exists in the east and in the department of the Orinoco.

I think it would be advisable for you to send Mérida on a mission to some other area; otherwise, he will make of Caracas a boiling cauldron for us. This scoundrel is worse than all the others that you have evicted. His character is accursed of Heaven, venom flows in his veins, and the spirit of Satan possesses his mind. Mérida is all vileness and villainy. Please, please deliver us from the Evil One!

I am your devoted

BOLÍVAR

286. To J[osé] Rafael Arboleda

[*Copy*]

Bogotá, February 7, 1828.

My esteemed friend:

Although I wrote you frankly and in detail concerning the topics of the day by the last post of the week past, I want to write again in reply to your favor of the 22d ultimo, which I have read with great interest. It is certainly a triumph for the right cause that our good friend, Joaquín Mosquera, has been elected by San Buenaventura, and it can be said that those from the south are also good men. These include P. Merino, whom you know, and Saa, who is an excellent sort. I am urging them all to hurry to Ocaña, especially since Santander will leave here next week. You must understand that he now boasts of having forty-seven *partidarios*[1] on his side. That is the choice word this gentleman uses to describe his faction, and certainly he could choose none better suited to the spirit that animates it. It is difficult to know or even to guess what the outcome of the convention will be. It will bring together diverse attitudes, conflicting ideas, and dissimilar men. Many friends of order will attend and, without doubt, some federalists, but all in all we must wait to see the outcome. I can tell you frankly that, if the federal system is adopted, it will destroy what remains of Colombia. It will be the signal for departure. I shall go far, far away.

If they partition Colombia, that will be less disastrous, but even that will only be a stay of execution. Hence, I can see no means of salvation other than that of strengthening the government in an effort to combat the demoralization of some and the passions of others. If this could be accomplished, I should be pleased to see anyone in the executive post other than myself.

Please give my respects to all your family and friends, and believe me to be your most devoted

Bolívar

---

[1] Partisans, adherents, or party men (ed.).

287. MESSAGE TO THE CONGRESS OF OCAÑA

[*Gaceta de Colombia,* May 1, 1828]

Bogotá, February 29, 1828.

TO THE REPRESENTATIVES OF THE PEOPLE AT THE NATIONAL CONVENTION.

Fellow-Citizens:

I congratulate you on the honor the nation has conferred upon you in placing her exalted destinies in your hands. In representing the ultimate sovereignty of Colombia, you are clothed with sublime powers. It is a very great privilege to return to you the authority that was placed upon my weary shoulders. You, whom the people have chosen, must assume the sovereign rights and the supreme power as you are the delegates of the supreme holder of power, the people, whom I serve as subject and soldier. To what higher power, then, could I relinquish the presidential gavel and the General's sword than to you? Wield freely these symbols of command and glory in behalf of the people's cause, and lay aside all personal interests that might impede a thorough reform.

As duty requires that I report to you upon the state of the nation, I shall have the ungrateful task of giving you an account of her trials and tribulations. Please do not conclude that I have exaggerated for the sake of producing a lurid picture or that this picture was created in the dark and mysterious recesses of fantasy. Its every shade and color has been applied in the light of notorious fact, even though the total picture may well appear to be but a figment of the imagination. But, if that were true, would Colombia have asked you to assemble?

The wounds of our country began to heal the moment her chosen elect assembled here to examine them. Your task is truly as difficult as it is glorious. And, although the difficulties have already shrunk by virtue of the fact that you represent a united Colombia, attentive to your voice, I feel impelled to tell you that we owe this priceless advance solely to the hopes raised by the convention—hopes that reveal to you the confidence of the nation and the full weight of the responsibility resting upon you.

You have but to review our history to discover the causes of our decline. Colombia, creator of her own existence, now lies dying. Once entirely devoted to the public interests, Colombians no longer esteem duty as the sole path to the country's salvation. Those who, during the struggle for independence, resigned themselves to poverty when the foreign debt was hardly three million have, in order to maintain peace, burdened themselves with new debts, with the most disquieting consequences. Colombia, which, when once confronted by the hosts of the oppressors, breathed only honor and love of country, is now indifferent to the loss of her national credit. Colombia once willingly accepted painful sacrifices and thought only of exalted service, but now she thinks only of her rights and not of her obligations. The nation would have perished had not a glimmer of public spirit impelled her to seek the remedy and save herself while on the very brink of the tomb. Only a terrible danger forced us to attempt the changing of the fundamental laws. Only this danger could overcome the devotion that we professed for the just and lawful institutions whose foundations had given us our cherished emancipation.

I should add nothing to this dismal description if my position did not require me to direct the nation's attention to the practical inadequacies of her laws. I know that I cannot do this without exposing myself to sinister imputations and without ambitious intentions being read into my words. But I, who have never declined to stake my life and reputation for Colombia, feel compelled to make this one last sacrifice.

I am forced to state that fundamentally our government is badly constituted. Without considering the fact that we had only just overthrown tyranny, we permitted ourselves to be dazzled by exaggerated aspirations that the history of every age has proved to be incompatible with human nature. At other times we have employed the wrong means and then attribute our failure to our not having adhered closely enough to the false guide that was leading us astray. We have ignored those who sought to follow the natural order of things and who wished to balance the various features of our Constitution and to make it, as a whole, more compatible with our background, customs, and political inexperience, lest we should venture upon treacherous, unknown seas.

Our many branches of government are not organized in keeping with our social structure and the needs of our citizens. We have made the legislative branch the sovereign body, whereas it should have only a limited sovereignty. We have made the executive branch subordinate to the legislative to which we have given a far greater part in the general administration of the government than the nation's true interests demand. By a great error, all power has been given to the popular will, while only weakness has been granted to the machinery and activities of the body politic.

The right to initiate legislation has been accorded exclusively to the legislative branch, which, by its very character, is far removed from the realities of government, its acquaintance with it being merely theoretical.

The veto power conceded to the executive is the more ineffective in that it offends the pride of Congress when it is used. Congress may prevail over the veto by a vote of a fifth or less of its members; hence, there is no way of escaping undesirable legislation.

The denial to the Secretaries of State of free access to the legislative chambers in order to clarify or make known the government's intentions removes this means of advising the legislature in cases where needed legislation has been rejected. Much could have been gained if a stipulated interval of time had been specified or a greater proportion of votes had been required, in order to pass laws over the executive veto.

Let it be noted that our already swollen code of laws, instead of contributing to our happiness, places obstacles in our path. Our laws are a patchwork. They lack coherence, method, classification, and even legal phrasing. They are conflicting, confusing, frequently unnecessary, and too often they defeat their own purpose. There have been instances where stringent regulations were necessary in order to check widespread destructive elements. The [new] law drafted for a particular purpose has often proved far less adequate than the old, as it has indirectly encouraged the evils it was designed to correct.

Seeking perfection, we adopted as a basis of representation a plan not yet permitted by our capacities. The lofty principle of popular representation has been degraded by excessive liberality. In some provinces, it appears, the people are indifferent, and it is small honor to represent them. This indifference, in part, has contributed to the discrediting of the laws. And what good can come of discredited laws?

The executive of Colombia is not the equal of the legislature or of the head of the judiciary. He is becoming a weak arm of the governing power in which he does not participate as he should, for Congress persists in interfering in the administrative, judicial, ecclesiastic, and military functions that properly belong to the executive. The government, which should be the source and driving force of public power, has to seek this power outside itself, and it must rely upon forces that should be subject to it. To be the center and hearth of power is the very essence of government, although it derives its motion from without. Once a government is shorn of its proper attributes, it lapses into a lethargy that brings disaster to the citizens and decay to their institutions.

This does not complete the list of the constitutional shortcomings with respect to the executive. A deficiency no less important than those mentioned is the lack of responsibility on the part of the Secretaries of State. For responsibility to rest exclusively with the head of the administration serves to defeat the purpose of the Constitution, since no effort is made to secure the greatest harmony and coördination among the administrative sections; furthermore, the number of guarantees for the observance of the law are correspondingly reduced. There will be a greater zeal in executing the law when moral responsibility is made applicable to the ministers, because responsibility will then be explicitly imposed upon them. They will have a more powerful incentive for good work. Should punishment unfortunately be necessary, it would not serve as the seed of greater evils, such as those that cause major upheavals and lead to revolution. The responsibility of an elected servant of the people will always be illusory, unless he voluntarily submits to it, or, what is most unlikely, unless he lacks the means with which to place himself above the law. Otherwise, such responsibility can never be made effective, unless the cases in which it is to be assumed and the penalties involved are clearly defined.

All have noted with dismay the paradox of an executive having a super-abundance of power coupled with extreme weakness. The executive has been unable to repel foreign invasion or suppress seditious plots except by resorting to dictatorship. The Constitution itself, as if to correct its faults, goes to extremes in order to provide in profusion those powers which it jealously guards. Thus, the government of Colombia is either a trickling fountain or a devastating torrent.

In no other nation has the judicial power been so eminently enthroned as in Colombia. Observing the manner in which the branches [of government] are constructed, one would never imagine that the functions of the state are merely to ascertain and enforce the will of the people. A third supreme agent has been added, as if the determination of what laws are applicable in a given case were not the primary function of the executive. To avoid undue influence upon such decisions, this power was completely isolated from the executive branch of which it is inherently a part. And, although the executive is required to keep constant watch over the prompt and proper administration of justice, no means are provided with which to discover when his intervention is needed and no specific limits are set as to how far such intervention should extend. Even the power to select personnel from among those qualified has been taken from him.

Not content with this anomaly, we have, by subsequent legislation, and contrary to the consistent practice of centuries, given the civil courts absolute control in military cases, thus impairing the authority that the Constitution confers upon the President and destroying discipline, which is the keystone of any standing militia. This additional legislation has granted the judiciary the right, which it should never have had, of passing sentence [in military cases]. The law on procedure has enormously complicated the legal process. In every region new cantonal courts and tribunals have been established, and everywhere their reform is being demanded by the unfortunate townspeople who are being sacrificed to the involved procedures and to the venality of the judges. On repeated occasions the Superior Courts, composed almost exclusively of laymen, have ruled on the proper or improper enforcement of the laws.

The executive has received bitter complaints about the knavery and corruption among the judges, but he does not possess the power to punish them. He has witnessed the public treasury a prey to the ignorance and hypocrisy of the courts without being able to remedy the situation.

The concentration of all administrative branches in the hands of the executive's direct agents in each department serves only to increase his impotence. Thus the intendant,[1] who is the custodian of civil order and internal security, finds himself burdened with the administration of the national revenues, for which a large staff is needed, if only to prevent a decrease in revenue. However expedient such a concentration of duties may appear, in reality it is not effective except as regards military authority, which in the maritime departments should be united with the civil; but the civil and revenue authorities should be separated if each of these branches is to render the people and the government satisfactory service.

The municipal governments, which could serve as advisory bodies

---

[1] The principal civil authority in each of the seven departments or major political divisions of the Republic of Colombia. Each department was divided into provinces headed by governors (ed.).

to the governors of the provinces, cannot be said to have performed their true functions. Some of them have presumed to take upon themselves the sovereignty belonging to the nation, while others have fomented sedition. Nearly every newly created local government has done more to harm its city than to promote welfare, health, and general improvement. Such local governments do not satisfy the purpose for which they are intended. They are disliked because of the taxes they impose and the hardship that they cause the very members who comprise them, so that in many places there are no others to fill their posts. What renders them especially odious is the obligation placed upon citizens of annually doing court duty, in the performance of which they spend their time and money and frequently sacrifice their conscience and their honor. It is not unusual for some persons to foresake their home towns just to avoid being appointed to this burdensome duty. Finally, to express what is in everyone's mind, I must state that no more popular decree could be conceived than one that would do away with the municipal governments.

As there is no law providing for a national police force, not even a shadow of one exists. As a result of this fact the state is a maze, or rather a mystery, to the subordinates of the executive, who must deal with the people individually. But people cannot be managed without an efficient and active police force, to act as a link between each citizen and the agents of the government. For lack of a police, the intendants are seriously inconvenienced in enforcing the laws and regulations within every section of their jurisdiction.

Security and peace, the only strong desires of the people, having been destroyed, it has been impossible for agriculture to raise itself from its present deplorable state. This condition has brought about the ruin of other branches of industry, thus discouraging the rural population and reducing purchasing power. All this has led to hopeless misery. In certain cantons citizens have reverted to a state of primitive independence, because, having lost their possessions, they have no ties with society and have even become the enemies of society. Foreign commerce has followed the same pattern as domestic industry, and it might be said that this commerce scarcely provides us with our most indispensable needs. This situation has been aggravated by frauds, encouraged by the laws and the courts, leading to numerous bankruptcies and destroying all confidence in a type of trade whose very foundation is good faith and credit. How can there be commerce without exchange and profits?

Our army was formerly the glory of freedom and a model for all America. Its obedience to the law, to the chief of state, and to its general were worthy of the heroic age of republican virtues. It bore only arms, for it had no uniforms. Suffering extreme privations, it lived upon enemy spoils and, scorning ambition, it lived for love of country and nothing more. These generous virtues have somehow been eclipsed by the new laws designed to regulate and control the army. The military is affected by every upheaval that troubles society, and all that is left to him is his devotion to the cause that he preserved and a wholesome respect for his own battle scars. I have made mention above to the pernicious effect which the subjecting of the military to civil tribunals has had upon discipline, as the resulting decisions and regulations are fatal to stern discipline and to that passive submission and blind obedience that form the basis of military strength, which is the prop of all society. The law permitting the soldier to marry without official permission has seriously affected the army's mobility, strength, and morale. It was reasonable to forbid the recruiting of heads of families, but, in effect, by adopting this new regulation, we have made soldiers heads of families. The attacks upon commanders by writers in the public press have also contributed greatly to the relaxing of discipline. Declaring arbitrary detention to be corrective punishment is tantamount to establishing the rights of man by ordinance and spreading anarchy among the soldiers—and who is more terrible or cruel than a soldier turned demagogue? Dangerous rivalries between civilians and the military have been encouraged by the press and by the debates in Congress. Our soldiers are no longer looked upon as liberators of their country, but as assassins of liberty. Can this be the just reward for the suffering they endured and the sublime sacrifices they made? Is this the reward reserved for heroes? Malice has reached a point where hatred and ill feeling have been fostered among the soldiers of different provinces; hence, neither union nor strength can exist.

I would prefer to forget the matter of granting clemency to military crimes during this fateful period. Every legislator knows full well the seriousness of such outrageous indulgence. What army, hereafter, will be fit to defend our sacred rights, if rewards are to be the wages of crime, and if glory no longer goes hand in hand with loyalty, and valor with obedience?

Since eighteen hundred and twenty-one, when we began to reform our financial system, we have tried one experiment after another, each leaving us more disappointed than the former. The lack

of vigor in the administration of each and every branch, the widespread tendency to evade taxes, the notorious corruption and negligence of the tax collectors, the creation of unnecessary positions at
small pay, and the very laws themselves—all have combined to ruin
the treasury. On various occasions efforts have been made to overcome this mountain of obstacles by recourse to the courts. But the
courts, under pretence of protecting the innocent, have acquitted
both the delinquent taxpayer and the accused tax collector in cases
involving dilatory court procedures respecting which Congress has
not had time to enact new laws. This situation has further weakened
the government's position. Congress has yet to audit the commis-
sioner's offices handling the largest revenues. Congress has yet to
investigate, for the first time, the administration of funds of which the
government is merely the trustee.

The continuance in Europe of the person[1] who, acting under instructions issued in 1823, is undertaking to account for the millions
owed on the loan contracted for and ratified in London; the dismissal
of the chargé d'affaires[2] that we once had in Perú, who was negotiating for the collection of the subsidies that we made to that Republic; and, finally, the wasteful distribution of national property
have forced us to charge many items against the debit column of
the nation which these factors could have served to cancel. The
treasury of Colombia has reached a critical stage. It cannot uphold
our national honor with those generous foreigners who, placing their
confidence in our good faith, loaned us their money. The army is receiving only half its pay, and the government employees, excepting
those in the treasury department, are in the utmost misery. For very
shame I hesitate to tell you that the nation is financially bankrupt
and the Republic assailed by a horde of creditors.

In describing the chaos that surrounds us, I have thought it all
but superfluous to speak to you of our relations with the other peoples of the world. These relations prospered in keeping with our
growing military glory and with the prudence of our fellow-citizens,
thus inspiring the hope that our civil and social organization would
ultimately attain the heights that Providence had intended for us.
The course of foreign relations has always been linked with maturity in governments and harmony among peoples. No nation has
ever won admiration except through the exercise of these virtues;

[1] Santos Michelena (ed.).
[2] Cristóbal Armero (ed.).

none has ever won respect without unity to make her strong. But what inducements can Colombia, torn by strife, despising her own laws, her credit ruined, offer to new friends? What guaranties can she make even to keep those she now has? By retrogressing instead of advancing in her civil life, she can arouse only scorn. Already she has been provoked and insulted by an ally who, but for our kindness of heart, would never have come into existence.[1] Your deliberations must decide whether or not our friends among the nations, regretting having recognized us, will strike our name from the roster of nations that comprise mankind.

Legislators, great and arduous is the task that the national will has set before you. By saving Colombia you can discharge the obligation that our fellow-citizens have placed upon you. Let your gaze penetrate to the innermost hearts of your constituents. There you will read the anxiety that torments them: Their profound yearning for security and peace. Your country is pleading for a strong, powerful, and just government. See her as she stands amidst the ruin and desolation created by depotism; pale with fear, she mourns the five hundred thousand heroes who have died for her and whose blood watered the battlefields and brought her rights into existence. Yes, Legislators, the living and the dead, the ruins and the tombs, all cry out to you for security. And now I, as I am about to return to my home as a plain citizen, one of the multitude, regain my right to speak out. I who am the last to demand the benefits of society, I who have served freedom and my country with a religious devotion cannot be silent on this solemn occasion. Give us a government in which the law will be obeyed, the statesman respected, and the people free; a government that shall see that the general will and the commandments of the people do not go unheeded.

Consider, Legislators, that vigor in the public services constitutes protection against weakness in the individual and is the scourge of the unrighteous and the hope of society. Remember that the corruption of a nation has its origin in the laxity of the courts and in impunity for crime. Consider that where there is no strength there is no virtue, and without virtue the Republic cannot survive. Finally, remember that anarchy destroys freedom, and unity preserves order.

Legislators! In the name of Colombia I plead with you and earnestly pray that, as the arbiters of our destinies and like the Provi-

---

[1] Doubtless Perú, which claimed territory in the southern part of Colombia (ed.).

dence you thus represent, you will enact, for the people, for the army, for the judge, and for the governor, a binding, an inflexible code of laws!

SIMÓN BOLÍVAR

---

288. To JOAQUÍN MOSQUERA

[*Biblioteca Popular* (Bogotá), No. 102]

Bogotá, February 29, 1828.

My dear friend:

I find encouragement in the hope that by now you are in Ocaña, struggling with your colleagues to save them from themselves. I am sending Colonel O'Leary, in whom I place the fullest confidence, to deliver my message to the great convention. It is written, to be sure, with some bitterness, or at best it is painted in the blackest of colors. I did not wish to do it, but the ministers insisted, and I yielded against my will. I am afraid to publish it, and as yet I do not know if I shall.

From every section of the country they write me that public opinion is opposed to the Constitution and to reform; that they do not want a constitution until peace has been concluded, and until the new governments in America have discovered what is the best system of government. They want a provisional government, empowered to preserve and organize the Republic. So far as I am concerned, I know neither what I want nor what is best; but I know definitely that Colombia will perish sooner or later, and that only a miracle can save her from impending doom.

My greatest desire is to get away, but should the great convention even succeed in part, I shall remain to see the outcome, and if it fails to establish a strong government, I shall leave as soon as I learn what changes it has made.

I am leaving for Venezuela on the 7th of next month to put down the disorders afflicting that unfortunate country and to be ready to depart when the time comes.

I should like you, in so far as it is possible, to work hand-in-hand with Castillo, forgetting the treasury argument. How harsh is my treatment of the treasury! My message states that Colombia is bankrupt and hounded by creditors. I have refrained from referring to the loan, except casually, and I make no complaint against the administration. I attribute almost everything to the law, since laws and constitutions are the point at issue, and every man must be appealed to in his own tongue.

O'Leary will tell you anything you want to know.

I am your devoted friend,

BOLÍVAR

P.S. Regards to your esteemed brother Rafael.

---

289. To J[osé] M[aría] del Castillo [y Rada],
PRESIDENT OF THE CONGRESS OF OCAÑA

[Blanco y Azpurúa, XII, 248]

Sátiva, March 24, 1828.

My esteemed friend and Sir:

My aide-de-camp Wilson has orders to go to Ocaña on his way to Cúcuta, where he is to bring me news of the installation of the Constituent Congress. At the same time he is to call on you to pay my respects. Wilson also carries letters and important documents relative to Venezuela for O'Leary, and news from Bogotá for your information and guidance. The entire country is inspired with a holy fear of anarchy and federation, and is, moreover, resolved to demand a nationwide referendum, unless the great convention acts in accordance with the general opinion. Popular protests against federation and weak government are pouring in from every region. Union and strength is the rallying cry, and you may be sure that this cry will not go unheeded, as tempers are inflamed. You must, therefore, my dear friend, bring this to the attention of the great convention, so that there will be no equivocation.

Please write, as only you can, to Cartagena, for you are heard with admiration and respect.

Ours will be a most unhappy land unless [the Congress of] Ocaña restores it to health, for the salvation of all. I pray more fervently and earnestly than for my own life that you too will enjoy the precious treasure of health. You are the hope of the great convention, and the great convention is Colombia's only hope. Be mindful, therefore, of your value and of the high esteem in which I hold you.

Be so kind as to pay my respects to Messrs. Rebollo and J. de Francisco, to whom I cannot write for lack of time.

I am your most affectionate friend and servant,

BOLÍVAR

290. To COLONEL DANIEL F[LORENCE] O'LEARY

[Copy]

Sátiva, March 24, 1828.

My dear O'Leary:

Major Wilson has orders to proceed to Ocaña, in order to learn whether or not the great convention is to be installed early next month, as we all earnestly hope. He will bring you various letters that will inform you of conditions in Venezuela, and he will also be able to report all the news between Bogotá and the towns thereabouts, which you can communicate to Castillo, Mosquera, Aranda, Juan de Francisco, and any others, as you think advisable, in order that they may use the information as they see fit. The letters that I am sending from General Páez and certain other friends may help to give insight into the true intentions of that General and of the Venezuelan people. The one in which he tells me of the steps that are being taken to inform the great convention of the people's wishes, I have sent to Bogotá. But you may have been informed of all this by General Briceño; he saw General Páez' aide-de-camp, who told him what he had seen and heard up to the time of his departure from Caracas on the 6th of this month.

From Bogotá, Tunja, and the south appeals are being made to the grand convention to the effect that the people desire neither a federation nor a weak government. The spirit in the capital has been excellent, as well as that in the towns of this department. They have asked that I again be granted extraordinary powers, as you no doubt know.

Since General Páez reports that conditions in Venezuela are satisfactory, I rather think that I shall move no farther from Cúcuta than Barinas, just in case anything important should occur. But if the majority of the delegates should show a proper frame of mind, I might perhaps leave and go where I am most needed, so as not to lose precious time in such circumstances. For this reason, I want you to send me detailed reports of the names and views [of the delegates]. Wilson will bring me this valuable report, together with the reply, if any, of the convention to my message. He will also bring me word as to whether or not Bernardo Herrera, who is the bearer of the Venezuelan petitions to the Congress, has arrived in Ocaña. You must remain in Ocaña until you can determine the results of the convention. Even after Ferguson arrives there, you are not to leave until you know the results. Have Castillo and P. Briceño Méndez read these communications, so that they will be fully informed. As regards Peña, I can tell you that he has written me very gracious letters, expressing the most cordial sentiments. As for the rest, General Briceño will tell you what he knows.

My only source of anxiety in Colombia is Cartagena. It would be a good idea if Ferguson were to go there to keep General Montilla informed, and if both you and Juan de Francisco were to write him along these lines and help him with your suggestions.

I feel that Castillo should give the people of Cartagena a good lecture. They will heed him like an oracle, for they love and respect him.

I shall close by saying that, unless wisdom inspires the convention and moderation guides the people, this very year will see the beginning of a civil war that will end God knows when. I feel certain I have influence enough with the people to hold them in check, but not so with the convention. The people's weaknesses can be remedied, but not the convention's. And so I shall be the first to leave the country.

Mendoza is not going to attend the great convention, and I believe half the delegates from the south will not attend either. I greatly fear the convention will be at loggerheads because the parties are about equally represented.

Good-bye, my dear O'Leary. I am your devoted

BOLÍVAR

291. TO GENERAL JOSÉ ANTONIO PÁEZ

[*Original*]

Bucaramanga, April 12, 1828.

My dear General:

In these last few days I have learned of the early meetings of the great convention, where the first developments favored our opponents. They, of course, refused to seat Dr. Peña and Dr. Bruzual, two of our friends. We are momentarily expecting my aide-de-camp Wilson with news of the official opening of that body and the election of its president.

Twenty-six members of the great convention enthusiastically applauded a dispatch from Padilla advising them of his revolt, and gave him a vote of thanks for his abominable conduct.[1] Both Montilla and Peña have complained to me officially, and I have written to the convention concerning these matters, saying what had to be said about having Peña admitted and demanding an explanation for the ignoble treatment accorded him. Both matters strike me as being of the greatest importance. By their treatment of Peña they sought to nullify my amnesty decree of January 1, and by supporting Padilla they meant to provoke a bitter revolution. Santander's party is both insolent and frantic; it will be a marvel if it does not wreck the Republic. I fear it greatly, for I do not see among my friends the fanatical zeal that the others possess. If the convention allows itself to be led by those scoundrels, countless ills will befall our country, because, although at first glance the success of the convention may seem natural and assured, the laws it adopts will cause powerful repercussions. Since a new constitution lacks full legality, its opponents are apt to believe themselves authorized and entitled to destroy it, while people of honor will show little interest, or they may even consider such plans for destroying it to be justifiable. Only law or the sanction of many generations can protect a government. Lacking these foundations, it is exposed to endless friction and quarrels, whereupon annihilation follows, because sheer fatigue permits that which is least desired to ensue. No other institution is so cruel and costly! For my part, I am far from willing to assume the direction of affairs under such calamitous conditions. I am ready to sacrifice

---

[1] General José Padilla, formerly in command of the Colombian navy, led a revolt against the government in Cartagena, which was speedily put down by the government forces (ed.).

a great deal to obey the lawfully expressed will of the people; but by no means will I accept so much as the title of citizen in a country which, lacking a constitution, is weak and divided.

As I have told you above, I am expecting Wilson today. We hope for little enough from Ocaña; nevertheless, he may bring some good news to console us among all these dismal prospects. If there is time I shall append his story at the end of this letter, which must leave this afternoon to catch the post for Venezuela at Pamplona.

The federalist party fell at Ocaña because the entire nation had turned against it. And now the opposition plans to so weaken the central government that it will be unable to govern. I shall have nothing to do with such a government even if they endeavor to force me to head it, for they know very well that I am not so much of a fool as to expose myself to trouble uselessly and against the public interest. These gentlemen intend to shake the structure of society by adopting new philosophical concepts of individual rights and establishing municipal governments that will be more cantankerous than the very *cabildos* that have been responsible for all the rebellions we have witnessed. The demagogues refuse to believe that freedom is kept alive only by the practice of virtue and that, where this reigns, tyranny is impotent. Therefore, as long as we are lacking in those virtues and as we cannot be free, let the nature of the state be what it will; and, as it has never been possible to reform a people corrupted by slavery, nations, too, need conquerors only, never liberators. History has proved this, and Montesquieu has recorded it. Consequently, our struggle will be eternal, and our ills will continue while we strive for the impossible. It would be necessary for us to alter our very natures in order to be able to live under an absolutely free government. We would have to change our habits and customs, become austere, and free ourselves of our baser passions, or else forego the chimera that forms our plans. I was the most deluded of all, and it has taken forty years of disillusionment for me to arrive at this pessimistic and despairing conclusion. We have wasted our time and wrecked our handiwork. We have piled error upon error and made worse the condition of the people, who will eternally deplore our inexperience.

The news from the south and from Bogotá gives us nothing to fear. In truth, there is no cause for alarm as long as hope in the convention survives.

From Cartagena, General Montilla writes to assure me that the country there is quieting down little by little but that General . . .

[Padilla]¹ has not yet been taken. Padilla must be tried according to the law and strict justice, as it is high time that an example is made of such mortal crimes, which, I am sure, are encouraged when allowed to go unpunished. As for myself, I do not yet know what I shall do. I shall remain here until conditions in the Magdalena area are completely tranquil; meanwhile, I shall carry on, resolved to go wherever danger or necessity call me.

Herrera writes that he has reached Ocaña and will pass by here in order to bring me news of the results of his mission. The Venezuelan delegates complain loudly of not having received a sufficient daily allowance. I should like an adjustment made, if not for all, at least for the poorer ones.

I am your devoted friend,

BOLÍVAR

The 13th. Since yesterday another post has come from Venezuela, but it brought nothing. Wilson is not yet here, and I am sending this off in order not to delay the post. Yours.

----

292. To General Pedro Briceño Méndez

[*Original*]

Bucaramanga, April 23, 1828.

My dear General:

I was deeply affected by your letter, which Ferguson brought me. O'Leary's letter is more or less in the same vein. Both offer me hopes and assurances, but I can foresee nothing but disappointment and defeat for all of you. Your opponents win on every hand, and they are highly elated over the success of their cause. You and your supporters, on the other hand, make it appear as if you were defending some crime, for your appeal is solely to compassion and humanity. I shall not draw you a comparative table of principles, developments, or personalities, as it would be superfluous to list what everyone knows. Your group will have to compromise with the federalists,

---

¹ The text reads "Montilla" (comp.).

since you lack the strength to support the cause of good sense and justice, inasmuch as virtue is gentle and crime violent. They will triumph without a doubt, after robbing us of glory, fortune, and hope for Colombia and outraging us in a thousand ways. I see all this very clearly, and, if I must say what is at the bottom of my heart, it is only for my country's sake that I regret it; as for my own sake, I rejoice. Every triumph of my enemies opens wider the door through which I can leave Colombia. I shall leave, and, from a distance of one or two thousand leagues, the frightful tumult of civil war will reach me. I shall assuredly not return a fifth time to a country from which I have been shamefully exiled on so many occasions. It matters little to me, therefore, by what means Colombia's downfall is decreed, since those gentlemen can at best choose only the palliatives, never the salutary remedies. Colombia is a chaos in which the anarchy of so many leaders can serve only to create an ever-increasing confusion among their followers.

I am awaiting the arrival of Herrera before making a final decision respecting my departure for Venezuela, as the arrest of Padilla has eliminated my reason for remaining here. Perhaps I shall never return, for this has been my intention since I first thought of leaving Bogotá. It was only to oblige my friends that I promised to help them save the country, but who can save his country when it is controlled by such monsters, when civic virtue is called monarchism and parricide liberalism, when the basest of thieves is considered the oracle of opinion and of principle? I do not propose to have anything to do with such riff-raff [canalla], and I will not coöperate with them for a moment.

If you want my opinion as to what you should do, I shall advise you to retire to Venezuela, as *you are suspected* of being the mouthpiece of my opinions. Those wretches ought to regard you as the finger of Providence pointing the way to their salvation. But, since they abuse us both, we should leave them to their suspicions and let them wallow in their own filth. Wretches, why I gave them the very air they breathe, and now I am suspect and my friends and relatives are scorned! A fine thing!

Tell O'Leary to regard this letter as his own, and that all I have to add on his account is to ask him to come to my General Headquarters immediately upon completing his assignment to obtain money for the delegates that need it. I feel that his presence at Ocaña is unnecessary, as it gives those gentlemen the idea that I need them for some purpose. I do not need them or Colombia for anything, and they do not have to point out to me that the popular will has been of no help to me, and, if by chance there have been some feeble voices raised in my behalf, they have spoken in vain. In spite of resistance and the popular will I gave this country freedom, and, as the glory of it is all that I own, no one can take it away from me.

A thousand regards to Castillo; tell him that I have not written because I am in a very bad mood and, moreover, Ferguson brought me no letter from him to which I could reply.

If you happen to have held back the messages, present them immediately, as I have ordered them to be published.

Tell Joaquín Mosquera that the same reasons that keep me from writing Castillo also prevent me from writing to him.

I am your devoted

BOLÍVAR

---

293. To J[osé] M[aría] del Castillo [y Rada]

[Blanco y Azpurúa, XII, 436]

Bucaramanga, May 15, 1828.

Dear friend and Sir:

After reading your two kind letters, brought by O'Leary and Herrera, I at once declared a truce with my sentiments and designs. I have suspended the course of my desires, making them subject to the wishes of my friends. This responsibility places upon them the obligation of justifying my confidence. What you tell me brings to mind the whole gamut of my former hopes. One paragraph of your letter tells it all; that paragraph is the prophecy I wish to see fulfilled. I shall repeat it, to be sure it is not forgotten: "We shall do nothing that is not entirely to the purpose; otherwise, we shall adjourn the sessions and postpone the reforms until another time. If nothing can be accomplished, we will depart, consigning the promoters of evil to public censure." This program is perfect and provides for every contingency. Therefore, I shall restrain myself and wait patiently for the good my friends will do. Herrera has said nothing, nor has O'Leary done more than confirm my faith that you are making every effort to save the Republic. This cause is exactly what induced me to change my plan, since it was no longer possible conveniently to put it into action. As I was determined not to serve Colombia except to good purpose, I was obliged to tell you and the others all that went on in my mind, and my confession was proof of the sentiments that I have always professed. These have been directed not to the accomplishment of any positive good but to the avoidance of evils which I consider inevitable. Our desperate situation compels us to choose from among the worst of the alternatives; consequently, come what may, there can be no new cause, and we can never hope to find a solution. In this horrible dilemma, desperation itself counsels me to remain inactive and accept fate. Nevertheless, you must never forget your own admirable dictum, that timid counsels never fail to lead to bad results. I shall adopt this motto on condition that you gentlemen swear to abide by it. You yourself have said it, and I therefore take you at your word and pledge myself to the same terms. Let our watchword, then, be, Death rather than timidity. When I hear talk of bravery and daring I feel my whole being restored; I am reborn, as it were, for my country and for glory. How happy we should be if wisdom could be guided by strength! Then I could promise the impossible; then Colombia and the rest of America could be saved. Consequently, let all our friends adopt this sentiment, and I shall banish from my lips forever all unworthy talk of danger and fear. Let them command me to uproot anarchy, and not even the memory of it shall remain. When the law authorizes me to act, I find nothing impossible. These promises that spring from the heart and from my feelings of patriotism are not idle boasting or mere pretense. No, my friend, one who has taken part in so many miracles is entitled to expect the best.

Please read the letter I have written to General Briceño. Though its tone is quite different, I have but one heart, and you may count on it in all things as that of your most devoted friend,

BOLÍVAR

294. To [José] Rafael Arboleda

[Copy]

Bucaramanga, June 1, 1828.

My esteemed friend:

Yesterday I received your very kind letter of May 6, which has given me a feeling of great satisfaction by virtue of the admirable spirit you say prevails in your important department. In this regard, I must thank you for the part you have played in the restoring of my reputation.

May I, to begin with, express my surprise that you still address me so formally. No, no! I, Excellency? ¡Por Dios! Stop tormenting me with so much etiquette, for it offends me. The title of friend alone is as good as a hymnal of verses or any distinction this world can bestow. As for the title of Excellency, you know I do not deserve it. I am content with being just; hence, I have no right to the superlative of excellence. Address me as plain you [usted] and, were we Romans, thou [tú] would be still more appropriate. Such is the title of friendship, confidence, and all genuine feeling.

You ask me to join in the rehabilitation of Colombia, and to this end you proffer me your services, which you term insignificant. No, my friend, that is not so. O'Leary and I have constantly regretted your absence from the great convention. Our friend Joaquín[1] is doing divinely and appears to be the best orator in the assembly; but he has lost some time because of his excessive caution. Rafael Mosquera, of whom you speak so highly, has proved to be quite mediocre, and sometimes he even opposes his cousin. On the whole there has been considerable improvement, and they are now fairly well set on their course, especially Joaquín, who is the delight of our friends. They say that his speech on federation was inimitable. Nevertheless, we have suffered so many setbacks that, very shortly, they say, the defeated will be put to flight. They are only delaying their withdrawal in hopes of submitting, as a last resort, a new constitutional plan containing ideas more vigorous than those submitted by Soto and Azuero. The plan of these two practically eliminates the executive and establishes a modified federal system. Our friends, therefore, have decided to abandon the field rather than seal the ruin of Colombia. This is a very dangerous step that will place me in an embarrassing predicament. As yet, I do not know what I shall do in case such a

---

[1] Mosquera (ed.).

scandalous event takes place. Furthermore, I do not know what the opposition will do; hence, I shall bide my time and act in accordance with the circumstances, without showing my hand too soon. I can therefore venture only one thought, which amounts to this: I am determined not to abandon my country in her hour of peril. I previously suggested to our friends in the great convention that, since we could not hope to achieve a government suited to the entire nation, we should divide the Republic and let each section govern itself according to its needs and desires. But our friends became alarmed and said that they would not be a party to such a plan. They earnestly pleaded with me not to desert them and promised to do anything rather than adopt an inadequate constitution. They are, therefore, determined to attempt everything, if it should be necessary. And so you see the dilemma in which I am placed, one from which I can see no escape. But, of course, I am counting upon all my friends in Colombia in the event we have to resort to extraordinary measures; and in that event I particularly rely upon my friend Arboleda and my friends in Cauca, from whom I expect the fullest coöperation. I presume, of course, that you will immediately arrange with the Intendant and Commanding General the best course of action. I believe that the said contingency will not arise until sometime early in June; thus it is possible that we may witness these events within a matter of fifteen or twenty days. When that time comes, I urge you to use your good sense and strong character. God grant that such noble efforts will not be in vain! Meanwhile, accept the devotion of one who holds you in the highest esteem and respect.

I am sincerely your friend,

BOLÍVAR

P.S. I am leaving for Bogotá within four days; as the situation is utterly hopeless, we shall have to act. The letters I receive from Ocaña indicate that the great convention is definitely about to come to a sudden and bad end; hence, the proposed constitution will not even get a hearing. Our friends are desperate, including Joaquín. His cousin, too, is expected to follow the others.

295. To [GENERAL DIEGO IBARRA]

[*Copy*]

Bucaramanga, June 2, 1828.

My dear Diego:

I am sending your brother to Maracaibo with these letters for Venezuela, so that General Páez will be informed of the state of affairs at Ocaña. My friends there write me in a very sorrowful, almost despairing manner, as you will see from what they say. They were about to introduce a draft of a very liberal constitution, but they fear that it will not receive support, for Santander's party is strongly opposed to it as are ten or twelve of the Venezuelan delegates. Moreover, there is a non-partisan group which is frequently found on the side of the trouble-making faction. Only the delegates from Cartagena, those from the south, and half of the Venezuelan delegates, some twenty-six in all, support the government. These are fully determined to withdraw next week, thereby dissolving the convention, unless the delegates can at least agree on a fair constitution or on a provisional government that can first ascertain the will of the people. They demand that, ultimately, the Constitution be submitted to a popular referendum for acceptance, modification, or rejection. If the stubborn *santanderistas* agree to neither of these alternatives, the respectable delegates will refuse to be a party to their iniquities even though the resulting scandal will greatly embarrass us, fill the country with rumors, and damage our standing abroad.

I suggested a resolution to my friends that might have conciliated the interests of the various sections of Colombia, but I could find no one who would venture to introduce it. Everyone has accused me of intending to abandon my country and even of bringing about her destruction, thus sacrificing the glory of my name and the most hallowed interests of Colombia. They sent O'Leary from Ocaña to prevail upon me. I had to yield, as it is my duty to save the Republic in a time of such imminent peril, for it has never been my intention either to sacrifice my country or to lose my reputation. My only thought has been to reconcile the bitterly opposed parties and interests.

I expect a terrible storm to break at any moment; we must, therefore, prepare ourselves to deal with it, taking all precaution to prevent the disorder from involving us in the horrors of a bloody anarchy. I am, however, refraining from so much as expressing an opinion so that the popular will can express itself regarding the initial establishment of a provisional government whose purpose shall be to organize the Republic in accordance with the wishes of the people. I insisted on the convocation of the convention in order that the nation's will might be carried out. But this aim has not been achieved; consequently, it becomes my duty to enable the nation freely to express its wishes, each person stating his particular wish, no matter what, provided that no attempt is made to act arbitrarily. I therefore earnestly beg and instruct you that, whatever party the people finally adopt, everything be made to proceed with perfect order and in conformity with the laws.

Caution, my dear Diego, must be exercised in everything, and everything must be done in conjunction with General Páez and General Salom, to whom you should send a copy of this letter, for them to act accordingly. Write to Lino[1] telling him what I have told you, and also to the Marquis.

Your devoted

BOLÍVAR

---

296. To J[osé] M[anuel] Restrepo,
    MINISTER OF THE INTERIOR

[Blanco y Azpurúa, XII, 569]

Bucaramanga, June 3, 1828.

My dear friend:

My respect and admiration for you have grown with the reading of your *Historia de Colombia*.[2] This is one of those works that create a stir and arouse criticism but which, in the judgment of ensuing generations, is wiped clear of the charges of calumniators. I put myself in the place of these later generations and, impelled by the sense of justice which inspires me, I declare: "The author has endeavored to ascertain the truth and has published it courageously. If at times he

---

[1] Lino de Clemente (ed.).
[2] *Historia de la revolución de la República de Colombia*. 10 vols. (Paris, 1827) (ed.).

has been partial to his friends, he has not on that account been unfair to his opponents. And if he has erred, this is only human. The earnestness with which he has sought the facts and the wisdom with which he has evaluated them excuse any unintentional errors into which he has lapsed. His judgments are severe upon those who have worked evil, and his indulgence of the good is irrefutable proof of the honesty of his principles. Though the accused may complain, I absolve Restrepo of the charge of ill-faith, but I do have one reproach to make—his severity with Madrid, who was more to be pitied than blamed, more deserving of praise than of censure, because a single moment of weakness should not erase a lifetime of service. It was his duty to preside over the funeral rites of his country." [1]

I can voice this opinion with the impartiality of an admitted friend, since you yourself have treated me with a similar indulgent impartiality. Each of us is perfectly right to a certain degree, for we do not depart from the facts in the slightest. It is no fault of ours if others see them in a different light.

Your pen has the gift of historicity, simplicity, accuracy, and thoroughness. I must confess that your work strikes me as being better than anything I expected; however, when you publish a new edition in Caracas, where there is a first-class printshop, you will set an excellent example of fairness and moderation if you add notes or corrections, after you have heard the opinions of others and the protests of the offended. If I were in your place that is what I should do. Appeal to the public to give you the facts, making it clear that you will reject nothing if it is accompanied by the proof of impartiality. An announcement of this sort, worded simply and effectively, might have excellent results. For my part, I can foresee that the openminded public will be with you, and I am certain you realize that you cannot take anyone to task without reprisal; hence, you should be prepared for all manner of vengeful attacks. No one can achieve fame with impunity, nor can anyone rise above the average and escape the backbiting of the envious. Let us, then, find consolation in these thoughts for the cruel rebuffs that merit must endure.

Accept the assurance of my gratitude and esteem.

BOLÍVAR

---

[1] Madrid had been under suspicion of treason (ed.).

297. To Estanislao Vergara, Minister
    of Foreign Affairs

[*Original*]

Bucaramanga, June 3, 1828.

My dear friend and Sir:

You are the best foreign minister on earth where polemics is concerned. Wonderful! What a neat thrust you delivered Villa.[1] If that gentleman had only known his trade, he would have made off promptly, with his fine passport of twenty sheets in quarto. Surely no diplomat has ever been given a more complete dismissal. This is what is known as being dismissed with the honors of war. You can be sure I did not mind the bit of well-proven evidence that you served upon the Peruvian. This is a case of a recalcitrant mule needing a hard driver. He came to us bent on a lawsuit, and you haled him to court right then and there. I suppose the judgment of God will decide the verdict; consequently, there will be no appeal. And so, my dear friend, brook no nonsense from this contemptible element whose placating explanations constitute only a renewal of outrages. If, in America, we continue in this fashion, we shall reach a point where our affairs are conducted in the gladiators' arena. How shameful! We scarcely know how to greet our friends. I have often regretted being an American, for there is nothing, however exalted, that we do not debase. At any rate, accept my thanks for your trouble in rebuffing these affronts.

I shall not reply to the other points mentioned in your letter, as the one that I have written General Urdaneta will be shown to you, so that you both may decide what is best. The bull is already in the ring, and now we shall see who are the valiant. I count you among that group and, if I must speak plainly, you are the best of the lot. Let us put fear behind us and save our country. You lured me on, and I allowed myself to become involved; therefore, it is essential that the two of you do your duty. You yourself should exert your tremendous influence and assume your rightful place in the public mind. The result will be to our best advantage, while otherwise we may lose out altogether. In short, you two decide what is best, and I shall come at once.

It would be wise to announce my expected arrival in the *Gaceta*. Accept the sincere expressions of my friendship.

BOLÍVAR

---

[1] Peruvian Minister to Colombia (ed.).

298. To José Fernández Madrid, Colombian Minister to England

[Copy]

Bogotá, June [28], 1828.[1]

My dear friend:

My letter from Bucaramanga must have upset you greatly, considering the feeling with which it was written. At that time I visualized Colombia afloat upon a sea of disaster. I could see her going down on the very ship that was to have saved her, and I, in a mood of despair, was determined to flee rather than witness the last rites of the Republic. The great convention, which was to have satisfied the demands and needs of the people of Colombia, was doing nothing to accomplish its sacred trust. Vengeance, hatred, and partisan spirit ruled the hearts of many of its members, who, under the banners of General Santander, combatted the efforts of the true friends of the Republic, the lovers of order and stability, who sought their country's welfare; or perhaps I should say those members abandoned their country in order to strike a blow against me. During the sessions and in their proposals and deliberations, they were concerned with but one thought—to crush and destroy the power of the executive, for no other reason except that I exercised it. While they flattered the people by appearing to grant an extraordinary measure of freedom, they were actually preparing the people's grave, ignoring their petitions, and, most dangerous of all, inciting the army. In brief, the thought of destroying me obsessed them completely. The friends of the government, the men of good intentions who attended, soon realized that they would be unable to accomplish anything during the convention and that they could only struggle in vain against the torrent of passions that drowned out their voices. The worthy José María Castillo took upon himself the noble task of harmonizing the views of the well-intentioned in order to present a solid front against Santander's group, which very early revealed their intentions and the perfidy of their politics. They were so carried away by their own passion that, even before they had been formally seated, they had the insolence to give a vote of thanks to General Padilla, who had just committed the scandalous action of bribing the troops in Cartagena and usurping the civil and military government of that

---

[1] The copy is erroneously dated June 4. Comparison with other letters of June 28 makes it apparent that this letter is of the latter date (comp.).

city. Yes, my friend, this was the first act of the federal party, of those who called themselves the friends of freedom and the foes of tyranny. The convention was scarcely installed before they openly flaunted the true colors of their party, and, being superior in number and in aggressiveness, they routed our friend Castillo, who had defended the nation's interests and stability. It would be too lengthy a story to enumerate, in this letter, the scandalous incidents, the treasonable proposals of these enemies of order, who, as I said before, forgot their country in order to . . . [attack me].[1] It brings to mind the days of the French convention. At last the moment to revise the Constitution arrived. This was the moment when the *santanderistas* poured out all the venom of their political views. They introduced a plan which, in reality, amounted to federation, without the advantages attributed to the federal system. Its tone was one of vengeance and its main element destruction, for, among other absurdities, it limited the executive in every way. It was easy to see that this plan was the work of Azuero and his companions. Castillo then presented his plan. This, though better adapted to our situation, was also too weak, in view of Colombia's present condition, her needs, and the indispensable power that her government must have in order to hold in check the passions and the fierce factional spirit that have erupted on all sides. Neither plan was accepted, and the convention was, therefore, deadlocked. My own decision, bitter as it was, had already been made; hence, I left to find a vessel that would carry me far from Colombia, far from the chaos of anarchy—but Providence, not intending to abandon us, inspired the people of this capital with what they believed to be the only means of salvation. On the 13th of this month, they proclaimed, in the main square, the resolution which you will see, delegating their sovereignty to me and entrusting me with their destinies, to regenerate a nation which everyone regarded as lost. This proclamation fired the enthusiasm and hopes of the other towns, which hastened to follow Bogotá's example. All this took place while the convention was breaking up because Castillo and his associates, refusing to underwrite the ruin of Colombia, had walked out. At this point I received a deputation from the capital and petitions from every town to accede to their pleas. Thereupon, though the sacrifice was great, I could hesitate no longer, and I assented, relying on popular support and the backing of all

---

[1] *Cascarme* (to break me) has been changed to *atacarme*, which is doubtless what Bolívar dictated (comp.).

good men. On the 24th of this month, I entered this capital, which welcomed me as if it were a day of triumph and overwhelmed me with such demonstrations of trust and consideration that once again they forced me to return to public office.

The Secretariat will officially inform you about all matters, including my present situation. It is true that this situation is due to a misfortune which we have fortunately avoided, but it also offers me the means of rebuilding the country, as I have mentioned, and of restoring morale, establishing justice, and, above all, replenishing the treasury, the source of public credit. This will be one of my first concerns, for it is the only means left to us with which to reëstablish Colombia's good name. My efforts toward these ends will prepare the road that may lead us to the stability we have thus far been unable to achieve.

To all this must be added the fact that Perú has just committed the outrage of invading Bolivia without prior declaration and quite without cause. Perú also maintains an army which constantly threatens the province of Guayaquil, and she is employing every ruse and device that she can in order to incite the departments of the south to revolt. In short, Perú is drawing us into a war which, ultimately, we will be unable to avoid except at the expense of our national honor and credit. Moreover, it must be borne in mind that, if the Peruvians invade our southern provinces, as has been asserted, that section will be left in utter ruin; it would even be dangerous for us to wage war in that region because of its present wretched state. We have therefore decided that it would be better for us to be the invaders rather than the invaded, and we are accordingly preparing for a campaign which, however regrettable, is necessary if we are to insure the tranquility of the south and to obtain the satisfaction and the indemnities that Perú owes us.

I am very much obliged to you, my dear friend, for the interest that you are taking concerning the matter of the mines, and I am very glad to know that the gentlemen there have agreed to pay the rentals, pending conclusion of the sales contract, which I trust will now be executed. Be so kind as to assure them that, upon that understanding, I shall waive the amount due for the last six months.

I repeat my request that you send us the statement of account for the mines.

Your affectionate friend,

BOLÍVAR [1]

299. To General J[osé] A[ntonio] Páez

[*Original*]

Bogotá, August 9, 1828.

My dear General:

I have received your kind letter and the Valencia proclamation, both brought by Revenga. The proclamation has made me very happy, because of your promptness and because it is in keeping with the one from Bogotá. Revenga has given me encouraging news about Venezuela, which has afforded me immeasurable satisfaction, for I am always extremely anxious about that country, especially since I know that the eastern region is restless and wretched, with poverty everywhere. I do not know what can be done to better the lot of that stricken area; its plight is of such a nature that only a drastic reorganization can help it, unless its leaders are clever enough to suggest a plan that will enable us to be of assistance.

Revenga has touched on several matters which you asked him to bring to my attention. I wholeheartedly agree with you that the police force should be enlarged and improved. In order to effect this change a set of general police regulations should be drafted, after which you could officially recommend such amendments as you deem advisable in order that we may speed this beneficial enterprise. I also agree that the judiciary should be organized as it was under the Spaniards, and you are hereby authorized to do so. I also believe that permission should be granted to export mules, but only under the following conditions: first, General Salom should be empowered to see that they are exported through the department of Cumaná, paying at least thirty *pesos* per head, to permit that impoverished department to reap the benefit. But I do not approve of their being removed through any other place, as my object is to let General Salom have this authority so that he, in turn, can guard against illegal exports at other points without his approval. Furthermore, I concur with you that Venezuela's plan of finances should not be changed; however, I want, even more, to have the nation's credit reëstablished. Accordingly, I have recommended that the taxes on exports should not be spent for any other purpose. The English [bankers], through their government, have already made representations for what is owed them and the Colombian public has begun to do the same, as Colombia's finances are painfully low.

I have already ordered the granting of a brigadier general's commission to your friend Colonel Ortega, to whom you will tender my personal congratulations. I want him to know how much I have done for him and how pleased I am with his promotions.

By post from the south we have learned, with great satisfaction, that General Gamarra has withdrawn from Bolivia by way of the Desaguadero River after occupying La Paz for several days and keeping that area in a state of alarm and apprehension. On that occasion the Bolivians proved their love of country and her institutions. No one was disloyal, and, in the midst of that terrible disaster, General Sucre named General Urdinenea as his successor.[1] Perú is placed, therefore, in a rather painful and embarrassing situation, for, having failed in her attempt, she finds her aims thwarted. You have probably seen in our papers that we have declared war on Perú. This does not mean that we can begin it immediately, for we must wait and see what comes of the Spanish expedition which looms as an imminent threat. I have written to you previously about this expedition, and because of it I was compelled to declare a state of emergency. You must shout this decree from the housetops in order to frighten off the Spaniards and silence the excitable demagogues. I do not believe, of course, that this decree can be carried out completely, but at least we will do what duty demands of us to save our country. The decree should be printed and distributed everywhere with all possible fanfare, and sent to the Antilles so that it will reach Havana.

Matters here are continuing as they began. Resolutions arrive with every post from the south, the latest from as far away as Quito, where the decree was adopted amidst indescribable enthusiasm. All have given me unqualified support, and, with the exception of an occasional follower of Santander, such as Soto, Azuero, and Gómez, New Granada is not a bit behind Venezuela in these sentiments.

I have learned from Revenga that you are very much pleased with Sanabria, the new secretary, and that all our friends are also satisfied with him. I implore you to keep him at your side, because everyone likes him. Let us not alienate anyone, for, frankly, we are in no position to court trouble. You would not accept Guzmán, so keep this new secretary as a special favor to me. I insist that Dr. Peña come and occupy his post in the Supreme Court, if only for a few days, for his own satisfaction and for the sake of the humiliation his enemies will suffer when they see him restored to an office from which

---

[1] Sucre had been elected President of Bolivia in August, 1826 (ed.).

they thought him removed forever. As you probably know, I am about to establish a council of state with one minister from each department. Revenga will represent Venezuela, since neither Peña nor Soublette, whom I had intended to appoint, is here. However, Soublette's name has been entered, although I understand that he will not be here for some time, as he does not want to return to office but would rather remain with his family and devote himself to farming. Everyone wants you to remain in Caracas most of the time and I, too, would appreciate your doing so, especially in view of the new office that you are to hold, namely, that of prefect of the three departments now under your command, which will be formed into provinces with the same names. There will be but one treasury intendant for all of them, and you will be the supreme head for war, treasury, justice, and administration, each government having to deal with you. The treasury intendant will be under your orders. In brief, it will be more or less a viceroyalty or *vice presidencia*[1] for the provinces of Barinas, Achaguas, Carabobo, Caracas, Barcelona, Cumaná, Guayana, and Margarita. I repeat, instead of intendents there will now be only governors. In Caracas there will be a political and military governor to rule the province, under the orders, of course, of the prefect or supreme head. Thus the intendants will cease to enjoy their privileges and influence, but you will have enough to keep you occupied, since your responsibilities and duties will be twice what they were. In the existing circumstances, I could not refrain from drawing up this new reform plan for the outlying sectors of Colombia.

I am your affectionate friend,

BOLÍVAR

---

[1] The *presidencia* was a Spanish colonial administrative unit (ed.).

300. To Dr. Cristóbal Mendoza, Governor
    of the Province of Caracas

[Original]¹

Bogotá, September 16, 1828.

Esteemed friend:

You wrote me a letter under date of August 6, which, on the one hand, fills me with sorrow, while, on the other, your words gratify me in a thousand ways. I cannot bear the thought of what you tell about your life and your family.² A man of learning never dies, because his work lives on, but his family suffers. I do not know how I can tolerate this thought, and, do what I may, I cannot bring myself to accept it as final. Why must you leave us, when so many of us who are undeserving of life survive? Be that as it may, I shall do everything that I possibly can for your deserving family, at least while I am in Colombia. You will leave many friends behind, and we shall all assist your family, for you can be sure that we respect and esteem them, which is unquestionably a great consolation to one who knows that fortune is nothing compared with virtue.

I am ever your most sincere and devoted friend; be confident of the assurance that, be it before the Creator of life or here below in this vale of afflictions, I am the one man in this world who most admires and esteems you as a paragon of virtue and good works.

I am your affectionate and tender friend,

BOLÍVAR

---

¹ From the collection of Dr. Cristóbal L. Mendoza, Caracas, Venezuela (comp.).

² Mendoza had written that he was about to die and that his family would be penniless (ed.).

301. To General Bartolomé Salom, Intendant
of the Department of Maturín

[*Original*]

Bogotá, September 29, 1828.

Dear General:

From the printed enclosure you will note the horrible conspiracy against Colombia and her government which came to a head in this city on the night of the 25th instant.[1] Many details might be added to this account, if there were time, but now we must all concentrate upon discovering whether or not any possible ramifications of this treasonable attempt remain in the provinces. As this is merely a renewal of the efforts made in Ocaña to dissolve and wreck the Republic, specific attention should be given to the subsequent behavior of those who, in the convention, approved the Padilla revolt in Cartagena. They must at least be expelled from the country, but those who are found to be associated with the conspirators here, must be tried immediately and given the full penalty prescribed by law. The most recent decree on conspiracy, that of February 20, includes all the necessary provisions for this purpose, according to the circumstances and the seriousness of the crime. The leniency which has hitherto been practiced by the government has only encouraged new crimes because their perpetrators expect to go unpunished. Colombia now cries aloud that justice be done and that justice alone prevail. This is the only way that Colombia can succeed in reëstablishing order and tranquility; it is the only way she will be able to preserve her existence.

I most particularly commend you to the greatest vigilance and to the prompt punishment of criminals. The situation could not be more solemn or more urgent, nor could the demands of the people be more reasonable or more unanimous. Let us, then, show ourselves as true to Colombia as she expects us to be.

It is impossible for me to write at greater length today, as the excitement and anger against those apprehended must be calmed, and, at the same time, justice must be done. These things require my

---

[1] An attempted assassination of Bolívar failed due to the sagacity of his mistress, Manuela Sáenz, who urged him to jump through a window to escape death. For further details of the conspiracy see Doc. 303 (ed.).

fullest attention. Let me again urge vigilance and ask you to believe me to be your friend.

BOLÍVAR

Bogotá, September 30, 1828.

You must take very special care to keep your department in a state of absolute peace and order, and to discover the accomplices in this conspiracy. I know that General Gómez left with secret instructions to organize it.

The writer has you always in his thoughts.

—————

302. To [GENERAL JOSÉ ANTONIO PÁEZ]

[Original]

[Bogotá, September 30, 1828]

My dear General:

While I was studying the correspondence that you sent me in the care of Carmona, a conspiracy directed against Colombia and myself broke out here. The printed enclosure will give you some of the details, and from it you will see that this conspiracy is but a continuation of the one which the patriotism of certain citizens at Ocaña rendered abortive. The present one, moreover, was precipitated by the fact that it was discovered that same afternoon of the 25th. Although the conspirators could not have labored with greater determination and purpose, they might possibly have accomplished more had the circumstances been different. An active search is being made to discover every accomplice and to bring the guilty to justice. Hereabouts their actions are regarded with the utmost abhorrence, for, in truth, it is impossible to judge in any other way an attempt at the most criminal of all crimes—the ruin of the Republic. The attempt was made against me because I was considered the main obstacle to her destruction. They corrupted the artillery corps stationed here; however, the other troops not only remained loyal but conducted themselves with the most admirable zeal and devotion to duty.

You could hardly expect me, considering these circumstances, to attend to any other matters. I have not yet been able to receive from Carmona the verbal report that I want from him. We must now, above all, take care to save the Republic and to purge her of her enemies. I urge upon you the greatest care and vigilance. All those who supported the Padilla insurrection in Cartagena must be made to leave the country. I repeat that, in every section of the country, the Republic's enemies will be severely punished. The latest decree on conspiracy authorizes whatever powers may be necessary for this purpose. It is time we put an end to it. Hitherto, leniency has borne no fruit but relapses. We must, therefore, let justice do its work.

In these circumstances you can see ever so much more reason why the intendant of Maturín must be a leader of men, as well as a man capable of prudence, firmness, and economy. I am writing General Mariño to this effect today. On your part, please write Salom, commending him to vigilance, extreme economy, and, above all, the maintenance of quiet in that department.

I have learned that Generals Gómez and Guerrero are, or at least they are believed to be, among the conspirators here, and that General Gómez left expressly in order to help organize the revolt in the departments of the east, and that the conspirators felt they could rely on General Guerrero, as he was discontented.

I am your affectionate friend,

BOLÍVAR

---

303. To José FERNÁNDEZ MADRID

[*Copy*]

Bogotá, October 14, 1828.

My dear friend:

Before you receive this, perhaps, you will have had word of a conspiracy that came to a head in this city on September 25. It was aimed at me and at Colombia, and, I might well add, against all America. The attack began at the palace and immediately spread to the barracks of the *Vargas* battalion. Had the conspirators not felt compelled to act hurriedly, for they suspected, as they had good reason to in

view of the arrest of one of their number, that they had been discovered, their treason might have resulted in greater havoc. It was
ostensibly headed by a certain Navarro and by Horment; Luis Vargas
Tejada, a delegate to the convention; Ramón Guerra, departmental
chief of staff; and by Carujo, attaché of the general staff. As Padilla
was to have placed himself at the head of the conspirators, the first
thing they did was to release him.[1] The cry of "Long live General
Santander, long live the Constitution of Cúcuta," was raised. This
cry was accompanied by that of "The tyrant is dead." From time to
time, the artillerymen were heard to say, "And now to their houses."
Indeed, it was not their fault that I was not murdered in my bed.

The people took no part whatever in this coup, which has everywhere been regarded with the abhorrence it deserves. The soldiers
of the ranks especially distinguished themselves by their devotion and
attention to duty. Carujo, Vargas Tejada, Florentino González, Mendoza, and other leaders have still to be apprehended. A search for
Mendoza is now being conducted throughout a certain block in this
city, where he is believed to be hiding. Seven of the others, including
Padilla, have already been executed. The less guilty have been confined in various places. Most of the artillerymen have been sent to
Cartagena, for, although only a few of them are guilty, they had begun to corrupt the entire corps with stories that my own guard had
mutinied, that I had to be rescued, and that the *Vargas* battalion had
also mutinied.

The traitors attempted to carry the conspiracy into the provinces,
and we know exactly how they went about it. But they had little or
no success. All the guile that the leaders possessed would not have
sufficed to secure any help from outsiders, whether voluntary or obtained through subterfuge.

At this very moment news has reached me that Mendoza has been
captured.

From the south, we hear that when the schooner *Guayaquileña* put
out to inspect a Peruvian sloop that was blockading the entrance to
Guayaquil, her only reply was cannon fire; thereupon a lively en-
gagement ensued, and just as the sloop was about to be boarded she
managed to escape. The Peruvian problem having been settled, I am
now anxiously awaiting the arrival of General Sucre, who is expected at any moment. The southern departments are unable to main-

---

[1] Padilla had been imprisoned following his unsuccessful revolt in Cartagena. See Doc. 291 (ed.).

tain the forces that are now concentrated there. They must therefore be ordered to march immediately or be disbanded.

Otherwise, the Republic is of one mind and demands, in no uncertain terms, to be preserved.

I remain your devoted friend and servant,

BOLÍVAR

—————————

304. To GENERAL ANTONIO JOSÉ DE SUCRE

[Copy]

Bogotá, October 28, 1828.

My dear General:

Blessed the day when you reached Guayaquil! I previously entertained the greatest fears regarding your fate, but now I base my fondest hopes upon your return. May your fortune be better than that which attended the Grecian heroes on their return from Troy! Heaven grant you happiness in the arms of your new Penelope!

I am sending a special emissary, namely Dr. Merino, for the purpose of delivering these papers to you. They contain your commission as absolute commander of the south. All my powers, for both good and evil, I delegate to you. Whether or not you make war or peace, save the south or bring about its ruin, you are the arbiter of its destinies. I have placed all my hopes in you. Consider the nature of things in all that you do, and let that which is of immediate concern guide you in making your decisions. Let circumstances pursue their own course; permit yourself to be carried away by them as by an irresistible impulse. Do this and you will always receive praise rather than blame. There is no other way; destiny must be our guide. As for me, I think that glory is a thousand times preferable to happiness, and the vindication of Colombia means more to me than the sordid pleasures of this life.

If by ill chance the inner defenses of Quito should be lost through the insurrection of the Cauca towns, you must center your attention upon Pasto, the principal base of our operations, in order to make sure of that place, which is the key to the south and our point of anchorage. If you are sure of that area, then we can consider further operations, which are of secondary importance.

From separate points, I am having three battalions and a squadron proceed to Popayán. These units are to be kept as a reserve for the Army of the South. I expect, and in fact I want, the Peruvians to come looking for us when they learn of our situation. They will then be able to occupy some portion of our territory, and we can surround and destroy them. Our measure of justice will be in proportion to their crimes. I believe that the Peruvians have dealt with us implacably and forbearance on our part would only encourage their arrogance. It would therefore be inexcusable to dissolve our army, though poverty and selfish interests might demand it of us. If the south were to be disarmed, the Peruvians would take it, and it would suffer threefold. I am ruthless with the ignominious, and I am convinced that Heaven, having sent me these obstacles to overcome, has also willed the *destruction of my enemies*. I am resolved to proceed to the south within a month, by which time I estimate the reserve troops will be prepared to advance. Meantime, I am crushing the abortive conspiracy. Every accomplice will be punished in one fashion or another. Santander is to be the first, but he is also most fortunate, for my generous nature is his shield. His party will be wiped out, and he will be rendered harmless for a long time. That is all I can say for the present. Otherwise, the Republic is progressing famously, though in human affairs nothing is certain.

Venezuela and Cartagena are bulwarks for our friends. Cumaná has been redeemed by General Salom, who is managing the place with remarkable success. He is the true peacemaker and benefactor of his country. I am sorry to add that in the east no one can accomplish anything, thanks to its former *caudillos*. You, my dear General, are the one man of untarnished reputation from that heroic but hapless land.

By the way, are you angry with me because of your family? If I explain, you will see that I am right ten times over, as I always place society before the individual. I shall, however, see that payment is made, for your sake and for the sake of justice. Moreover, if you are really angry with me, I should think that the rest of mankind would be justified in murdering me outright, for I have never offended you, nor have I been tempted to do so.

I am not replying by this courier to Flores or O'Leary or anyone else. That is why I want you to read this letter to them, for I want them to know I have vested in you the very being of Simón Bolívar.

Yes, my dear Sucre, you are one with me, except for the goodness of your heart and the fate that is mine.

I am sending you the official proclamation of this fact; it is to be published, so that it will serve the implicit purpose of its every word.

That your happiness be a thousandfold, dear General, and your glory a thousand times greater is the wish of him who loves you best in this world, though less than you deserve.

BOLÍVAR

P.S. I cannot speak highly enough of the commanders of the south, or of my aide-de-camp, who deserves special mention.[1] Where is there another Flores?—or the incomparable Illingworth, the generous Torres, the shrewd Heres, the noble González, the courageous and heroic Sandes, Urdaneta, and the other brave men of that army, each of whom I love as a particular friend.

---

305. To General José Antonio Páez

[*Original*]

Bogotá, October 30, 1828.

My dear General:

Excepting General Sucre's arrival in Guayaquil, we have nothing to report by this post. General Sucre was in Callao, where he had occasion to observe the Peruvian government's behavior toward us. La Mar issued a furious proclamation against me, and, in an insolent reply, he rejected the friendly notes General Sucre had sent him with a view to settling Perú's differences with Colombia. La Mar has come to take command of the army along our border, and a break may be expected very shortly, especially since Obando's revolt in Patía will greatly encourage our enemies, who will lend it greater importance than it yet possesses, although it may become serious if the *pastusos* rebel, as is quite possible, considering the ill will they bear Colombia. I have given the command in the south to Sucre, with authority to make war or peace or do whatever he thinks best. Our troops number

---

[1] Daniel F. O'Leary (comp.).

6,000 veteran soldiers who are capable of checking Perú; but, should those towns revolt, we will always need troops in that vicinity to maintain order and insure respect for the government. It is necessary, therefore, that the number of troops in those departments be increased; hence, you are to send me, immediately, as many as you can, for we are in a very critical position. I also repeat my request that the *Granaderos* battalion and the Zulia squadron be sent to Tunja. You are to replace your [Maracaibo] garrison with another that you can trust implicitly. This is to be done at once, so that Maracaibo will not be left unguarded and perhaps be temporarily taken from us.

We hear nothing now about the Spaniards. Every day the news is more encouraging from this quarter, and it finally appears that we are no longer of concern to them. In the present circumstances, this is a great relief.

As matters now stand, I should like Diego Ibarra to come and join me; you can replace him at Puerto Cabello with General Valero, to whom I promised that post should it be vacated. In that fortress we need a mutual friend, one who is loyal to us both, as otherwise there will be disputes or suspicions, which tend to be aggravated in circumstances that already have everyone worried. General Carabaño can do whatever Valero is doing, and do it better, as he is a man of thrift, a virtue to be commended to Valero, who lacks it and generously squanders all that he can.

I am urgently requested by General Sucre to see that payment is made to his brother in Cumaná for the silver that he deposited in Guayaquil. I have decided that you should permit them to export mules sufficient in number to cover the debt by levying [a tax of] thirty *pesos* per head, and also to allow the brothers to sell the export license to the merchants who are to ship the animals. However, great care must be taken to see that they ship no more than those authorized, for a contractor is always part smuggler.

I am writing Colonel Sucre to apply to you for permission to ship the mules duty-free, as I have indicated above.

I am your affectionate friend,

BOLÍVAR

P.S. The trial of the conspirators is almost over, but Santander will escape punishment as his aids have made it a point not to talk. That he knew of the conspiracy has been virtually established, and in reality he was behind the whole affair.

In addition, I want to ask you to pick a dozen young men of excellent character who are anxious for a military career and send them to Magdalena, for General Montilla to place them as he sees fit in the battalions and squadrons of that district. Some could also come to Bogotá—from captains on down, and all Venezuelans.

I want General Silva to go to Barinas, to raise one or more companies of cavalry, so that he will be ready to come to this capital when he is so ordered.

---

306. To General Mariano Montilla

[*Original*]

Bogotá, November 14, [1828].

My dear General:

I can imagine what your feelings were when you heard the news regarding the clemency shown Santander and his clique! I realized full well what was coming but I could not prevent it. First, my *judicious* friends said there should have been no conviction without conclusive evidence and that it would be unwise to enforce it.[1] And, finally, they impressed upon me that the glory of my name meant more than my country. I have preserved my reputation for magnanimity, and my country has suffered an irreparable blow. I am deeply regretful, but it is now too late for me to do anything about it.

Montebrune will tell you what went on here. I am so disturbed that I am going to the country for a few months, to recover from my despair and from the urge to leave at once and forever. Urdaneta is going to do the same; everything here will be left in the hands of Castillo and the other council members. However, I am to be consulted in everything. Everything will be done in my name. I am going to an Indian village four leagues from here.

Tell Juan de Francisco not to forward anything more and to hold for me whatever may come from London. If the great convention is to meet, it is best that I leave here.

Yesterday, the Council of State discussed the question of whether

---

[1] Santander was sentenced to death by a special court, but Bolívar's Cabinet recommended that he be exiled (ed.).

or not the great convention should be convoked, but no decision was reached. The ministers thought it *should not be,* and Revenga, Espinar, and Osorio thought it should be. We shall know tomorrow. It was I who made the motion, for I can no longer bear the increasing ingratitude. I am no saint, and I do not seek martyrdom. Only my concern for the fate of my *few* friends keeps me in this chamber of horrors.

Good-bye, my dear General, I am your devoted

BOLÍVAR

1829

307. To General J[osé] A[ntonio] Páez

[*Original*]

[Pasto, March 9, 1829]

My dear General:

You have doubtless heard that we ended our civil war by decree and our foreign war with victory. This is something worth telling our friends about. We entered here like newly reconciled brothers, and perhaps we shall do the same in Perú, and as easily. Generals Sucre and Flores have worked wonders with our valorous troops, whose heroism increases from day to day. I am beside myself with joy at these unusually favorable developments, and I am sending congratulations to all my friends as quickly as they congratulate me. So please accept mine, and the most heartfelt . . . [torn].

Since our victories, we have no lack of soldiers and *friends* here at home. I leave tomorrow for Quito to reap the fruit of our glories. We have no end of laurels, but we need money and rest, both of which I expect to obtain as the harvest of this season's wars. Everyone opposed war, which, in the end, proved necessary, just, and useful. The Peruvians and La Mar behaved abominably; they added every crime to their scandalous list of evils and abominable deeds. Providence . . . [torn] always comes, favoring us in every way.

Good-bye, my dear friend; I am your devoted

BOLÍVAR

P.S. A thousand regards to Briceño, Soublette, and my other friends.

308. To Dr. José María del Castillo y Rada,
    President of the Council of State

[*Copy*]

Quito, March 19, 1829.

My dear friend:

The pacification of Pasto and the favorable outcome of the campaign in the south have restored me to health and allowed me to take a brief rest in this city, where I have received a cordial welcome.

The communications sent from Cumbal by my Secretary-General to the Secretary of War have doubtless informed you of the high-minded vengeance that our generals exacted after the victory of Tarqui. Perú's commissioners begged ours not to subject them to harsh and humiliating terms, and I am, in fact, more than pleased with the generosity extended the vanquished in the name of Colombia. General Flores, however, has written me, and O'Leary has informed me personally, that they doubt whether Perú will faithfully comply with the treaties. If these suspicions are confirmed, I shall be very much disappointed, as I definitely want peace.

The orders respecting the surrender of Guayaquil and the instructions for our fleet were sent from Cuenca on the 7th instant. Since that date we have had no news from the commissioners, but we expect to hear from them at any moment.

General Heres has gone to Loja to establish order in that province. He writes in his letters that the remnants of the Peruvian army are returning home in complete disorder.

I have already begun work on the organization of the departments here. The treasury is in a deplorable state. I do not know where or how to find the means with which to maintain the army until the definitive treaty has been signed with Perú.

I intend to form a *junta,* composed of deputies from these departments, in order that this group can suggest to me the changes they believe this country needs. This procedure will please the south and it will prove very effective, as it did in Venezuela. General Sucre will remain in complete charge. I am extremely pleased with his conduct in the present situation.

I have received a communication from the government of Chile, offering mediation, jointly with Buenos Aires. The note is extremely cordial. In due time I shall forward it to the Secretary of Foreign Relations.

Be so kind as to show this letter to the other secretaries, and give them my regards. I have no time today to write them individually.

Remember me kindly to your esteemed wife, and believe me your sincere and devoted friend forever,

BOLÍVAR

---

309. To JOAQUÍN MOSQUERA

[*Biblioteca Popular* (Bogotá), No. 102]

Quito, April 12, 1829.

My dear friend:

Unfortunately I was denied the pleasure of answering, by the last post, your esteemed letter of March 21, which I read with extreme interest and pleasure.

General La Mar has written General Sucre an official note in which he advances many frivolous reasons for violating the treaty obligations and continuing the war. This is all either *childishness or senility,* fit only for the idlest parlor talk. He asserts that our men killed some prisoners while the combat was in progress and that we decreed a vote of thanks that was an offense to Perú. Even if true, all this occurred prior to the Treaty of Girón. Let me inform you as to what did happen before and after that treaty: first, the Peruvians killed General Mires and several officers, after their capture in mid-February; second, they have violated the terms of the Guayaquil capitulation on every count; third, they have forced the population to bear arms for their enemies; fourth, they have violated the treaty of Girón by refusing to return Guayaquil; fifth, they have burned Bava, killing the women, children, and even the priests; and sixth, in the course of their retreat, they razed the provinces of Loja, killing the Valdiviesos, attacking the women, despoiling everyone, and carrying off the slaves. By now, my friend, you will have heard that the United States is anxious to mediate our differences with Perú, and I can only hope the mediator realizes how strongly we are in the right.

General Flores is marching with sufficient troops to take Guayaquil, but he will be unable to accomplish this before the end of May, when the rains stop. The moment he reports that he has occupied that city, I shall set out for Bogotá, as I intend to arrive there as soon as possible. In any case, I feel sure we will have peace by June, brought about in one of the following ways: first, by the recapture of Guayaquil and the resulting threat to Perú; second, by the arrival of our naval forces in the Pacific; or, third, by the simultaneous revolt of Gamarra and Santa Cruz, who is already in power in Bolivia. This is almost certain; however, until it happens, nothing can be settled as regards Santander. To prove this I shall quote you a passage from a letter written from Loja by General Heres to General Urdaneta. It reads as follows: "I am making some remarkable discoveries here. At a public dinner, in toasting Santander, La Mar added that they had come at his request and that he had suggested the invasion plans. The plan was to penetrate as far as Juanambú, convene a congress in Quito, and create a separate republic in the south, to be known as Ecuador. La Mar, as a native son of Azuay, was to be its president, and Gamarra president of Perú, with Bolivia again to form a part of Perú." What do you think of that? Santander was hand in glove with La Mar; he sent for him and pointed out the way for completing the project. Nevertheless, when the time comes, I shall duly take into consideration whatever you may have to say about this base, perfidious, and traitorous man.

Convey my respects to your wife and my regards to your father and to the rest of your esteemed family, and believe me to be your good and devoted friend,

BOLÍVAR

---

310. To GENERAL JOSÉ A[NTONIO] PÁEZ

[*Original*]

Samborondón, June 20, 1829.

My dear General:

I received your kind letter of the end of March, and I am very sorry to learn that you are in poor health.

We have held possession of this point since the 16th, when we expelled the Peruvians who were holding it with 800 men, and, though they had not planned to defend it, they suffered 150 casualties, dead, wounded, and missing.

When you receive this letter, you will already have been informed of the burning of the *Prueba* and the recent developments between Gamarra and La Mar at Piura, because we reported these matters to you from Baba, before our departure and as soon as we had received the information. Furthermore, I can now tell you that all this has definitely been confirmed by all parties and most recently by the envoy who has just returned from Guayaquil, where I sent him yesterday. At Piura, La Mar was deposed as president and banished to Guatemala, and Gamarra has taken control in Perú. Necochea relinquished his command in Guayaquil on the 17th and, either through choice or necessity, departed, together with his aides-de-camp and other officers, all enemies of Gamarra. Gamarra and General La Fuente, who is in Lima, are working hand-in-hand to seize the government, which they already virtually control. Perú, therefore, is in a state of complete anarchy.

Yesterday I warned the city of Guayaquil, and I have received a very satisfactory reply. They have offered to accept an honorable surrender, complete with the proper formalities, but they request an armistice first, to allow them time to communicate with Gamarra in Piura, who has the same desire for peace that I have. Tomorrow I plan to move nearer the city, to watch it more closely and to cover all the principal points. I shall then send an envoy to Gamarra, and we shall suspend hostilities for a few days, in the course of which the city will be taken, and then we will be able to negotiate a peace. I shall tell Gamarra that I will listen to no proposals whatsoever while any portion of Colombia's territory is occupied; as long as this situation exists, we shall continue hostilities wherever duty commands. I believe that everything will work out to our satisfaction. Perú's condition is too deplorable for that country to oppose us, and public opinion there is daily more in my favor. Bolivia is governed by Santa Cruz, and the Bolivians are our friends. What with this and a thousand other factors favoring us, everything is proceeding very well, which for you and our other friends, who are concerned about Colombia's welfare, should be most welcome news.

Very likely I shall return to the capital as soon as I have taken Guayaquil.

We have just learned that in that town they have arrested Icazas, Luzarraga, a certain Villamil, the vicar, and twenty other leading citizens, for being involved or, rather, they are accused of having been involved in a plot to help us, with members of the Third Division, who are also under arrest. Utter confusion, therefore, on the part of both factions exists in Guayaquil. One priest is in the death house and is to be hanged for the same reason. Twenty thousand *pesos* were demanded of the city, which yielded eight thousand. The troops want to sack the town as they are miserable and without pay. We are no better off, but we are not complaining; on the contrary, we are united and in excellent spirits.

From the interior of the Republic, I receive favorable reports. It would seem that there, as in the north, there are no new developments. I can therefore assure you that everything is progressing admirably. You have only to regain your health, and everything will be perfect.

I am, as ever, your devoted friend,

BOLÍVAR

---

311. To Bruno Espinoza

[*Copy*]

Camp Buijó, before Guayaquil, July 11, 1829.

My esteemed friend:

I have duly received your esteemed letters, whose dates escape me. I was unable to answer them when they reached me, as I was on the march and had a thousand matters to attend to; moreover, there was no one to do my writing.

I thank you for the newspapers you enclosed, and I am greatly obliged to you for the sentiments of friendship and regard that you have expressed in all your letters.

Our affairs here are proceeding quite satisfactorily. The Peruvians have been converted to our way of thinking. They have admitted the injustice and unreasonableness of the war they were waging against us, and they have deposed La Mar, who has been exiled to Guatemala. The new government has, to date, exhibited a desire for peace, which I have promised them as soon as they have effected the withdrawal of all their troops from Colombian territory. At present, we are maintaining a provisional armistice, which, either today or tomorrow, will be ended or extended, in order to negotiate the peace; for in this time one of my emissaries will have reached Piura and seen General Gamarra, who commands their army. The evacuation of Guayaquil has begun, and we expect that city to be turned over to us within the week. The current success of our arms and policy not only presents the most auspicious prospects for Colombia but it should reassure us of the hope of ultimately achieving the full measure of our national happiness, were it not for the fact that the rest of our America is so busy spreading the fire of revolt that we are more and more fearful of being enveloped in the general collapse.

Revolts in Chile and Buenos Aires multiply daily because of the infernal differences of opinion. Mexico offers no hope of survival. Guatemala keeps us wondering, for there they destroy each other in a most atrocious manner. No one knows why, as there are no royalists, centralists, or advocates of a life-term presidency. The provinces have captured the capital and committed other outrages. Is not the latest development in Perú, then, although it has, for the moment, taken a favorable turn for us as far as this war is concerned, a sorry forecast for the future of that country and a far-reaching example of disorder? Colombia alone is in a happy position today, but her happiness hangs by a thread that cannot possibly save her from the hazards of the immense whirlpool of disorder which assails the rest of America. These thoughts give me good cause to be despondent. I am only waiting until peace in Perú is assured before returning [to Bogotá] to see if it is at all possible to provide our country with some sort of organization and if I am at last to be left in peace.

Meanwhile, I remain your very affectionate friend,

BOLÍVAR

312. To Dr. Estanislao Vergara, Minister of Foreign Affairs

[*Original*]

Camp Buijó, July 13, 1829.

My dear friend:

I have received your esteemed letter of June 8, and I note what you tell me about France, the United States, and the favorable turn of the elections in the cantons, as well as your many other comments regarding our America.

I agree with you that the American continent is attracting attention by its scandalous behavior, which cannot but cause Europe alarm respecting the maintenance of social order. We, who have been more judicious, realize that it is only by chance that we are better off, although we are in no position to inspire confidence anywhere. America's prospects have kept me in such a state of despondency of late that neither the fall of La Mar nor the advantages gained from Perú's change of attitude have consoled me. On the contrary, they have only increased my pessimism, as they clearly show that order, security, life, and everything else are constantly moving farther and farther away from our continent, which is fated to destroy itself and become the slave of Europe. I believe all this to be inevitable, as no one can hold this unbounded revolution in check. Because of this conviction, I feel that the most that can be achieved by this Congress is a fundamental law of brief duration, which even I will have the greatest difficulty in upholding.

So far I have said yes, yes, to everything that you gentlemen have suggested, without venturing to express my true opinion, fearing that my letters might be intercepted and turned against the government or used to discredit the Council in the eyes of the masses.

My views are of long standing and I therefore consider them to have been carefully thought out.

First. I cannot continue to be the head of the government forever, and, when I leave, the country will be broken up by civil war and frightful disorder of every kind.

Second. To avert the horrible disasters that will surely come to pass before another ten years have elapsed, it is to be preferred that the country be legally divided and enjoy peace and harmony.

Third. If the people's representatives in Congress feel that such a settlement would be favorably received by the people, let them effect it openly and deliberately, and, at the same time, issue a declaration concerning mutual rights and interests.

Fourth. If the representatives are of the opinion that they are not sufficiently empowered to take such an important step, they might ask for a ruling of the electoral colleges of Colombia, in order that the latter can voice their opinions and desires and provide Colombia with a government in conformity with them.

Fifth. If none of these measures can be adopted because the Congress opposes them, no other alternative should be entertained but that of a government with life tenure,[1] as is the case in Bolivia, and a hereditary senate such as I proposed in Guayana.[2] This is the most that we can do for the stability of the government, a stability which, as regards Venezuela and New Granada, I consider to be illusory, since antipathies exist in both countries that cannot be overcome. On this point the Páez and the Santander factions are in complete agreement, although others in the country have different opinions about it.

The idea of a foreign monarchy taking over the reins of government from me, however promising of results, is impractical for a thousand reasons:

First. No foreign prince would accept the legacy of an anarchic principality that offers no security.

Second. The national debt and the poverty of the country cannot provide the means with which to maintain a prince and his court, however penuriously.

Third. The lower classes would become alarmed, fearing the effects of aristocracy and inequality.

Fourth. Neither the generals nor those who lust after power could bear to see themselves barred from supreme authority.

I have said nothing of the obstacles that Europe might put in the way, as it is conceivable that, given a rare combination of favorable circumstances, none might arise.

As for myself, you may well believe that I am weary of serving and disgusted with the acts of ingratitude and the crimes that are daily committed against me. You have seen how the great convention confronted me with the alternatives of either abandoning the country to its fate or saving it at my own expense. The article of which you speak, the most favorable that has been written in my behalf, states simply that my usurpation of power is a fortunate thing and for the public good. I, a usurper? I usurp power? My friend, this is horrible. I cannot tolerate the thought. It arouses within me such hor-

---

[1] See Doc. 251 (ed.).
[2] See Doc. 70 (ed.).

ror that I should prefer Colombia's ruin to having this epithet attached to my name. I retort that, as our country will tolerate neither freedom nor slavery, a thousand revolutions will produce a thousand usurpations. This is fact, my friend, and, however viewed, the events of 1828 have sealed my fate.

You will see, through the Secretary-General, what the government of Perú has written in ordering the surrender of the city of Guayaquil under an armistice which has probably already been arranged and which I presume our emissary Guerra will bring here in a day or so.

I might mention in passing that, if you gentlemen adopt the policy that I have suggested above, namely, the establishment of a separate government for each section, you will most definitely assure your future. You gentlemen will, without doubt, assume the leadership of public opinion, and even my enemies will regard you as the true saviors. My friends are many, and Santander's are too few to be noticed. If you join forces to this end, you will rout the latter and strip them of the weapons they rely upon. In executing this plan you can count upon all the generals that are devoted to me, including those of Venezuela, as I understand exactly how they think and I know they will always prefer the sounder party. To be sure, I do not believe that Santander should, for the present, be a part of this government, as he has many enemies in every region, and the means that he might use to destroy them would be criminal and therefore harmful. If you gentlemen adopt this counsel and oppose Santander outright, you can be sure of the south, as General Sucre, Flores, the army, and all the influential persons in that section would prefer to join with you rather than stand divided, for they fully realize that alone they are entirely at the mercy of Perú, while to the north Pasto remains an ever-present menace.

Please show this letter to the ministers for them to consider and decide what they think best.

A country that depends on the life of one man runs a risk as great as if its future were daily staked upon the cast of a die. And if that man has suffered greatly for twenty years, has many enemies who would gladly destroy him, is weary of public office and thoroughly loathes it, then the problem of maintaining such a state becomes infinitely greater. Such is the situation, my dear friend, I give you my word. I do not want to deceive you gentlemen, nor to be my own undoing. I cannot go on, and my heart reminds me of this a hundred times a day. Put yourself in my place and you will understand; and, if you will carefully analyze your own position, you will surely see that what I say is true. We must both reach a decision—you yours, and I mine. Through such a policy all of us will benefit, at least to some extent.

I remain your devoted

BOLÍVAR

---

313. To General Rafael Urdaneta

[*Original*]

Guayaquil, July 22, 1829.

My dear General and friend:

At last we are in Guayaquil. It was occupied by the Peruvians for over five months, and, as might be expected, the city's population is overjoyed. In addition, all goes well in the south. The elections have been held, and the delegates are to my liking; at least they are sensible men who probably will not decline, which is an accomplishment for this part of the Republic.

General Cerdeña came to see me at Buijó, and I found him as affable and friendly as ever. He told me that he had been invested with broad powers to treat with me concerning the surrender of Guayaquil, and he was surprised that Gamarra had been so ungenerous in the armistice. He doubts whether or not Perú can attain stability in the hands of those who are now, or will be, in control. It is expected that Gamarra will assume the presidency but will not hold it for long, so that ultimately the Peruvians will be obliged to call upon me. I replied that my mind was made up never to go to Perú, as I have too much to do in Colombia; and that, moreover, I have lost all taste for office. I asked General Cerdeña to convey to my friends and enemies my ideas on peace and my irrevocable determination never to return to that country unless war should force me. The latter possibility is hardly to be feared, as I do not have the slightest doubt but that we can negotiate a satisfactory peace if Perú does not persist in being unfair to Colombia. He thereupon informed me that Santa Cruz, La Fuente, and Gamarra, who were in agreement, were all great admirers of mine and had always opposed the war against Colombia. He made me a thousand protestations on this score which I thought sincere, as he seems to be his own natural self and a devotee of mine. He also assured me that the ministers who are to negotiate the peace will soon be appointed. Accordingly, I expect them next month, and I suppose that by September the negotiations will have been completed, or at least the bases agreed upon, unless the negotiations fail and are broken off. I intend to demand no more than is strictly just and necessary, which they naturally will be unable to refuse.

In Chile the government was attacked by troops the very day the revolt took place in Lima, and now Buenos Aires is engaged in a horrible civil war.

From Paris, Palacios has sent me some of Benjamin Constant's replies to De Pradt, concerning my usurpation of power and the severity of my behavior in Perú and Colombia. He states that many of his liberal friends share this opinion; hence, you see the comfort my enemies receive from so eminent an authority. Palacios tells me that he could have answered him, but thought it best to ignore him. But I think differently. Constant is not a man to be ignored. All this worries me considerably and confirms my original intentions, for it is very unpleasant to hear nothing but criticism on all sides.

Good luck, and believe me your affectionate and devoted

BOLÍVAR

---

314. To Colonel Belford Hinton Wilson

[*Copy*]

Guayaquil, August 3, 1829.

My dear aide-de-camp:

I have had the pleasure of receiving your several letters, dated between February 10 and April 1, but I have not received the items you sent me from the United States. They may have arrived at

Cartagena, but I have no information. In any case, I thank you, and shall never cease to recognize in you a most faithful and loyal friend.

I am well aware of the current opinion in the United States respecting my political conduct. It is unfortunate that we cannot achieve the happiness of Colombia with the laws and customs of the [North] Americans. You know that this cannot be; it is even less probable than for Spain to be like England.

I do not know what to say to you regarding Murat's son, as you know the obstacles we must face in everything. Nevertheless, you may tell the erstwhile King of Spain[1] that I am honored and pleased by the confidence he has chosen to repose in me by offering to place under my orders the nephew of the great Napoleon and the son of the world's greatest soldier, but that I cannot accept this honor, as my authority is due to end early next year with the convening of the Constituent Congress, to whom I propose to return the supreme authority, which I am firmly resolved never to assume again.

As this is my final decision, your letter will probably reach the United States shortly before the news of my resignation, so that Prince Joseph will see that I am neither deceiving nor rejecting him.

I shall ask General Sucre for the letter you mention, but it cannot be sent promptly as it is with his papers in Chile. I shall forward it to you as soon as it comes. This letter is really of the utmost importance, as is another that the General has in his possession. I shall write to Miranda in Bogotá to send you the medals you request, for there are none here.

I again want to thank you for the interest you have taken in the undeceiving of the former President and Secretary of State of the United States.[2]

I was pleased with the reply of the deaf-mutes and still more so with your kind comment on it. In truth, the mute speak better than the long-tongued, the loud-tongued, and the sharp-tongued, which are fitting descriptions for those gentlemen who want China to be governed like England. The fact is I am sick and tired of all this charlatanry, and, therefore, I am fully determined to return to private life. I have already wasted too much time serving my fellowmen, who, as Voltaire said, do not deserve to have rulers.

Very shortly, my dear Wilson, you will see me in England, and

---

[1] Joseph Bonaparte, who was living in the United States at that time (ed.).
[2] John Quincy Adams (ed.).

I shall have the pleasure of seeing you again and personally meeting the most distinguished of my friends, the illustrious General Wilson, whom you will congratulate for me upon his victory in behalf of the Catholics, who, no less than their courageous protectors, fully deserve it.

You have no doubt heard, from our friends in Bogotá, of the constitutional projects that rattle about in the heads of the many statesmen in that capital. For my part, I have had nothing whatsoever to do with the plans for new constitutions and monarchies. Knowing my ideas as you do, this cannot surprise you. I am engaged solely in bringing Colombia peace with Perú, which is all that now concerns us.

You will have heard of what happened to La Mar, who richly merited it. They bound him like a beast and, at the point of their bayonets, forced him to resign. They placed him aboard a vessel, which must have gone down, and shipped him off toward the coasts of Guatemala. His conduct was execrable. He cursed Colombia day and night and clamored for the extinction of the Colombian people. He was stricken with madness, and by now it has doubtless developed into hydrophobia.

Generals Gamarra and La Fuente have taken command, and both have laid claim to the presidency. It has been reported that the military favor Gamarra and the civilians La Fuente. Both protest their friendship for me, but La Fuente seems the more sincere, and his public utterances are more candid and outspoken. I already foresee that eventually Gamarra will head the La Mar party and La Fuente mine. The only thing that seems beyond question is that they will clash and depose each other, and that a civil war will take place shortly.

In my earlier letter, addressed to your father, I requested him to acquaint himself with the facts concerning the events of the past year with which you are familiar, and to please print a defense of my conduct in the papers. I trust that you have already done this, and I beg you to do so again whenever possible.

By now the Congress of Perú will probably have convened and sent envoys to negotiate the peace. Gual will represent us, and I expect he will manage very well.

Bolivia is being governed by Santa Cruz, who is doing nicely. The Bolivian papers praise me warmly, saying that my proclamation of Quito is the most glorious document in American history. Thus you can see that Bolivia is well disposed.

I am enclosing a letter for the Count de las Cases and beg you to be so kind as to forward it.

I remain, my dear Wilson, your devoted friend,

BOLÍVAR

---

315. To COLONEL PATRICK CAMPBELL, BRITISH
    CHARGÉ D'AFFAIRES, BOGOTÁ

[*Copy*]

Guayaquil, August [5], 1829.[1]

My esteemed friend and Colonel:

I have the honor of acknowledging receipt of your kind letter, dated May 31, at Bogotá.

I can only begin by thanking you for the many fine things that you say in your letter respecting Colombia and myself. Yet do you not have every right to our gratitude? I am abashed when I recall how much thought you have given and how much you have done, since you came among us, to assist this nation and uphold her leader's glory.

The British minister resident in the United States does me too much honor in saying that he has hopes only for Colombia because Colombia alone has a Bolívar. But he does not know that Bolívar's physical and political existence is seriously weakened and soon will end.

What you are good enough to tell me regarding the latest plan for appointing a European prince as successor to my authority does not take me by surprise. I had been informed of it in part, although with no little mystery and some trepidation, because my thoughts on the subject are well known.

I know not what to say to you about this plan, which is surrounded by a thousand drawbacks. You must know there is no objection on

---

[1] Erroneously dated August 25. The Archivo del Libertador contains another copy in O'Leary's hand, with which this copy has been collated and corrected (comp.).

my part, as I am determined to resign at the next Congress. But, who will appease the ambitions of our leaders and the dread of inequality among the lower classes? Do you not think that England would be displeased if a Bourbon were selected? Will not all the new American nations, and the United States, who seem destined by Providence to plague America with torments in the name of freedom, be opposed to such a plan? I seem to foresee a universal conspiracy against our poor Colombia, which is already greatly envied by all the American republics. Every newspaper would issue a call for a new crusade against the ring-leaders in the betrayal of freedom, those supporters of the Bourbons and wreckers of the American system. The Peruvians in the south, the Guatemalans and the Mexicans at the Isthmus, the peoples of the Antilles, Americans and liberals everywhere would kindle the flame of discord. Santo Domingo would not remain inactive; she would call upon her brothers to make common cause against a prince of France. Everyone would become our enemy, and Europe would do nothing to help us, for the New World is not worth the price of a Holy Alliance. We have good cause to think this way, judging from the indifference which greeted our launching and maintaining of the struggle for the liberation of half the world, which is soon to become the richest source of Europe's prosperity.

In short, I am far from being opposed to a reorganization of Colombia that conforms to the tested institutions of sagacious Europe. On the contrary, I would be delighted and inspired to redouble my efforts to aid an enterprise that might prove to be our salvation, one that could be accomplished without difficulty if aided by both England and France. With such powerful support we could do anything; without it we could not. I, therefore, reserve my final opinion until we hear the views of the English and French governments respecting the above-mentioned change in our system and the selection of a dynasty.

I assure you, my esteemed friend, with the utmost sincerity, that I have told you my thoughts fully. I have concealed nothing. You may use this statement as your duty and Colombia's welfare may require. That is my only condition, and so I beg you to accept the personal assurances of affection and regard of your very obedient servant,

BOLÍVAR

A true copy.—Urdaneta.

316. To Joaquín Mosquera

[*Biblioteca Popular* (Bogotá), No. 102]

Guayaquil, September 3, 1829.

My dear friend:

I have received your discouraging letter, every word of which suggests that you are not yet resigned to the eternal law that governs man's fate. In truth, death is a terrible thing, and it is all the more depressing because it also brings an end to the intelligent and the righteous whom we are wont to liken to divinity. Human life saddens you; yet this is an obvious contradiction. You desire an impossibility which, if attained, would bring martyrdom to one who has earned repose. I would prefer not to mention it, but regrets of this kind have always seemed to me to be related to egoism. We feel grief for those who have departed, though we know life is evil. Take consolation, then, in the reward that has come to the best father on earth. I loved him too, and at first I felt the sharp pangs of bereavement; but all this is but the mechanical response of our instincts. Reason then told me to rejoice, for death heals all our sorrows.

What you say about the problem of organizing Colombia is proof of what I have just said. We can do nothing for this country, in which the counsels of reason are like mortal assaults that lead only to plans of iniquity. Bogotá, some years ago, became the headquarters of demagogy, and, as this system was deleterious, the provinces received it with open arms; and now that the leading figures in the country have sought to correct this unfortunate tendency, they are, as you say, disappointed.

As I, on occasion, must identify myself with the people, my words and thoughts reflect those of the people on the main points to be dealt with in the Congress, namely, the Constitution and the choice of a government. It is my opinion that this Congress should separate New Granada from Venezuela, as this is what is most ardently desired, while the contrary is a wild dream, wholly impracticable. The men of greatest stature in this country admire the Venezuelan leaders least, and, as the latter know that the capital of the Republic is located in New Granada, they can imagine no other corrective to offset this advantage than to have a government headed by a Venezuelan. The bitterest animosities have arisen over this point. You have witnessed all this clearly among certain leaders whom you know but whom I will not name.

Unless separation is agreed to, Congress should at least accept my resignation and organize Colombia in conformity with the majority opinion. Federation may be the system most favored by the people; if so, let them adopt it, and we shall have no more contests to decide with the provinces. If they want the Constitution of Cúcuta, or twenty departments with twenty departmental assemblies, nothing could be simpler, as they will not even have to go to the trouble of drawing it up. They do not want a monarchy, or a life-term presidency, or, most emphatically, an aristocracy, so why do they not hurl themselves outright into the tempestuous, rolling sea of anarchy? This is a popular notion, and therefore it must be right, for it is my maxim that the majority has to be infallible.

For my part, I have no intention of going to Bogotá to influence the Congress, from which I shall accept no authority. I convoked the Congress in order that it might provide for a constitution and choose a government; hence, it would not be proper for me to receive the slightest consideration from their hands, still less for me to suggest a program of legislation.

The time has come for me to take my pleasure and do as honor dictates. Authority now weighs heavily on my hands. I undertook to fight for the liberation of Colombia. Spain herself is contemplating recognition, and when that is accorded Colombia's future will be assured forever.

When I returned from Perú the parties took alarm, even the Venezuelan which was then in power. They have all quieted down, so there is no justification for destroying them.

The war with Perú has ended and peace will be concluded shortly, though without guaranties; there is no way to obtain them, as a revolutionary government cannot provide them. This is what I have been able to accomplish in twenty years of labor. I doubt that it could rightly be demanded of me that I die upon the cross. Yet, were it only the cross, I could suffer it with endurance as the last of my agonies. Christ endured thirty-three years of this mortal life; mine has extended over forty-six. But then I am no impassive deity; if I were, I could bear up through all eternity.

Here, my dear friend, you have my general confession and my decision to mend my ways. Santander will see to the confession of my sins. Could greater repentance be asked? I doubt it.

Be so kind, my dear friend, as to forgive me for this tedious letter. It is born of a melancholia that consumes me and has kept me ill these many days; for this reason I have gone a mile out of the city to enjoy the country air, but no exercise, as I am located on an island that, owing to the nature of the terrain, allows no freedom of movement.

We are momentarily expecting the minister from Perú, to conclude the peace treaty with Gual.

Why do you not have the people of Popayán express their opinions on government? Many months ago I wrote the ministers that they should have the electoral colleges give written instructions to the delegates. They failed to comply, and I wrote to Venezuela to have it done. I am now giving orders that the people in all parts be invited to speak out and give their views. Let Popayán do so freely.

If you receive any money for me, send it by the post.

Your devoted

BOLÍVAR

---

317. To General Daniel F. O'Leary

[Blanco y Azpurúa, XIII, 629][1]

Guayaquil, September 13, 1829.

My dear O'Leary:

You have probably been informed that I am recovering from a liver complaint which has left me in a very weak condition and with the conviction that my strength is nearly all gone.[2] My condition is incredible, considering the fact that I have been active all my life. Whether it is my mental powers that have greatly declined or my constitution that has been completely undermined, the fact remains that I do not possess the strength for anything, and nothing in all the world can revive it. A complete calm, or rather absolute apathy, has gripped me and dominates me completely. I am so convinced of my inability to go on with public life that I feel obliged to reveal to my

---

[1] Taken by Blanco and Azpurúa from *El Porvenir*, of Bogotá (Number 14, December 18, 1855). The first five paragraphs have been corrected by reference to O'Leary's version of the incomplete rough draft. See O'Leary, XXXI, 516 (comp.).

[2] In reality he was suffering from tuberculosis (ed.).

closest friends how imperative it is that I relinquish the supreme command forever, so that they, on their part, can make their decisions accordingly.

At first sight you and my other friends will view this development as an extraordinary and unfortunate emergency, and yet nothing is more natural or inevitable, regardless of the effect that it will produce. Consider the life of a man who has served for twenty years, the better part of his youth having been behind him, and you will realize that he has little or nothing left to offer, in the natural order of events. If, in addition, you consider that he has aged before his time, that his life has been very active, and that every physical and moral ailment has afflicted this individual, then it must follow that he can expect to live only four to six years longer—four or six years of little capacity for work and of great agony for the sufferer. I form this judgment without prejudice, without personal concern, and as impartially as I am able. And so I judge, I say, that, however great the loss, there is no cause for regret; it is rather to be welcomed as a lesser evil when compared with what is to be feared.

Let us review the state of the Republic, which at first glance presents, on the one hand, imminent chaos, and, on the other, a prospect of triumph. We have defeated Perú and the domestic faction. Doubtless everyone will more or less agree that we acted rightly and reasonably in warding off our enemies, who were also the enemies of Colombia's well-being. Those citizens who hold the offices, influence, and power are the very ones who shared with me the sacrifices of war and public service. They are in the prime of their physical and spiritual capacities; they are clothed with public authority; they possess the necessary means with which to maintain it; and public opinion generally encourages and supports them in the task of saving the country. These persons today enjoy youth and vigor of mind; therefore, they have the necessary ability to defend the state and their own positions. Four or six years hence this will no longer be true. By then they will be what I am now; age, having taken its toll, will have put them at the mercy of their enemies or their successors. When that day comes, without doubt, neither I nor any of those who now support me will be present. Consequently, every pillar of this edifice will suddenly collapse, and its fall will prove fatal to those within. What remedy is there for so severe a blow? Would not the social order be weakened and fall at a stroke? Would this not be the greatest possible catastrophe? It most certainly would be. It would be better then, it seems to me, to prepare for this catastrophe in advance, as we cannot hope to avoid it even by making the most superhuman of efforts.

The momentum of things and events propels our country toward this great upheaval, or, if you will, this political transformation. I am not immortal. Our government is democratic and elective. Accordingly, the changes that may be made in it do not have to be permanent, for we agree that our position or social structure is strictly transitional in nature. We all know that the union of New Granada and Venezuela holds together solely because of my authority, which must sooner or later come to an end, whenever Providence, or man, so determines. Nothing is so fragile as the life of a man; therefore, have the prudence to prepare for the time when my end will come. Once I am dead, what good can I do this Republic? Then, when there is no mediator, no friend, no common adviser, it will be realized how expedient it would have been to anticipate the separation of these two sections during my lifetime. Instead, all will be discord, bitterness, and strife.

Let us suppose that the Constituent Congress, to be assembled in January, will be wise enough to undertake successful legislative reforms. What might these be? Consider the size of Colombia, her population, the prevailing spirit, the trend of opinions today, the continent in which she is located, the bordering states, and the widespread resentment to the establishment of a stable order. We thus face a chain of fearsome threats that we cannot ignore. The size of our territory requires one of two entirely different types of government, both of them extremely unfavorable to the country's welfare: Monarchy or general confederation are the only forms suitable for the ruling of this far-flung empire. I cannot even conceive of the possibility of establishing a kingdom in a country which is essentially democratic. The lower and most numerous classes claim their prerogatives, to which they have an incontestable right. Equality before the law is indispensable where physical inequality exists, in order that the injustices of Nature can, in some measure, be corrected. Moreover, who would be king in Colombia? No one, as I see it. No foreign prince would accept a throne surrounded by dangers and misery, whereas the generals would be compelled to submit to someone else and to renounce forever the supreme authority. The people, frightened by this innovation, would consider themselves sacrificed to the numerous consequences they would foresee in the structure and foundations of a monarchy. The agitators would rouse the people with deceitful arguments, and their persuasiveness would be irresistible, for everything conspires to make this spectre of tyranny appear odious; its very name strikes terror. The poverty of the country does not permit the establishment of an expensive government, favoring every abuse of luxury and dissipation. The new nobility, indispensable in a monarchy, would stem from the people as a whole, and so it would have all the envy of one group and all the arrogance of the other. No one would patiently endure such an aristocracy, steeped in poverty and ignorance and animated by ridiculous pretensions. Let us speak no more, then, of this chimera.

Nevertheless, I am less inclined toward the federal form of government. Such a system is no more than organized anarchy, or, at best, a law that implicitly prescribes the obligation of dissolution and the eventual ruin of the state with all its members. I think it would be better for South America to adopt the Koran rather than the United States' form of government, although the latter is the best on earth. Nothing more can be added; simply witness the unhappy countries of Buenos Aires, Chile, Mexico, and Guatemala. We, too, may recall our own earliest years. These examples alone tell us more than entire libraries.

There remains no alternative for Colombia but to organize, as best she can, a centralized system duly proportioned to the size of her territory and the nature of her inhabitants. A civilized state based on the European model offers less resistance to government, on the part of the people and of nature, than does a small province in America, by reason of the ruggedness of our terrain and the ignorance of our people. For these very reasons we are compelled to give our institutions greater stamina and energy than would be considered necessary in other countries. Colombia is not only as large as a European state, but she could hold several nations of Europe within her borders. What problems and obstacles shall we not encounter in administering a far-flung empire when the government is equipped with tools barely sufficient to rule a single province, and that badly?

If I am to speak my mind, let me say that I have seen nothing whatsoever in Colombia resembling government, administration, or public order. It is true that we are beginning a new career, and that war and revolution have directed all our attention toward fighting. We have appeared to be transfixed by the contemplation of our dangers and by the anxiety to avert them. We did not know what it meant to govern, and, while we were engaged in defending ourselves, we did not have the time to learn. But now it is time to think deeply and earnestly of repairing all these losses and insuring our national existence.

The present government of Colombia is not adequate for ruling and administering extensive provinces. The center is too far removed from the outlying sections. Force is dissipated by distance, and the central administration lacks the necessary means to deal with the immensity of its far-reaching responsibilities. I repeatedly observe evidence of this fact. There is no prefect, no governor, who does not invest himself with supreme authority, principally as a matter of absolute necessity. It might be said that each department has a government distinct from the national, modified by local conditions or circumstances peculiar to the area, or even personal in nature. All this exists because the whole is not compact. Our social ties are too loose to stabilize, bind, and hold together the remote sections of our country. We suffer from such utter confusion and we are so incapable of remedying this evil that, unless we reorganize, this disease will make dangerous progress.

The Constituent Congress must choose one of two courses, the only ones open in the present situation:

1. The separation of New Granada and Venezuela.

2. The creation of a life-term presidency and a strong central government.

In the former case, the separation of the two countries must be complete, just, and peaceful. Once this is adopted, each region should reorganize as it sees fit and each should confer separately respecting matters of common interest and mutual relations. I believe that New Granada should remain intact, so that she will be able to defend herself on the south against the Peruvians and to prevent Pasto from becoming a cancer. Venezuela must also remain intact, as she was prior to the unification of the two regions.

However much one may wish to avoid this separation, all things conspire to bring it about. It has many inherent difficulties, but who can resist the demands of passions and immediate interests? I see no way of soothing local antagonisms or shortening enormous distances. These factors, in my opinion, are the great obstacles to forming a single government and a unified state. We shall always founder upon this reef, and it is a challenge to our valor to overcome it with firmness. Let two governments be formed, and, allied against common enemies, conclude a pact to establish their mutual relations—the rest will come with time, which has endless resources.

So long as we were obliged to continue the war, it seemed, and perhaps it was, expedient to create the Republic of Colombia. When domestic peace followed, and with it new relationships, we found that this laudable plan, or rather this experiment, did not live up to the hopes we had placed in it. Men and conditions cry out for separation, because the dissatisfaction of each region makes for a general unrest. Spain herself has now ceased to threaten us. This is final proof that the union is no longer necessary, for it served only to concentrate our forces against our former rulers.

The day this act of separation is consummated will be blessed by the active elements of the population, and above all by those who direct it and are, in effect, the true agents of society.

The formation of a life-term government or any other system that should be desired—but always in accordance with the popular will—is the other possibility that the Congress might adopt. The preservation of the Republic of Colombia offers, of course, genuine advantages and prestige abroad. Spain will have greater respect for us; Perú will honor any treaties she signs; and the nations of America generally will continue to look up to us. The citizens of both countries will be less inclined to engage in border clashes, and the national debt will offer less occasion for dispute. All this is of great importance. If only we could preserve this beautiful union!

Colombia must forget her illusions and make her decision, for I cannot rule any longer. This is fact, so let us draw our conclusions.

What will Congress do to appoint my successor? Will he be a Granadan or a Venezuelan? An army man or a civilian?

The Granadans doubtless want a president from their country, for a Venezuelan has ruled them for more than ten years. The Venezuelans will say that they are subject to the capital of New Granada and to the influence of her sons, and that their only hope is for a Venezuelan to be the head. Thus there are many drawbacks in either case, but this is not all.

Are the military always to rule, sword in hand? Will not the civilian population complain of the despotism of the army? I admit that the existing Republic cannot be governed except by the sword, and yet at the same time I must concede that the military spirit is incompatible with civilian rule. The Congress will inevitably be forced to consider the matter of dividing the country, because, select whom they will, their choice of a president will be questioned.

Nevertheless, I shall do my part to support him. I will, with an indefatigable zeal, watch over the government night and day. I shall bring all my influence to bear in behalf of the supreme authority. I shall speed to the provinces to defend them with whatever arms are provided me. In short, the government will be strong, insofar as it depends on my power and that of my friends, whom I pledge in behalf of our common cause.

I am your devoted

BOLÍVAR

---

318. A PANORAMIC VIEW OF SPANISH AMERICA[1]

[Blanco y Azpurúa, XIII, 493]

In this review of Spanish America we shall begin with the Argentine Republic, not because this country occupies the vanguard of our revolution, as her citizens have fatuously chosen to believe, but because she lies farthest to the south and, as it happens, affords the most typical example of anarchic revolution.

On May 25, 1810, the city of Buenos Aires began its political existence. As its example was not followed by the other provinces, it was necessary to use force in order to compel them to espouse the revolutionary cause. While so engaged, the troops of Buenos Aires set a precedent for their subsequent harsh and ignorant behavior by killing the Viceroy Liniers, who had earlier freed that country from the British troops.[2] At the same time they began to persecute the pastors of the Church, in the person of a bishop who was guilty of nothing more than obedience to his vows.

Continuing their operations, the troops, commanded by the people's representative Castelli, reached the Desaguadero River after a period of six months. Such fortunate beginnings promised a most auspicious future for the Argentine Republic. But, whether because of the inexperience of that revolutionary commander, or because of the people's and the army's complete ignorance of military and political science, the fact is that the philosophic conqueror and his entire

---

[1] This article was written in Quito in 1829 and published anonymously in a periodical in Ecuador (ed.).

[2] A British expedition invaded Buenos Aires in 1806-1807 (ed.).

army were crushed not far from the Desaguadero, and its remnants were pursued as far as Córdoba. Since that time disasters have followed one after the other without interruption.

The Río de la Plata has had but one man who proved capable of serving his country nobly and well. Saavedra quickly proved himself capable of presiding over the destinies of that Republic, but his death soon deprived the country of its one remaining hope. Since that time there has been no order or pattern in Argentine affairs. The federal government took possession of the land, and the land became its victim. Every province recovered its individual sovereignty, which God has given to every man, but that every man tacitly relinquishes to society, which thereupon assumes responsibility for the individual's safety. Nothing is so perilous as inconsistency between a political system and natural law. Each province governed itself, and every military expedition sent against them went down in humiliating defeat. The towns armed and fought each other like enemies. As a result of federation, the nation fell heir to blood, death, and crime of every description, due to the unleashing of the passions of a people who, although they had broken their chains, were devoid of the concepts of right and duty, and could only avoid enslavement by becoming tyrannical themselves.

Elections were characterized by riots and intrigue. Many times armed soldiers marched to the polls in formation, something unknown even in ancient Rome or in the island of Haiti. Force, faction, and bribery determine everything. And to what purpose?—momentary control amidst times of trouble, battle, and sacrifice. Virtually every government official has been replaced by a blood-stained victor, and those who are removed are made to suffer the misfortune of banishment, proscription, or violent death. Rare are the elections that are free of terrible crimes, and fewer still are the government leaders who have held their posts for the term provided by law or have been succeded by legally elected leaders.

Today we barely recall the name of Rodríguez, the governor of Buenos Aires, who preceded Rivadavia. How did Rodríguez come into power?—through force, plunder, and bloodshed. Rivadavia was unable to stay in office half the legal term; he resigned, virtually forced out because of the incompetence of his administration and the parties opposing him. Notwithstanding this fact, his maneuverings gave no respite to Dorrego, who occupied the post after López had been President for several months.

After Dorrego had been called upon to govern the Republic by the acclamation of all the provinces, including Buenos Aires, he conducted the war against the Emperor of Brazil with ability and distinction. When he took office the nation was in desperate straits: the government lacked funds, leaders, and military forces. For these reasons Rivadavia resigned, and, not content with this act of weakness, he raised new issues when the time came for peace with Brazil. He then dared to call in General Lavalle, a bold and unscrupulous man, a soldier worthy of Catiline, whose career has followed the path that normally leads a felon to the gallows.

As a soldier he was insubordinate; as an officer, mutinous; as a commander, a murderer and plunderer, as Ica woefully recalls; and, finally, he was a rebel who killed his country's leader. He seized the supreme authority, doubtless in the hope of legalizing his usurpation of power through the criminal action of the corrupt delegates of the people, who, as in Mexico, are prone to sanction the atrocious conduct of so depraved a man.

However, let us be fair to the Río de la Plata. What we have just described is not peculiar to that country: its history is that of all Spanish America. We shall again see these same principles, these same processes, these same consequences in every republic, one country differing from another only incidentally, and modified only by circumstances and regional variations.

Throughout America we shall see but a single trend in public affairs. The cycles are similar, varying at most according to time and conditions, but otherwise paralleling the stages and the events in the other newborn states.

Nowhere are there legal elections; nowhere do those elected come to office according to the law. If Buenos Aires has produced one Lavalle, the rest of America is plagued with many Lavalles. If a Dorrego has been assassinated, assassinations are also being committed in Mexico, Bolivia, and Colombia—September 25 is too recent a date to be forgotten.[1] If Pueyrredón plunders the public treasury [of Buenos Aires], there are those in Colombia who do the same. If [the Argentine province of] Córdoba and Paraguay are ruled by bloody hypocrites, Perú has its General La Mar in a donkey-skin, with the claws of a tiger and an insatiable lust for American blood. If anarchic movements occur in every Argentine province, Chile and Guatemala set such horrible examples that we can scarcely hope for peace. In the Argentine provinces, Sarratea, Rodríguez, and Alvear

---

[1] See Docs. 304-306 (ed.).

have compelled their country to house, in the capital, bandits who call themselves liberators. In Chile, the Carreras and their henchmen have committed similar acts. Freire, the director, destroyed his own government, the control of which he has obtained only by subjecting the Congress to extreme violence; moreover, as a result of his inability to govern, anarchy soon held sway. Urriola legislated for the legislature, after first defeating the government troops and the Director himself, who had led them with distinction. And is there any crime of which Guatemala is innocent? The lawful authorities have been removed; the provinces have rebelled against the capital; brother wars upon brother—a horror which the Spaniards had prevented—and this war is to the death. Town fights town; city stands against city, each with its own government, and every street is a self-constituted nation. In Central America all is bloodshed and terror!

Though it is true that a government in Buenos Aires lasts scarcely a week, it is equally certain that Bolivia has now followed this monstrous example. No sooner had the illustrious Sucre left that unfortunate country than the traitor Blanco seized, through intrigue, the government which legally belonged to General Santa Cruz. Yet Blanco did not hold it five days before he was captured and killed by a dissatisfied faction, to be followed by a legitimate head, Velazco, who was in turn succeeded by Santa Cruz. Thus, hapless Bolivia has had four different leaders in less than two weeks! Only the Kingdom of Hell could offer so appalling a picture discrediting humanity!

We are amazed at the almost infinite number of subdivisions in the territory of the Argentine, whose condition resembles that of the baronies of old, so that this federation under freedom is like the feudal estates under monarchy. The barons imposed levies, built castles, and ruled as they pleased; they thus defied their sovereign, and on occasion they even fought him. Buenos Aires, Chile, and Guatemala imitate and surpass the practices and doctrines of those barons; thus, extremes clash, and, for the same reasons, personal ambition.

But recent events in Mexico dwarf everything that we have so ruefully mentioned respecting the Río de la Plata and the rest of America. Buenos Aires must, therefore, bow before opulent Mexico, now a rabble-ridden city. Horror and crime stalk that fair land. A new breed of sans-culottes, or rather sans-chemises, occupies the seats of government and controls everything. The rudderless rule of usurpation and plunder is enthroned in the capital and in the provinces of the Federation. A wild man from the southern coasts, the vile

issue of a savage Indian woman and a barbaric African,[1] has climbed
into supreme power over two thousand dead bodies and at the price
of twenty millions in property destroyed. This new Dessalines stops
at nothing; he holds nothing sacred. He robs the people of their
liberty, the citizens of their possessions, the children of their lives,
the women of their honor. Every crime committed is at his command
or on his behalf. Unable to attain office by the path of law or popular
election, he joined with General Santana [sic], that most depraved of
men. First they destroyed the Empire and murdered the Emperor,[2]
because they could not occupy the throne. Then, in order to seize
control of the provinces and finally the capital, they proclaimed a
federation, hand-in-hand with other demagogues, as unscrupulous as
themselves. They joined the Masonic Order to win proselytes; they
also threatened General Bravo, a worthy champion of honest men,
and, since his honesty hindered them, they drove him from the
country together with hundreds of deserving officials, after they had
created discord in order to unseat him.

This cruel soldier, who like Pizarro could neither read nor write,
was rejected in the general elections. The overwhelming majority of
the electorate, with Bravo gone, voted for General Pedraza, in conformity with the Constitution and the hopes of all. But the ambitious
soldier did not hesitate to go to criminal lengths. In collaboration with
Victoria, a disgrace to the presidency, he bathed the capital in blood,
and, setting the entire rabble upon the propertied classes, he overran
the finest city in America with the scum of the earth. The filthy
lepers, led by generals of their own ilk—Guerrero, Lobato, and Santana—seized everything, and, like Attila's Huns in Rome, plundered
and wrecked the city's freedom, government, and wealth. What men,
or what demons, are these? From one end to the other, the New
World is an abyss of abominations, and, were anything lacking to
complete this terrible chaos, Perú could more than supply it. A partisan of the tyrannical Spaniards during the war for independence,
Perú, with her liberty not yet fully won, in the very first days of her
existence, was the scene of a fratricidal struggle. The country had
been cleared of Spaniards from Trujillo to Ica by valorous General
San Martín, at the head of the Chileans and Argentines. In the
eyes of the people of Lima there was no more of Perú to liberate;
thereupon, some promptly undertook to rid the country of San Mar-

---

[1] Vicente Guerrero (ed.).

[2] Iturbide, who, although exiled returned to Mexico in an attempt to regain his throne (ed.).

tín, whose services were most urgently needed. This act of ingratitude interrupted all political progress in Perú, and she rushed forward
headlong to Girón,[1] where the most damnable thing happened—but
let us go on.

Luna Pizarro—he is worthy of both names—detested Riva Agüero
and Torre Tagle, and yet he conspired with them to oust San Martín. Succeeding in this, the triumvirate had no thought of dividing
the Incan Empire among themselves; instead, each hoped to possess
it entirely for himself, but without fighting or running any risks
to obtain it. Luna Pizarro matched La Mar against the others. He
triumphed with ease over two rivals less crafty than he, though more
discredited and unscrupulous. Guided by his teacher La Mar, and
through the command of Alvarado, lost the army of San Martín at
Torata and Moquegua, thereby opening the country's gates to the
Spaniards. Then General Santa Cruz, joining with Riva Agüero, deposed the traitor La Mar and forced him to flee the country. These
new chiefs applied to Colombia for the auxiliaries which La Mar had
craftly returned to their own country, lest they interfere with his
treasonable plans. Once more the Colombians went to Perú, to free
that country of her enemies. President Riva Agüero, deposed and
proscribed by the Congress, then offered to sell his country to the
Spaniards. The Congress named Torre Tagle president, and, incredible as it may seem, also welcomed the Spaniards and turned
Lima and Callao over to them—such was the behavior of the most
traitorous triumvirate history has ever produced. Never, never have
there been three successive heads of one nation, who, in succession,
surrendered her to crueler enemies of independence and political
freedom.

The Liberator returned to Colombia, leaving Perú without leadership. He had hardly turned his back when news reached him of the
insurrection of the Colombian auxiliaries in Lima. And what did the
government of Perú do at this juncture? It decided, without hesitation, to send these traitors to invade their own country in order that
they might rob it of much of its territory and dispose of it for a sum
which the infamous Bustamante offered to pay. General La Mar, a
Peruvian, lent this insurrectionary movement powerful support, and
he was soon able to take possession of Guayaquil by having himself
named head of that department by his friends and relatives.

------

[1] See Doc. 309 (ed.).

As a reward for this incredible treachery the Congress of Perú, or rather Luna Pizarro, appointed La Mar President of the Republic. This unworthy Colombian lost no time. Without warning, he gathered together all his forces and invaded Bolivia, where he committed political atrocities to enable him to make war upon his own country. He finally declared war and laid waste his native land. He ordered the sacking of the town in which he had first seen the light of day, and he carried the fury of war to a pitch not matched by the most savage barbarian. Nor was Perú any less the victim of his crimes.

A coward as well as a parricide, La Mar fled Guayaquil like a madman. He fled from a child who commanded a handful of soldiers. At Saraguro, he and the entire reserve of his army retreated from 20 men of the *Yaguachi*; at Portete he fled from the same battalion, and especially from its commander Alzuru. On reaching Girón, he saw that he was lost; hence, he signed a treaty, which he soon violated after it had served to save his life from Colombia's vengeance; and later he again made war upon Colombia, in reward for our extreme generosity.

There is no good faith in America, nor among the nations of America. Treaties are scraps of paper; constitutions, printed matter; elections, battles; freedom, anarchy; and life, a torment. Such, Fellow-Americans, is our deplorable situation. Unless we change it, death is to be preferred. Anything is better than endless conflict, the indignity of which appears to increase with the violence and the duration of the movement. Let us not delude ourselves—this evil, which increases revolts and mutinies in the armed forces, will eventually compel us to reject the very first constructive principles of political life. We lost all individual rights when, in an effort to obtain them in perfect form, we sacrificed our blood and all that we cherished most, prior to the war—for, if we look back at that time, who will deny that our rights were then more respected? Never were we as badly off as we are at present. At that time we enjoyed positive and tangible benefits, whereas today we have dreams bordering upon illusion, hope feeding upon the future, and disillusionment forever tortured with the bitterness of reality.

Enough then of twenty years of hostilities, misery, and death. We yearn for a stable government, fitted to the actual state of our affairs, compatible with the character of our people, and capable especially of rescuing us from that hydra, from that bloody monster, unfettered anarchy, that feeds upon the best of the Republic, and whose despicable nature reduces men to a state of frenzy that inspires all of them with an insane love of absolute power and an implacable dislike for obedience to law.

This nightmare-like picture is a faithful portrayal of the revolution that we have experienced in the past, but it also awaits us in the future, unless we exert ourselves in rescuing the social order which is about to destroy itself. Our country looks forward to the day when Congress shall convene to remind us of our duty to save her. Then shall she say:

Colombians, you have suffered greatly and sacrificed much but to no avail, for you have not found the path to salvation. You were seduced by freedom and deceived by her potent charms. But, since freedom is as dangerous as beauty in women, whom all desire out of love or vanity, you have not kept her as innocent and pure as she was when she descended from Heaven. Power, the born enemy of human rights, has excited personal ambition in all classes of our society. The second man to head the Republic assassinated the first; the Third Division invaded the south; Pasto rebelled against the Republic; Perú laid waste to her benefactors' territories; and there is hardly a province that has not exceeded its powers and prerogatives. Throughout this ill-fated period there has been nothing but blood, disorder, and destruction. There is nothing left for you to do but to muster all your spiritual strength and establish a government strong enough to bridle ambition and safeguard freedom. Otherwise, you will become the laughingstock of the world and the victims of your own undoing.

May the citizens and the government, the provinces and the armies heed the bitter cry of their country and, uniting to form an impenetrable wall against the violence of factions, envelop the nation's representatives in Congress in all the virtue, power, and genius that Colombia has to offer!

SIMON BOLIVAR.

D'après l'original présenté par lui peu de temps
avant sa mort à M. WATTS consul de S M B a Carth.

Bolivar in 1830
From an original by Meucci.

1830

319. Message to the Constituent Congress
   of the Republic of Colombia

[*Gaceta de Colombia*, January 24, 1830]

Bogotá, January 20, 1830.

Fellow-Citizens:

Allow me to congratulate you upon the gathering of this Congress which, in behalf of the nation, is to fulfill the sublime duties of lawgiver.

Arduous and great is the task of creating a nation out of a people emerging from oppression through the path of anarchy and civil war, a people lacking the necessary preparation with which to profit from the salutary reforms to which they aspire. But the lessons of history, the examples of the Old World and the New, the experience of twenty years of revolution, must serve you as so many beacon-lights amidst the dark uncertainties of the future. I am confident that your wisdom will reach the heights necessary to dominate courageously the passions of the minority and the ignorance of the masses, and to consult duly, for enlightenment, the keen understanding of those judicious men whose respected opinions are of priceless aid in resolving problems of statecraft. You will, moreover, find valuable counsel in the very nature of our country, which extends from the high peaks of the Andes to the torrid banks of the Orinoco. Survey this land in its entirety, and you will learn from Nature, that inexorable mistress of mankind, what laws the Congress must decree in order to insure the well-being of Colombia's people. You will learn much from the study of our history, and much from an investigation of our needs; but more convincing still will be the cries of the people against the woes that they suffer because of the lack of established order and freedom.

Glory to the Congress if it succeeds in endowing Colombia with those invaluable prizes, for it will merit the most hallowed of blessings!

The Congress has been convened to draft the fundamental code by which the Republic is to be governed and to choose the higher administrative officers; therefore, it becomes the duty of the government to inform you of the facts known to the respective ministries concerning the present state of the country, so that your legislation may conform to the nature of things. The Presidents of the Council of State and of the Council of Ministers are to report to you upon their labors during the past eighteen months. If these labors have not fulfilled the hopes we have entertained, at least they have overcome the obstacles to administrative progress caused by the troubled conditions of foreign war and domestic insurrection, evils which, by the grace of God, have given way to the benefits of clemency and peace.

Allow me to direct your sovereign attention to the origin and course of these unsettled conditions.

The unfortunate disturbances which occurred in 1826 obliged me to return from Perú, despite my determination not to accept the chief magistracy under the Constitution, to which I had been reelected during my absence. Urged, pleaded with, to return and reestablish harmony and avert civil war, I could not refuse my services to my country. I accordingly accepted that new honor and the other indubitable proofs of the confidence reposed in me.

The nation's representatives proceeded to examine the causes of the discontent that agitated the minds of men, and, having discovered their nature, they realized that radical steps had to be taken and they submitted to the necessity of advancing the time for the gathering of the great convention.[1] That body convened at a time when partisan feeling was at its height, and so it adjourned before its members could reach an agreement upon the proposed reforms. As the Republic was threatened with complete dissolution, I was again obliged to sustain it during so grave a crisis. Had not national sentiment demanded that deliberations respecting the preservation of the Republic be held immediately, it would assuredly have been destroyed at the hands of its own citizenry. The Republic then chose to honor me with its trust, a trust that I was bound to respect as the most sacred commandment. With my country about to perish, how could I hesitate?

The laws, which had been violated amidst the clash of arms and the disturbances in the towns, eventually lost their force. The legislature, having recognized the necessity, had already decreed the con-

---

[1] The Congress of Ocaña, 1828 (ed.).

vocation of the assembly that was to revise the Constitution; that assembly subsequently unanimously declared that such a revision was most urgently needed. This solemn declaration, added to others that preceded it, dealt a fatal blow to Colombia's political system. According to the general opinion and in actual fact, the Constitution of the year '11 was no more.[1]

Our country was in a terrible situation, and my position was even more terrible, for I had set myself up as a target for misinterpretations and suspicions. I was not deterred, however, by threats to a reputation earned by innumerable services, for, in rendering them, sacrifices like this had frequently to be made.

The organic law, which I decreed on August 27, 1828, should have convinced everyone that my most ardent desire was to lay aside the insupportable burden of unlimited authority and to see the Republic reëstablished by its representatives. But I had hardly begun to exercise the duties of supreme chief when the opposition erupted with all the violence of passion and the ferocity of crime. Attempts were made on my life; civil war broke out. The latter development, among other things, encouraged the government of Perú to invade our southern departments for the purpose of conquering and usurping them. This, Fellow-Citizens, is no mere conjecture—the facts and documents attesting to it are authentic. War was inevitable. Our forces, in a splendid and glorious victory, routed the army of General La Mar at Tarqui. The remnants of the enemy's troops were spared only through the generosity of the victors. Colombia's magnanimity notwithstanding, General La Mar, flouting the treaties, reopened the war by renewing hostilities. I replied by again offering him peace; his response was an outpouring of slander and abuse. The department of Guayaquil fell victim to his fantastic plans.

Lacking a naval force, beset by the winter floods and other obstacles, we were obliged to await a more propitious season to recover that city. During this interval the "verdict of the nation," in the words of Perú's own Chief Magistrate, vindicated our conduct and freed that country of General La Mar.[2]

This change in the political complexion of that Republic opened the way to negotiations, and we recovered Guayaquil by means of an armistice. Finally, on September 22, we concluded the treaty of peace, thus ending a war in which Colombia had successfully defended her rights and honor.

[1] The Cúcuta Constitution of 1821 (ed.).
[2] See Docs. 311, 312 (ed.).

I congratulate the Congress and the nation upon the satisfactory outcome of our affairs in the south, not only because of the end of the war but also because of the unmistakable tokens of good will demonstrated by the Peruvian government, which has generously avowed that depraved ambitions provoked us into war. Never has one government given as much satisfaction to another as has Perú. Such greatness of spirit is deserving of our most whole-hearted esteem.

Fellow-Citizens! Peace has been concluded with the moderation that is to be desired between brother peoples who, in fact, should never have taken up arms consecrated to liberty and mutual defense. We were equally lenient with the unhappy people of the south who allowed themselves to be dragged or tricked into a civil war by the enemy. I am happy to say that, in settling our domestic feuds, not a single drop of blood has spoiled the vindication of our laws. And though a valiant general and his followers died upon the field of battle, their punishment came from the hand of the Almighty, whereas from us they would have enjoyed the clemency which we granted the survivors. They were all freed, despite their errors.

We will always recall with grief these misfortunes, from which our country has suffered so severely. If anything can assuage our deep affliction, it is the consolation that we had no part in its origin and that we were as generous toward our adversaries as our situation permitted. We deeply regret that certain delinquents were sacrificed upon the altar of Justice, and, though execution is little-deserving of consideration, nevertheless, at my hands, many of them, perhaps the most vicious, received it.

Let this picture of horror, which I, unfortunately, have been obliged to reveal to you, be an example to us. Let it serve us in the future, like those trials and blows which Providence, for our correction, is wont to visit upon us during a lifetime. It should warn Congress not to pluck sweet fruits from this bitter tree, or at least to withdraw from beneath its noxious shade.

Had I not been charged with the honored task of calling you together to represent the rights of the people and to shape or improve our institutions in conformity with the desires of your constituents, this would be the place to reveal to you the experience of twenty years devoted to the service of the country. But I must refrain from suggesting that which every other citizen is free to demand of you. All can and should make known their opinions, fears, and desires to those whom we have chosen to relieve our sick society of its fever and weakness. I alone am forbidden to exercise this civic duty, for, as it was I who convened you and defined your powers, I am not permitted in any manner to influence your deliberations. Moreover, it would be presumptuous of me to repeat to the chosen representatives of the people what Colombia has made public in characters of blood. My only duty consists in submitting, without reservation, to the code of laws and the officials that you are to give us, and my sole desire is for the will of all the people to be heard, respected, and carried out by their delegates.

To this end, I have made ample provision to enable every section of the country to express its opinion in complete freedom and safety, with no restrictions other than those which order and moderation prescribe. This has been done, and in the petitions to be submitted for your consideration you will find the untrammeled expressions of popular desires. All the provinces await your resolutions; in every region the meetings held to this end have been conducted in a spirit of order and respect for the authority of the government and the Constituent Congress. We have only to deplore the intemperate action of the *junta* of Caracas, which your prudence and wisdom will have to judge.

I fear, and not without reason, that my sincerity will be questioned when I speak to you of the magistrate who is to head the Republic. But the Congress must realize that their honor forbids them to consider me for that post, and that mine forbids me to accept it. Would you, by chance, return this precious authority to him who has delivered it to you? Would you, conceivably, to the detriment of your good name, cast your votes for me? Would this not mean that I had voted myself into power? Far be it from you or me to stoop to such behavior.

As it is your obligation to organize the Republic into a well-established government, you will find, both within and without your own august number, illustrious citizens who are capable of discharging the office of president with glory and success. All, all of my fellow-citizens, excluding none, enjoy the great good fortune of being held innocent of suspicion; only I am branded as aspiring to become a tyrant.

Shield me, I beg you, from the disgrace that would be mine were I to continue in a post that stamps me inescapably with the odium of ambition. Please believe me—the Republic vitally needs a new chief magistrate. The people wonder if the time will ever come when I shall cease to rule. The nations of America regard me with a certain misgiving which may some day embroil Colombia in unfortunate situations similar to that of the war with Perú. Europe, too, does not lack those who fear that my conduct may discredit the noble cause of freedom. Ah! Witness the many conspiracies and wars we have suffered, aimed at my authority and person! These attacks have brought injury to entire peoples, whose sacrifices might long since have ended if the legislators of Colombia had not forced me to assume a burden that has weighed more heavily upon me than war, with all its horrors.

Fellow-Citizens, prove yourselves worthy of representing a free people by banishing the belief that I am indispensable to the Republic. If any one man were indispensable to the survival of a state, that state should not, and in the end could not, exist.

The chief magistrate that you are to select, will, without doubt, be a mediator of domestic harmony, a bond of brotherhood, a comfort to the repudiated factions. Every Colombian will rally around this fortunate man. He will receive them all in the arms of friendship and make them one family of citizens. I shall obey this lawful magistrate with the profoundest respect. I shall follow him as if he were the angel of peace. I will support him with my sword and with all my might. Everything will add strength, respect, and obedience to the one you elect. I swear it, Gentlemen, and I promise it in the name of the people and the army of Colombia. The Republic will be blessed if, on accepting my resignation, you select as president a citizen beloved of the nation, but the Republic cannot survive if you insist that I remain in command. Hear my entreaties; save the Republic; save my glory, which is Colombia's own.

Do as you will with the presidency, which I respectfully deliver into your hands. Henceforth, I am but a citizen-in-arms, ready to defend my country and obey her government. My public duties are forever ended. I formally and solemnly deliver to you the supreme authority conferred upon me by the express wish of the nation.

You come from all the provinces; you are their finest citizens; you have served in every public office; you are familiar with local and national interests; and you possess all the means for reviving this Republic, which stands tottering in every branch of her administration.

Allow me, as my last official act, to commend to you the protection of the holy religion that we profess, the fountain-head of heavenly blessings. The national treasury must claim your attention, especially the system of revenues. The public debt, Colombia's cancerous sore, demands that its sacred obligations be honored. The army, which has innumerable claims to the nation's gratitude, is in need of thorough reorganization. Justice demands codes capable of protecting the rights and the honor of free men. All this is for you to create. You must prepare the groundwork for prosperity by establishing the general foundations of our political organization.

Fellow-Citizens, I am ashamed to say it, but independence is the sole benefit we have gained, at the sacrifice of all others. Yet independence, under your sovereign auspices, opens the gates to the recovery of these others, in all the splendor of glory and liberty.

SIMÓN BOLÍVAR

---

320. To José Fernández Madrid

[Copy]¹

Fucha, March 6, 1830.

Esteemed friend:

I have duly received your most recent letter by the latest post, and I understand therefrom that the gentlemen who purchased the mines are requesting new documents; but you do not say, nor can I imagine, which documents. The fact is that my position is daily becoming more critical; I do not have so much as the hope of being able to live abroad except as a pauper. If the mines are not sold, they may be confiscated, on one pretext or another, by the Venezuelan government, because of the animus against me on the part of certain officials there. Taking all this into account, I would suggest that you approach the gentleman and arrange for him, as the new owner of the mines, to assume my rights, claiming to be already in possession of them by virtue of the contract which has been executed by both parties. As the aforementioned purchaser has a contract which long

¹ Copied by Pedro Fernández Madrid and reproduced in José Manuel Groot, *Historia Eclesiástica y Civil de la Nueva Granada.* 5 vols. (Bogotá, 1870), III, 685, with the phrase "and he is a scoundrel" (y éste es un canalla), in reference to Pando omitted (comp.).

antedates the present revolution, no one has the right to place obstacles in the way of this legitimate sale.

There is no need to remind you to discuss the matter with a lawyer to assure that the necessary documents are issued in favor of each party, and to obtain for ourselves every possible guarantee to make sure that we will not be cheated in any way and to enable us to collect the proper amount when the time comes.

The Congress is continuing its labors, and it has already drafted a constitution which is very republican and liberal, one that is designed to appeal to all the moderate elements. This Constitution is to be ratified within a month, at which time new elections for president and vice president of the Republic will be held. By that time we shall also know the outcome of the mission that Congress sent to Venezuela, although it will probably result in nothing more important than a repetition of previous reactions. As a consequence, Congress will decide whether or not the separation of the two countries is to be voted upon. Of this there is little doubt, since public opinion favors avoiding war.

You can, of course, be sure that I, come what may, will not be president again, and that I will seek respite from further vexations by leaving the country and going wherever my limited fortune permits. You will learn more about this matter in the next mail.

I had intended to send you the papers concerning my public life, but I have learned from Colonel Wilson that his father, the General, has the work in sixteen volumes; you might ask him to lend them to you so that you can reply to the slander that is being spread about me.

Do not hesitate to deny positively any assertion contrary to what you know of my character.

First, I have never sought to establish the Bolivian Constitution in Colombia; nor was it I who introduced it in Perú. The people and the Ministers of State did so of their own accord. On this point you might read the Pando declaration of that time, and Pando is a scoundrel who would not hold back anything that might reflect upon me.

Second, every act of treachery, duplicity, or deceit attributed to me is unmitigated slander. Whatever I have done or said has been in earnest and with no secrecy whatsoever.

Third, you should categorically deny any cruelty toward the patriots and point out that, if at any time I dealt severely with the Spaniards, it was in reprisal.

Fourth, you can deny any act of self-interest attributed to me, and you may unhesitatingly affirm that I have dealt generously with most of my enemies.

Fifth, you can assert that in war I took no step dictated by prudence or reason that can be ascribed to cowardice. My every action was prompted by calculation, and, more, even by daring. The incident at Ocumare was the most extraordinary event in the world.[1] I was deceived both by an aide-de-camp of General Mariño, who was a traitor, and by the foreign seamen, who were guilty of infamy, for they left me on a deserted shore, surrounded by my enemies. I was about to turn my pistol against myself when one of them J. B. Videau returned from the sea in a rowboat and rescued me. This incident demands a more detailed explanation.

In short, my dear friend, the documents concerning my life contain an adequate supply of defense material, though most [of the records] relating to the earlier period of my history are missing. However, since the most recent years are more often under attack, you can always find evidence in the facts as they were witnessed and recorded.

I am sending you today's *Gaceta,* which will afford you some satisfactory explanations; moreover, you will note that I have left Caicedo in charge because of the state of my health, which is not serious, however. I shall never return to take the supreme power as I now find it insufferable in every way. Fortunately, it cannot be said that I abandoned my country, since it was the country that rejected me, shamefully and criminally. I am not as virtuous as Phocion, but in the services that I have rendered, I resemble him; and while I do not feel that I have been as ill-used as he, there is a certain parallel in the ingratitude of our fellow-citizens.

General Ibarra has just arrived from Venezuela, where he had the opportunity to observe public opinion carefully. He assures me that all the people favor me, except for a few plotters who, behind the cloak of terror, have brought about the revolt. Only those who know the [Spanish] American people will be able to believe this. Look where you will on our continent, and you will see the same thing. History long since has taught us the influence of demagogues on Greece and Rome. Given these examples, nothing else could be expected.

---

[1] See p. xxiv. (ed.).

Good-bye, my dear friend. Watch your health, and believe me to be your firm and devoted friend,

BOLÍVAR

---

321. To GENERAL ANTONIO JOSÉ DE SUCRE, GRAND MARSHAL OF AYACUCHO

[Copy]

Turbaco, May 26, 1830.

My dear General and good friend:

Your esteemed, undated letter, in which you take leave of me, has filled me with emotion; if it pained you to write it, what of me, for I am leaving not only a friend but also my country! You speak the truth when you say that words fail to convey one's innermost feelings in circumstances such as these. Forgive me, then, for my own lack of words, and accept my heartfelt wish that you may prosper and be happy. I shall forget you only when those who love glory forget Pichincha and Ayacucho.

You will be pleased to know that on my way from Bogotá here I received a thousand testimonials in every town. This department has especially distinguished itself. General Montilla has borne himself like a perfect gentleman.

Convey my very kindest regards to your wife, and be assured that nothing on earth is more sincere than the affection with which I once more remain, my dear friend, your

BOLÍVAR

322. To Mariana Carcelen de Sucre

[*La Opinión Nacional*, Caracas, October 28, 1879]

Cartagena, July 2, 1830.
My dear Madam:

Profoundly shocked by the horrible rumor that is abroad respecting the death of your distinguished husband, the Grand Marshal of Ayacucho, I venture, perhaps indiscreetly, to express to you my heart's overwhelming grief, grief which his wife, his son, his country, and his glory will share.

My mind cannot conceive the depths of anguish that this loss, as irreparable as it is great, has caused you. I can only presume to judge by my own feelings what must be those of a wife who has lost everything, so suddenly and so cruelly.[1] Our one consolation, if there is any, is to be sought in the flow of tears that all Colombia and half of America must shed in tribute to a benefactor of such heroic stature. For my part, please accept this expression of my immense and indescribable grief at the death of a friend, who, above all others, deserves my eternal gratitude for his loyalty, his character, and all that we owe him.

Forgive me, Madam, for not saying more in this letter, but I do not know how to express my feelings of sorrow for you and for myself.

With sentiments of the most profound respect and high regard, I am your most devoted servant,

Q. B. S. P.
Bolívar

---

[1] Sucre was assassinated at Berruecos, Colombia, on June 4, 1830 (ed.).

323. To General Rafael Urdaneta, Provisional President of Colombia

[*Memorias de Urdaneta*, p. 481]

Cartagena, September 18, 1830.

My dear General:

Yesterday the commissioners arrived, bringing me the resolution and all the most important news from the capital. Much as I would have liked to yield to the arguments and exhortations of these commissioners, of the friends I have in this country, and even of the letters that have come from Bogotá, I could not bring myself to accept a command that rests on nothing more than two resolutions of two municipal councils. Moreover, Mosquera has not relinquished his title, and by tomorrow he will have himself recognized elsewhere as the lawful president.[1] This event is not far distant. It will take place upon his arrival in Popayán, as Obando and López will attend to it. Mosquera, thus far, has taken counsel from these two monsters only. He will then be the lawful president and I the usurper. Try as I may to overcome my repugnance, I cannot bring myself to accept such a situation.

Santa María tells me that, unless I accept the command, fearful anarchy will inevitably follow; but what am I to do about the iron barrier that keeps me from the presidency? That barrier is the matter of lawful possession. This I do not have, and he who holds it has not surrendered it. We must, therefore, await the elections. Following these, I will be duly cloaked in legitimacy, unless a new president is elected. The political horizon will have cleared, and, in short, we shall know whether or not we have a fatherland. Then, and only then, could I vest myself with the executive power, always assuming that the elections are held in conformity with the law.

I cannot be accused of having abandoned my fellow-citizens to anarchy, because I have had no part in their conflicts and, moreover, because you head the government, and you are clothed with all the necessary powers to meet such a crisis. As a citizen and soldier I offer my services to the Republic; none will serve her more devotedly, for I shall support the government with all my prestige and strength.

---

[1] On September 5, Urdaneta led a revolt in Bogotá against Mosquera, who had been elected President by the Congress of 1830. Urdaneta hoped to restore Bolívar to power and thereby prevent the division of the Republic of Colombia (ed.).

There is still another circumstance which renders me useless to this administration: actuality precedes improvement. We must first bring our country back into existence, as she has been dissolved and cannot, therefore, be well governed until she is reunited by force of arms. I offer my services for the most difficult and perilous of the tasks ahead, and thus I shall escape the charge of personal aggrandizement.

I enclose a proclamation containing statements that will please those who most favor me. This will serve to dispel some of the misunderstanding, and, in the meantime, all those gentlemen can be told that I am marching toward Bogotá at the head of 2,000 men, to help reëstablish public order and to support the present government, and that when I arrive it will definitely be made known whether or not I accept. This will give rise to entreaties and supplications, and every problem will find a solution. Austria has orders to mention any of these things in order to placate the people and to enable me to avoid responsibility and yet be helpful in this situation.

My official letter in reply to yours should be published in order that the people may see that I propose to support the new administration. I shall also write to all my friends and ask them to back you, because you are the indispensable man in that section. I shall, moreover, act in such a way that the people's hopes will be encouraged and not lost altogether.

You must not complain that I am not doing all I can for the public interest just because I cannot take the ultimate step, for I find that to be impossible.

It is now my turn to ask you not to abandon us to the mercy of this fearful anarchy. You cannot be accused of ambition in view of the fact that you have made every effort to persuade me to return, and you have never vied with anyone for the supreme power. You are under a greater compulsion than I, as you held the position of minister when the government fell and you are now holding office for only a few days, *pro tempore*, until I arrive. I am proceeding to the capital, which might make it appear that I am considering taking office. It is true, of course, that, if I set foot in Bogotá, I cannot tell what will happen, pressed as I will be on all sides, by the Church on the one hand, the army on the other, and the people everywhere! In the capital I might lose my head, my friend, and I could not be sure of myself. These fanciful hopes and many others may serve to keep the public spirit high, while you yourself will meantime act sternly and firmly, as the cruel circumstances of the moment imperiously demand. Governments must be merciless when conditions are hopeless; if you save Colombia from her present chaos, you will achieve immortal fame and distinguish yourself forever.

I believe that the leading citizens of Cartagena have not been especially pleased with the composition of the present ministry. They think well of Vergara only. I know that you could select no better; hence, I do not know what you are to do on this score. Our friends want you to use García del Río. He seems to me to be a valuable man for any post, particularly that of foreign relations, as he is familiar with the field and is a good man for it. They complain also of the indulgence that they expect will be shown to the traitors and assassins. On this I will say no more, as you must know what has to be done; moreover, the responsibility is yours.

I believe it to be absolutely imperative that a competent commander, accompanied by good officers, arms, and munitions, be sent to the Cauca Valley. If you make Jiménez a general, he will do best; otherwise, Mugüerza or Castelli. I heartily recommend all these gentlemen, as I do all those who have distinguished themselves. The troops to be sent to Antioquia would make excellent reinforcements for Cauca. Popayán and Patía will fight us for a long time, but the valley is an excellent base. Direct your attention exclusively to that quarter, and I will see to the rest, from the Magdalena to Venezuela, including Boyacá. But I repeat that we need money in Cúcuta. That will be your greatest miracle. The dissidents should be made to pay, even at a sacrifice, and the well-intentioned should make sacrifices for their own security—in fact, everyone must pay, to assure our political, and indeed our physical, existence.

Should anything further develop, I shall write you by the post that leaves tonight.

The officials here want the government to grant them the special powers it possesses by virtue of the act legally required by the Constitution, but subject to the exceptions necessary to keep up the new regime. Here, therefore, as the officials will be left without troops, their authority must necessarily be reinforced, so that a healthy respect for them will prevent criminal outbreaks.

Remember me kindly to your esteemed wife, and believe me your devoted

BOLÍVAR

Addendum. Notwithstanding what I say above, I have an idea that Borrero could do a great deal to influence the union of Cauca and Cundinamarca, and for this reason he should not leave his present position unless he himself insists. I am writing to urge him to remain in the Cabinet.

---

324. To GENERAL RAFAEL URDANETA, PROVISIONAL PRESIDENT OF COLOMBIA

[*Anales de Venezuela*, IV, 261]

Santa Marta, San Pedro, December 7, 1830.

My dear General:

I must confess that the last letter I received from you, dated the 21st ultimo, caused me no little concern, as the differences between you and Briceño[1] may lead to considerable trouble.[2] I have previously mentioned this matter to you, and I trust that my counsels and predictions arrived shortly after you wrote me the letter under reply. But this is not all that troubles me. Your comments have affected me strangely, for I cannot imagine what you had in mind when you made them. If you believe that I would conceal any adverse opinion from you, after dealing with you as frankly as I have, you do me an injustice which you cannot say that I do you, as I have lost patience with those who have presumed to give me assurances of your sincerity, which seemed to me quite uncalled for. If the differences between you and Briceño have their origin in anything other than personal resentment, I fail to understand why you make statements so alien to the friendship that I choose to believe exists between us. But I shall speak no more of this unpleasant subject, which I trust will not recur in the future as a fresh source of discord. It seems to me that my advice to you on this point is sufficient if you care to take my hints; if, on the other hand, these are not in harmony with your views, there would be no point in my repeating them to you. Nevertheless, I shall rejoice if my fears fail to materialize and if such trivial matters as these do not lead to more serious consequences. To this end, I have

---

[1] Justo Briceño (ed.).

[2] See Doc. 326 (ed.).

called on General Briceño[1] to serve in the Ministry of War. You know him well, and you are acquainted with his integrity and loyalty. I am inclined to believe he may be able to resolve some of the difficulties. Blanco likewise can sway Justo Briceño. This friend, they say, is very ill, and it might be for the best, in any case, if he were to be stationed in Boyacá.

Eight Venezuelan commanders have arrived here, among them Generals Infante, Silva, and Portocarrero. Some of them are going to your city and some to Cúcuta, to be of service as best they can. The news they bring from Venezuela is very encouraging, but doubtless you have learned about this through other channels.

I must ask a favor of you, namely, that you send letters of appointment to Silva and to Andrés Ibarra, so that they will at least have salaries to live on. The latter, it seems to me, has earned a promotion, and I should be obliged to you if you would grant him one.

I was pleased with the news from Cauca, and I think the arrangements you have made for that area are very satisfactory. I am not replying to the official letter that you addressed to me, as I am still very ill, and, indeed, this is the only reply I have been able to make.

Colonel Guerra, who was in Venezuela on a commission from Flores, has returned, they tell me, in fine spirits. He wrote me from Cartagena before going on, telling me that he did not come to see me, as he had intended, so as to reach Guayaquil the sooner, that the south was doing excellently, and that he had every intention of conveying to me personally the sentiments he had always cherished for me. Everyone keeps telling me that, after his arrival, Flores may change his politics. I wrote to him through Urbina and strongly urged him to proceed against the assassins of Sucre, and this, at least, I believe he will not fail to do.

I have been very ill, and my physicians thought me in danger, and, although I took ship and came to Santa Marta, I felt no improvement until yesterday, when I arrived at this hacienda. Today I have felt much better and I now have hopes of recovering quickly, especially if the climate where I intend to go to convalesce agrees with me.

Good-bye, my dear General, I remain your devoted

BOLÍVAR

P.S. Do not believe a thing they say about me. I disapprove of Briceño's conduct more strongly than you do, and whatever I write to him is for the purpose of holding him in check, if possible.

---

[1] Pedro Briceño Méndez (comp.).

325. PROCLAMATION TO THE PEOPLE OF COLOMBIA

[Original]

SIMON BOLIVAR, Liberator of Colombia, etc.

Santa Marta, December 10, 1830.

Colombians:

You have witnessed my efforts to establish liberty where tyranny once reigned. I have labored unselfishly, sacrificing my fortune and my peace of mind. When I became convinced that you distrusted my motives, I resigned my command. My enemies have played upon your credulity and destroyed what I hold most sacred—my reputation and my love of liberty. I have been the victim of my persecutors, who have brought me to the brink of the grave. I forgive them.

As I depart from your midst, my love for you tells me that I should make known my last wishes. I aspire to no other glory than the consolidation of Colombia. You must all work for the supreme good of a united nation: the people, by obeying the present government in order to rid themselves of anarchy; the ministers, from their sanctuary, by addressing their supplications to Heaven; and the military, by unsheathing the sword to defend the guarantees of organized society. *Colombians!* My last wishes are for the happiness of our native land. If my death will help to end party strife and to promote national unity, I shall go to my grave in peace.

Hacienda de San Pedro, in Santa Marta, December 10, 1830. The 20th [year].

SIMÓN BOLÍVAR

---

326. TO GENERAL JUSTO BRICEÑO

[Blanco y Azpurúa, XIV, 462]

San Pedro, December 11, 1830.

My dear General:

In these last moments of my life, I am writing this to ask you, as the final token of affection and esteem that you can give me, to be reconciled in good faith with General Urdaneta and to join with him in supporting the present government. My heart, dear General, assures me that you will not deny me this last tribute to friendship and to duty. It is only at the sacrifice of setting personal feelings aside that our friends, and Colombia herself, can be saved from the horrors of anarchy. The person who carries this, who is a friend of yours, will bear witness to the desires I have expressed for unity and order. Receive, my dear General, the last farewell and the devotion of your friend,

BOLÍVAR

---

327. TESTAMENT OF SIMÓN BOLÍVAR

[Blanco y Azpurúa, XIV, 463]

Santa Marta, December 10, 1830.

In the name of Almighty God, Amen. I, Simón Bolívar, Liberator of the Republic of Colombia, born in the city of Caracas in the department of Venezuela, legitimate son of Juan Vicente Bolívar and María Concepción Palacios, both deceased, late residents of the said city; being gravely ill but sound in mind, memory, and natural understanding; believing and confessing, as I do firmly believe and confess, the high and sovereign Mystery of the Most Blessed and Most Holy Trinity, the Father, the Son, and the Holy Ghost, three distinct persons and only one true God; and all the other Mysteries believed, preached, and taught by our Holy Mother, the Roman Catholic and Apostolic Church, in whose faith and belief I have lived and profess I shall live until I die, as a true Catholic and Christian; in order to have my testamentary dispositions ready when death shall claim me, do under divine invocation hereby make, provide, and order this my testament in due form as follows:

1. First, I commend my soul to the Lord God who created it from nothing, and my body to the earth whence it sprung, leaving to the discretion of my executors my funeral and burial, and the payment of the tithes that may be due for charitable works, as provided by the government.

2. I declare that I was lawfully wed to Teresa Toro, deceased, such marriage being without issue.

3. I declare that, when joined in matrimony, my said spouse brought to our marriage no dowry or any other goods, and I brought all that I had inherited from my parents.

4. I declare that I possess no other goods than the lands and mines of Aroa, situate in the province of Carabobo, and certain jewelry which appears in the inventory to be found among my papers; said jewelry is in the keeping of Juan de Francisco Martín, a resident of Cartagena.

5. I declare that my only indebtedness is for a sum of *pesos* due Messrs. Juan de Francisco Martín and Powles and Company, and I charge my executors to examine and verify the accounts that these gentlemen shall present and satisfy them from my estate.

6. It is my will that the medal presented to me by the Congress of Bolivia in the name of that people be returned to that country as promised, in token of the true affection which, to my very last moments, I shall have for that Republic.

7. It is my will that the two books given me as a gift by my friend General Wilson, which formerly belonged to the library of Napoleon, namely, *The Social Contract* by Rousseau and *The Art of War* by Montecuculi, be donated to the University of Caracas.

8. It is my will that there be paid eight thousand *pesos* out of my estate to my faithful steward José Palacios in consideration of his ever-faithful services.

9. I order the papers in the keeping of Mr. Pavageau to be burned.

10. It is my will that upon my demise my remains be buried in my birthplace, the city of Caracas.

11. I instruct my executors that the sword given me by the Grand Marshal of Ayacucho be returned to his widow, for her to have and to hold in token of the love I have always cherished for the aforesaid Grand Marshal.

12. I instruct my executors to give my thanks to General Robert Wilson for the noble conduct of his son Colonel Belford Wilson, who so faithfully remained with me to the last moments of my life.

13. For execution and payment of this my last will and testament and the bequests herein made, I name and appoint as my testamentary executors, trustees, and administrators General Pedro Briceño Méndez, Juan de Francisco Martín, Dr. José Vargas, and General Laurencio Silva; that they may jointly and severally take possession, use, and dispose of my estate at auction or otherwise, even after expiration of the legal term of one year of executorship, as I hereby grant them

such extension of time as they may require for the free, clear, and general disposition thereof.

14. And this, my testament and the bequests therein contained, having been executed and fee paid, I do appoint and name as my sole and universal heirs to the residue of all my goods, assets, rights and actions-at-law, as well as to any inheritance or inheritances to which I shall have fallen or may hereafter fall heir, my sisters María Antonia and Juana Bolívar and the children of my deceased brother Juan Vicente Bolívar, to wit: Juan, Felicia, and Fernando Bolívar, with the provision that my estate be divided into three parts, two for my said two sisters, and the third for the aforesaid children of my aforementioned brother Juan Vicente, to have and to enjoy by the blessing of God.

And I do revoke, annul, and void, as having no force or effect, any other testaments, codicils, powers-of-attorney, or memorials whatsoever heretofore given in writing, by word of mouth, or otherwise, same not to have validity as evidence of proof in any court of law or elsewhere, saving these presents, which I now execute as my last and deliberate will, or in such manner and form as shall have greatest force of law. In witness whereof I do so execute same, at this hacienda of San Pedro Alejandrino, district of the city of Santa Marta, this tenth day of December, in the year of our Lord eighteen hundred and thirty.

And His Excellency the testator, whom I, the undersigned, a registered notary public of this district do certify as being to me known, and who to all appearances is of sane and sound mind, memory, and natural understanding, did so declare and execute and subscribe, before me in the house where he resides; and it is so recorded in this my current register of public deeds, the witnesses being General Mariano Montilla, General José María Carreño, Colonel Belford Hinton Wilson, Colonel José de la Cruz Paredes, Colonel Joaquín de Mier, Major Juan Glen, and Dr. Manuel Pérez de Recuero, all present.

SIMÓN BOLÍVAR

Before me,
José Catalino Noguera, Notary Public.
True copy.—Cepeda, Secretary.
True copy.—Cartagena, January 12, 1831.

The Secretary of the Prefecture:
Juan B. Calcaño.

INDEX

INDEX

Abilities, 262, 264, 272, 281, 284, 291. See also Bolívar, *Ability*.

Absolutism, 110-111.

Achilles, 447, 521.

Acosta, José de, comment on Quetzalcoatl, 121

Acuerdos del Consejo de Gobierno de la República de Colombia, xxxiv.

Aeneas, combat with Turnus, 522.

Aeneid, mentioned, 521.

Africa, continent of, savage hordes from, 267; fratricide in, 603; mentioned, 43.

Agriculture, destruction, 19; importance of to America, 79; restricted by Spain, 111.

Aguirre, Vicente. Colonel and brigade commander, named Governor of Province of Quito, 360, 365; mentioned, 382.

Albión battalion, requests discharge, 348.

Albuera, regiment of, defeated, 86.

Alcántara, Francisco de Paula. Squadron commander, carries news of armistice, 248; at Santa Ana conference, 248.

Aldama, Juan. Spanish colonel, 141.

Aldao, Francisco. Major, 430.

Alexander I. Czar of Russia, will head coalition against Britain, 78; 574.

Alexander the Great, 485, 572, 591, 656.

Alliances, of European monarchs, 77; for America, 122; with Great Britain, 512-13, 563; against Brazil, 554; of Mexico, Guatemala, and Colombia, 631.

Allies, of Europe, meet with Castlereagh, 76.

Almagro, Diego de. Peruvian conquistador, kills Atahualpa, 108; cruelties of, 109; family, 447.

Alvarado, Rudecindo. Peruvian general, leading general in Perú, 299, 314; defeated at Moquegua, 302, 361; army of, 308; commands Callao, 420, 422; leaves Upper Perú, 596; betrays army of San Martín, 746; mentioned, 308, 375, 423.

Álvarez, ———. Aide-de-camp, 282.

Álvarez, Ignacio. Argentine general, envoy to Perú, 491-505.

Álvarez, Manuel de Bernardo. President of Cundinamarca, letter to, 84-85.

Alvear, Carlos María de. Argentine general, envoy to Bolivia, 531; and Francia, 533; suggests union of Argentine and Bolivian republics, 551; letter to, 553-555; suggests federation of Buenos Aires, Chile, and Bolivia, 588; mentioned, 743.

Alzaga, Félix, 416.

Alzuru, Juan Eligio, commands *Yaguachi* battalion, 747.

Amador, Juan de Dios. Governor of Province of Cartagena, letter to, 89; 421.

America, multiple governments in rejected, 56-57; aided by fall of Napoleon, 70; Britain will aid, 78; commerce and industry, 79; knowledge of kept mystery, 104; fate of native monarchs, 109; general conditions in, 110; people of on level with serfs, 111; causes of independence, 112-113; plight, 121-22; effect of Spanish revolution, 234; cause of abandoned, 435; domestic peace in, 461; anarchy in calls for

debt to, 767; writings placed in hands of, 767; mentioned, 686, 715.

Frankfort, public declaration of, 76.

Franklin, Benjamin, and science, 525; mentioned, 267.

Freedom, value of, 229, 306-307; guarantees for, 456; superior to tyranny, 473; upholds social order, 602; defeats tyranny, 689; dangers of, 747-48; of press, 74, 550; of speech, 550.

Freire, José Ramón. General and Supreme Director of Chile, letter to, 392, 423; sends congratulations, 409; in Concepción, 508; fall of predicted, 563; heads expedition against Chiloé, 563; government of, 744.

Froster, Captain, Chilean navy, 452.

Fucha, 755.

Fundamental Law of 1819, creates Colombia, 212-13, 220, 221, 237; ordered distributed, 214-15.

Funds, lack of and requests for, 14, 157-58, 208, 225, 228-29, 242, 282, 444-45, 517.

Funes, Gregorio. Dean, 548.

Gaceta de Caracas, letter to Monteverde in, 40; censorship of, 74; mentioned, xxxiii, 41.

Gaceta de Cartagena, charges against government appear in, 466; mentioned, 542.

Gaceta de Colombia, 538.

Gaceta del Gobierno (Perú), 496, 574, 587.

Gaceta de Guayaquil, 365.

Gaceta del Patriota (Guayaquil), 327.

Gaceta de Santiago de la Vega, 124.

Galindo, León. Major and battalion commander, in command at Huari, 426-27; mission to Potosí, 566; mentioned, 429.

Gallegos estate, Bolívar seeks settlement of, 14.

Gamarra, Agustín. Peruvian general, President of Perú, letter to, 616-619; will coöperate with Santa Cruz, 617; withdraws from Bolivia, 704; as president of Perú, 720; seizes control in Perú, 721; admires Bolívar, 727; and surrender of Guayaquil, 727; claims presidency in Perú, 730; mentioned, 428, 635, 723.

Gámeza, 211.

García de Ortigosa, Salvador. Priest, mission of, 44.

García del Río, Juan. Peruvian diplomat, opinion of, 762.

García Rovira, Custodio. President of United Provinces of New Granada, 93.

García, José Antonio. Lieutenant, joins Patriot ranks, 141.

García, Pedro. Captain, death of, 8.

García, Pedro Antonio. Colonel, retirement of, 293.

Garcilaso de La Vega, 510.

Garzal, 382.

Gaul, and Rome, 516.

Geography, political importance of, 749.

George IV. King of England, letter to respecting British volunteers, 668.

Germans, in Brazil, 466.

Geneva, Republic of, 306.

Genoa, 19.

Genghis Khan, 111, 176.

General Santander, vessel, 446.

General Staff, lack of, 498.

Gibraltar, 439.

Girardot, Atanasio. Colonel, 46; death of, 62.

Girón, Treaty of, between Colombia and Perú, 719; mentioned, 747.

Glen, John. Major, witness to will, 768.

Goajira Peninsula, 119. Campaign in, 305.

godo, defined, 87, n. 1.

Gómez, Juan María. Captain, mission to Santander, 345.

Gómez, Francisco Esteban. Division

supports Portugal against Spain, 652; upholds rights of world, 655; Foreign Enlistment Act of, 668, n. 1; and monarchy in Colombia, 732; invades Buenos Aires, 741.

Greece, failure of democracy in, 183; and defensive league against Holy Alliance, 380; liberation of, 503; under protection of England, 565; mentioned, 19, 484.

Greeks, return from Troy, 711.

Grita, 30.

Guacara, 6, 48.

Guadalupe, Virgin of, proclaimed Queen of the Patriots in Mexico, 121.

Guajibos, of Casanare, 267.

Gual, Pedro. Minister of Foreign Affairs, *xxi*; Governor of Cartagena, letters to, 91-93, 265-66, 282-83, 579, 631-32; opinion of, 92, 526-27; appointed Minister of State, 260; recommended for vice presidency, 262; requests presence at Congress of Cúcuta, 282; advice of sought respecting boundary dispute with Perú, 327-28; laws of Nature demand restrictions, 331; rights of majority prevail over minority, 331; reviews problem of Guayaquil, 331-334; mission to the Congress of Panamá, 526, 546; views on Colombian-Peruvian boundary, 610; negotiates peace treaty with Perú, 730, 735; mentioned, 282, 449, 481, 548, 576, 587, 594, 595.

Guanare, 265.

Guárico, 267.

Guasdualito, 199, 201-202, 204, 236, 239.

Guatavita, mines at, 481.

Guatemala, confederation of, 119; funds and troops requested of, 434, 440, 437; and federation, 461; colonial dependency of New Spain, 470; recognized by Mexico, 491; joins the confederation, 492; and military alliance, 631-32; population, 632; La Mar exiled to, 722;

anarchy and civil war in, 723, 743; rejects monarchism, 732.

Guatémoc. See Quauhtemotzin.

Guayana, province of, liberated, 139, 143; enemy plans to attack, 171; sends funds, 208; news from, 238; sister visits, 517; mentioned, 58, 137, 142, 144, 154.

Guayaquil, expedition against planned, 277; Patriot losses in, 286; arrival in, 293; recognition of Colombian sovereignty sought, 312f., 322, 323, 329-33; under jurisdiction of Viceroy of Perú, 317; returned to jurisdiction of audiencia of Quito, 319-320; port of vital to Ecuador, 322; defended by Colombian troops, 322; seizure of, 324; to be permitted to choose between Perú and Colombia, 325; Peruvian troops near, 325-26; considered Colombian territory, 327-28; must be retained by force, 328; factional strife in, 329; persuasion should be used to win, 333; future of lies with Colombia, 333; arrival of San Martín in, 334; meeting of Bolívar and San Martín in, 336f., 348; elections in, 343, 344; settlement of question of possession, 345-46; defense of, 364; garrison of, 407; treatment of citizens of, 407; reinforcements sent from, 457; does not favor Santander, 564; proclaims Bolívar dictator, 636-37; arrival in, 1826, 631, 634; favors federalism, 659; insurrection in, 659; remains in union, 664; Sucre in, 711; surrender of, 1829, 718, 719, 721, 726, 727, 751; held by Perú, 719; evacuated by Peruvian forces, 723.

Guayaquileña, brig, 406, 407, 595, 710.

Güere, victory at, 172.

Guerra, Antonio de la. Colonel, sent to Venezuela by Flores, 764.

Guerra, José de la. Major, commands *Vargas* battalion, 427.

730; peace negotiations with, 719, 722-23, 728, 734, 751; Gamarra controls, 721; armistice with Colombia, 723; rejects monarchy, 732; defeated, 736; under La Mar, 734; caudillism in, 746.

Perú Number 4 battalion, 454.

pesos fuertes, defined, 52, n. 1.

Petion, Alexander. President of Haiti, powers of, 599; mentioned, *xvii*, 129.

Petre, Francis Loraine, *Simón Bolívar, xxxvi.*

Pey, José Miguel. President of New Granada, letter to, 101-103.

Pezuela, Joaquin. General and Viceroy of Perú, 447.

Philadelphia, visited, *xv.*

Philippine Islands, Spanish fleet sails for, 462.

Phocion, 757.

Piar, Manuel de. Division general, success of, 146; fate of, 646; mentioned, 137.

Pichincha, Battle of, *xviii*, 292, 758.

Pichincha battalion, ordered to Perú, 342; bound for Venezuela, 613; mentioned, 377, 406, 595, 608, 615.

Pichincha, sword of, 497.

Pierson, William Whatley, quoted, *xxiii.*

Pilate, 508.

Pildain, José Francisco. Lieutenant Colonel and aide-de-camp, 169.

Piñango, Francisco. Major, 133, 134.

Pineda, ———, revolt of, 420.

Piñerez family, friendship for, 93.

Pinto, Francisco Antonio. General, troops under, 402; support of, 422; withdraws troops from Callao, 423; in Coquimbo, 508.

Pisba, 203.

Pisco, San Martín in, 249; expedition to, 399; customs payments at, 524.

Piscobambo, 429.

Pisistratus, accomplishments of, 183; mentioned, 64.

Piura, grants funds, 445; mentioned, 325, 721.

Plato, 228, 235, 266, 555.

Plaza, Ambrosio. Colonel, at Carabobo, 268, 269.

Plural executive, weakness of, 180.

Pizarro, Francisco, and death of Atahualpa, 108.

Pizarros, 447.

Polignac, Prince de. French minister of state, favors monarchies in America, 479.

Police, nature of, 602-603; enlargement of, 703.

Political virtues, absence of among people, 21.

Ponte. See Tovar Ponte, Martín.

Ponte, Gabriel, wounded at Valencia, 7.

Popayán, people of abandoned by Bishop, 291; news from, 363; opposition in, 671; revolt in, 762; mentioned, 97, 100, 211, 289, 360, 637, 712, 735, 760.

Pope, Alexander, poet, 521; works of translated by Olmedo, 522.

Populations, estimates of, 105-109.

Porras Barrenechea, Raúl, editor of *Archivo Diplomático Peruano, El Congreso de Panamá*, 525, n. 1.

Portugal, King of, returns to Lisbon, 272.

Portugal, Kingdom of, proposes league against Holy Alliance, 379-80, 388; relations with Britain, 652; mentioned, 307, 484.

Port-au-Prince, 127.

Portete, Battle of, 747.

Porto-Viejo, province of favors Colombian rule, 333.

Portobelo, 610.

Portocarrero, Mariano. Peruvian general, mission of, 368; reaches Santa Marta, 764.

Postal system, 635.

Potosí, Argentine envoys arrive in, 528; conditions in, 565; climate of, 613; mentioned, 477, 539.

Powles and Company, English mer-